Celebrating Research

Rare and Special Collections from the Membership
of the Association of Research Libraries

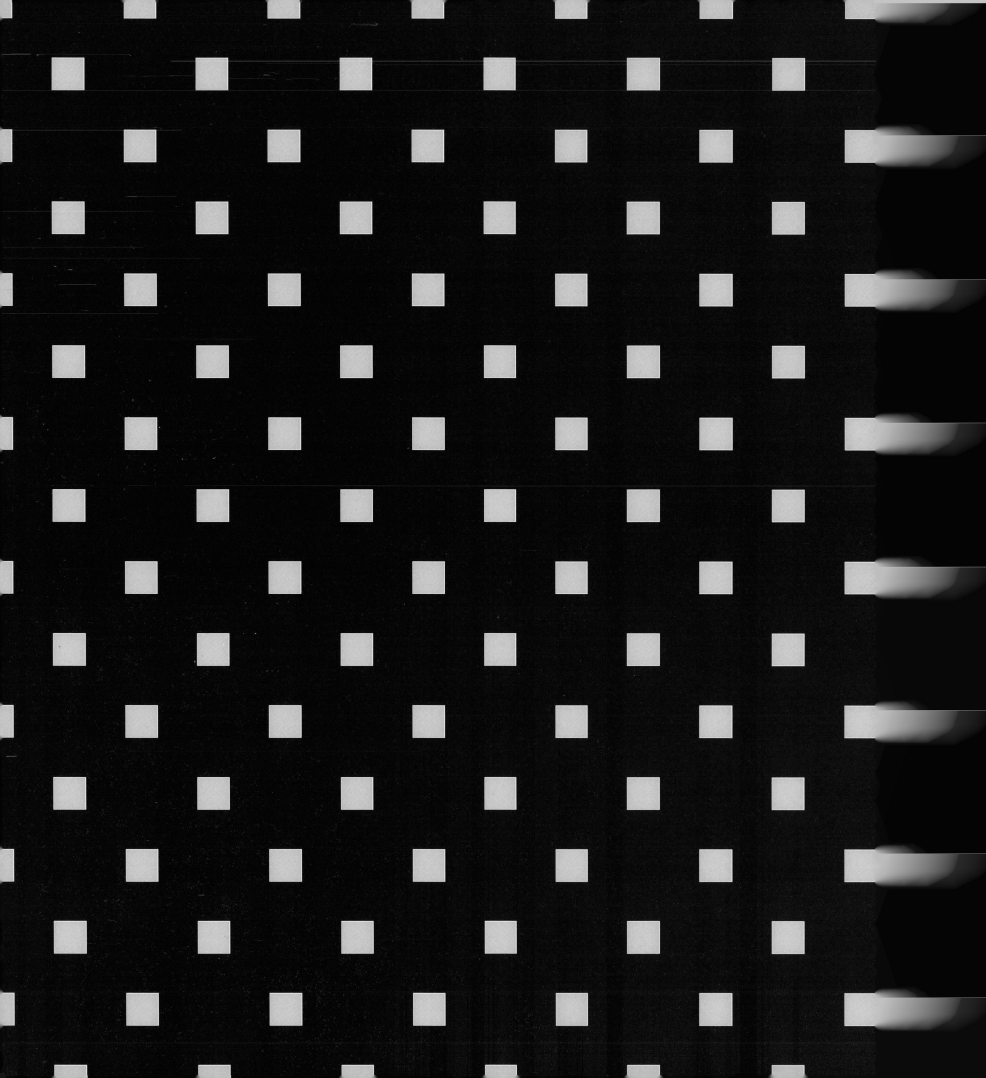

Celebrating the 75th Anniversary
of the Association of Research Libraries

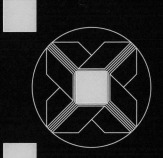

Celebrating Research

Rare and Special Collections from the Membership
of the Association of Research Libraries

Editors

Philip N. Cronenwett
Special Collections Librarian Emeritus
Dartmouth College Library

Kevin Osborn
Research & Design, Ltd.

Samuel A. Streit
Director for Special Collections
Brown University Library

Introduction by Nicolas Barker

Association of Research Libraries

Washington, DC

Acknowledgments

The Association of Research Libraries acknowledges and thanks the following for their generous support of the preparation and production of *Celebrating Research* in commemoration of the Association's 75th anniversary.

The Gladys Krieble Delmas Foundation
OCLC Online Computer Library Center
Brown University Library

EBSCO Information Services
Otto Harrassowitz, Wiesbaden, Germany

The many people in ARL libraries
who contributed essays and photographs.

♾ The paper used in this publication meets the requirements of ANSI/NISO Z39.48-1992 (R1997) Permanence of Paper for Publications and Documents in Libraries and Archives.

ISBN 978-1-59407-769-2

Editors
Philip N. Cronenwett
Special Collections Librarian Emeritus
Dartmouth College Library

Kevin Osborn
Research & Design, Ltd.

Samuel A. Streit
Director for Special Collections
Brown University Library

Introduction
Nicolas Barker

Index
Trudi Olivetti

Editorial Support
Kaylyn Groves
Jaia Barrett

Brad Leifer
Michael O'Connor
Timothy Tulenko

Design
Kevin Osborn, Research & Design, Ltd., Arlington, Virginia, with Anne-Catherine Fallen

Printed in the United States of America
by Schmitz Press, Sparks, Maryland

Preface

THIS compendium is a sampling of the remarkable abundance of collections available for use in the member libraries of the Association of Research Libraries (ARL). It is not a comprehensive view or a directory but instead an array of profiles that exemplify a spectrum of rare and special collections in research libraries. Special collections have been broadly construed to encompass the distinctive, the rare and unique, emerging media, born-digital, digitized materials, uncommon, non-standard, primary, and heritage materials. Each profile tells a story of a single collection, briefly recounting how the resources were acquired and developed and, importantly, how they are being used.

The volume is the result of a collaborative effort among 118 ARL member libraries on the occasion of the Association's 75th anniversary. Hundreds of people from research libraries across the US and Canada were involved in the identification of potential collections to be profiled and in the writing and photography used in the volume. From these nominations, a single collection was selected from each library by an editorial team comprised of Philip N. Cronenwett, Special Collections Librarian Emeritus, Dartmouth College Library; Kevin Osborn, Research & Design Ltd.; and Samuel A. Streit, Director for Special Collections, Brown University Library. Each expert in their own right, together these three provided experienced leadership and creativity that brought the essays and illustrations together in a way that is appealing both intellectually and aesthetically.

Significant anniversaries present occasions to celebrate past accomplishments and to anticipate the future; ARL's 75th anniversary volume does both. The essays salute the stewardship of past decades and celebrate the research enabled by these collections. Taken together, the essays also represent a window into the future of research libraries. They illustrate some of the active library collaborations underway with faculty, students, and local and remote communities to encourage use of these materials and to identify new resources of all formats that are important to collect and steward for future users.

Put aside any lingering images of special collections as a domain reserved for specialists and enjoy this tour of how research libraries and their communities of users are engaging rare and special collections in the early 21st century.

Sherrie Schmidt
University Librarian
Arizona State University
ARL President

Duane E. Webster
ARL Executive Director

October 2007

Contents

About ARL

The Association of Research Libraries was established in 1932 to serve and represent the interests of libraries that are distinguished by the breadth and quality of their research-oriented collections as well as the characteristics and magnitude of the multidisciplinary communities they serve. ARL has remained an important and distinctive association because of the nature of the institutions represented. The members of ARL are libraries that are part of comprehensive, research-extensive institutions in the United States and Canada that share the same research mission, aspirations, and achievements. These institutions comprise notable communities of scholars across many disciplines who are actively engaged in research and teaching and who have high levels of need and expectations for library collections and services.

In the 75 years of the Association's history, much has changed in North American society and within libraries. In the past decade alone, the changes in systems of scholarly communication and in research library roles have been dramatic. Digital technology and ubiquitous networking have transformed scholars' and students' access to knowledge and to one another and, as a consequence, have transformed the process of teaching and learning, as well as the conduct of research. Everything seems to change in this highly digital networked environment: the context, methods, objects, and outputs of research change and so too have people's expectations about access to information and the use of these resources.

In this environment of creative, fast-paced, and unsynchronized change across disciplines, research libraries are responding in many new ways. Longstanding library strategies to support novice and experienced researchers are being adapted to meet new needs. Libraries are assuming such new roles as managing digital repositories for text, images, and data generated by and for research. Importantly, libraries are forceful advocates for change in institutional practices and scholarly and research behavior that will lead to innovations in systems of scholarly communication. At the same time, core library responsibilities are sustained: research libraries continue to collect, preserve, and provide services to enable discovery and use of research knowledge in all formats. Especially as research and higher education subdivides knowledge into disciplines and subdisciplines, comprehensive research library collections and services serve as bridges that facilitate the synthesis of information that advances interdisciplinary understanding and inquiry.

ARL provides a forum for its members and acts as an advocate on behalf of these libraries to shape and influence this changing environment of scholarly communication and the public policies that affect their diverse communities. ARL also serves as a venue in which its member libraries come together to identify and articulate strategies for integrating library services into research, teaching, and learning. With 123 libraries as members, ARL is a small association and yet it represents an extraordinary North American community of considerable influence working together to support the current and future needs of local, national, and international scholarship.

Association of Research Libraries
21 Dupont Circle NW, Suite 800
Washington, DC 20036
(202) 296-2296 (t)
(202) 872-0884 (f)
http://www.arl.org/

ARL Member Libraries

The date in parentheses following each library name is the year that library joined ARL.

University of Alabama Libraries (1967)
University at Albany, State University
    of New York, Libraries (1975)
University of Alberta Libraries (1969)
University of Arizona Library (1967)
Arizona State University Libraries (1973)
Auburn University Libraries (1992)
Boston College Libraries (2000)
Boston Public Library (1933)
Boston University Libraries (1962)
Brigham Young University Library (1974)
University of British Columbia Library (1967)
Brown University Library (1932)
University at Buffalo, State University
    of New York, Libraries (1967)
University of California, Berkeley Library (1932)
University of California, Davis Library (1969)
University of California, Irvine Libraries (1981)
University of California, Los Angeles Library (1937)
University of California, Riverside Libraries (1979)
University of California, San Diego Libraries (1973)
University of California, Santa Barbara
    Libraries (1973)
Canada Institute for Scientific and
    Technical Information (1982)
Case Western Reserve University Libraries (1969)
Center for Research Libraries (1962)
University of Chicago Library (1932)
University of Cincinnati Libraries (1932)
University of Colorado at Boulder Libraries (1946)
Colorado State University Libraries (1975)
Columbia University Libraries (1932)
University of Connecticut Libraries (1962)
Cornell University Library (1932)
Dartmouth College Library (1932)
University of Delaware Library (1983)
Duke University Libraries (1932)
Emory University Libraries (1975)
University of Florida Libraries (1956)
Florida State University Libraries (1962)
George Washington University Library (1998)
Georgetown University Library (1962)
University of Georgia Libraries (1967)
Georgia Tech Library and
    Information Center (1983)
University of Guelph Library (1979)
Harvard University Library (1932)
University of Hawaii at Manoa Library (1976)

University of Houston Libraries (1975)
Howard University Libraries (1971)
University of Illinois at Chicago Library (1988)
University of Illinois at Urbana-Champaign
    Library (1932)
Indiana University Libraries Bloomington (1932)
University of Iowa Libraries (1932)
Iowa State University Library (1932)
Johns Hopkins University Libraries (1932)
University of Kansas Libraries (1932)
Kent State University Libraries and
    Media Services (1974)
University of Kentucky Libraries (1952)
Bibliothèque de l'Université Laval (1985)
Library and Archives Canada (1971)
Library of Congress (1932)
Louisiana State University Libraries (1938)
University of Louisville Libraries (2002)
McGill University Library (1932)
McMaster University Libraries (1976)
University of Manitoba Libraries (1981)
University of Maryland Libraries (1962)
University of Massachusetts Amherst
    Libraries (1969)
Massachusetts Institute of Technology
    Libraries (1932)
University of Miami Libraries (1976)
University of Michigan Library (1932)
Michigan State University Libraries (1956)
University of Minnesota Libraries (1932)
University of Missouri–Columbia Libraries (1932)
Bibliothèques de l'Université de Montréal (2001)
National Agricultural Library (1948)
National Library of Medicine (1948)
University of Nebraska–Lincoln Libraries (1932)
University of New Mexico Libraries (1979)
The New York Public Library,
    Astor, Lenox, and Tilden Foundations (1932)
New York State Library (1969)
New York University Libraries (1936)
University of North Carolina at Chapel Hill
    Libraries (1932)
North Carolina State University Libraries (1983)
Northwestern University Library (1932)
University Libraries of Notre Dame (1962)
Ohio State University Libraries (1932)
Ohio University Libraries (1996)
University of Oklahoma Libraries (1962)

Oklahoma State University Library (1962)
University of Oregon Libraries (1962)
University of Pennsylvania Library (1932)
Pennsylvania State University Libraries (1962)
University of Pittsburgh Libraries (1962)
Princeton University Library (1932)
Purdue University Libraries (1956)
Queen's University Library (1976)
Rice University Library (1971)
University of Rochester Libraries (1932)
Rutgers University Libraries (1956)
University of Saskatchewan Library (1980)
Smithsonian Institution Libraries (1971)
University of South Carolina Libraries (1975)
University of Southern California Libraries (1962)
Southern Illinois University Carbondale
    Library (1967)
Stony Brook University, State University
    of New York, Libraries (1975)
Syracuse University Library (1962)
Temple University Libraries (1962)
University of Tennessee Libraries (1962)
University of Texas Libraries (1932)
Texas A&M University Libraries (1962)
Texas Tech University Libraries (1997)
University of Toronto Libraries (1932)
Tulane University Library (1967)
University of Utah Library (1962)
Vanderbilt University Library (1946)
University of Virginia Library (1932)
Virginia Tech Libraries (1976)
University of Washington Libraries (1932)
Washington State University Libraries (1962)
Washington University in St. Louis Libraries (1932)
University of Waterloo Library (1984)
Wayne State University Libraries (1962)
The University of Western Ontario Libraries (1976)
University of Wisconsin–Madison Libraries (1932)
Yale University Library (1932)
York University Libraries (1979)

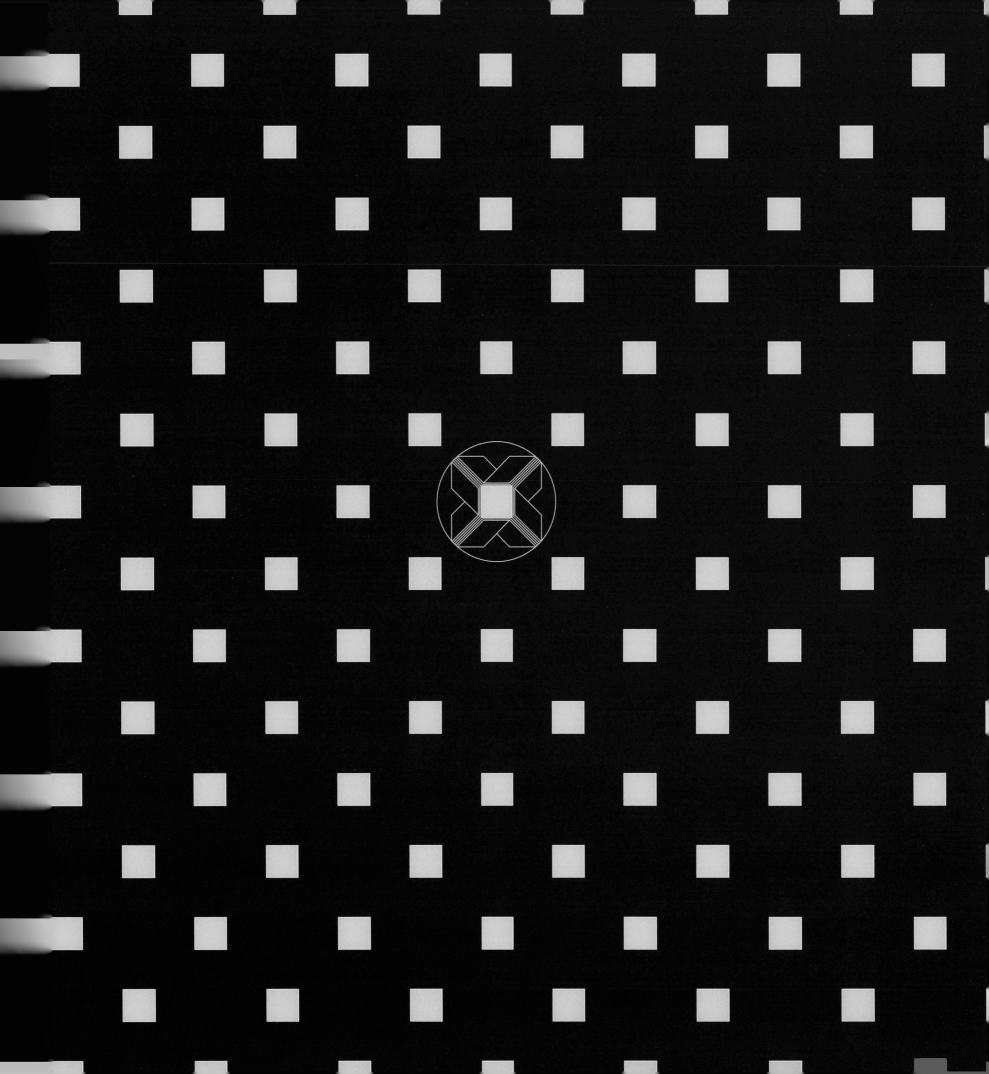

Introduction

by Nicolas Barker*

THE Association of Research Libraries (ARL) was born on 29 December 1932, three weeks after the present writer. For half our lives thereafter, we pursued different courses, and it was only in 1970 that our paths first crossed. At the beginning of that year I went on a pilgrimage that took me from the east to the west of North America and back again. In 31 days and 35 flights, I visited 70 campuses and libraries in places other than universities. Mohawk, Eastern, Piedmont, Delta, Braniff, PanAm, Ozark, and other forgotten names shimmered on what seemed always the same plane, as I sped from New York to New Haven, up to Syracuse and down to Washington, DC, plunged south to Raleigh and Atlanta, across to Baton Rouge and Austin, on to Los Angeles (stopping five times en route on what was then Continental's only out-of-state flight), north to San Francisco and Vancouver, east to Chicago, deviating to Toronto, Urbana, and St. Louis, and finally to Boston and Providence.

It was the first and most intensive journey of many since that have taken me to, I think, 46 of the places where the Association of Research Libraries has member libraries. Although it was not the main reason for my journey in 1970, I visited all the special collections and rare book libraries I could on the way. In those days, there were fewer than there are now. The collections themselves were, it seemed to me then, less the result of deliberate acquisition, more often of accidental accumulation. Books acquired from older institutions, a seminary that had closed, from the private library of a deceased faculty member, an unsolicited gift from alumnus or neighbour, mixed with books simply segregated, on the grounds of age or worth, from the general stacks. There was not much pattern, still less an acquisitions policy, in evidence.

If some of the books were, so to speak, an odd lot, so too were some of the librarians. Many of them seemed to have drifted into position, rather than being appointed to it. Many of them had problems, some general (dilapidated stock, unsatisfactory accommodation, neglectful administration), some more personal, particularly that they too were neglected. But what united them all was a love of books, above all those in their care. It was impossible not to be moved by the passion that burst out on any provocation, and I did not find it hard to provoke or fail to be moved by its expression. I quickly grasped that one immediate cause of complaint was that they had few visitors of any kind, let alone one prepared to share their enthusiasms or woes.

Like many another innocent abroad, I was tempted to generalise, and, like most generalisations, mine was a gross caricature. There were already many exceptions—for example the still new Beinecke Library at Yale, the older Houghton and William Andrews Clark Libraries at Harvard and UCLA, with a well-defined sense of purpose and staff well able to meet it. But speculation thus induced could not be repressed, and over the years since I have continued to ponder the meaning and purpose of names like "Special Collections" and "Rare Book Library."

The use and abuse of the word "rare" in the context of American libraries was the subject of a memorable enquiry by Gordon Ray, begun in 1965 and repeated in 1975, a decade of considerable change. The merits or otherwise of rarity had already had a long history. In 1691 a British auctioneer, crying up his wares, could write, "nothing more truely recommends any Collection of Books, to the Judicious Lovers of Learning, than that it contains not the Common and Obvious, but the Outer-Course and more obscure Authors." But at the same time Jean Le Clerc, who had a temper as sharp as his common sense, was dismissive: "Some of the rarest books are, if you consider the matter candidly, the least useful, a fact you can deduce from their very rarity: what benefit can be got from what has been but rarely or never printed?" Off stage, behind both these statements, is the question of monetary value. Books are valuable for many more reasons than what they cost: why then do some cost more than others? In 1975, reflecting with Ray on a decade that had seen much change, I wrote in the *Book Collector*:

> If rare books are rarer than they used to be, they will cost more and deserve closer examination. Equally,

current financial stringencies will impose on libraries and universities and other places where rare books are studied a further need to define terms. It would be grand to be able to maintain the old nineteenth-century vision, panoptic and egalitarian, that all books deserve the same attention, but the books are too many and money too short for this to be possible: it is thus further necessary to define how and for what rare books are to be *used*. [emphasis added]

Creating a "rare book room" was, I thought, in itself a retrograde step. It was true that the books in them would probably be harder to replace now than they were when acquired, but the reason for these enclaves was not the difficulty but the cost of replacing the contents. An increasing tendency to measure utility in cash terms brought new needs to justify the existence of libraries.

Scholars ought not to need much explanation of the attractions of a library, but administrators, let alone the general public, have to be met more than halfway. In 1975 Ray noted the arrival of new demands and new ideas for libraries, the "museum function," the duty "to instruct and amuse the general public in an informal way," the uncomfortable arithmetic of user capitation counts, "community outreach" mediated through "Friends" groups—all these reflected the intrusion of cost-efficiency arithmetic into libraries. "Balancing the books" was to take on a wider connotation, and now, with increasingly pressing monetary preoccupations, it is harder than ever for a library to maintain its integrity. How to keep faith with scholarly users and the public, how, above all, to keep faith with benefactors who see their gifts as a memorial not to be wantonly destroyed by casual sales of "duplicates"—all this stretches "library resources" to the full. It is, in a changing world, an exhilarating prospect to be responsible for the preservation of the evidences of civilisation, but it is also an exacting one.

The desire to erect a monument to this sense of mission, and, at the same time, a repository for the books, might fit with the impulses that brought new schools, colleges, and universities into being, or with the other impulses that led to the foundation of the proprietary and circulating libraries. But the shape of the buildings reflected the institutions less than the veneration felt for the books themselves. Often literally built in the form of classical temples, they conveyed the iconic status of their contents. Surrounded by Ionic pillars, pediment surmounting the name of the library in Roman capitals, steps leading up to the bronze doors, they inspire awe appropriate to books that are, in mass, more valuable than the sum of their parts. If the physical form of the building offered a sense of security for the contents, it was not as consonant with new demands for access. A frame as well protected may inculcate respectful handling of its contents; it may, however, frighten off the casual or even the learned visitor. More insidiously, it may sow in the minds of the custodians a feeling that such visitors ought to be kept at arm's length. If some of the special collections librarians that I met in 1970 were lonely, they were not always aware that what was familiar and comfortable to them had the opposite effect on those that they were anxious to help, with whom they might share the treasures in their care.

New Roles & Expanding Scope of Collections

The last 30 years have seen many changes that have altered such directly contradictory impulses as preservation and access. Far from lonely, the librarians and curators of today have put in place programs of exhibitions and seminars that have encouraged visitors to come to libraries with no fear that they will be subjected to some alarming questionnaire or test before they are allowed in. Outreach takes librarians and curators to meet schoolchildren, laying down a relationship of mutual trust and interest for the future. Writers and artists in residence have come to work within the library, and thus are encouraged to add creatively to the library's resources. Closer links between library and faculty or community have encouraged both sides to interpret a mutual sense of shared purpose. Acquisitions have come to follow a much more specific pattern, reflecting the same shared purpose. More than anything else, the use of the Internet as an extension of all the library's activities in every field, has increased its scope, and with it many more ways of engaging with different kinds of users, as likely to be remote as present.

The proper contents of a library have been a matter of study and scholarly interest since classical times. De Bure's *Bibliographie instructive* and Brunet's *Manuel* merely canonised, in their time, ways of dividing up the subject matter of books corresponding with categories that were far older. Theology, the classics, history, jurisprudence, literature, fine and applied art, architecture, civil and military, geography and voyages, natural history, science and technology, provided a structure to which every library, including its special collections, was supposed to conform, within whatever classification system had been adopted for them. Archives, whether internal or external, followed the same principles, adopting archival standards and cataloguing systems.

A glance at the list of contents of this volume will show how far the role and scope of the special collections or rare book library has moved on, since this Procrustean formula was devised. Here again the Internet and international databases have had a liberating effect on individual libraries, their contents, and how they are treated and used. Synergy, hitherto undreamed of, has grown up between libraries and researchers geographically distant. These links have born fruit in joint cataloguing and research projects, shared exhibitions, and other activities. Isolation is no longer an endemic problem.

Special Collections as Distinctive Signifiers of Excellence

The variety of the material covered in the profiles of their collections selected by 118 of ARL's members for this volume is in itself remarkable, the more so if we reflect that this is in each case simply one part of a collection that contains much more. Each choice tells you something about the special collection that is its home. It also tells you how much the libraries' expectations of special collections have changed: where once special collections were regarded as the top dressing on the solid cake of main library management, they are now regarded as distinctive signifiers, almost trademarks. Indeed, the choice of special collections as an appropriate subject with which to celebrate ARL's 75th birthday, rather than intellectual property or preservation or diversity or networked information, tells you something about the way the research library world has changed over the last 30 years. ARL libraries want to be

known for their distinctive collections, not by some characteristic shared with every other library.

This is itself not a new phenomenon. Each of these characteristics serves to distinguish its library from others. To be unique in some definable way, however recondite, makes it the object of an attention that it would not otherwise attract. In 1974, deputising for John Carter who was not well enough to come, I went to Indiana University at Bloomington to meet his old friend and colleague David Randall and speak at the opening of an exhibition on the theme of "Printing and the Mind of Man" at the Lilly Library. I was housed in the Faculty Center in a building that also housed the university bookstore. There I discovered a more than respectable stock of academic books on a wide variety of subjects, which, however, also contained a collection, not just respectable but (I could recognise) comprehensive, of books on and in the Tartar languages. Sitting that evening next to the Chancellor, Hermon Wells, who more than made up a lack of inches in energy and imagination, I commented on this. He was pleased:

> "Yes," he said, "when I came to IU it was just
> another state university; it needed something to
> make it different from the rest. So I looked around
> for a subject, and lit on Tartar languages. No one
> else specialised in that. Now we are the world
> center. People even come from Ulan Bator to use
> our collections."

I could see the force of this, and others have followed this example as is demonstrated by the collection profiles selected for this commemorative volume.

At the same time, the old categories used by libraries since time immemorial have not dropped off the map; since, ultimately, it is books that determine how libraries dispose of their resources, and they in turn correspond with market expectation, it would be surprising if they had. But theology, once the staple of every library, is here recognisable in only four collections. Boston College, the largest Jesuit educational establishment in the country, celebrates the history of the Society of Jesus with a collection of Jesuit authors and materials about the society prior to its suppression in 1773. The University of California, Santa Barbara holds the American Religions collection of J. Gordon Melton, Methodist minister and author of the *Encyclopaedia of American Religions*, whose speciality has been "less documented religious groups," the newer Asian religions, American Islam and New Age organizations, not to mention Wicca and Neo-Paganism and flying saucer religions. The Hamilton Family fonds at the University of Manitoba record one of the longest running experiments in the history of spiritualism, which made Winnipeg an automatic port of call for visiting spiritualists from 1913. More conventionally, the University of Chicago boasts the collection made by its professor of New Testament and Early Christian Literature, Edgar J. Goodspeed, of 65 manuscripts from the 7th to the 19th century, Greek, Syriac, Ethiopic, Armenian, Arabic, and Latin. Believing, as he did, that "manuscripts are to research in the humanities what laboratories and laboratory materials are to the natural sciences," he would be delighted to know that his collection is used by his successor for students to confront medium and message together.

Any collection with medieval manuscripts in it is special, but apart from specialists they are more often admired than used. At the University of Houston, however, 12 manuscript books and 7 leaves are made to work hard. Faculty interest ranges from art history to music, and "assignments are not uncommon." One student constructed a full-size scribe's desk, another "a large folio detailing the Martha Stewart trial," while the Gothic Voices ensemble sang chant from a 15th-century Italian service book. The University of Missouri–Columbia owns *Fragmenta Manuscripta*, 217 leaves, from the 8th–15th centuries, rescued from bindings in the dissolution of Archbishop Tenison's Library in 1861 (I know it well, for I catalogued it before and after its sale in 1968); it is good to know that it is finding new use as one of the 29 participants in the Digital Scriptorium project. The University of Michigan shares in a similar project, APIS (Advanced Papyrological Information System), which makes its 12,000 papyrus fragments over two millennia from Karamis, excavated by the university in 1924 to 1935, accessible to the 25 partners who share comparable papyrus hoards.

Princeton's collection of 9,500 Islamic manuscripts, the major part given by Robert Garrett in 1942, is the largest and most comprehensive collection of its kind in America; work has begun on making the manuscripts digitally available. At Arizona State University they have 390 Sinhalese palm-leaf manuscripts, and at the University of Utah they have the Aziz Atiya collection of 1,700 Arabic papyrus and paper fragments from the 8th–16th centuries. The University of British Columbia boasts a collection of Japanese maps of the Tokugawa period. More recent events are commemorated in the Center for Research Libraries collection of Chinese pamphlets collected by a Far East news correspondent, real street literature, not "high-end" propaganda made for export; in the University of Maryland's Prange collection of the entire printed output of Japan in the MacArthur era; and in the University of Washington collection on the evacuation and internment of Japanese Americans, "put together by members of the community for safe-keeping." Yet more recent is the University of California, Irvine's Southeast Asian Archive, charting the lives and works of immigrants since war ended in 1975, started only in 1987 by the lone figure of UCI librarian Anne Frank but now grown far beyond its first filing cabinet.

Collections of the papers of the famous have been a staple of libraries before special collections, as such, were distinguished. These collections make special demands of library staff, need special cataloguing, and present special preservation and storage problems. At Indiana University the Lilly Library has the papers of Orson Welles, documenting not only his films but also his stage and radio career; to this have been added the papers of his cameraman and attorney, and the Pauline Kael manuscripts add another perspective on the great man. The result of collecting in this depth has paid off: Simon Callow's definitive biography could not have been written without these papers, and they are also used in the English, film studies, and telecommunications departments of the university. Only last year Welles's love letters to his wife Rita Hayworth were acquired; they had been "preserved for years in her travelling cosmetics case." The University of Oregon corralled the work of its alumnus James Ivory, filmmaker and founder of Merchant Ivory Productions, in 1999. The documentation of one of the most creative partnerships of the cinema, with Ismail Merchant as producer and Ruth Prawer Jhabvala as novelist-scriptwriter, brought to bear on the work of novelists from Henry James to Ishiguru, is already a much-used historic resource, to which Ivory is to add.

By contrast, Boston Public Library has the special privilege of looking after the books, 2,700 volumes in all, of President John Adams, deposited in 1894 and subsequently donated. Many of them are annotated, and this feature was the subject of an exhibition "John Adams Unbound," now supplemented by complete digital copies of 33 books. Another famous political figure is commemorated at the University of Rochester in the Seward papers, presented to the university between 1945 and 1951; there are 160,000 items, principally those of William Henry Seward, Governor and later Senator of New York, later again Lincoln's Secretary of State. In Canada, McMaster University has made itself world-famous as the home of the papers of the philosopher Bertrand Russell; it is also the center for the edition of Russell's complete works.

The libraries and papers acquired by a family over time, including estate archives, often present the same or greater problems of sorting and classification than those of important single figures. In 1938, the University of Georgia acquired the Wymberly Jones De Renne collection, once housed at Wormsloe plantation near Savannah. The collection's content goes back to the foundation of Georgia as a colony in 1732, including the 1861 Ordinance of Secession printed on silk, and the only known copy of *The Death Song of the Cherokee Indian* (1762). The New York State Library has the Van Rensselaer Manor papers, the documents of the first colonists sent out by the wealthy Amsterdam merchant Kiliaen van Rensselaer in 1634, and their descendants. Letters, contracts, accounts, maps, and ledgers trace the growth of the community in detail; there are barn plans and the blacksmith's bill for making cowbells, and family letters and accounts of the colonists' relations with the native peoples.

Native American peoples are also commemorated at the University of Alberta, thanks to the gift of 2,300 books on those of

South and North America by Albert Javitch who, a Russian Jew, felt a natural affinity to the oppressed in his adopted country, while the books and papers of the splendidly named Lucullus Virgil McWhirter, preserver of the cultural history of the first peoples of the Columbia Plateau, are at Washington State University. Other relics of the West are preserved at Brigham Young University, in the L. Tom Perry collection on Western and Mormon history in the 19th century; at the University of Arizona, where the Harvey hotel and resort chain's photographs and promotional material are in such demand as to spur a Web site; at the University of New Mexico, where Tony Hillerman preserves, in person and print, the stories of the Southwest; and at Colorado State University, whose Water Resources Archive preserves the work of Delph Carpenter, architect of the Colorado River Compact, the first such water-sharing agreement, and his successors.

Further north, the North is similarly celebrated. At Dartmouth College there is the collection of Vilhjalmur Stefansson, explorer himself in 1913 to 1918, and subsequently a tireless propagandist for exploration. At the University of Laval, *nordicité* is a special subject, with a remarkable polar exploration library, films, and a collection of artefacts; while McGill boasts the Canadiana collection of Lawrence Lande, beginning with Thévet's archetypal if oddly titled *Les singularitez de la France antarctique, autrement nommé amérique* (1558). From a more official point of view, the Library and Archives Canada's Prime Ministers Collection documents the careers, and often the personal lives, of 20 of Canada's prime ministers, beginning with Sir John A. Macdonald at the inception of the Canadian Confederation in 1867.

The history and plight of Africa is profiled in the collections of two libraries. Boston University's African Studies Library is strong in the history of Uganda and Ethiopia, while Northwestern University's Winterton collection of 7,610 photographs documents daily African life and culture throughout East Africa, 1860 to1960. African-American history is vividly recalled in Emory University's archive of Carter G. Woodson, the "Father of Negro History," the subject of a recent exhibition, while the University of Massachusetts Amherst has the archive of W.E.B. Du Bois, the first African-American to receive a doctorate from Harvard. Howard University boasts the Moorland-Spingarn Research Center Collection of books, manuscripts, newspapers, oral history recordings, photographs, and a myriad of other resources, one of the nation's most extensive collections on the African-American experience. At the University of Alabama they have an unexpected treasure in the Lupton collection of African-American cookbooks, visited by researchers from afar. One was encountered by a local reporter who exclaimed, "You've come all the way from New York to see *these*?", a cry familiar in other forms to most rare book librarians, not least, perhaps, at Waterloo University, where they have, thanks to Seagram, "the world's finest collection on the beverage alcohol industry."

Another oppressed but articulate minority is that of the Chicanos. The University of California, Berkeley began to document the Third World Liberation Front from the late 1960s, and has in its Chicano Studies Collection the best collection of contemporary and older Chicano literature. It is now part of the Ethnic Studies Library, where the Chicano Database is based, controlling access to the *Chicano Thesaurus* of "specific cultural terms…politically sensitive to the Chicano experience." At the University of Texas at Austin they look further south, thanks to the Nettie Lee Benson Latin American collection. The link began when representatives of the university, in Mexico for the inauguration of President Obregon, picked up a copy of Bernal Diaz's 1632 history of the conquest of New Spain. Over many years the collection was built up by Carlos Castañeda, adding the entire Icazbalceta library and the best collection of the works of Sor Juana, and has grown from 30,000 books in 1943 to 960,000 now. Nearer the US-Mexico border, the University of California, San Diego has the remarkable Southworth collection on the Spanish Civil War.

Other links with the Europe from which so much of America's past has sprung are celebrated at the University of California, Los Angeles. Thanks to the generous prescience of UCLA Chancellor, Franklin D. Murphy, whose spiritual home was in Italy, the vast archive of the famous Orsini family was acquired in 1964; another donation has enabled the creation of a digital finding aid that makes it possible

to reunite the archive with the residue, still in Rome, a remarkable example of modern technology creating a complete "virtual archive." At the University of Wisconsin–Madison, is the collection of Italian History and Culture formed by a former professor of physics, Jack Fry. Anticipating Clifford Geertz and Carlo Ginsburg, Fry was fascinated by "micro-history," how the broader sweep of time and space could be studied in the smallest events, and accumulated manuscripts, documents, and printed ephemera illustrating this from 1500 onwards, notably in the fascist period. Still in Europe, a dramatic epoch of French history is well illustrated through Florida State's Napoleon and French Revolution Collection, which has nourished no fewer than 100 graduate degrees since its foundation in 1961.

Literary collections are one of the traditional staples of the special collections library, none more so than the Houghton Library at Harvard. Characteristically, the "Dickinson Room" there was the gift of an alumnus, Gilbert H. Montague, a remote cousin of Emily Dickinson, who bought her manuscripts and letters from a descendant of the poet's niece. With her manuscripts and letters have come her books, her "famous bureau," the bedside table on which she wrote, pictures and other objects, her herbarium and family photographs. This is no static shrine, but the core from which the standard editions of her poems and letters, the "variorum edition" of 1998, and now an electronic edition, have grown. Dickinson's whole life was spent at Amherst, Massachusetts. At the University of Nebraska–Lincoln, they celebrate Willa Cather, who grew up there and was deeply influenced by the place and by the expansion of the West. The author's niece gave the university the manuscripts of 12 of her novels, photographs, and letters.

At Queen's University, Kingston, Ontario, they have incomparably the best collection of Canadian literature. Lorne Pierce, minister and editor of the Ryerson Press, was all in all to the Canadian writers of his time. Beginning in 1928, he gave the university their works, established a fund to buy more, and bequeathed his own collection and papers. He knew Bliss Carman, Charles Roberts, and Major John Richardson, whose manuscripts as well as books joined his.

The libraries of Mazo de la Roche and George Whalley are among the supporting collections.

A common theme links the University of Pennsylvania and the University of Illinois at Urbana-Champaign. Both have important Shakespeare teaching collections: at Penn the Horace Howard Furness collection made by the editor of the great "New Variorum," which concentrates on performance, with promptbooks and even Yorick's skull signed by several Hamlets; at Urbana-Champaign, it is the collection of T. W. Baldwin, author of *William Shakespere's Small Latine & Lesse Greeke*, and appropriately concentrating on his reading and contemporary pedagogy. At the University of Kentucky they have the wonderful collection of W. Hugh Peal, whose literary interests were kindled by the gift of a copy of *Lamb's Tales from Shakespeare*, given to him "to keep him occupied and away from horses." From this grew a collection, notably strong in the Romantics, made by Peal, by then a New York lawyer, who gave it to the library in 1982.

At the University of Virginia is the collection of Clifton Waller Barrett, incomparably rich in first editions of American authors, amplified by manuscripts, among them those of Whitman's *Leaves of Grass*, Crane's *The Red Badge of Courage*, and Steinbeck's *The Grapes of Wrath*. The University of Delaware has the Ezra Pound collection of Robert A. Wilson, proprietor of the Phoenix Bookstore, acquired by gift and purchase in 2004. The farther shores of literature are explored at the University of California, Riverside, which houses the collection of J. Lloyd Eaton, one of the earliest to take science fiction seriously. Eaton's 7,500 volumes were bought for Riverside by an equally far-sighted if sadly short-lived librarian, Donald Wilson. The University of Florida has the Ruth Baldwin collection of children's books, specializing in those read by children, rather than chosen by adults for them to read. Begun in her spare time as a professor at Louisiana State University, Florida persuaded Baldwin to come as curator of the collection that they bought in 1977, an imaginative stroke of developments.

But the most remarkable and, in its time, innovative literary collection is that started in 1937 by Charles D. Abbott, then Librarian at the State University of New York at Buffalo. His object was to collect all first editions of poetry in English printed since 1900, not at the time an expensive undertaking. But he also wrote to as many living poets as he could, asking for the contents of their wastepaper baskets, discarded drafts of letters, anything. Flattered, a surprising number responded generously. Two generous donations added James Joyce manuscripts, the second of Sylvia Beach's Joyce archive. From this has grown a catholic collection of British and American poets, in print and manuscript. The records of poetry magazines have also been acquired. This achievement would be remarkable anywhere; to have come about in a state university without special funding is little short of a miracle.

Not surprisingly, the records and documents of industry, technology, and commerce, as well as the books relating to them, are a common theme in special collections all over the country. The Trade Literature Collection of the Smithsonian Institution is one of international as well as national importance. Trade catalogues normally have a short life expectancy, and here, with over 500,000 catalogues in every field of human endeavour, from heavy engineering to seed and nursery catalogues, there is a record of incomparable importance, used by many more than industrial historians. Local patriotism, the need to catch the documents of invention and the tools of trade before they are forgotten or destroyed, has played its part.

At Auburn University (where I once helped open a new library building, beside the football coach who had raised most of the money for it), they have the corporate records of Eastern Air Lines with the personal papers of Eddie Rickenbacker, founder of the airline, but before that the air-ace hero of World War I, and after that racing car driver; the records of his equally heroic struggle for survival in the Pacific in World War II are the stuff of legend, a film, and a biography. At Case Western Reserve University they celebrate a different hero, Charles F. Brush Sr., who anticipated Edison in producing the first commercially viable system for outdoor electric lighting and invented the windmill for generating electric power. A lifetime of exploring and developing the practical use of electricity and electromagnetic phenomena is documented in a multiple archive.

At Georgia Tech they have the records of the Fulton Bag and Cotton Mills, rescued from neglect in the basement of the defunct business. The history of packaging and its attendant labor disputes can be read here (the mill has been converted into "a mixed-income community of 182 loft apartments"). The University of Guelph, Ontario, is home to the extensive archive of the Massey-Harris-Ferguson agricultural machinery business. The settlement of Upper Canada was an open field for mechanical aids to cultivation, and the original Massey and Harris founded their businesses, specialising in farm implements and iron foundry in the mid-19th century. The two joined in 1891, the company growing to become an international giant. Its records, annual reports, posters, trade catalogues and repair and maintenance manuals, photographs, even 16mm film, form a matchless record from 1847 to 1986. At the University of Hawaii at Manoa they have the records of the Hawaiian Sugar Planters Association, a representative body for the industry as a whole, which, in addition, providently collected the records of individual plantations, and gave them to the university in 1995.

The University of Louisville has preserved the records of the Louisville and Nashville Railroad from 1836, some 255 linear archival feet and 600 photographs. Those studying the general, e.g., the industrialization of the New South, or the particular, e.g., "the shape of the inner bolt on the wheel assembly of a particular freight car," find this a gold mine; it is particularly useful for the legion of historical conservators of surviving railroad stock. Best of all, Louisville enjoys the support of a former official of the railroad, a man so eminent that he has a stretch of existing track named after him, who is a living oracle, capable of interpreting for library staff and many users what the records meant to those who used them. Pennsylvania State University also keeps the archives of a local institution of more than local importance, the records of the United Steelworkers of America. From the 1940s the union held its annual Summer Labor Institutes and Leadership Academies on the campus, and the link was consolidated by the union's gift of its records to the university, which has devoted a Steelworkers' Room to deploy them.

In 1928 Purdue University gave a home to the collection of a former Dean of the Engineering School, William Freeman Myrick Goss, 900 volumes mostly on locomotives and railroads. Over time, this collection has grown and spread to include civil, electrical, and hydraulic engineering; metallurgy; and branches of science less directly connected with engineering. This was celebrated in an exhibition in 2004, "Voices that Changed the World."

In 2006, Ohio State University received as a gift from its owner the historic fonds of the Curtiss Show Print business, a unique resource that forms a bridge between industrial records and those of show business. Curtiss Show Print started in 1905 at Kalida, soon moving to Continental, Ohio, where it was on the railroad. This proved a crucial asset in establishing a reputation for quick delivery. Posters, heralds, tickets, and letterheads went expeditiously to the various travelling vaudeville companies, minstrel shows, and numerous circuses. Playbills have, since their earliest days, been a showcase for brightly coloured lettering and blocks, and the Curtiss collection contains no less than 1,200 printing blocks, as well as photographs, correspondence, job tickets, and ledgers, together with file copies of what was printed. The donor, Nyle Stateler, still keeps the business going, but its earlier relics have become invaluable to the Ohio Center for Book Arts as demonstration material for handpress printing. It has made a lively Web site, and the collection and the donor starred in a 2005 film, *Continental, Ohio*.

The University of Cincinnati preserves an equally important and unique dramatic record in the 99 notebooks of William Lawrence, who devoted his energies to researching the history of the Dublin stage from 1630 onwards in local newspapers, parish registers, and other public records. All this went in his neat handwriting into the notebooks, amplified with portraits from programmes and press cuttings. After his death his notebooks drifted into the book trade, whence the majority were acquired by William S. Clark II, professor of English at Cincinnati, on whose death they were acquired by the university; another 20 are in the University of Bristol theatre collection, a useful opportunity for collaboration. Cincinnati has added the printed texts of Dublin plays to round out its collection.

Joseph Urban was one of the most creative stage designers of the first half of the 20th century, first at Vienna, then Boston and New York. His *Nachlass* at Columbia University reveals his work, not only for the stage, but also as an architect and designer for films, exhibitions, interiors, automobiles, furniture, store windows, roof gardens, and ballrooms. The collection presents special conservation problems, and in 2002 the National Endowment for the Humanities provided a grant for the preservation of the models and to create a digital archive of the collection. Urban was "director of light" for the 1933 to 1934 Century of Progress exposition at Chicago, celebrating the city's incorporation a century earlier. This was a landmark fair, not only in the thoroughness with which it covered every aspect of Chicago's growth and progress, but in the innovative techniques used to display them. In 1968 the University of Illinois at Chicago (UIC) acquired the papers of Lenox Riley Lohr, the fair's general manager, now used by city historians and schools as a result of UIC's outreach programs.

At Ohio University is the equally important dance collection of Alwin Nicolais, the "father of multimedia theatre," and Murray Louis. They choreographed over 250 works, developing in the process a joint theory of dance and a means of teaching it. Their manuscripts, scores, dance notation, photographs, video, and audio records are sampled on the university's Web site, and 16 dances are viewable in "streaming video" on the site as well. Even more remarkable is the donation by Katherine Dunham to Southern Illinois University Carbondale of her material in the same media, covering all the various phases of her life, as dancer, choreographer, and African-American anthropologist. Her correspondents included Josephine Baker, Harry Belafonte, W. C. Handy, and Butterfly McQueen. Her field recordings preserve folk music from Haiti. As the record of the woman who introduced African and Caribbean dance to a North American public, it is an archive of unique importance.

The collection of Gilbert Sigaux has given Vanderbilt University an unrivalled resource for the study of French theatre in the 20th century. A man of enormous energy, Sigaux participated in almost every aspect of the theatre in his lifetime, not merely in Paris but in the provinces.

A very different kind of theatre is represented at the University of Iowa in the Redpath Chautauqua Records, 1890 to 1944. The Chautauqua "circuits" represent a uniquely American way of combining instruction and entertainment. Originally founded to provide better training for Sunday school teachers, the Chautauqua movement quickly increased in popularity and scope. The supply of performers and demand were unbalanced, and Keith Vawter, a Cedar Rapids manager for the Redpath Lyceum Bureau, solved the problem by organising a system of booking for 15 Iowa towns. This spread to become a national organisation. Chautauqua to Theodore Roosevelt was "the most American thing in America." It dwindled with the Depression, movies, and radio, but the record preserved by Vawter remains its monument. A detailed inventory is on the library's Web site, with a related Web site, "Travelling Culture," that displays almost 800 publicity brochures for Chautauqua events.

Music features in quite a number of special collections, and the four represented here illustrate very clearly what makes them "special," as they would be even if they formed part of a mainline music library. At Johns Hopkins they have the Lester S. Levy collection of sheet music. Levy was a wealthy man, who was not deterred by cost, nor interested in bulk (too easily amassed) but in the capacity of what he bought to illustrate or record historically important trends or events. He made this policy clear in his *Grace Notes in American History: Popular Sheet Music 1820–1900* (1967): "the song after the event has been the reporter and interpreter of history." As well as major events, trends and fashions could be reflected in pictorial covers and song titles. By 1976 when Levy began to donate the collection to his alma mater, the collection amounted to 29,000 pieces, not large, but it is no surprise to learn that it is one of the most visited parts of the Johns Hopkins collection, both actually and virtually through scanned images online. The Peabody Conservatory student who wrote and produced an opera based on one song in the collection was using special collections material as it should be used. Mr. Levy would have been delighted.

Rutgers University has taken a different, almost complementary line in embarking on a Jazz Oral History project, encouraged by the

National Endowment for the Arts. Between 1972 and 1983, 120 artists were recorded, among them Count Basie, Charlie Mingus, and other famous figures. Of the 120, only 2 are still alive, a very striking example of the need to take time by the forelock where oral history is concerned. At Tulane University, they have the William Ransom Hogan Archive of New Orleans Jazz, named after its inventor, head of the History Department, "who wrote the initial grant proposal" (a novel kind of immortality). Beginning in 1958, the archive has had a start before Rutgers, if with a more limited focus. With 2,000 reels of taped interviews, supported by books, photographs, recordings, 55,000 pieces of sheet music, 225 linear feet of vertical files, phonograph cylinders, and even historic instruments, this is a very serious historic resource.

At the other end of the musical scale is the University of Western Ontario's Mahler collection. This was originally put together by the composer's sister, who married the violinist Arnold Rosé; their descendants managed to preserve what was a joint family archive. It is the best source for the composer's early life, and of his gifted brother-in-law; it also records the life of his niece Alma, also gifted, whose life ended tragically at Auschwitz. Alma Rosé's life is known to students of the Holocaust, and two other special collections featured here hold materials devoted to the record of the Jews and others who perished and those who escaped only in exile. The University of Southern California is host to the Survivors of the Shoah Visual History Foundation, established by Steven Spielberg in the wake of the success of *Schindler's List*. The foundation's collection now contains 52,000 videotape interviews conducted in 56 countries and 32 languages. These interviews were contemporaneously indexed so that users can search a million names and 50,000 keywords, thus making them instantly historically useful. Over 30 years ago, John M. Spalek, professor of German at the State University of New York at Albany, began an oral history project to record the experience of German-speaking academics who fled Europe in the 1930s. Many of them came to New York, where a "University in Exile" was founded in 1933. To their recorded voices, a number of former members of the university added their papers, to be preserved at Albany.

Both these collections exemplify a theme that runs through all these essays, the need for libraries to catch material in time, as does the acquisition by the George Washington University of the Westwood Mutual Broadcasting System (MBS) Records at the point when MBS ceased operation in 1998. As a result, 65 years of American history and popular culture were preserved for posterity. Like Charles Abbott at Buffalo, Richard Schimmelpfeng, Head of Special Collections at the University of Connecticut, saw the need to preserve what was not then called the "alternative press." With Richard Akeroyd, a student and later Librarian of the University, he collected first local relics of student protest, then, finding himself providentially at San Francisco for the American Library Association meeting in 1967, he added posters and other print picked up in Haight-Ashbury. If the bulk of the collection still concerns the era of Vietnam protest, it now goes back to 1800 and forward to the protest movements of today, especially the liberation and civil rights movements. Cornell too has its Human Sexuality Collection, founded with gifts from the founders of liberation movements, notably the Human Rights Campaign. Duke University points out that its holdings on women and their rights were, until the foundation of the Sallie Bingham Center for Women's History and Culture in 1999, "for the most part collected along with the papers of fathers, husbands, or other male relatives." This has now been put right, and the center ranges from Victorian etiquette books to "the papers of cyberpunk novelist Kathy Acker." There is a proper emphasis on the documents of the suffragettes and the women's liberation movement. Symposia are a regular part of the new center's mission. Virginia Tech has built up a remarkable International Archive of Women in Architecture, begun in 1985. It now holds 1,200 cubic feet of primary sources on over 300 women, and has a biographical database that lists 650 women from 51 countries. The Zaha Hadid archive would add the capstone to an already remarkable edifice.

The Library of Congress, itself a remarkable edifice, is the repository of the Historic American Buildings Survey, Engineering Record, and Landscapes Survey Collections, which grew out of a scheme to employ out-of-work architects during the Great Depression.

These are among the library's most heavily used collections, not surprisingly, since, with more than 35,000 surveys, 60,000 measured drawings, and 250,000 photographs, they are incomparably the fullest record of America's built and inherited landscape, much of it available online. The Great Depression produced a similar initiative in the Louisiana and Lower Mississippi Valley Collection, now at Louisiana State University (LSU). The Works Progress Administration's Louisiana Historical Records Survey employed Edwin Davis, an instructor at LSU. He in turn persuaded the university to house the survey's archive in a separate department, which he headed from 1935 to 1946. In addition to this primary source, the archive now has 120,000 books, 200,000 photographs, as well as maps and newspaper holdings.

The Downtown Collection at New York University is more sociological than architectural, but it is perhaps unique in preserving the physical traces of a society and its members. Its focus is indicated in the 2006 exhibition "The Downtown Show: The New York Art Scene 1974–1984," brought to life in flyers and art-show programmes, and papers of major participants such as Richard Hell, the man for whom the term "punk rock" was invented. In so far as a library can capture anything so evanescent as a zeitgeist, NYU's Fales Library has done it.

Imagery of all sorts is a common denominator of many special collections, the more so as exhibitions become an increasing part of their work. At the University of Colorado at Boulder there is a remarkable collection of photo-illustrated books, begun in 1991 when the Tippit collection was bought. At the University of Kansas, there are 30,000 glass plate negatives, the archive of Joseph J. Pennell, a commercial photographer at Junction City from 1890 to the 1920s. At Texas A&M University an innovative experiment in "textual iconography" has brought together 1,200 illustrated editions of Cervantes and 15,000 independent engravings and drawings, from 1573 to a Chinese translation of *Don Quixote* (2001). The Fisher Library at the University of Toronto has one of the most remarkable collections of graphic art in any library, with that made by Sidney Fisher of the engraved work of Wenceslaus Hollar, complete and in almost every known state.

Maps and cartography are another staple, at the University of Minnesota's James Ford Bell collection, begun in 1953 with 600 items on European westward expansion, now with 30,000 on exploration worldwide, and at Yale, whose collection of 11,000 pre-1850 maps is, despite recent thefts (a sad and salutary warning that the simple monetary value of "special collections" brings hazards as well as advantages), paramount in America, and also, through its link to geographic information systems (GIS) and the Global Positioning System (GPS), capable of comparison with the latest satellite-based surveys.

Kent State University houses the Borowitz True Crime Collection, made by a corporate (not criminal) lawyer, whose spare-time occupation it was. By 1983 he had more than 12,000 books, including a fine set of Conan Doyle's Sherlock Holmes stories, so much truer to life than reality. With the collection comes the collector's own manual of the subject, *Blood and Ink* (2002). The collection is a valued source of loans, notably by the National Library of Medicine, who borrowed books for a forensic medicine exhibition. The National Library of Medicine itself, less sensationally, has built up a remarkable bank of public health films, drawn from many sources, including the Public Health Service. Almost all of them were made for propaganda purposes, especially during World War II, but they are also invaluable sociological records of changing habits and attitudes. The Rosen Collection at the University of Saskatchewan, acquired in 2004, is a notable assemblage of books on veterinary science, with 500 books, journal titles and ephemera, the earliest the 1528 *Scriptores de re rustica*; it has a special strength in veterinary education.

Natural history is reflected in the National Agricultural Library's Pomological Watercolor Collection. Painting the different types of apple accurately is a specially fascinating branch of horticultural draftsmanship. The year after the Department of Agriculture set up its Division of Pomology in 1886, it appointed an artist, William Henry Prestele, to document new species and grafts, and over the next 40 years he and other artists who joined him built up a collection of some 7,700 different drawings. The National Agricultural Library has had the drawings indexed, and has developed an online database from which every variety, grower, and place can be retrieved. North Carolina State University has a world-class collection on entomology, originally created by Zeno Payne Metcalf, professor at the university 1912 to 1950, to which Eugène Séguy's fine folio prints have recently been added. The University of South Carolina can boast possession of the copy of Audubon's *Birds of America*, originally bought by the state on December 17, 1831 (by a narrow vote, 51/50), when barely a quarter of the drawings were available.

The more abstruse realms of science can be found, not surprisingly, at the Massachusetts Institute of Technology (MIT), whose DSpace@MIT archive exists as "an open source digital repository platform…to capture, store, index, preserve, and redistribute digital assets" of the research and teaching output of MIT. The archive already holds 24,000 items ranging from a scientific technical report or thesis to complex objects such as multi-file Web sites. The Stony Brook University provides a home for the AIDC 100 Archives. "Automatic identification and data capture" (AIDC) is the name given to a remarkable digital enterprise that aims to record the way that scientists and businesses are developing the means of automatic information retrieval. Founded by two pioneers, George and Teddy Goldberg, the archive has now enlisted 100 professionals in the field whose records form the basis of the collection. It is growing at the rate of 100 cubic feet per annum; its progress can be charted in *SCAN Newsletter*, founded by the Goldbergs in 1977.

On more familiar ground, the University of Oklahoma has its Galileo collection. Begun with the loan, later converted into a gift, of 129 books by Everette DeGolyer, the collection was spurred on by the discovery (attested by the Galileo scholar, Stillman Drake) that the copy of Galileo's *Dialogo* (1632) was corrected in the author's hand. As remarkable, in a different field, is the collection at Washington University in St. Louis made by Philip Mills Arnold, an engineer with Philips Petroleum, who became fascinated by semiotics. He built up a collection on the symbols used to convey meaning, excluding Braille and shorthand whose symbols have no meaning, but including early works such as the first edition of Rabanus Maurus *De Laudibus*

Sancte Crucis Opus (1503), with its Christological diagrams, and Blaise de Vigénère's pioneering work on ciphers.

Georgetown University has the Russell J. Bowen collection on espionage. The collector, formerly a colonel in the CIA, after amassing 14,000 books on the subject, has encouraged successive directors of the CIA, latterly Richard Helms, to deposit their papers, apparently without breaching national security. Brown University's Anne S. K. Brown collection of militaria extends from every work on warfare to an unrivalled army of model soldiers. It is one of the most used parts of the library, and has recently produced a digitised version of a Japanese scroll of Admiral Perry's expedition, which fascinates schoolchildren. Notre Dame has a comprehensive collection on sport, in all its forms, begun by buying the entire stock of a dealer in sports literature, with books, the earliest Mercuriale *De arte gymnastica* (1573), journals and 18,000 college, and 3,500 professional, football programs. It was a prescient move since it anticipated the 1980s boom in the market for such material, and with it the growing academic application of "scholarly methodologies to the study of sport." Michigan State University, equally prescient, invested in comic art, beginning in the 1960s with a donation of 6,000 comic books by two students. Syracuse University specialises in cartoons and cartoonists, with 20,000 original items by 173 artists, beginning with Bud Fisher, originator of *Mutt and Jeff* (1907) and spanning the 20th century. Searchable online finding aids are available for the work of 70 artists, and are used increasingly by social historians.

I have left until last three collections that share common features, but features so uncommon elsewhere as to stand out in this brief survey. All three concern the environment, not a subject found other than peripherally in other special collections. All three were built by people who lived to a very great old age. All three donors saw the environment as the product of the interaction of human and natural factors, which they strove to support equally. At Oklahoma State University are the papers of Angie Debo (1890–1988), whose long lifetime was devoted to the study and preservation of the Southwest. Pioneering ethno-history with a prize-winning study of the Choctaw

Republic in 1934, she could not get a job until, in 1947, she became curator of maps in the Oklahoma State University Library. A "scholar warrior," she set up a national network to preserve nature and the needs of native peoples to preserve it. Michael Harrison (1897–2005) spent an even longer life, first in the National Park Service at the Grand Canyon, then in the Bureau of Indian Affairs, studying and preserving tribal ways. He also collected over 21,000 books (including the great Curtis *North American Indian* portfolio of photographs), analysing the contents of each book by his own "Harrison Peculiar System," whose 700,000 cards are a comprehensive guide to his work; all this is now at the University of California, Davis. Margery Stoneman Douglas (1890–1998) came to Miami in 1915 as a journalist, joining the University of Miami the year after it was founded. She campaigned to preserve the unique ecosystem of Southern Florida, and the Everglades became a National Park in 1947, the year that *The Everglades: River of Grass*, first of her many books, was published. She founded the Friends of the Library in 1960 and gave the library her papers in 1987, documents of a long life spent fighting for an area of unique beauty.

Developing North America's Cultural Assets

The record of all the special collections in this book covers an astonishing variety of matter, and a pattern of equally various and growing use of these collections. If most of it is American in content, that is as it should be. But the non-American holdings are no less remarkable, and it should be remembered that all the holdings described here are but one collection in libraries and institutions with larger and wider coverage. This compilation is a snapshot of work spread over a century, sometimes two centuries, among libraries that have grown in number as well as size over that time. I have enjoyed reading this account of them, as I have enjoyed visiting those I have seen and worked in. I am only sorry that there has not been more space to mention more of the librarians as well as the donors who put the collections together. I think of Bill Jackson at Harvard and Fritz Liebert at Yale, Karl Gay at Buffalo and Larry Powell at Los Angeles,

among a host of other librarians, no longer the lonely figures of 40 years ago but a community. I also remember the booksellers, often vital intermediaries in the gift as well as purchase of collections, like bees carrying pollen: at Seven Gables, Mike Papantonio, friend to many; and John Kohn, co-architect of Waller Barrett's collection; Dave Magee, a notable builder at Brigham Young; and Jake Zeitlin, all in all to the libraries of Southern California and beyond.

Over all these decades the Association of Research Libraries has served as a forum where the leadership of these North American research libraries convened to address the key issues facing their institutions and the diverse communities of users they serve. Through ARL, research libraries identified and pursued strategies to increase the visibility of special collections, and this, in turn, has opened the door to all the different kinds of new uses that its members now provide. Those who founded ARL just after Christmas 1932 set on foot something that has enabled their successors to grow and develop local assets into a whole that is one of North America's greatest cultural assets.

---

* About the Author

Nicolas Barker is editor of the *Book Collector*, "the leading English-language journal on book collecting, and the only one that bridges the worlds of the scholar, the librarian, the bookseller, and the private collector." He has written many books, among them *Stanley Morison* (1972), *Bibliotheca Lindesiana* (1977), and *Aldus Manutius and the Development of Greek Script and Type in the 15th Century* (2nd ed. 1992). He is the editor of John Carter's classic *ABC for Book Collectors* and in recent editions its author.

Nicolas Barker was the first head of conservation at the British Library, and in 1986–87 William Andrews Clark Visiting Professor at UCLA; he is a faculty member at the Rare Book School at the University of Virginia, and is a familiar figure in North America, having been a regular visitor at special collections here from coast to coast.

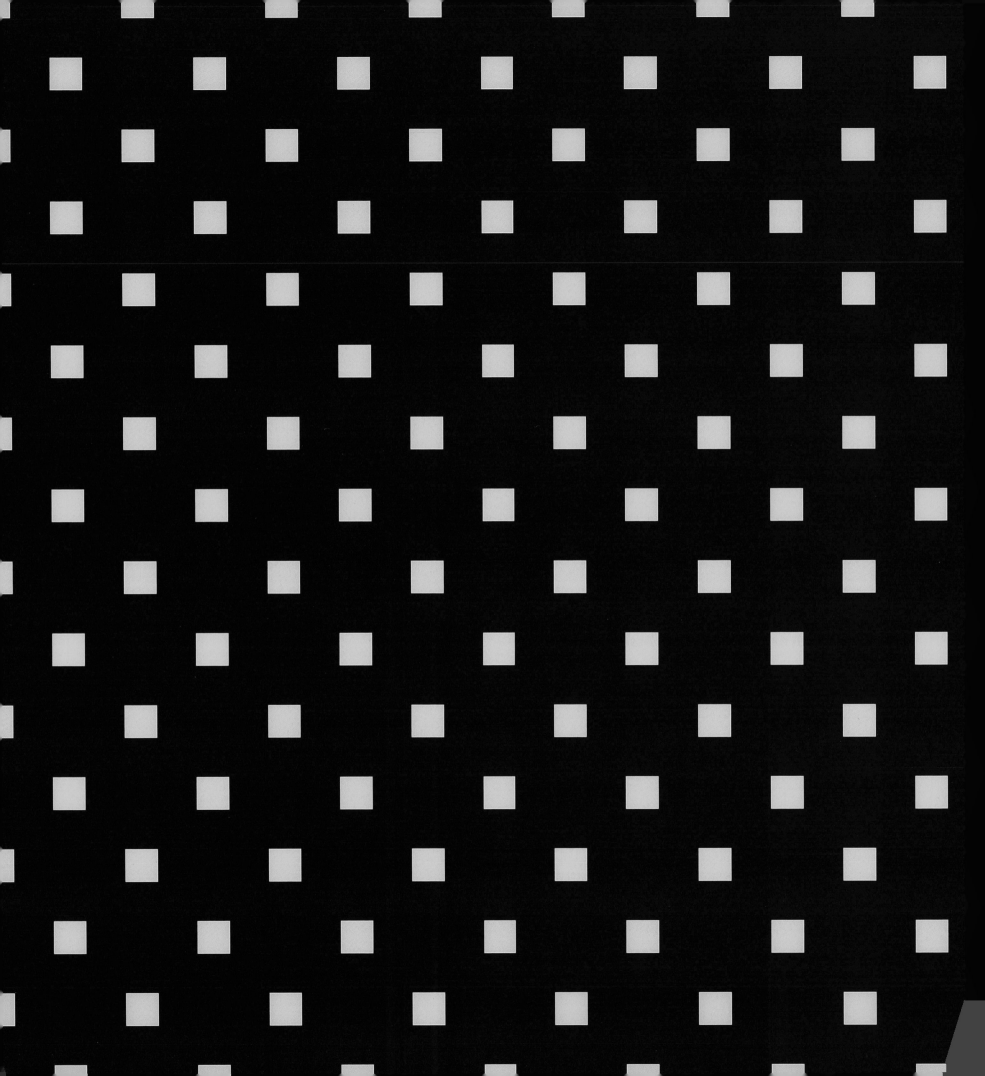

Collection Profiles

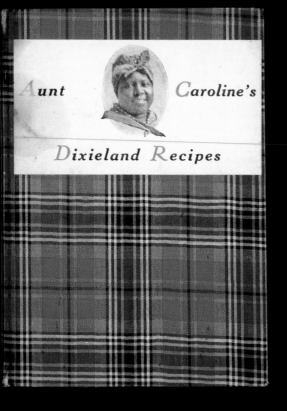

Aunt Caroline's

Dixieland Recipes

The
EBONY
COOKBOOK

A DATE
WITH
A DISH

By Freda DeKnight

The
GEECHEE
COOK BOOK

Introduction
"OPINION"

By JOHNNY MERCER

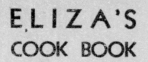

ELIZA'S
COOK BOOK

FAVORITE RECIPES
Compiled by
NEGRO CULINARY ART CLUB

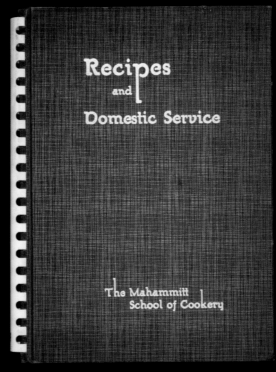

Recipes
and
Domestic Service

The Mahammitt
School of Cookery

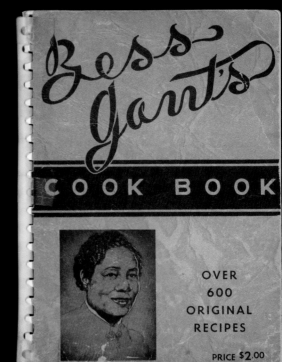

Bess
Gant's

COOK BOOK

OVER
600
ORIGINAL
RECIPES

PRICE $2.00

University of Alabama Libraries
W.S. Hoole Special Collections Library

The David Walker Lupton African American Cookbook Collection

A LOCAL reporter had arrived to do a story on our new collection of African-American cookbooks. A librarian was explaining the significance of the collection when a researcher walked in and asked to see the Lupton collection. "What a coincidence," the librarian said, "this reporter is doing a story about it. Perhaps she'd like to hear of your interest." As the researcher explained her interest in the collection, she mentioned where she was from. The reporter was stunned. "You've come all the way from New York to Alabama to see these! Why?"

David Walker Lupton put together his collection of 450 volumes because, in the words of his wife, "David had a deep conviction that cookbooks compiled by individuals in America of African heritage needed to be identified and preserved." His collection covers the period from 1827, when the first book with recipes by an African-American was published, through the year 2000. When Mr. Lupton, a collateral descendant of former University of Alabama president Nathaniel Thomas Lupton, was considering a permanent home for his collection, the University of Alabama seemed to offer the ideal context both geographically and institutionally. His widow, Dorothy R. Lupton, finalized arrangements for transferring the volumes in 2004.

Some of the cookbooks represent the work of talented African-American chefs responsible for much of the elegant cuisine in fine restaurants, hotels, clubs, and dining cars, but the beginnings of the soul food movement are well documented also. Many of the cookbooks are community-based fund raisers from churches, women's clubs, and sororities. These are often the most difficult to identify and locate because they usually do not receive wide publicity or distribution beyond their contributors.

Because culinary texts are written from the point of view of an individual or a community, they have much to say about ethnic identity, family and community life, social history, the roles of women and men, values, religion, and economics, as well as the more obvious fields of diet and nutrition, use of agricultural products, the food supply, and general food history. Almost every title in the Lupton Collection suggests more than recipes: food is linked with music, humor, social satire, cultural and religious celebrations, and other aspects of African-American life.

The Lupton collection has been used by students, faculty, and researchers from across the country. One researcher used the collection for research for a book and for a talk to be delivered in Africa on African foodways in America. A class on cooking and culture used the collection for group research projects, culminating in presentations complete with dishes prepared by the students. In an ethnography class, one student project resulted in tying recipes in several of the cookbooks to specific family traditions. Interest in the collection continues due to the initial press release and the information about the collection put on our Web site.

http://www.lib.ua.edu/lupton.htm

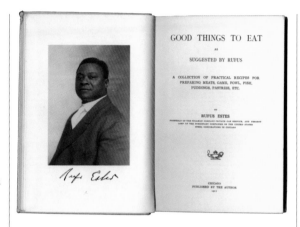

(ABOVE)
Good Things to Eat as Suggested by Rufus: A Collection of Practical Recipes for Preparing Meats, Game, Fowl, Fish, Puddings, Pastries, Etc. Rufus Estes. Chicago: The author, 1911.

Born a slave in Murray County, Tennessee, in 1857, Rufus Estes became one of the most highly regarded chefs of his day. US presidents, European royalty, explorers, and major industrialists were among those who enjoyed his culinary talents. His cookbook is widely held to be the first cookbook authored by an African-American professional chef.

(OPPOSITE TOP LEFT)
Aunt Caroline's Dixieland Recipes. Emma and William McKinney. 1922.

(OPPOSITE TOP CENTER)
The Ebony Cook Book: A Date with a Dish. Freda DeKnight. 1962.

(OPPOSITE TOP RIGHT)
The Geechee Cook Book. Episcopal Churchwomen of the Diocese of Georgia. 1956. Cover.

(OPPOSITE BOTTOM LEFT)
Eliza's Cook Book: Favorite Recipes. Compiled by Negro Culinary Art Club. 1936.

(OPPOSITE BOTTOM CENTER)
Recipes and Domestic Service. Sarah Helen Tolliver. Mahammitt School of Cookery, 1939.

(OPPOSITE BOTTOM RIGHT)
Bess Gant's Cook Book. Bessie M. Gant. 1947.

University at Albany, State University of New York, Libraries
M.E. Grenander Department of Special Collections & Archives

German and Jewish Intellectual Émigré Collection

DURING the early 1970s, Dr. John M. Spalek, then Chair of the State University of New York at Albany's Department of Germanic Languages and Literatures, initiated an oral history project to interview German-speaking academics who immigrated to the United States in the 1930s. Dr. Spalek and his team of researchers established contacts with hundreds of émigrés and their families and discovered that many still possessed important historical materials pertaining to their immigration. In 1976, recognizing the urgent need to save and preserve these papers, he proposed the establishment of what is now the German and Jewish Émigré Collection.

During the 1930s, totalitarian countries expelled thousands of intellectuals who opposed the rising power of the National Socialist (Nazi) Party. In Germany roughly 4,000 academics lost positions, and 1,700 of those scholars came to the United States. This enormous "brain drain" during the Hitler years cost Germany and Austria many of their most noted scholars. Some of these individuals would become Nobel Prize winners.

Many émigrés came to New York City and were hired by the newly created Graduate Faculty of the New School for Social Research, a "University in Exile" formed in 1933 to provide a safe haven for academics who had lost their positions in Germany. One member of the University in Exile, economist Hans Staudinger, was the first to agree to donate his papers to the University at Albany. Other New School faculty members soon followed his example. Within the next few years, Albany became home to the papers of political sociologist Hans Speier, economist Gerhard Colm, writer/philosopher Erich von Kahler, and political journalist Karl Otto Paetel. Over the last three decades, the papers of many other émigré social scientists, humanists, writers, and artists have been added to the collection.

Today the German and Jewish Intellectual Émigré Collection is preserved and accessible at the University Libraries' M. E. Grenander Department of Special Collections and Archives. While the papers of former faculty members of the University in Exile of the New School for Social Research form the core of the collection, the current Émigré Collection consists of 108 collections comprising more than 1,500 cubic feet of personal papers, organizational records, political pamphlets, tape recordings, photographs, and related research materials documenting the German intellectual exodus of the 1930s and 1940s. The collection has been used by scholars from many European and American universities, colleges, and other research institutions to produce scores of doctoral dissertations, theses, books, articles, conference papers, exhibits, and videos.

http://library.albany.edu/speccoll/emigre.htm

(ABOVE TOP)
The March of Evil. A.R. Lerner. 1945.

(ABOVE BOTTOM)
Jewish Unity for Victory. Alexander Bittelman. 1943.

(OPPOSITE)
"Harpsichordist Yella Pessl in New York City."
Photograph by Larry Gordon. Circa 1940.

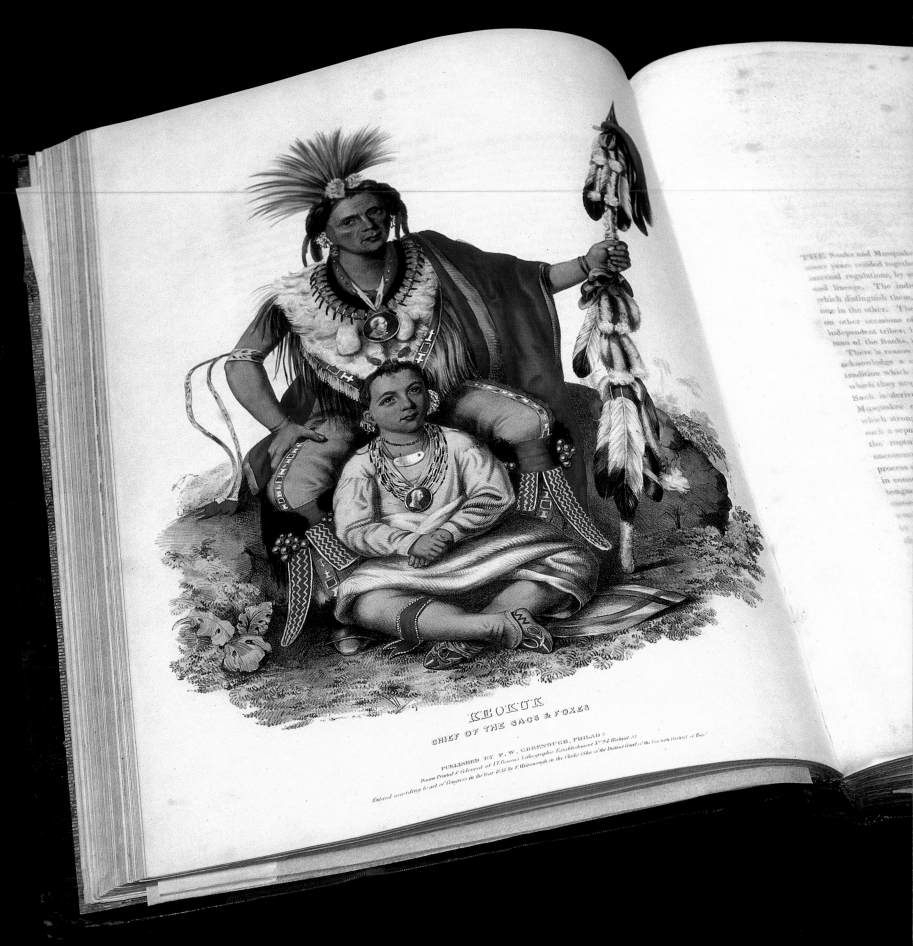

KEOKUK

CHIEF OF THE SACS & FOXES

PUBLISHED BY F. W. GREENOUGH, PHILAD.ᵃ

Drawn Printed & Coloured at I.T.Bowens Lithographic Establishment Nᵒ 94 Walnut St.

Entered according to act of Congress in the Year 1838 by F.Watsonough in the Clerks Office of the District Court of the Eastern District of Penn.ᵃ

University of Alberta Libraries
Bruce Peel Special Collections Library

The Javitch Collection

THE Javitch Collection of more than 2,300 volumes on North and South American aboriginals was the finest in private hands in Canada when Gregory Javitch offered it to the University of Alberta in 1980. Javitch was born in Russia in 1898 and moved in 1922 to France, which was his home for the next 20 years. In 1942 he took his wife and two sons to Palestine to escape from the Nazis, and in 1950 they came to Canada. Javitch became increasingly interested in the history of the Americas and began collecting rare books that offered a balanced view of indigenous civilizations. The resulting collection provides in-depth perspectives on the legends, ceremonial dances, music, and daily lives of aboriginal peoples.

Javitch was extremely sensitive to the fact that these people, the original inhabitants of the Americas, had been persecuted, displaced, and nearly annihilated by Europeans. It appeared to Javitch to be a form of genocide, and, having fled from such persecutions himself, he was sympathetic. As a Russian Jew, Javitch well understood what was involved in the persecution, displacement, and attempted annihilation of a whole race.

The Javitch Collection contains a number of subdivisions, and one of the most important, and painful, is called "A Well Digested Plan." The phrase first appeared in a letter from American President James Monroe to the Congress, in 1824, when Monroe began the policy of forcing the removal of aboriginals from their own lands. The implementation of that policy in the United States and Canada can be traced through 181 different treaties, laws, and documents in the Javitch Collection.

Legends, myths, and tales form another part of the collection. Although Europeans often regarded aboriginals as devoid of religious feelings, more patient inquirers realized that their religious ceremonies vie with those of any other culture or society, ancient or modern, for allegory, symbolism, and intricacy of ritual. Javitch also had a shrewd eye for useful, modestly priced books, including many children's stories which are retellings of aboriginal legends. Their narrative liveliness can be vividly appreciated, particularly since many of these authors have been deeply respectful of the original oral versions.

Javitch's fascination with the visual portrayal of aboriginal life also led him to acquire many remarkable 19th-century illustrated portfolios depicting views and costumes. Among these are such landmark works as Sir Robert Schomburgk's *Views in the Interior of Guiana* (1840) and the vibrant multicolored chromolithographs of Frederick Catherwood's *Views of Ancient Monuments in Central America, Chiapas and Yucatan* (1844). Numerous books contain illustrations of ceremonial dances. In Javitch's published checklist on this subject (Montreal, 1974), 97 titles are indexed by dance.

Further material on native culture is found in the collection of aboriginal-language books, comprising 120 volumes in 36 languages, from Abenaki and Biloxi to Wyandot and the hieroglyphs of the Mayans. The Javitch Collection, a cornerstone of the Bruce Peel Library holdings, continues to grow through the acquisition of further titles that complement and broaden the collection.

(ABOVE)
Aus dem Leben der Indianer. Herausgegben von der Orientalischen Cigaretten Compagnie, 19—.
   Cigarette-card book with pictures of Indians of North America.

(OPPOSITE)
"Keokuk: Chief of the Sacs & Foxes." In *History of the Indian Tribes of North America, with Biographical Sketches and Anecdotes of the Principal Chiefs*, vol. 2. Thomas L. McKenney. Philadelphia: D. Rice and J. G Clark, 1842.

University of Arizona Library
Special Collections

The Fred Harvey Hotels Collection

(ABOVE)
"El Tovar Hotel Entrance." Photograph from
National Park Service. Early 1900s.

(OPPOSITE)
"Telescope Tower, The Lookout, Grand Canyon,
Arizona." Photo by Santa Fe Railroad. Circa 1915.

How Fred Harvey became synonymous with the development of the American West is documented in a collection of photographs, ledger books, and other ephemera that Fred Harvey Inc. donated to the University of Arizona Libraries Special Collections in 1971. The Fred Harvey hotel and restaurant chain along the Atchison, Topeka, and Santa Fe Railway lines represents one of the most successful American business partnerships of the late 19th and early 20th centuries. By 1945, the Fred Harvey establishments extended from the Great Lakes to the Pacific Coast and the Gulf of Mexico.

Included in the collection are approximately 2,000 black-and-white photographs showing exterior and interior views of the Harvey establishments in Arkansas, Arizona, California, Colorado, Illinois, Kansas, Mississippi, Missouri, New Mexico, Ohio, Oklahoma, Tennessee, and Texas. It also includes correspondence sent to the Harvey Company dating from 1896 to 1944, a few scrapbooks, and other supplemental materials.

Many of the photographs appeared in early publications and promotions by Fred Harvey and his company. Being products of various photographers (for example, some bear the stamp of the Detroit Photographic Company), these photos illustrate American history in an era when rail travel thrived. They also confirm the contributions made by many single, well-mannered, and educated ladies who were waitresses in Harvey establishments. These young women, given one-year contracts as "Harvey Girls," came west to work and forged a new social history in the process.

The Fred Harvey Collection also includes examples of promotional materials about the Grand Canyon: travel brochures, publications, advertisements, and newspaper stories that influenced the growth of tourism in western states. Traffic to the Grand Canyon either by train or car grew from 44,000 in 1919 to over 300,000 in the mid-1930s. Fred Harvey hotels, newsstands, restaurants, and dining cars supported and also benefited from tourism and boosted the popularity of train travel.

Harvey's employment of architect Mary Colter in the early decades of the 20th century resulted in some of the Southwest's most famous landmark hotels. Colter completed 21 projects for Fred Harvey. Of her buildings still standing, certainly the best known are her Harvey-sponsored endeavors at the Grand Canyon: Hopi House, Hermit's Rest, the Lookout Lounge, the Watchtower, Bright Angel Lodge, and Phantom Ranch.

The photographs in the collection have also appeared in a variety of more recent publications. For instance, 30 photos were used in Virginia L. Grattan's *Mary Colter: Builder upon the Red Earth* (1992).

Demand for images from the collection resulted in the creation of an online Web exhibit:

http://harvey.library.arizona.edu/

Finding aid: http://harvey.library.arizona.edu/finding_aid/welcome.html

Arizona State University Libraries
Department of Archives and Special Collections

Guardian of the Flame Sri Lanka Manuscripts Collection

FEW students of Buddhism or scholars of Sri Lankan culture would expect to find primary sources relating to their work in Arizona, but thanks to a Phoenix physician the largest publicly accessible collection of Sinhalese palm-leaf manuscripts in the Western Hemisphere now resides at Arizona State University (ASU).

The donor of the Guardian of the Flame Collection became entranced by Sri Lankan art as a result of gifts he received from his father, a Sri Lankan national. He subsequently built a large collection of artistic works as well as hundreds of manuscripts acquired for their beauty, but he was unable to read all the manuscript texts. The donor contacted faculty at the ASU Center for Asian Studies, the Herberger College of Fine Arts, and the Department of Religious Studies to explore the potential for building curricula in Sri Lankan and South Asian studies. His plan was to donate materials from his collections to spark interest and investment in teaching students about Sri Lanka and Buddhism.

The Guardian of the Flame Sri Lanka Manuscripts Collection consists of 390 individual manuscripts comprised of palm leaves stacked upon each other, placed between wooden boards, and tied together with string and buttons or coins. Some wooden boards are ornate, displaying intricate design, carving and/or painting techniques. Writing is applied to the palm leaves by embossing them with a specially designed stylus, then rubbing lampblack into the resulting relief.

Most texts are written in the hand of one individual, and some of the texts are written in multiple languages. The majority of the collection is written in Pali, the traditional language of Theravada Buddhist monasteries, and presented in Sinhalese or Sanskrit script. Some of the texts present freehand illustrations.

The texts are predominantly Theravada Buddhist religious texts, but some texts present medicinal or astrological information. The textual content originates from as early as the third century AD, although these copies of the texts date from 1700 to 1910. The texts were transcribed by Buddhist monks, who received spiritual honor for copying and thus disseminating the words of the Buddha and his disciples. As a result certain texts are repeatedly presented in several manuscript objects.

Since the initial gift of manuscripts in 2005, ASU faculty in Fine Arts and Religious Studies have collaborated with University Libraries staff to engage scholars with the requisite language skills who can assist ASU with preliminary identification and cataloging of the materials. This collaboration has precipitated two guest lectures at ASU, class presentations, and an international scholar's consultation entitled "Buddhist Objects: Knowledge, Ritual and Art" hosted by ASU in October 2006. There, several visiting scholars examined the collection for the first time and confirmed the exceptional research value of these materials. A preliminary catalog has been produced from the scholars' descriptions, and it will be encoded for Internet access using the international standard. Conservation and selective translation and digitization will be conducted over the next several years. A scholar's consultation Web site is available at:

http://www.asu.edu/clas/religious_studies/lanka/collection.htm

(ABOVE)
Pratimoksha Sanne (Bhikshu-pratimokshayehi-padartha). N.d. Detail.

A Sinhala gloss on *Vinaya* text with lotus wheels.

(OPPOSITE: TOP TO BOTTOM)
Pratimoksha Sanne (Bhikshu-pratimokshayehi-padartha). N.d.

Folded.
Partially unfolded.
Fully unfolded.

Auburn University Libraries
Special Collections & Archives

History of Flight Collection

AUBURN University has had a mission to teach "mechanics" since 1872, when the state of Alabama accepted the provisions of the Morrill Act. Throughout the 19th and 20th centuries, the school's engineering programs have reflected the evolution of that field. Today, Auburn University supports teaching and research not only in aviation engineering, but also aviation management and the history of technology, the latter with a strong emphasis upon the history of flight.

The Special Collections & Archives Department of the Auburn University Libraries holds rare books, manuscripts, still pictures, motion pictures, sound recordings, and digital collections related to the history of both military and commercial aviation. These materials document not only the development of aircraft as weapons and instruments of commerce, but also tourism, labor-management relations in the aviation industry, popular culture, the evolution of engineering, and individuals significant to the history of flight.

The latter include the personal papers of Eddie Rickenbacker, founder of Eastern Air Lines, as well as corporate records of that company. In addition to Rickenbacker's career as a pioneer in commercial aviation, these materials document his days as a race-car driver, his airborne exploits as America's ace-of-aces during World War I, the relationship between this American hero and the members of his family, the 21 days during October and November 1942 when he was lost at sea while on a secret mission for Secretary of War Henry L. Stimson, and his devotion to conservative causes during the 1960s.

The 21 days during October and November 1942 may have been the single most dramatic episode in Rickenbacker's life, as well as the lives of the B-17 crew members adrift with him in the Pacific Ocean. In 1998, one of the remaining survivors, John Bartek, came to Auburn and provided a first-hand account of their long ordeal and dramatic rescue. Bartek's story resides among the documents found in Auburn's history of flight collection, as do the Rickenbacker scrapbooks that contain post-rescue press accounts referring to "Iron Man Eddie" and calling the World War I hero "one ace that can get out of any hole." Hollywood even dramatized this episode in a motion picture, a copy of which is also in the collection.

Scholars, graduate students, and undergraduates from Auburn University and other institutions of higher learning have employed the history of flight collection in the production of senior theses, master's theses, doctoral dissertations, scholarly articles, and books issued by the academic press. Most notably, these have included *Eddie Rickenbacker: An American Hero in the Twentieth Century* (2005), by W. David Lewis, a member of Auburn University's Department of History. Professor Lewis and others in his department have been instrumental in working with the Auburn University Libraries to build the history of flight collection.

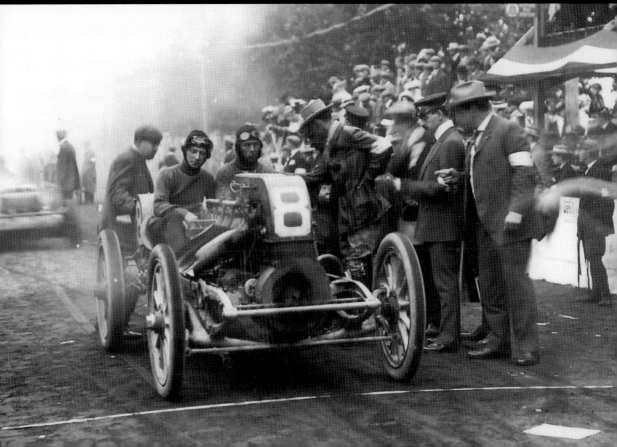

APPARET CHRISTVS SEPTEM DISCIPVLIS AD MARE TYBERIADIS.

Ioan. xxi.

A. Non multo post venerunt omnes Hierosolymis in Galilæam; erant ad mare Galilææ; alij alijs locis, Petrus, & Filij Zebedæi Bethsaidæ.

B. Ostendit Petrus velle se piscatum ire, offerunt se illi comites sex

C. Piscantur tota nocte, nihil capiunt

D. Stat IESVS mane in littore; rogat numquad pulmenti habeant; hoc est aliquid piscium pro obsonio

E. Respondent simpliciter, vt emptori vulgari; Non.

D. Subiungit IESVS; Mitte in dexteram nauigij rete, & inuenietis.

E. Mittunt, concludunt piscium ingentem copiam; quod cum sentirent,

F. Agnoscit IESVM Ioannes, & dixit Petro; Dominus est.

G. Quod Petrus audiens, succingit se tunica, & mari venit ad IESVM.

H. Panis & Piscis, quæ parauerat Christus in littore.

Boston College Libraries

The John J. Burns Library of Rare Books and Special Collections

The Rev. J. Donald Monan, S.J. Collection of Jesuitana

IT is only fitting that the largest of the 28 Jesuit colleges and universities in the United States should boast the premier Jesuitana collection in the nation. Exhibitions, catalogs, and conferences in the past focusing on the collection have given the library the opportunity to publicize its Jesuit treasures. The collection represents a wealth of material that is critical to a fuller understanding and appreciation of the many Jesuit contributions to early modern thought and culture, not only in Europe, but also in the New World and the Far East. Some highlights include seminal works in science and mathematics from Christopher Clavius (1538–1612), Gaspar Schott (1608–1666), and Athanasius Kircher (1602–1680); devotional material by Gerónimo Nadal (1507–1580); and travel literature, one outstanding example being the first comprehensive account of Asia to be published in English by Richard Willes, *The History of Travayle in the West and East Indies and Other Countreys Lying Eyther Way Towards the Fruitful and Ryche Moluccaes* (1577).

In 1986, Boston College published the first print catalog of its rather modest but important collection of Jesuit material. Since then, the Jesuitana collection has grown tremendously and is currently one of the most dynamic special collections in the Burns Library. In the 1990s came three major acquisitions from the Weston School of Theology in Cambridge, Massachusetts; the Jesuit Library from the Rue Dauphine residence in Old Quebec City, Canada; and the Bibliothèque des Fontaines in Chantilly, France. In 1996, the collection was named the Rev. J. Donald Monan, S.J. Collection of Jesuitana at Boston College, in honor of Boston College's outgoing, long-serving president. Currently, the collection numbers some 15,000 titles, covering virtually the entire spectrum of human knowledge, including many rare and seminal works in the fields of theology, philosophy, Biblical exegesis, mathematics, science, history, politics, and travel. It is especially rich in pre-Suppression (i.e., pre-1773) materials. In addition, the collection includes three original letters from Jesuit saints— Francis Borgia, Robert Bellarmine, and Francis Xavier.

Cataloging of the collection has progressed steadily, but the Chantilly acquisition has proven especially challenging because of its many "bound-with" volumes, each of which contains numerous pamphlets requiring separate title analysis. Growth has also continued in other areas of the Jesuitana Collection due to generous gifts from the Jesuit Community of Boston College and the Jesuit Institute of Boston College, as well as the efforts of a number of independent booksellers who have taken a special interest in helping Boston College strengthen this important scholarly resource. In late 2006, Boston College converted the temporary cataloging appointment into a permanent one, underscoring the college's commitment to sustaining, extending, and show-casing this unique collection. The Jesuit Institute has been instrumental in helping widen scholarly access to the collection. In 2004, the institute created a Traveling Research Grant available for research in any field of the humanities making use of the Jesuitana Collection, with preference given to scholars specializing in the early modern period.

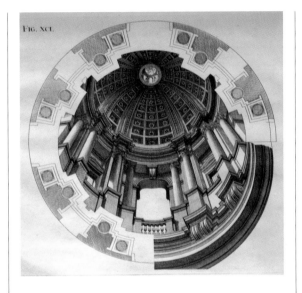

(ABOVE)
"Pozzo's Trompe-l'oeil Dome at Sant'Ignazio." Illustration from *Rules and Examples of Perspective Proper for Painters and Architects*. Andrea Pozzo. 1707.

    Pozzo's theoretical manual on perspective was one of the earliest of its kind.

(OPPOSITE)
"Resurrected Christ's Appearance in Galilee while His Disciples Are Fishing." Illustration from *Evangelicae historiae imagines*. Gerónimo Nadal. 1593.

    Ignatius Loyola meditated in front of paintings everyday in his apartment in Rome; Nadal created this engraved cycle to provide others images to meditate by.

The Personal Library of President John Adams

Le monde primitif, analysé et comparé avec le monde moderne.
Antoine Court de Gébelin. 1773–84. Detail.

Between 1812 and 1816, John Adams embarked on a systematic, comparative investigation of ancient religions. This nine-volume *Primitive World, Analyzed and Compared with the Modern World*, explored ancient cultures and argued that early civilizations were far more enlightened than many had suspected. In his diary, Adams recorded dining with author Gébelin at least twice in 1778 while serving as diplomat in France and described him as "silent, soft, and still. His mind always upon the Stretch."

Transcription of Adams's commentary:

Truths sublime indeed and eternal! The Unity of the Universe, its Author, Government, and End are the Sublimest Conceptions of which any Intellect is capable! Dupuis may call the Acting Power Matter if he will: I call it Spirit and I know what I mean as well as he does.

Le monde primitif, analysé et comparé avec le monde moderne.
Antoine Court de Gébelin. 1773–84. Pages.

DEPOSITED with the Boston Public Library in 1894, the John Adams Library includes over 2,700 volumes collected by President John Adams as well as hundreds of additional volumes donated by family members. Adams's book collection constituted one of the largest personal libraries collected in America during his lifetime (1735–1826) and—at 3,510 books—the library remains one of the largest early American libraries still intact. This remarkable collection represents the intellectual tastes of an influential thinker, writer, and political philosopher who helped shape the Constitution of the United States and drafted the Massachusetts Constitution, the oldest functioning written constitution in the world. Adams set forth quite deliberately to educate himself by collecting books on an immense variety of subjects and by engaging the great thinkers, philosophers, and political minds across time and place through their writings. The John Adams Library spans the fields of classics, literature, history, politics, government, philosophy, religion, law, science, mathematics, medicine, agriculture, linguistics, economics, and travel.

The John Adams Library Collection is of particular interest to scholars and historians because Adams recorded thousands of interpretive and critical manuscript annotations in the margins of hundreds of his books. His engagement was active and argumentative, as evidenced by the voluminous personal commentary he scrawled into the margins of his books. In these annotated volumes, many of which were hand-dated by Adams, researchers will encounter an intimate and candid conversation that engaged Adams at every stage of his long life with the wider world of self-culture through books—as a boy, university student, Boston lawyer, revolutionary, founding father, diplomat, president, and elder statesman of the early American Republic.

In 2003, the Boston Public Library was awarded two major federal grants to fund the preservation, electronic cataloging, digitization, and physical exhibition of the John Adams Library collection. The following components of the John Adams Library Project have now been completed: electronic cataloging of the complete John Adams Library collection, accessible from the Boston Public Library's main catalog as well as from the John Adams Library Web site; typed transcriptions of Adams's manuscript annotations for all books with comments or interpretive notes by Adams; the opening of a major gallery exhibition, "John Adams Unbound"; development and launch of the independent John Adams Library Web site; and digitization of 33 complete volumes from the John Adams Library Collection. Through the development of this multi-faceted project, researchers and the general public are now privileged to look over Adams's shoulder at the extraordinary revolutionary times in which he lived and to explore his deeply personal reflections preserved in the margins of this remarkable library.

http://www.johnadamslibrary.org/

de & languissante, elle sera vive, variée & pleine de gaieté chez les autres: favoris de la Nature, sur-tout dans des Climats qui font tout pour eux, sans soucis, sans ambition, sans études pénibles, leur imagination que rien n'émousse se portera avec force à peindre la Nature, & à chanter ses heureux effets.

C'est sur-tout dans les développemens des vérités abstraites de la Morale & de la Religion, que cette imagination déployera ses richesses. Ces vérités nécessaires à tous les hommes, ne peuvent être facilement saisies de ceux qui livrés aux travaux les plus pénibles de la société, ne sont pas habitués à suivre de longs raisonnemens, & n'ont ni le tems, ni la volonté de s'enfoncer dans des recherches Métaphysiques.

§. 9.

Nécessité des Allégories pour communiquer & pour conserver ces connoissances.

Ces connoissances étoient cependant nécessaires pour le bonheur des sociétés & pour celui de leurs individus; il falloit donc les leur rendre sensibles à tous, en ébranlant leur imagination & leurs sens plus aisés à émouvoir que leur entendement.

Ce fut le triomphe de l'imagination de ceux qui instruisirent les humains dans ces premiers tems. Imitant la Nature qui par les merveilles qu'elle nous présente, nous élève aux idées les plus spirituelles, & nous fait connoître une classe d'êtres qu'elle n'offre point à nos yeux, ils eurent recours pour instruire les Hommes, à des Symboles physiques, & à des Allégories ingénieuses, & conservèrent ainsi au milieu des Nations éclairées, les lumières auxquelles elles étoient redevables de leur grandeur & de leur prospérité.

De-là, ces Processions à chaque renouvellement de l'année & des saisons, ces emblèmes des deux sexes qu'on y portoit avec tant de vénération; Images de la Nature fécondée & du grand Être auquel elle devoit toute son efficace; ces coffrets mystérieux qu'on y portoit, ces corbeilles sacrées, placées sur la tête de Vierges choisies, les fleurs, les grains, les étoupes dont elles étoient remplies; ces Statues, emblèmes des vertus de la Divinité, ces Hymnes & ces Fables Allégoriques, ces voiles brodés & ces vaisseaux représentatifs qui constituoient le culte des Nations anciennes; & sous des figures physiques, peignoient les idées les plus sublimes & les leçons les plus simples & honnêtes, les leçons les plus consolantes.

A la vue de ces spectacles brillans, de cette pompe, de cette magnificence, de ces objets frapans & significatifs, le cœur de ces Peuples embrasé de reconnoissance pour tant de biens & éclairé sur ses devoirs les plus essentiels, s'affermissoit de plus en plus dans une route aussi agréable, & dans l'observation

l'observation de laquelle il trouvoit son plus grand intérêt: il en revenoit satisfait, consolé & instruit.

Ces usages furent de tous les siécles & de tous les Peuples. » Dieu lui-» même établit des Cérémonies religieuses pour perpétuer la mémoire des » bienfaits dont il avoit comblé la Nation qu'il choisit d'abord, & faire en-» trevoir ceux qu'il préparoit à l'Univers entier «. Tous les Rits & les Fêtes du Peuple Hébreu, tous les ornemens du Temple, l'Arche de l'alliance elle-même, furent autant de monumens destinés à conserver parmi ce Peuple le souvenir des merveilles que la Divinité avoit opérées en leur faveur, & de Symboles propres à les élever à la connoissance des vérités les plus sublimes.

Il falloit nécessairement alors de grands moyens, des moyens frapans pour instruire les hommes, pour les réunir, pour leur donner de plus en plus l'esprit & le goût de société; pour les élever aux idées les plus sublimes & les moins matérielles de la vertu & de leurs devoirs.

Ces moyens consistèrent, & ne purent en effet consister que dans ces Spectacles Allégoriques qui réunissant les hommes par le plaisir & la suspension de leurs Travaux, leur présentoient les biens infinis qu'ils retiroient de la Société; & les remplissoient de la plus vive reconnoissance pour l'Auteur de tant de biens.

Ils sont donc de tous les tems & de tous les Peuples: ce n'est que lorsque les Sciences forment une classe à part dans la Société, que lorsqu'elles sont cultivées d'une manière plus particulière par les personnes les plus distinguées par leur rang & par leurs richesses, que ce genre d'instruction symbolique, devient moins universel, & se borne à la portion laborieuse de la société, tandis que l'on invente pour ceux dont le goût est plus exercé, de nouveaux genres d'amusemens instructifs, plus analogues à leurs connoissances & à leur génie.

Mais plus cette portion de la Société se perfectionne & s'instruit, & plus l'autre retombe dans l'ignorance; car non-seulement elle n'est plus soutenue par l'exemple de ceux qui s'en sont séparés, mais son instruction se trouve négligée, parce qu'elle ne peut y suffire, se trouvant désormais seule; parce qu'elle a toujours moins de goût pour un genre d'instruction qu'elle voit dédaigné de ceux qui tiennent le haut bout dans la Société, & qui semblent mériter sa confiance par leurs lumieres; jusqu'à ce qu'il arrive des Sages, qui étonnés de voir tant de lumiere d'un côté, & tant de ténèbres de l'autre, rétablissent en quelque sorte l'égalité entre tous, par des préceptes qui ramenent les Sociétés à l'ordre primitif, sans lequel elles ne peuvent subsister, & qui ne se trouve que dans l'instruction de tous.

Cependant, on n'aura pas recours alors à l'Allégorie, comme dans les premiers tems, parce que les Sociétés ont pris plus de consistance, parce

Génie All. T

KINSHIP TERMS:

FATHER— WON , WORA—my father) ,ABA,ABANA

MOTHER— MA

SON ** WOD

DAUGHTER—NYAKO

BROTHER— OMERA (my Bro) OMIN, (Brother)
(Child of own Ma and another Fa.)
(Child of own Fa and another Ma.)   OMERA
Elder brother   )   OMERA
Younger brother   )

SISTER— LAMERA (my Sist) LAMIN
(Child of own Ma and another Fa.) LAMERA
(Child of own Fa and another Ma.)
Elder sister   ) LAMERA
Younger sister   )

FATHER'S BROTHER—Omin WORA

FATHER'S BROTHER'S WIFE— CHI WORA

FATHER'S BROTHERS SON— OMERA

FATHER'S BROTHER'S DAUGHTER—LAMERA

FATHER'S SISTER——WAYA,or LAMIN WORA (Wora)

FATHER'S SISTER'S HUSBAND— CHWA WAYA or(Wona)

FATHER'S SISTER'S SON—   WOD PA WAYA Wonow
                          OKEYA o speaking
FATHER'S SISTER'S DAUGHTER—NYA PA WAYA Woman
                          LAKEYA o speaking

MOTHER'S BROTHER*— NERA
Mother's Brother's WIFE— CHI NERA
Mother's brother's SON— NERA
Mother's Brother's DAUGHTER— MA

MOTHER'S SISTER— MA,or LAMIN MA
Mother's Sister's HUSBAND——WORA !
Mother's Sister's SON——OMARA
Mother's Sister's Daughter——LAMARA

Father's FATHER   KWARA
FATHER'S MOTHER   DAA

MOTHER'S FATHER— KWARA
MOTHER'S MOTHER— DAA

GRANDCHILD: LAKWARA
Son's Son   ) LAKWARA
Son's Daughter   )
Daughter's Son   ) LAKWARA
Daughter's Daughter)

Sister's Daughter's Husband CHWA NYARA.
Sister's Daughter's Children LIKWAYA.

Husband's Sister's HUSBAND—CHWA PA WAYA
HUSBAND— CHWA, (my husband) CHWARA
Husband's FATHER— KWARA
HUsband's MOTHER— DAA
Husband's BROTHER— YUERA
Husband's SISTER— WAYA
Husband's Brother's WIFE— NYIRKA (my co-wife)
Husband's Brother's CHILDREN— LATINNA (my child)
Husband's SIster's Children— Nya and Wod PA WAYA

WIFE— DAKO
Wife's Father— ORA
Wife's MOTHER—MARA
Wife's BROTHER—ORA
Wife's SISTER—YUERA
Wife's BROTHER'S WIFE—MARA,or CHI ORA
Wife's SISTER'S HUSBAND— OMARA
Wife's BROTHER'S CHILDREN,Nya or Wod Pa ORA
Wife's SISTER'S CHILDREN—

SON'S WIFE'S PARENTS:(Man Speaking)
Son's Wife's FATHER **— LAREMA (my friend)
SON'S Wife'S MOTHER — MARA

Son's Wife's Father—   (Women speaking)
Son's Wife's Mother— JOANNA, (my friend)

BROTHER'S CHILD— LATINNA (my child or (w.s.)
                 LATIN OMERA   (m.s.)
SISTER'S CHILD: LATINNA.   (w.s.)
                LAKEYA.   (m.s.)

DAUGHTER'S HUSBAND'S PARENTS:
Daughter's Husband's Father—
Daughter's Husbands Mother   (m.s.)

Daughter's Husbnd's Father—
Daughter's Husband's Mother   (w.s.)

DAUGHTER'S HUSBAND CHWA NYARA.   (w.s.)
Daughter's Husband OMARA.   (m.s.)

SON'S WIFE CHI WODA.
                                   (w.s.)
Son's Wife—CHI WODA   (m.s.)

BROTHER'S WIFE CHI OMERA.

SISTER'S HUSBAND YUERA

SISTER'S SON— Okeya OKEYA   (MABRO. speaking)
SISTER'S DAUGHTER—LAKEYA   (MA.BRO. speaking)

SISTER'S SON   LATINNA   (Ma Sis pealing)
SISTER'S DOUGHTER " "   (MA.SIS.speaking)

SISTER'S SON   LOKEYA   (FA.BRO.speaking)
SISTERS DAUGHTER LAKEYA   (FA BRO. speaking)

SISTER'S SON   LATINNA.   (FA SIS. Speakin)
SISTER'S DAUGHTER   (FA. SIS.Speakin)

SIster's Son's Wife CHI LATINNA
Sister's Son's Children LIKWAYA.

Boston University Libraries
Mugar Memorial Library

African Studies Library

STUDENTS using the African Studies Library (ASL) usually begin their research with its substantial collection of books, journals, and electronic resources. Beyond these conventional materials, ASL also offers primary research sources: government publications, dating from colonial to contemporary, and published letters and accounts of travelers. Recently, donations outside the original scope were added: ethnographic field notes and diaries from research on the Acholi people of northern Uganda in the mid-1950s, including transcripts of provincial and district court proceedings for which the anthropologist Paula Hirsch Foster was a paid interpreter; a hand-written copy of the Psalms of David in Ge'ez, the liturgical language of Ethiopia, with marginal notes, straw bookmarkers, and bits of candle wax testifying to its frequent use over the years; and site notes and maps of excavation in the 1970s of the ancient city of Axum in present-day Ethiopia.

This and similar raw material for academic research also provides exciting opportunities for students to learn how to use primary sources. The Axum collection on one day might be consulted by visiting archaeologists from Italy and by a student learning what excavation field reports actually are—not Indiana Jones fare, but precise lists of ceramic fragments. Students hired to work on the Foster archive learn how to match unlabelled slides with segments of the text and to find a lab capable of processing the 50-year-old undeveloped film.

The collections invite creative synthesis of secondary and primary resources. Forrest Whitaker's Oscar-winning portrayal of Ugandan dictator Idi Amin in *The Last King of Scotland* or the documentary *Invisible Children*, portraying the plight of children abducted to serve as soldiers in Uganda's Lord's Resistance Army might inspire a paper topic. Students not only can read a wealth of books, articles, and documents on both eras but can also explore the Foster field notes for clues on what might have led to these horrific events. Guided exercises are being devised for students to learn how to investigate the archival collections and how to use the texts they find there.

Stories of donors add rich context to the collections. The personality of Paula Hirsch Foster leaps out between the lines of her meticulous notes of court cases and interviews; 16mm film segments even include scenes from her wedding. Charles Samz included a chapter describing his adventures as a petroleum geologist from his autobiography-in-progress, which accompanied his gift of an early 18th-century Ethiopian manuscript.

From these collections, students come to understand that it's not "all on the Internet," and that vital information isn't always conveniently packaged. ASL prepares guides and finding aids for its collections, but the answers to some questions can only come from reading page after page of material in the hopes of hitting the revealing passage. This is an acquired taste, but the appetite and the skills students develop by using these collections may enrich their entire lives.

(ABOVE TOP)
"Acholi, Uganda, Village Festival." Photograph from Paula Hirsch Foster Archive. 1956.

> The print was made in 2006 from canisters of exposed but undeveloped film found among the papers.

(ABOVE BOTTOM)
Diary pages and postcards.
Paula Hirsch Foster Archive. 1956.

> The diary includes notes on personal events, District Council meetings, and interview schedule. The postcards were found in the diary.

(OPPOSITE)
Typed notes on Acholi, Uganda, kinship terminology.
Paula Hirsch Foster Archive. 1956.

Brigham Young University Library
L. Tom Perry Special Collections

19th Century Western and Mormon Collection

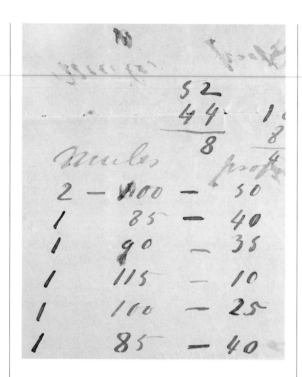

(ABOVE)
Letter from Kit Carson to Brevet Major J. H. Carleton.
Fernandez de Taos, New Mexico, May 13, 1854. Detail.

In this letter, Carson asked Carleton, Commander of
the First Dragoons encamped near Taos, to send
troops immediately to protect settlers and stock at the
Rayado settlement, which Carson, as "Indian Agent,"
believed was in imminent danger of attack from
Apaches in need of provisions for their journey to the
"extreme south." The numbers indicate provisions
sent by the Army, e.g., number of mules.

(OPPOSITE)
Pages of journal. Emmeline B. Wells.
April 1844–February 1846.

In the opening pages of her journal, Emmeline B. Wells
describes her departure from Massachusetts in April
1844 to join other members of the Church of Latter-day
Saints in Nauvoo, Illinois. She later describes her
crossing of the Mississippi River in February 1846
following the expulsion of the Latter-day Saints
from Nauvoo. In her journal, Wells writes detailed
entries about daily chores, children, difficult traveling
conditions, and her relationships with other women
on the journey to Iowa. She frequently mentions the
status of neighboring Mormon immigrant companies.

FROM the prayerful utterances of Joseph Smith in 1820 to the international church of today with a membership of over 12 million members, the Church of Jesus Christ of Latter-day Saints (LDS Church) has embraced many peoples and cultures. The LDS Church was formally organized on April 6, 1830. From that time to the present, the church has encouraged its members to keep a record of their daily activities and accomplishments. Many of these records have been preserved and are now being collected by the L. Tom Perry Special Collections.

The 19th Century Western and Mormon Manuscripts Collection seeks to document the experiences and accomplishments of latter-day saints from all walks of life by collecting as many of their written records as possible. As a result, the collection of 19th-century manuscripts is composed of virtually every kind of written record, including journals, diaries, letters, minute books, speeches, photographs, drawings, and scrapbooks. One treasure trove is the collection of missionary diaries that document the rise of the early church. Also included in the manuscripts are the papers of community and academic leaders, artists and writers, social activists, and environmentalists.

In addition to collecting the records of individuals and families, the Lee Library strives to ensure that the collection is a valuable asset to scholars as they enhance their understanding of the beginnings and early development of the LDS Church and its interactions in the world. The collections supporting research on the 19-century church and the history of the West range from single documents to collections comprising hundreds of boxes. With the rise of the church internationally, the proliferation of its membership, and its acceptance into the American mainstream, historians will continue to research and write for new generations. In addition, there are significant areas of church history that still await serious treatment.

The collection also seeks to document the church's role in the settlement of the American West. These materials provide an important context for the Mormon experiences in the world of 19th-century America, with a specific focus on the history of the American West. The collections cover such diverse topics as westward migration, Native American history, mining and related activities, the environment, religion, literature, and other topics that help establish the Mormons in the larger history of the region and nation.

Deaths

Rozetta Adeline Hinckley Died
Sept 30 1844

Died on her Birthday

Died on his Birthday

---

among

Journal of the church of
Jesus Christ of Latter day Saints.

Friday Feb 27. 1846.

Mrs. Whitney
Sarah Ann and myself crossed the
river to go to the encampment of
the saints. Br. Lot and his wife took
Mrs W. and myself in their carriage
We crossed the river a part of the
way on foot, and then went on to
the encampment about 7 miles
beyond; we reached the destined
place about dusk it came in when we view
it looked like pictures I have seen
of the ancients pitching their
tents and journeying from place
to place with their cattle and their
goods. We repaired immediately
to Br. H. C. Kimballs tent

University of British Columbia Library
Rare Books and Special Collections

Collection of Japanese Maps of the Tokugawa Era

GEORGE Harry Beans, owner of the Philadelphia Seed Company, began his collection of Japanese maps in the 1930s and continued to collect maps of the Tokugawa (or Edo) period (1600–1867) until 1963. Previously, amongst other things, he collected stamps, atlases, and Italian maps.

Beans was a born collector. It is interesting to note that he did not speak a word of Japanese or Italian, yet he assembled world-renowned collections. For more than 30 years after selling his collection of Italian maps, Beans methodically built his private collection of Japanese maps with the assistance of map dealers and other collectors. Assisted by Professor Kazutaka Unno, Beans published a catalog of his collection: *List of Japanese Maps of the Tokugawa Era* (1951). Originally published by his press, Tall Tree Library, Beans issued three supplements in 1955 (A), 1958 (B), and 1963 (C) as he continued to build his collection. He also included in this catalog all of the maps known to have been published during the Tokugawa period, extant or not.

In 1965, Basil Stuart Stubbs, Special Collections librarian at the University of British Columbia (UBC) learned that Beans had placed his collection on the market. UBC, located in Canada's hub for Asia-Pacific trade, has a strong Asian Studies program, so the library made the decision to purchase the collection for $15,000. The purchase was announced in the international journal for the history of cartography, *Imago Mundi.* Throughout the years, the library has continued to add to the collection, and most notably, in 1986, purchased 59 maps of the Tokugawa and Meiji periods from George Schlegel Bonn.

Today the collection is one of the three best collections in the world of maps from the Tokugawa Era. It includes a large number of sheet maps, several scrolls, some screens, *Fukanzus* ("bird's-eye views" of landscapes), many "atlases," and geographies. Unlike most of the collections outside Japan, this one does not hold many government or administrative maps. Its focus is on privately published and travel-related maps and guides published in Japan during the Tokugawa period. There is world coverage, although the majority of maps are of the whole or parts of Japan. A number of prominent Japanese *ukiyo-e* (woodblock print) artists are represented, including Katsushika Hokusai, Ando Hiroshige, and Hashimoto Sadahide.

Continuing in the spirit of learning and scholarship that Beans exhibited, research is encouraged and many publications on the collection have been produced by scholars from around the world. In anticipation of the Early Modern Komonjo and Kuzushi Workshop, co-hosted by UBC and Stanford University, in July and August 2006, 285 maps in the collection were digitized and are now available online. These beautiful maps, which previously were so difficult to use because of their fragility or great size or length, are now available and easy to access and use.

http://www.library.ubc.ca/spcoll/beans.html

(ABOVE)
"Shoho Teiyu." Hand-painted woodblock print by unknown artist. Late 17th century.

This companion to a Shoho map of the world depicts a diversity of the world's people.

(OPPOSITE)
"Fuji ryodo ichiran no zu, Fugaku dochu ichiran [Panoramic view of two ways to climb Mt. Fuji and Panoramic view of routes to Mt. Fuji]." Hashimoto Sadahide. 1859.

Brown University Library

The John Hay Library

Anne S. K. Brown Military Collection

VISITORS to Brown University's John Hay Library are often surprised to find a collection of 6,000 miniature toy soldiers on display in the third-floor gallery. The building has been home to the Anne S. K. Brown Military Collection since 1981, when it was donated by Mrs. John Nicholas Brown who married into the family of the university benefactors in 1930. In fact, it was on her honeymoon to Europe that year that she purchased a number of sets of military miniatures from toy shops. Upon examining the figures, Mrs. Brown became fascinated by the range and variety of military costume to the extent that she devoted the rest of her life to the study of military uniforms.

What began as a hobby quickly turned into an obsession to comprehensively acquire graphic and textual documentation. The destruction of such material in Europe during the Second World War only made her more determined to create an all-inclusive collection devoted to the history and iconography of soldiers and soldiering from all periods, especially circa 1500 to 1945.

In addition to books, she purchased portraits of soldiers, military caricatures, engravings of battle scenes, watercolors of soldiers on campaign, luxurious volumes of colored lithographic plates of uniforms, original photographs, sheet music covers bearing images of obscure militia units, sheets of paper soldiers, and illustrated manuscripts. While uniforms were the main focus, she bought complementary material on early military science, weapons, flags, medals and heraldry, world royalty and ceremony, regimental and unit histories, army lists, and thousands of albums, sketchbooks, scrapbooks, and portfolios. While Europe and North America are most heavily represented, there are sections on virtually every country that has ever employed armed forces.

This endowed collection continues to grow and still enjoys the support of the Brown family. Gifts have been an important source of new material, none more so than the World War II art collection. A chance meeting with the granddaughter of a World War II official artist led to a major project to acquire original artwork created by artists who served in the armed forces of the United States between 1942 and 1945, and material is still being added to this major archive, which currently numbers over 1,600 items.

The Military Collection is recognized as a leading source for images by national and international publishers, filmmakers, scholars, and museums. While there are national collections of military history and iconography around the world, the unique aspect of the Browns' collection is that it is international in focus. The collection serves a major role in the Brown community as a source for research and exhibitions, as it contains extensive material for historians and students of visual arts in virtually all media. Recent student projects have included the digitization and study of an original watercolor scroll painted by a Japanese artist depicting scenes from Admiral Perry's expedition in the early 1850s; this has subsequently been used by schoolchildren and students as well as scholars in Japan.

http://www.brown.edu/Facilities/University_Library/collections/askb/

http://dl.lib.brown.edu/napoleon/

http://dl.lib.brown.edu/askb/

(ABOVE)
"The Retreat from Moscow." Miniature lead soldier group by Madame Metayer. N.d.

(OPPOSITE TOP LEFT)
"Colonel John Whitehead Peard" (a.k.a. "Garibaldi's Englishman"). Watercolor by Thomas Nast. 1860.

(OPPOSITE TOP RIGHT)
"A Foot Soldier and His Wife." Etching by Daniel Hopfer. Circa 1521.

(OPPOSITE BOTTOM LEFT)
"War Bonds Are Cheaper than Wooden Crosses." Tempera painting by Ardis Hughes. 1944.

(OPPOSITE BOTTOM RIGHT)
"The Strongest." Photogravure by Fortunino Matania. 1915.

War Bonds

ARE CHEAPER THAN WOODEN CROSSES

BUY MORE THROUGH PAY ROLL SAVINGS

At a town in which acacias grew, he lay
On his balcony at night. Warblings became
Too dark, too far, too much the accents of
Afflicted sleep, too much the syllables
That would form themselves, in time, and
  communicate
The intelligence of his despair, express
What meditation never quite achieved.

The moon rose up as if it had escaped
His meditation. It evaded his mind.
It was part of a supremacy always
Above him. The moon was always free from him,
As night was free from him. The shadow touched
Or merely seemed to touch him as he spoke
A kind of elegy he found in space:

It is pain that is indifferent to the sky
In spite of the yellow of the acacias, the scent
Of them in the air still hanging heavily
    In the hoary-hanging night. It does not regard
      This freedom, this supremacy, and in
        Its own hallucination
          never sees
        How that which rejects it
          saves it in the end.

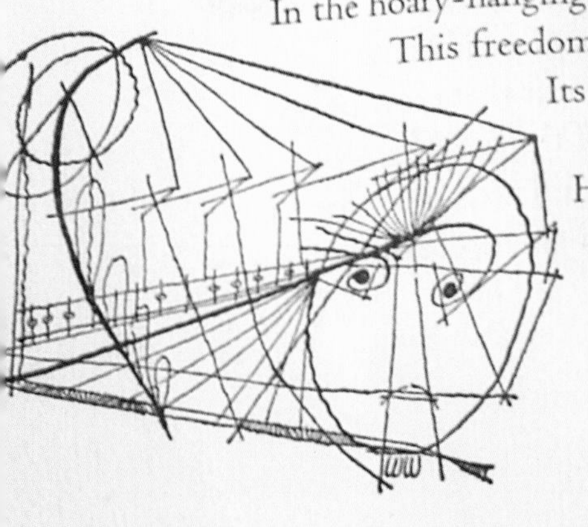

His firm stanzas hang like hives in hell
Or what hell was, since now both heaven and hell
Are one, and here, O terra infidel!

The fault lies with an over-human god,
Who by sympathy has made himself a man
And is not to be distinguished, when we cry

Because we suffer, our oldest parent, peer
Of the populace of the heart, the reddest lord,
Who has gone before us in experience.

If only he would not pity us so much,
Weaken our fate, relieve us of woe both great
And small, a constant fellow of destiny,

A too, too human god, self-pity's kin
And uncourageous genesis. . . It seems
As if the health of the world might be enough.

It seems as if the honey of common summer
Might be enough, as if the golden combs
Were part of a sustenance itself enough,

As if hell, so modified, had disappeared,
As if pain, no longer satanic mimicry,
Could be borne, as if we were sure to find our

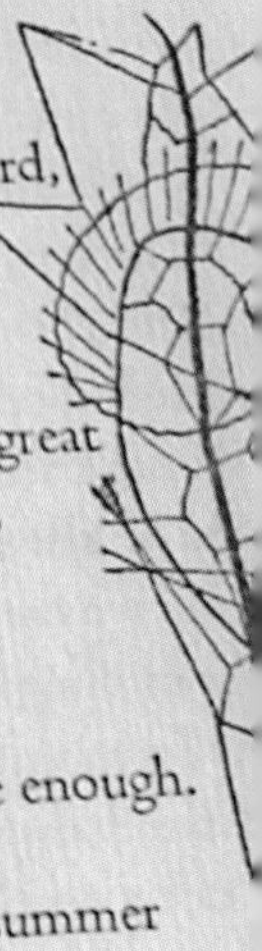

University at Buffalo, State University of New York, Libraries
Special Collections

The Poetry Collection

Charles D. Abbott began the Poetry Collection in 1937, shortly after he was appointed Director of University Libraries at the University of Buffalo. A Rhodes Scholar and book collector, Abbott intended his "Poetry Project" to be poetry's library of record and to serve scholarship in poetry. To achieve his vision, Abbott designed a narrow but exceedingly liberal book collecting policy: to collect all first editions of books of poetry published in English after 1900. First editions were gathered from across the United States, Canada, England, Ireland, Australia, New Zealand and the entire English-speaking world. This policy remains in place and the first edition collection now numbers more than 100,000 volumes. To study the evolution of poetry, Abbott also initiated the collecting of the little entrepreneurial literary magazine. This premier collection now numbers more than 5,000 titles.

Shortly after two collecting junkets to England and adding Mary Barnard as the Poetry Collection's first curator, Abbott embarked upon collecting the manuscripts and literary letters of living poets. In the late 1930s, this was a bold move. Abbott wrote hundreds of letters literally asking poets for the contents of their wastepaper baskets. Poets from across the English-speaking world responded by donating manuscripts and letters. Contemporary genetic scholarship locates its origins in Abbott's fascination with the creative process.

To add to the manuscript collection, in 1949 the Wickser family purchased a collection of James Joyce manuscripts, books, and portraits. This Joyce collection was augmented in 1958 by the Stafford family who purchased Sylvia Beach's Joyce archive. These archives combined to make the Poetry Collection home to the world's largest James Joyce archive. In 1960, Mildred Lockwood Lacey purchased the poetry manuscripts of Robert Graves for the collection. The collection also holds the papers of William Carlos Williams, Dylan Thomas, Wyndham Lewis, and Ezra Pound. Today the collection boasts more than 100 unique archives. Among these significant holdings are the papers of the Jargon Society and the *Wormwood Review* and the manuscripts of Robert Kelly, Theodore Enslin, Kenneth Rexroth, Basil Bunting, and Helen Adam.

Today, as poetry's library of record, the collection has expanded its parameters to include an authoritative collection of poem cards and broadsides. The collection also acquires cheaply made poetry zines and fine press books of poetry. It has one of the largest collections of concrete and visual poetry in any institution. As an extension of visual poetry, the collection boasts a healthy mail art archive.

Charles Abbott believed that a research library's purpose was to mesh with and serve evolving scholarship. To this end, the Poetry Collection regularly hosts international researchers, graduate students, and faculty from all points in North America and each year supports dozens of books and dissertations. The collection's books and manuscripts travel the world as parts of exhibitions. To better serve the world's scholars, an ambitious conservation project has begun, and detailed finding aids to the manuscript collection are being prepared.

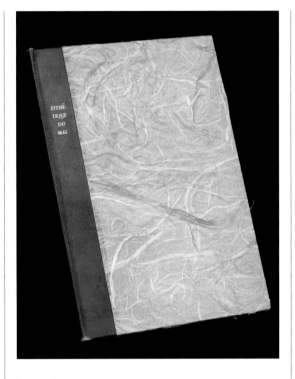

(ABOVE)
Esthetique du mal. Wallace Stevens. Cummington Press, 1945. Illustrated by Wightman Williams. Cover.

(OPPOSITE)
Esthetique du mal. Wallace Stevens. Cummington Press, 1945. Illustrated by Wightman Williams. Pages.

University of California, Berkeley Library
Ethnic Studies Library

Chicano Studies Collection

I N March 1968, Mexican-American students in several East Los Angeles high schools walked out of their classrooms demanding a better education. One of their complaints was the lack of information about their own history and culture. In February 1969, a coalition of ethnic student groups at the University of California, Berkeley also protested for a better education. The Third World Liberation Front strike called for the inclusion of Chicano, Native American, African-American, and Asian-American courses in the university curriculum. Students formed small alternative reading rooms to collect and share the newspapers, newsletters, pamphlets, posters, and flyers that documented their revolutionary era.

One reading room became the Chicano Studies Collection, whose main goal has been to continue what these students began: to collect, preserve, and make accessible the historical and cultural documents of the Chicano experience. The serials collection was especially important because it was historical evidence of the political and literary expression of an entire cultural group. Although periodical literature had always been an important expression of the Chicano community, bibliographic access to it was only minimally available. In fact, one scholar had asserted that there was not very much literature about Mexican-Americans mainly because Mexican-Americans had not written about themselves. This belied a long tradition of Spanish-language periodicals and personal accounts which later scholars would acknowledge and place in its context within Chicano literary history.

A turning point was the 1960s and the Chicano Movement, which brought forth a blossoming of political and cultural publications along with an assertion of civil rights. In the mid-1970s, a group of Chicano librarians established the Chicano Periodical Indexing Project, whose goal was to index the contents of the journals, newspapers, and magazines that conveyed the intellectual and cultural expression of that civil rights movement. They were resolved that the literary output of Chicanos would never again be forgotten or overlooked because of lack of access. In 1976, the Chicano Studies Collection made a commitment to develop and sustain an automated database and thus institutionalize this major effort. Important Chicano Movement era publications indexed in the database include *El Grito, Aztlán, Caracol, De Colores, Regeneración*, and *Revista Chicano-Riqueña*.

The Chicano Studies Collection, which in 1997 became a component of the Ethnic Studies Library at the University of California, Berkeley, has continued to produce the *Chicano Database* to the present time. The database evolved over the years from a printed index published commercially, to an in-house library publication, to a CD-ROM database (the first ethnic studies bibliographic database available in that format), to a Research Libraries Group database, and now to an OCLC database distributed to research libraries across the United States. Its unique contribution to subject access is the controlled vocabulary of the *Chicano Thesaurus*, which includes specific cultural terms in both English and Spanish and terms politically sensitive to the Chicano experience. A companion microfilming project of the Chicano Studies Collection preserves and makes accessible Chicano community newspapers and journals from the 1800s to the present.

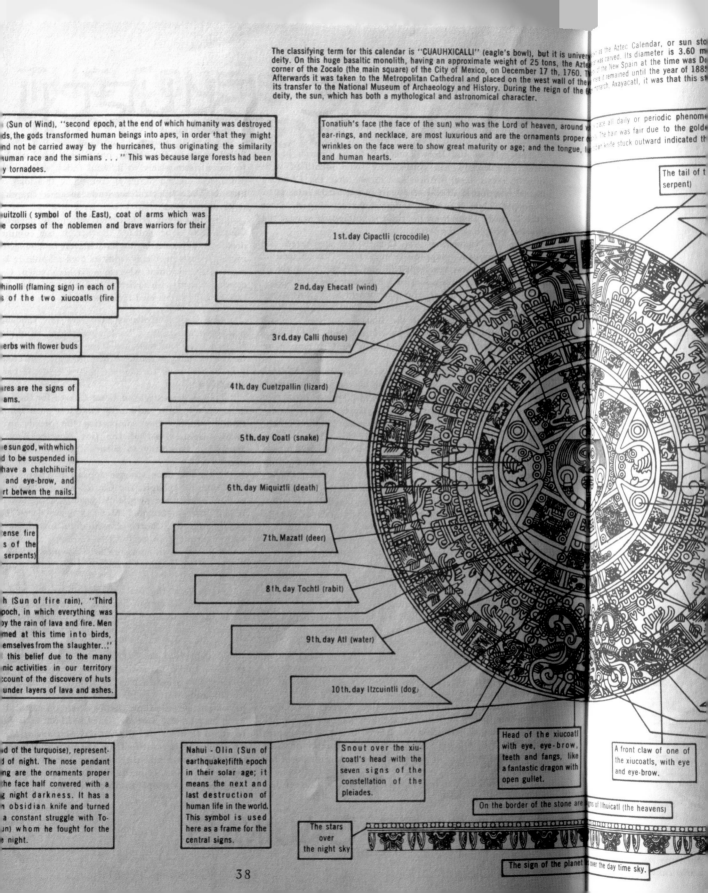

The classifying term for this calendar is "CUAUHXICALLI" (eagle's bowl), but it is univer... [as the] Aztec Calendar, or sun sto... deity. On this huge basaltic monolith, having an approximate weight of 25 tons, the Azte... [it] was carved. Its diameter is 3.60 m... corner of the Zocalo (the main square) of the City of Mexico, on December 17 th, 1760. T... [of] the New Spain at the time was De... Afterwards it was taken to the Metropolitan Cathedral and placed on the west wall of the... [wh]ere it remained until the year of 1885... its transfer to the National Museum of Archaeology and History. During the reign of the 6... [mon]arch, Axayacatl, it was that this st... deity, the sun, which has both a mythological and astronomical character.

[Nahui Ehecatl] (Sun of Wind), "second epoch, at the end of which humanity was destroyed ...ds, the gods transformed human beings into apes, in order that they might ...nd not be carried away by the hurricanes, thus originating the similarity ...human race and the simians . . ." This was because large forests had been ...y tornadoes.

Tonatiuh's face (the face of the sun) who was the Lord of heaven, around w... ear-rings, and necklace, are most luxurious and are the ornaments proper... wrinkles on the face were to show great maturity or age; and the tongue, l... [obsidi]an knife stuck outward indicated th... and human hearts.

The tail of t... serpent)

...quitzolli (symbol of the East), coat of arms which was ...e corpses of the noblemen and brave warriors for their

1st. day Cipactli (crocodile)

...hinolli (flaming sign) in each of ...s of the two xiucoatls (fire

2 nd. day Ehecatl (wind)

...erbs with flower buds

3 rd. day Calli (house)

...res are the signs of ...ams.

4 th. day Cuetzpallin (lizard)

...e sun god, with which ...d to be suspended in ...have a chalchihuite ...and eye-brow, and ...t betwen the nails.

5 th. day Coatl (snake)

6 th. day Miquiztli (death)

...ense fire ...s of the ...serpents)

7 th. Mazatl (deer)

...h (Sun of fire rain), "Third ...poch, in which everything was ...by the rain of lava and fire. Men ...med at this time into birds, ...emselves from the slaughter..!' ...l this belief due to the many ...nic activities in our territory ...ccount of the discovery of huts ...under layers of lava and ashes.

8 th. day Tochtl (rabit)

9th. day Atl (water)

10 th. day Itzcuintli (dog)

...d of the turquoise), represent- ...d of night. The nose pendant ...g are the ornaments proper ...the face half convered with a ...g night darkness. It has a ...h obsidian knife and turned ...a constant struggle with To- ...un) whom he fought for the ...night.

Nahui - Olin (Sun of earthquake)fifth epoch in their solar age; it means the next and last destruction of human life in the world. This symbol is used here as a frame for the central signs.

Snout over the xiu- coatl's head with the seven signs of the constellation of the pleiades.

Head of the xiucoatl with eye, eye-brow, teeth and fangs, like a fantastic dragon with open gullet.

A front claw of one of the xiucoatls, with eye and eye-brow.

On the border of the stone are [si]gns of lihuicatl (the heavens)

The stars over the night sky

The sign of the planet... over the day time sky.

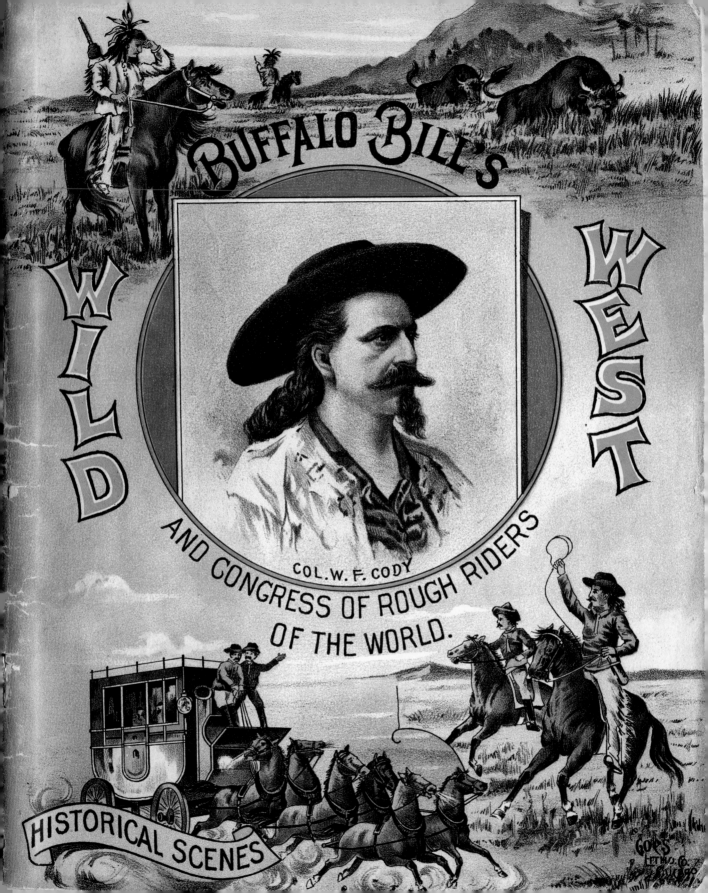

University of California, Davis Library
Department of Special Collections

Michael and Margaret B. Harrison Western Research Center

WHEN Michael Harrison (1897–2005) chose to work in the National Park Service at the Grand Canyon in 1922, he could not have guessed that his life in the West would lead to the building of one of the finest Western Americana research collections in private hands. Michael Harrison, known as Mike to his friends, assembled the collection with his wife, Margaret B. Harrison, whom he met while working as a ramrod at a dude ranch in California in 1931. The collection, donated in its entirety in 2006, consists of more than 21,000 volumes relating to the history of the Trans-Mississippi West. It is made up of rare and fine press books, serials, pamphlets, maps, and other printed items.

Michael Harrison's passion for the American West was the driving force behind the collection, while Margaret B. Harrison supported his efforts by gaining the skills to become a fine hand-bookbinder. Harrison began to collect books in the 1920s, starting with government publications on southwestern history and Native American cultures. After his employment with the Park Service at the Grand Canyon National Park, he worked in New Mexico and California for the Bureau of Indian Affairs. As part of his responsibilities he traveled around northern California evaluating Indian tribal conditions for the Commissioner of Indian Affairs (1934 to 1947). A major focus of his collection is the history and treatment of Native Americans, with a highpoint of the collection being the spectacular Edward S. Curtis *North American Indian* 40-volume set (1907–30). Subject strengths of the collection include Native Americans, cowboys and cattlemen, western military history, Custer and the Battle of the Little Big Horn, western art, transportation, trails, and national parks. The collection also contains prime examples of artwork including paintings, etchings, and lithographs; Native American baskets and pottery; bronze sculptures; and memorabilia.

With the arrival of each new book, Harrison would begin the painstaking process of cataloging the book using the "Harrison Peculiar System," often working late into the night at his manual typewriter. The resulting card catalog of over 700,000 cards leads researchers to numerous indexed subjects for books and journal articles not found in a standard library catalog. Although the collection has only recently been opened for research in an academic setting, correspondence to Michael Harrison provides a record of the collection's long history of supporting the research of numerous western historians, museum directors, faculty, students, and history buffs. The correspondence also shows Michael Harrison's efforts to support Native American causes, debunk western myths, and his insistence that researchers support their claims with documentation.

A unique relationship developed with the General Library, University of California, Davis to assist Harrison in building and cataloging the collection into his centenary years. Michael Harrison died at 107 years of age on April 5, 2005, after 80 years of collecting. The General Library celebrated the Harrisons' contributions and the opening of this remarkable collection in October of 2006.

http://www.lib.ucdavis.edu/ul/libcoll/harrison/

(ABOVE TOP)
"Not-o-way (the Thinker)." George Catlin.
In *The North American Indians*, vol. 2. Philadelphia:
Leary, Stuart, and Co., 1913.

(ABOVE BOTTOM)
The North American Indians. George Catlin. Philadelphia:
Leary, Stuart, and Co., 1913.

(OPPOSITE)
"Buffalo Bill's Wild West and Congress of Rough Riders of the World." Program. Chicago: The Company, 1893.

University of California, Irvine Libraries
Department of Special Collections and Archives

Southeast Asian Archive

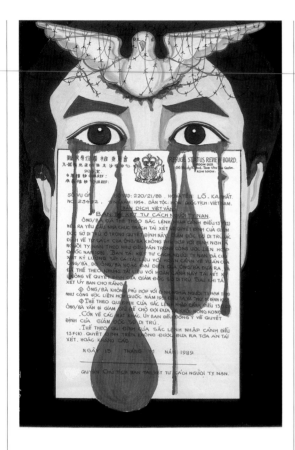

THE Vietnam War was an immense tragedy for many Americans, but far greater losses were suffered by the people of Vietnam, Cambodia, and Laos, whose nations were devastated by years of land warfare and bombing. The decades-long diaspora that began at the war's end in 1975 was caused by political and religious persecution and led to the exodus of more than two million refugees. Many of these forced emigrants spent years in refugee camps in Asia. Others, including the "boat people," suffered shocking privations in their efforts to flee. Even those who were fortunate enough to be airlifted to safety in 1975 were faced with starting new lives, often without family, belongings, money, or the ability to make a living, while also adjusting to utterly foreign cultures and climates. More than 30 years later, vibrant Southeast Asian–American communities have grown up throughout the United States, following patterns similar to those of earlier immigrant groups. New generations are thriving, but the road to success is long and arduous.

UC Irvine's Southeast Asian Archive is the most significant collection in the United States that focuses on documenting the refugees and immigrants from the former Indochina—Vietnam, Cambodia, and Laos—since the Vietnam War ended in 1975. Its national prominence was confirmed by receipt of a major grant from the National Endowment for the Humanities in 2004 which enabled both processing of all archival collections and creation of a digital resource accessible via the Internet.

The archive is a prime example of a collecting effort begun in the right place at the right time, given that the largest expatriate Vietnamese-American community in the world, known as "Little Saigon," is located 12 miles from campus. In addition, 40 percent of the nation's Southeast Asian refugees reside in California. The archive was founded and nurtured almost single-handedly by librarian Anne Frank (who retired in 2007 after 40 years of service to UCI), who was inspired and assisted by members of the local Vietnamese-American community. In the years since the archive began in 1987 as a small collection of pamphlets in a filing cabinet, it has grown to contain more than 3,000 publications, 75 linear feet of vertical file ephemera and serials, and 300 linear feet of archival material.

The archive was founded years before UCI's Department of Asian American Studies was launched in the 1990s. The collection's strength and prominence were significant factors in the successful campaign to establish the program, and the archive has played a central role in research and instruction ever since. Students taking courses in Asian-American, Southeast Asian-American, and Vietnamese-American history visit the archive to locate primary and secondary sources for their research projects. Scholars from throughout the United States and abroad visit to conduct in-depth research.

Anne Frank has received numerous awards from Southeast Asian–American community organizations in recognition of the archive's contribution to the preservation of their history, and the Southeast Asian Archive Advisory Board helps steer a straight course and maintain strong community relations. Finding aids are widely accessible via the Online Archive of California at:

http://www.oac.cdlib.org/

TƯỞNG NIỆM
những người đã
chết trên đường
tìm TỰ DO

People VN

Pianta del Sito della Terra di Vallata, e sua Abitazione

di cap.ta tutto il corpo di essa _____ 19; M. 9; P. 18.

Il suo circuito, è di passi _____ n° 598.

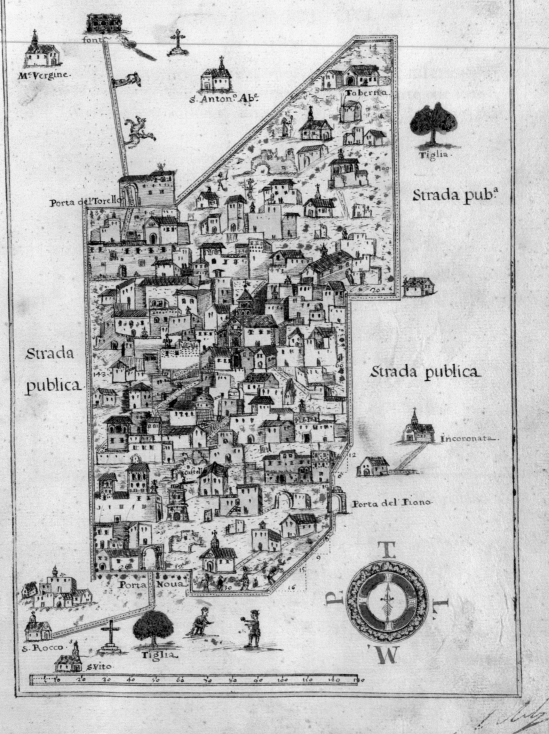

M.a Vergine.

fonte

S. Anton.o Ab.e

Taberna

Tiglia.

Porta del Torello

Strada pub.a

Strada publica

Strada publica

Incoronata.

Castell

Porta del Piano.

Porta Noua

S. Rocco

Tiglia.

S. Vito

University of California, Los Angeles Library
Department of Special Collections

Orsini Family Papers

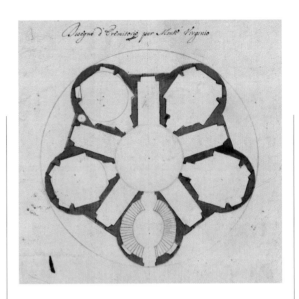

THE Orsini, one of Italy's most ancient and illustrious families, used the *orso*—the bear—as their heraldic device. Coincidentally, the bear is also the mascot of UCLA, which houses the Orsini Family Papers. The papers have been in Los Angeles since 1964, when they were sold by the family and bought by the Department of Special Collections of the Charles E. Young Research Library. The 540 boxes of documents, dating from circa 1300 to 1950, constitute a significant portion of the family's private archive.

Based in Rome, the Orsini have been one of Italy's leading families since the Middle Ages when they acquired much land across central and southern Italy. Over the following centuries, their private armies and enormous wealth made them crucial players in the complicated power-game of Italian politics. The family cultivated close ties with the Medici, and so formidable were the Orsini that Lorenzo il Magnifico considered taking an Orsini bride to be a step up in the world. His son Piero also married into the Orsini family, as did Isabella de' Medici several generations later. The Orsini eventually boasted three popes and thirty cardinals, and kinship ties with the royal houses of France, Spain, England, Denmark, Sweden, Norway, and Poland.

The Orsini Family Papers are a window into the public and private lives of the Orsini over the centuries, and especially from 1500 to 1800. Much of the material concerns the administration of property. The papers include measured maps and registers of rural lands, and plans and inventories of houses and palaces in town. There are records of grain yields, appointments of personnel, reports from estate managers, and a great number of rentals and concessions. Dowries and wills, disputes and settlements, both of Orsini family members and of their subjects, attest to the complicated business of administering such a vast and powerful family, as well as the life-and-death concerns of ordinary people living on their properties. Legal papers record quarrels over successions and patrimony, and testimonies from provincial courthouses in the Orsini family's lands preserve tales of marauding soldiers, lecherous vicars, thefts of livestock, nighttime brawls, and village murders.

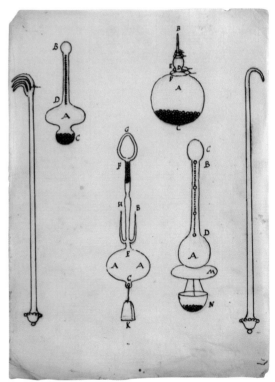

Until 2005, the papers remained largely uncataloged. Thanks to a gift from the Steinmetz Family Foundation, Special Collections was able to undertake a two-year project to create a digital finding aid for the papers. In addition, selected items from the collection were digitized and linked to the online finding aid. Now the archive is not only widely accessible to scholars, but it has also been reunited—in a virtual manner—with the remainder of the Orsini archive housed in the Archivio Storico Capitolino in Rome.

In early 2007, the Department of Special Collections mounted an exhibition of material from the collection and organized and hosted a major international conference on the family. UCLA Library's Department of Special Collections has not only made an important and hitherto hidden collection available, but has also actively promoted new scholarship on these unique materials.

http://catalog.library.ucla.edu/cgi-bin/Pwebrecon.cgi?DB=local&CNT=50&v2=1&BBRecID=2470436

(ABOVE TOP)
Plan for a hermit's dwelling to be built at a hermitage endowed by the Orsini in Montevirginio, near Rome. 17th century.

(ABOVE BOTTOM)
Drawings of hydrometers used by the Orsini to gauge the quality of drinking water from their lake at Bracciano. Mid-17th century.

(OPPOSITE)
View of the town of Vallata. From a register of properties owned by the Orsini in southern Italy. 1723.

University of California, Riverside Libraries
Special Collections

J. Lloyd Eaton Collection of Science Fiction, Fantasy, Horror, and Utopian Literature

(ABOVE)
Stalking the Nightmare. Harlan Ellison. Limited-edition first-edition copy in carved box. 1982.

Interior of box showing book cover and signatures of artist and author on inside of box lid.

(OPPOSITE TOP)
Stalking the Nightmare. Harlan Ellison. Limited-edition first-edition copy in carved box. 1982.

Detail of box lid.

(OPPOSITE BOTTOM)
Stalking the Nightmare. Harlan Ellison. Limited-edition first-edition copy in carved box. 1982.

Box.

WHEN the family of the late Oakland physician Dr. J. Lloyd Eaton (1902–1968) sought a home for his 7,500-volume collection of science fiction, they were not met with much enthusiasm among academic librarians. At that time, science fiction was considered an inferior literary product—pleasant enough as a diversion, but unworthy of serious academic study. As even public libraries did not regularly acquire science fiction, there was no public collection anywhere with a comprehensive collection.

Donald G. Wilson, then University Librarian at UC Riverside, was alone in recognizing that the vast popularity and influence of science fiction rendered it worthy of academic analysis and study. Although many ridiculed his decision, Wilson acquired the collection of Dr. Eaton, saving it from the hands of a book dealer who had intended to sell it piecemeal.

When the collection was examined in detail by the scholar Michael Burgess (a.k.a. Robert Reginald), its full value was recognized. At his urging, a curator was hired for the collection. The choice was Dr. George Slusser, who held a doctorate in comparative literature from Harvard University. Dr. Slusser launched the Eaton Conference in 1979, bringing noted writers and scholars annually to the Riverside campus, and producing more than 20 volumes of conference proceedings.

During George Slusser's 25-year curatorship, the Eaton collection grew to more than 100,000 volumes, ranging from the 1517 edition of Thomas More's *Utopia* to the most recently published titles in all languages. The collection also includes journals, comic books, and 300,000 fanzines, enriched by donations from collectors Terry Carr, Bruce Pelz, Fred Patten, and Rick Sneary. In recent years, films, videos, DVDs, film scripts, and illustrated narratives have been added, most of which have come as donations. The archival holdings comprise the papers of leading science fiction and fantasy authors, including Richard Adams, Gregory Benford, David Brin, F. Busby, Michael Cassutt, Robert L. Forward, Anne McCaffery, Lewis Shiner, Colin Wilson, and James White.

From its humble and controversial origins, the Eaton Collection has established itself as the largest publicly accessible collection in its field, visited by students, scholars, filmmakers, and enthusiasts from around the world. Dozens of dissertations, hundreds of monographs, and thousands of scholarly articles have been produced from its holdings. Curator George Slusser, now retired but still active in the collection's development, is considered the leading scholar in science fiction studies.

While it is unfortunate that Donald Wilson, who died in 1976 at the untimely age of 45, did not live to see the development of the collection, his vision has been vindicated by the fact that more than 30 other major university libraries worldwide are now building similar collections. Indeed, it is the rare academic curriculum that does *not* include courses in science fiction studies. Today the entire staff of Special Collections participates in ongoing outreach efforts, which include answering thousands of electronic reference queries annually, creating Web and *in situ* exhibitions, speaking at conferences, and providing tours to enthusiasts of all ages.

http://eaton-collection.ucr.edu/

http://library.ucr.edu/?view=collections/spcol/fanzines.html

http://lib.ucr.edu/spcol/eaton/

University of California, San Diego Libraries
Mandeville Special Collections Library

Southworth Spanish Civil War Collection

Spain's Second Republic (1931–1936), the Spanish Civil War (1936–1939), and the post-war years of the 1940s form the foci of the collection, named for Herbert Rutledge Southworth, who began collecting these materials during the war. Southworth was an American journalist closely associated with the Republican government both in Spain and in exile. He contributed numerous anti-Franco articles to the *Washington Post* during the war and, after the war, served as secretary to Fernando de los Ríos, the Spanish Republic's ambassador to the United States. Southworth's collecting interests continued while he served as a radio correspondent in Tangier during the 1940s and 1950s. In addition to histories, memoirs, and other books relating to Spain during the 1930s and 1940s, Southworth also assembled a substantial number of propaganda pamphlets and short-lived journals and newspapers of extremely limited circulation that appeared during the war years.

Since the acquisition of Southworth's collection in 1966, UCSD has continued to add materials to make it as comprehensive a collection as possible. Currently, the collection includes more than 13,000 items, including monographs, pamphlets, periodicals, photographs, drawings, newspapers, posters, and manuscripts. Publications by Republicans, Falangists, Catholics, anarchists, communists, socialists, agrarian reformers, and regional political parties are all represented, as are those by Spanish exiles and partisans. The collection holds all works by such prominent writers as Diego Martínez, Juan Negrín, Indalecio Prieto, José Antonio Primo de Rivera, and Fernando de los Ríos; commentaries by non-Spanish writers as diverse as Ernest Hemingway and Joseph Goebbels are also collected.

Of special interest are publications that were printed in small editions and subject to destruction through censorship or war, such as 3,500 political pamphlets from a variety of parties, a copy of the mimeo newssheets printed by the Falangists inside the besieged fortress of Alcázar, and a plethora of ephemera published by the Partido Comunista de España and produced in Madrid. More than 600 drawings made by Spanish children during the war are particularly evocative of the human tragedy of such conflicts, and more than 100 original photographs by non-Spanish journalists working in Spain provide unprecedented graphic visual coverage of the war. More than 80 colorful posters published during the war illustrate the work of artists as propagandists.

Modern Spain has remained a focus of UCSD's Department of History since the establishment of the campus in 1960. The Southworth Collection is frequently used by students and the larger community of scholars, and images from the collection are often included in films, publications, and exhibitions—all testament to Herbert Southworth's passion and perseverance. Digital versions of portions of the Southworth Collection may be viewed at the following sites:

Posters: http://orpheus.ucsd.edu/speccoll/visfront/index.html

Children's drawings: http://orpheus.ucsd.edu/speccoll/tsdp/index.html

Photographs: http://orpheus.ucsd.edu/speccoll/swphotojournalism/index.html

Communist ephemera of Madrid: http://orpheus.ucsd.edu/speccoll/calltoarms/index.html

(ABOVE TOP)
Drawing by Rafael Barber, age 10. 1937.

(ABOVE CENTER)
"Victoria, hoy mas que nunca." Poster by Josep Renau. 1938.

(ABOVE BOTTOM)
"Spanish Refugees in France." Photograph from London News Agency Photos Ltd. January 1939.

(OPPOSITE)
Drawing by Luisa Rodríguez, age 11. 1937.

University of California, Santa Barbara Libraries
Department of Special Collections

American Religions Collection

JONESTOWN, Waco, Heaven's Gate—all names in the headlines that continue to capture our interest. The American Religions Collection at the University of California, Santa Barbara contains printed, manuscript, and ephemeral material relating to these and thousands of other religious movements, figures, and events. The driving force behind the collection has been J. Gordon Melton, Methodist minister, prolific author of works such as the *Encyclopedia of American Religions* (1978), expert witness at numerous "cult" trials, and founder of the Institute for the Study of American Religion (ISAR). Since the late 1960s Melton and ISAR have been seeking materials relating to America's many new and alternative religious and spiritual groups in the short time before they disappeared from distribution. In 1985, Melton moved from Illinois to Santa Barbara and donated this burgeoning collection to the UCSB library. With his help, it has continued to grow dramatically and today contains more than 30,000 books, several thousand serial titles, 1,000 linear feet of manuscripts, and hundreds of audiotapes, videotapes, CDs and DVDs.

Some of the American Religions Collection's holdings date from the early 19th century, but the bulk is from the mid- and latter 20th century. The emphasis has been on less documented religious groups, with strengths in the newer Asian religions, American Islam, esoteric and New Age organizations, religious healing, the metaphysical religions, astrology, independent Catholicism, and smaller Protestant denominations. There are particularly substantial holdings for Buddhist, Christian Science, evangelical Christian, Hindu, Mormon, Scientology, Theosophical, and Unification movements, as well as religious broadcasting, Wicca and Neo-Paganism, and flying saucer religions.

Alongside the core collection donated by Melton are more than 60 other discrete manuscript collections. The Nori Muster Betrayal of the Spirit Collection, for example, contains correspondence, diaries, interviews, and other material from a former member and associate editor of *ISKCON World Review: Newspaper of the Hare Krishna Movement.* The Anthony U. Leitner Memorial Collection focuses on hundreds of Buddhist groups, many in the greater Los Angeles area, where Leitner attended and often recorded services. The Cult Awareness Network (CAN) Collection includes files on hundreds of organizations whose activities were considered suspect, as well as detailed records of CAN's annual conferences which often featured sessions on deprogramming, psychological evaluation, and abuse issues.

Use of the American Religions Collection has mushroomed as word of the broad scope of its holdings has spread. Some of the use comes from religious studies faculty and students, but the bulk comes from independent religious scholars, devotees and debunkers of specific movements, researchers in American studies, sociology of religion, women's studies, gender/sexuality (ordination of women, gay/lesbian issues), as well as those studying Muslim, Buddhist, Hindu, and other immigrant groups in America. The collection has served as the source for many of Gordon Melton's works, as well as numerous other publications. Further information, including new acquisitions, can be found on the following Web pages:

    http://www.library.ucsb.edu/speccoll/aguides.html

    http://www.library.ucsb.edu/speccoll/arc.html

ARTIFICIAL MOONLIGHT.

The Brush Electric Light Mast.

THE MAST SOON TO BE ERECTED IN THE PUBLIC SQUARE BY THE BRUSH ELECTRIC LIGHT AND POWER COMPANY.

THE MAST SYSTEM

A New Application of the Electric Light.

Description of the Masts or Towers

By Which the First, Second and ... method of putting them up that is both novel and interesting. It is briefly as follows: The first section of the mast is composed of boiler tubing eight inches in diameter and about 20 feet long, to this are riveted other pieces of tubing made of boiler iron which gradually increase in size toward the butt of the mast, until about 100 feet of the mast is complete. This is then set upon end by the ordinary means of putting up poles and spars. After this the mast is lifted bodily from the ground and shoved skyward like a telescope, by a powerful hydraulic jack. It is kept in a perpendicular position by means of strong guys, and section after section riveted on to the lower end until it is of the required hight. It is in this manner that the masts in Akron have already perfected arrangements to try the system. Albany last week gave a contract to the Brush Company of that city to light the entire city with electricity by means of a combination of the mast and low lights such as are now in use in the Public Square.

By clippings from London *Engineering* and the *Electrician* of last month, it appears that the Anglo-American Brush Company have secured contracts to light large portions of Dublin and Edinburg by a combination of the mast and low light system.

Further proof of the demand for the light is the fact that the Brush Electric Company are again to increase the present great capacity of their new works, so that employment for fifteen hundred men will be given and products manufactured to the value of eight ... tricity as power, under absolute control, and with a minimum of trouble and expense. Such being the case, we may expect to witness an enormous development of the applications of electricity, assuming, of course, that the Faure battery is capable of indefinite reproduction on a practical scale. There are not wanting those who entirely dispute the value of the invention, and who ridicule the ideas set forth by Sir William Thomson. Professor Osborne Reynolds, of Owens College, Manchester, for instance, points out that, after all, one million foot pounds is a very small matter, being in fact just as much "energy" as is contained in one and one-half ounces of coal. Coal, indeed, is to be our standard, according to Mr. Reynolds, and he predicts the utter failure of the plan for storing electricity. Professor Ayrton also comes forward as a critic, albeit one of a milder type. He admits the truth of the statement that 1½ ounces of coal

ENGLISH NEWSPAPERS.

Their Treatment of the News About the President.

Commendable Enterprise on the Part of Some of Them---Minister Lowell's Work in Distributing the News.

NEW YORK, July 19.—Mr. Smalley writes the following interesting letter to the *Tribune* about the reception of the news of the assassination in England.

LONDON, July 7.—The dispatches to the London papers respecting the tragedy at Washington have been very full, those to the *Daily News* and the *Standard* filling many columns, on Monday, the other papers contenting themselves with less voluminous narratives. Never before has the London press shown so much interest in any American event, or spent so much money in preparing accounts by cable. And the accounts have been for the most part very good accounts. The dispatch to the *Daily News* of Monday was a very lucid and complete piece of writing, six columns in length.

That supplied to the *Standard*, which we hear has lately set up a bureau in New York, was less remarkable for literary merit, and has been followed by others remarkable for passages which might, with advantage, have been omitted. If the correspondent of the *Standard* is an Englishman, it may be regretted that he should think this a good moment to paint in such black colors a picture of American political life. If he be an American, his act deserves condemnation without reserve. No censure can be too strong for a man who takes foreign pay for reviling his own country. The English public is full of respectful sympathy for its cousins across the water. The *Standard* correspondent encourages this feeling by depicting what he calls a condition of political rottenness that is appalling, and he goes on thus:

"Civil service reform is a wild dream in the presence of the hideous nightmare of corruption which demoralizes the public life here, and paralyzes it by the action of the government. Politics have sunk to the level of a game of cards, in which both sides play with a marked pack, and consider it no dishonor to cheat."

We shall owe the *Standard* little thanks for its enterprise if it is going to give publicity to wholesale libels upon the people and government of the United States. Such things, of course, are copied. There are people, I dare say, who think them spicy. They are read at a time when the interest in American affairs is keen beyond precedent.

They are, however, wholly inconsistent with the opinions which lie at the root of the general feeling in England, and the opinions expressed editorially in the paper which prints this insulting and caluimnous paragraph. Of course they do mischief. I hope the mischief is lessened by the indignation at the cruel outrage upon the President, who lies low under an assassin's bullet. For the President is the chief of a party as well as of the Nation, and it is he who is likened by this writer to a blackleg and card sharper. I don't think we should endure many allusions of that sort very patiently.

The dispatches to the *Telegraph*, like all such dispatches, are of interest, but if a suspicion of partisan purpose could be entertained in such a case, I should say they were conceived in Mr. Conkling's interest. They do certainly appear to proceed from somebody who has close relations with the journal which has of late been Mr. Conkling's New York organ. I hope my conjecture may give offense to no one. It is a pure conjecture. I have no notion who the author of these telegrams is—of these or of any of the other telegrams on which I comment, save one. Whoever he may be, he does beat the Conkling drum very loudly indeed in the ear of the small shopkeeper, who is supposed to be the most valued integer in the constituency of this particular ournal.

Perhaps I am wrong in attributing this partiality to the supposed author of the supposed telegrams in the *Daily Telegraph*, He had a talent for silence on Monday, when the *Daily News* had six columns and the *Standard* its five columns and even the *Times* two columns. The special dispatches to the *Daily Telegraph* and its shopkeepers amounted in all to one-eighth of one column. On Tuesday, however, it made up for its previous want of energy, publishing a bad caricature of President Garfied, as it had the week before published one of the Brighton murderer, Lefroy, and a picture of the White House. It published also a column and a half of what purported to be dispatches from its correspondents in New York, a part of which bore close resemblance to parts of telegrams in its contemporaries of the day before, only much watered and padded, so much so that the Conklingism which seems to be the ear mark of genuineness in their accounts is quite choked and stifled. But the Conklingism reappears here today, and this morning we now learn that the political excitement arising out of charges wrought by the administration press is subsiding, and that there is a reaction in favor of Arthur and Conkling, more especially as an examination of the assasin shows that his sympathies have always been with Conkling's opponents. He opposed Grant, it appears, in the Chicago Convention, and has sought office from President Garfield as an enemy of Conkling. This again is highly interesting and novel intelligence. What surprises us is that no story of the same sort appears in the other London papers.

The *Telegraph's* correspondent remarks that the published declarations of Mr. Conk- ... ter, which I know must have been of comment with you, it is in hope omission may be repaired, and that glish public, like the American, may opportunity of reading at full len expressions of Mr. Conkling's s with President Garfield, which he m uttered, but which have so unacc dropped out of this Philadelphia di

Mr. Lowell's post during all thi ment has been anything but a The first news of the attempt rea legation a little before 5 o'clock on afternoon, by private hands. Mr. was just leaving for a visit over to Mr. Matthew Arnold, to w at once telegraphed his regrets that hour down to the pres legation has been beset by ca every rank, and by inquiries from of England by telegraph, post and me The details of these visits, so far as late to persons of importance, you ready. The interviewer, naturally as matters go now, appeared on th early, and has remained late, though think he has taken much by his p ance. The English variety of this s but a feeble copy of the American and even the American adept, a W was baffled by the imperturbable of his victim. If I may hazard an on such a point, Mr. Lowell felt the of the situation much too deeply to be to give publicity to his sentiments ions in the form of what Mr. C calls a statement, and the legatio short-handed by reason of Mr. Hopp ness, there was official work enough a Minister's hands busy. Dispatch Washington to the various Courts of are sent in the first place to the leg London, and transmitted by the here to the other Ministers on the co All Mr. Blaine's telegrams were fo also in full to the Queen, to the P Wales and to many others who as them. Of the distinguished persona called many were not satisfied with cards, but desired to hear from Mr. himself the latest news. And the duties of the legation, which are ma to go on as usual. G.

FUN ON A TRAIN.

Mark Twain Tells of His Travel perience.

I got into the cars and took a seat taposition to a female. That fema was a perfect insurance company—it her against ever getting married to but a blind man. Her mouth looke crack in a dried lemon, and there more expression in her face than th a cup of cold custard. She appe though she had been through one and had got about two-thirds thr other. She was old enough to b grandmother to Mary that had th lamb. She was chewing prize pop-c carried a yellow rose with a band- cotton umbrella nestled sweetly by I couldn't guess whether she was on sion of charity, or going West to saw mill. I was full of curiosity her speak, so I said:

"The exigencies of the times requi circumspection in a person who is ing."

Says she, "What?"

Says I, "The orb of day shines r ent in the vault above."

She hitched around uneasy like, raised her umbrella and said, "I do any of your sass—get out," and I got

Then I took a seat alongside of fellow, who looked like a ghost of lengthened out. He was a stately cuss, and he was reading.

Said I, "Mister, did you ever see opard?" I said camelopard becaus pious animal, and never eats grass getting down on his knees. He hadn't seen a camelopard. Then "Do you chew?"

He said, "No, sir."

Then I said, "How sweet is natur

He took this for a conundrum and didn't know. Then he said he was interested in the history of a gr "Alas!" he exclaimed, "**we are but**

I told him I knew made my cooking stove was a great

Then he asked, "Would I read?"

Says I, "What have you got?"

He replied: "Watt's Hymns, Rev Moonlight, and How to Spend the S

I said, "None of them for Hannah he had an unabridged business dire New York city I would take a little

Then he said, "Young man, look gray hairs!"

I told him I saw them, and that man got to be as old as he was he o die. Said I, "You needn't think th hairs are any signs of wisdom; it' sign that your system lacks iron, and vise you to go home and swallow a cr

He took this for irony, and wh *entente cordiale* there was between spoiled. It turned out that he was lain of a base-ball club.

When we got to Rochester I calle bowl of soup. I send you the rec making it: Take a lot of water, wash and boil it until it is brown on both then carefully pour one bean into it it simmer. When the bean begins restless sweeten it with salt; then pu in air-tight cans, hitch each can to and chuck them overboard and the done.

The above receipt originated with in Iowa, who got up suppers on odd oc for Oddfellows. He had a receipt for soup, leaving out the salt.

Speaking of Iowa reminds me of t I got my money to pay for my tick that fellow's supper. I bet a fellow that I could tell him how much wat quart went under the railroad bridg the Mississippi at Dubuque in a year. the bet, but after all the supper awful swindle.

Case Western Reserve University Libraries
Department of Special Collections

The Charles F. Brush Collection

THE Department of Special Collections in the Kelvin Smith Library celebrates the life of a pioneer in American electrical technology and industry, Charles F. Brush Sr. (1849–1929) with a collection of over 25 linear feet of materials. An inventor, entrepreneur, and business leader, Brush figured prominently in the rise of Cleveland as an important center of technological innovation and manufacturing in the late 19th century. The Brush collection brings together two separate sets of materials originally gathered by Dorothy Brush Walmsley, the wife of Charles F. Brush Jr., and Charles Baldwin Sawyer, a friend and business partner of Brush Jr. The materials were loaned to the Case Institute of Technology in 1962. After Sawyer's death in 1964, a single, consolidated collection was donated to Western Reserve University. (Case Institute of Technology and Western Reserve University federated in 1967 to become Case Western Reserve University.)

The Charles F. Brush Collection showcases Brush Sr.'s lifelong interest in electricity and electromagnetic phenomena, as well as his engineering and business acumen in the invention and large-scale production of municipal arc lighting systems. Brush preceded Thomas Edison in producing the first commercially viable system for outdoor electrical lighting, and he became the first person in America to illuminate public streets with electricity. In the course of his career as an inventor, Brush made significant contributions to electrical generation and storage technology. Brush is also considered by many to be the father of wind-powered electrical generation.

The Brush Collection includes professional and personal correspondence, laboratory notes, instrument diagrams, manuscripts of scientific papers, patent specification and litigation documents, photographs of Brush and his inventions (including arc lamps, batteries, generators, and his famous windmill for home electricity generation), and documentation of his numerous scientific, professional, and civic awards. Other holdings include business contracts and financial records, product catalogs, and selected shipping/sales ledgers from the offices of the Brush Electric Company during the 1880s. Audio and video reminiscences of Brush, recorded in the 1950s and 1960s by former associates, are also stored in the collection. In addition, the research materials of biographers and historians have been collected.

The Brush Collection significantly enhances our understanding of the history of electrical technology, as well as the role of entrepreneurship and regional business consortia in the evolution of American industry. Along with other holdings in the Department of Special Collections, such as the Warner & Swasey and C. B. Sawyer collections, as well as related collections in the Western Reserve Historical Society, the Brush papers also illuminate the development of Cleveland as a national center of technological innovation during the latter half of the 19th century. The Brush Collection continues to provide faculty and researchers in the Case community, as well as scholars from around the world, with resources for academic research in the history of technology and the history of business. The collection receives regular attention from museums, historical societies, media outlets, publishers, business firms, secondary and undergraduate students, and educators with requests for the use of Brush collection materials in exhibits, documentaries, news programs, and research projects.

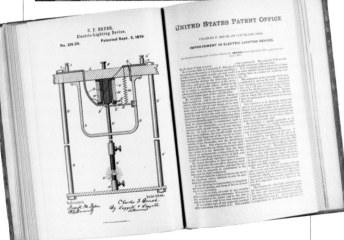

(ABOVE TOP)
"Charles F. Brush." Photograph by unknown artist. N.d.

(ABOVE BOTTOM)
Patent for electric lighting device (patent 219,211) in volume 1 of patents awarded to Charles F. Brush. September 1879.

(OPPOSITE)
"Artificial Moonlight: The Brush Electric Light Mast." In the *Cleveland Leader*, July 23, 1881.

Chinese Pamphlets: Political Communication and Mass Education in China

(ABOVE)
Man hua, no. 7. December 1950. Page.

(OPPOSITE TOP LEFT)
Man hua, no. 7. December 1950. Back cover.

(OPPOSITE TOP RIGHT)
Man hua, no. 7. December 1950. Front cover.

(OPPOSITE BOTTOM LEFT)
Man hua, no. 17. October 1951. Back cover.

(OPPOSITE BOTTOM RIGHT)
Man hua, no. 17. October 1951. Front cover.

THE holdings at the Center for Research Libraries (CRL) are especially rich in primary documents of political communication. The pamphlets, reports, newspapers, and other kinds of printed materials held by CRL chronicle the activities of political figures, parties, and organizations around the globe. Such documents are vital source materials for history and area studies, but tend to be produced erratically and disappear quickly. The center's collection of Chinese pamphlets used for mass education in the early period of the People's Republic of China, compiled by Edward Hunter, is one such collection.

An analyst of propaganda and mass education, Edward Hunter (1902–1978) had a long career in journalism and intelligence. As a correspondent and foreign editor for newspapers and news services in the Far East, Hunter covered hostilities in Manchuria during the 1930s. During World War II he served in the Morale Operations Section of the US Office of Strategic Services for two years, mainly in Asia. After World War II Hunter became a vociferous anti-Communist and popular lecturer on propaganda and psychological warfare. He was publisher-editor of the monthly journal *Tactics,* a contributor to mass-market magazines like *Esquire* and *Harper's,* and an expert witness for the Senate Internal Security Subcommittee and the House Committee on Un-American Activities. His best-known book was *Brain-Washing in Red China: The Calculated Destruction of Men's Minds* (1951).

The Hunter Collection consists of mass education materials published in Hong Kong and in Mainland China during the years 1947 to 1954. These include approximately 200 cartoon books, pamphlets, postcards, and magazines, heavily pictorial in content, on such topics as foreign threats to Chinese security, Chinese relations with the Soviet Union, industrial and agricultural production, and marriage reform. The materials were produced by both Kuomintang (Chinese Nationalist) and Communist regimes, and appear to be directed at the general youth and adult populations of China. Unlike the high-end, made-for-export propaganda held by many Western libraries, this is the "street literature" of the revolution: the comic books, leaflets, and other ephemera distributed to the population of the provincial cities and villages.

Accompanying the Chinese publications were a small number of pamphlets from a series entitled Cartoon Propaganda Reference Materials, published in Beijing by the People's Art Publishing House. The Cartoon Propaganda Reference Materials offer insights on contemporary readings of the images and picture stories and on party leaders' expectations of the artists who created them. Although cartoons were popular in China since the 1920s, they had not been used for political purposes by the warlord governments and the Kuomintang. In China prior to the Revolution it was more common for critics, rather than supporters, of the government to employ cartoons and pictorial materials to communicate their message.

The collection came to the Center for Research Libraries as a deposit from the University of Wisconsin–Madison, which received it directly from Edward Hunter. In 2006, a corresponding digital collection was released at CRL's Annual Meeting as one of the cornerstones for its e-collections.

http://ecollections.crl.edu/cdm4/index_hunters.php?CISOROOT=/hunters

漫画 7

蛇蝎美人　・張文元・

美國真相　采智

漫画 7

漫画 17

等於一張廢紙　・尚岳・

MADE IN USA

漫画 17

慶祝偉大的祖國建國二週年特輯

我們的祖國從今走向繁榮富強

University of Chicago Library
Special Collections Research Center

The Edgar J. Goodspeed Manuscript Collection

How did a 9th- or 10th-century Gospel lectionary travel from Argos, Greece, to a restaurant in Chicago owned and frequented by gangland figures, and then to the University of Chicago Library? Is a small hand codex of the Gospel of Mark a very early exemplar or a later forgery? Does a mystery novel, *The Curse in the Colophon* (1935), accurately depict the activities of its author, New Testament scholar Edgar J. Goodspeed?

These are just some of the research possibilities to be explored in the Edgar J. Goodspeed Manuscript Collection. The Goodspeed Collection comprises 65 early Greek, Syriac, Ethiopic, Armenian, Arabic, and Latin manuscripts ranging in date from the 7th to the 19th centuries. Edgar J. Goodspeed (1871–1962), Chairman of the Department of New Testament and Early Christian Literature at the University of Chicago, spearheaded the acquisition of these hitherto unknown manuscripts because he believed that "manuscripts are to research in the humanities what laboratories and laboratory materials are to the natural sciences." Along with Harold R. Willoughby and other colleagues, Goodspeed used the manuscripts to transform the textual and iconographic study of the New Testament and to teach a generation of students who would go on to further their work.

Among the manuscripts of incomparable beauty, research significance, and teaching potential in the collection are the 12th- or 13th-century Rockefeller McCormick New Testament, a Byzantine manuscript of the entire Greek New Testament except the Book of Revelation, containing more than 90 miniatures; and the Elizabeth Day McCormick Apocalypse, dated ca. 1600, the only known illustrated Apocalypse in Greek, with 69 miniatures.

Decades after the collection was named in honor of Edgar J. Goodspeed in 1948, a collaborative effort of library staff, faculty, and technology experts at the University of Chicago is advancing Goodspeed's goal of teaching students at Chicago and making the texts available to others. Funds from the university supported a pilot project to begin producing high-quality digital images of complete manuscripts in the Goodspeed Manuscript Collection. An award from the Institute for Museum and Library Services is now supporting completion of the project to make all 65 manuscripts available to the public online.

Professor Margaret M. Mitchell, Professor of New Testament and Early Christian Literature, taught a course on the Gospel according to Mark and the "media revolution" in earliest Christianity that focused on the mysterious "Archaic Mark" in the Goodspeed collection. Students explored the relationship between medium and meaning in gospel interpretation through direct encounters with this manuscript in class, and studied and contributed annotations to a digital version of the codex accessed online outside of class. Professor Mitchell and her teaching assistant, Patricia A. Duncan, published a journal article that introduced the digital "Archaic Mark" to the scholarly world and made available the first full collation of its text. Thanks to new tools, the Goodspeed Manuscript Collection continues to advance scholarship and enrich learning into the 21st century.

http://goodspeed.lib.uchicago.edu/

(ABOVE)
"Christ's Entry into Jerusalem." In *Red Gospels of Ganjasar.* Armenian, 13th century.

(OPPOSITE)
"Portrait of St. Luke" and Gospel of Luke text. In *Red Gospels of Ganjasar.* Armenian, 13th century.

The William J. Lawrence Notebooks on the History of the Dublin Stage

A TRAVELING salesman's early career on the road proved to be an interesting path to the creation of a prodigious body of work documenting nearly three centuries of British and Irish theatrical productions. Born in Belfast in 1862, William J. Lawrence was educated at Methodist College, and at the end of his formal schooling became a commercial agent for a wine and liquor wholesaler. Seeking to enliven an existence for which he quickly found himself ill-suited, Lawrence began to delve into old periodicals in Dublin libraries, jotting down the anecdotes and accounts he found of the city's stage heritage. By 1892, he had published his first book, *The Life of Gustavas Vaughn Brooke, Tragedian,* and shortly thereafter, resigned his position to conduct research and contribute reviews to a variety of publications.

The Lawrence collection consists of 99 handwritten notebooks containing his research on the Irish stage from 1630 to 1911. For his sources, Lawrence sought out copies of the Dublin daily newspapers, parish registers, the collections of Trinity College, and the Public Records Office—any slight bit of information that he could gather to illuminate the world of the theater. The notebooks are like those of a schoolboy's small, lined essay books, with Lawrence's careful handwriting supplemented by tipped-in news clippings, images of actors taken from programs and pamphlets, and the occasional typed transcription of a play. His attention to detail was remarkable; there are not only day-by-day notes on the theaters and their productions, but lists of actors, ticket prices, and management concerns as well. In many cases, he also provided insights on the personal lives of the players. For an 1865 performance by G. V. Brooke in *Othello*, for example, Lawrence noted that the actor "appeared as Iago…I say 'appeared' advisedly, since he was much too intoxicated to play the part." What Lawrence compiled offers a vibrant, cogent look at the cultural life of Dublin.

Lawrence's critical writings and historical research received occasional recognition during his lifetime, and he was awarded honorary degrees from Queen's University Belfast and the National University of Ireland. However, when he died in 1940, Lawrence was blind and impoverished. After his death, his collections of notebooks found their way to the used-book trade where most of them were obtained by William S. Clark II, a professor of English at the University of Cincinnati, to add to his own research in Restoration literature and theater. Another 20 of Lawrence's notebooks, the focus of which are on scenery, production records, and prompt books, were purchased by theater historian Richard Southern and are now part of the University of Bristol Theatre Collection. When Clark died in 1969, the University of Cincinnati's Charles Phelps Taft Library Fund bought the notebooks from his estate. The collection has been microfilmed and listed by volume in the university's online catalog. Over the decades it has been supplemented with hundreds of 18th- and 19th-century Irish plays, and is actively used for both scholarly work on Lawrence and on British drama, as well as by students interested in Irish urban history.

Mrs Barry

Character of Rosalind in the

As you like it.

E. VERHAEREN

SVÍTÁNÍ

Nové vydání

Odeon

THE GRANDEUR OF THE GORGES

DONALD MENNIE

in Colorado

Heart of the Rockies

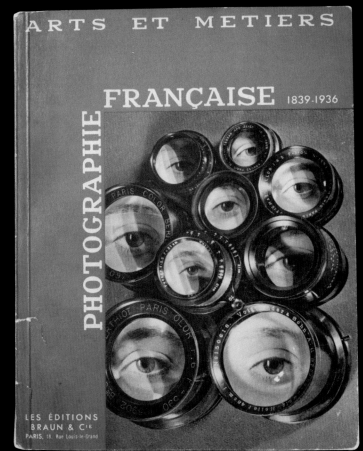

ARTS ET METIERS

PHOTOGRAPHIE FRANÇAISE 1839-1936

LES ÉDITIONS BRAUN & Cie
PARIS, 18, Rue Louis-le-Grand

University of Colorado at Boulder Libraries
Special Collections Department

Photobook Collection

THE University of Colorado at Boulder Libraries (CU Boulder) owns a significant photo-illustrated book collection containing over 15,000 volumes. The collection is interdisciplinary in nature and contains a dizzying array of images and artists from the iconic to the virtually unknown. The foundation of the Photobook Collection was laid with the purchase of two separate collections. The first was acquired in 1991 from collector David H. Tippit who began formation of the collection in 1978. The Tippit collection focuses on books that illustrate the works of important 20th-century American and European photographers whose original photographs are either too rare or too expensive to purchase. It includes first edition photobooks in their original dust jackets, exhibit catalogs, and rare serials providing the researcher with the convenience of being able to view, in one place, a broad range of images by any given photographer. The second collection, purchased in 1994 from Alan Scuba, emphasizes architectural, travel, and ethnographic photography. The scope of the combined collections has since been expanded to include new subjects and processes as well as an international array of lesser-known and emerging male and female photographers.

Within the history of books and printing, the 20th century is a rich period in the art and technique of the photographic visual record. CU Boulder art professor and photo historian Alex Sweetman observes that "the invention of photography culminates in the development of photomechanical processes and the creation of the modern world. Just as writing stabilizes language by making it exactly repeatable and multiplying its effectiveness (action at a distance and across times), picturing stabilizes vision and creates visual language(s)." Illustration of the written word transformed as the photo-mechanical process evolved in the 20th century.

Today traditional photography, which uses light-sensitive silver salts to record images, is quickly being replaced by the electronic image. Images are now recorded, manipulated, stored, and disseminated digitally, heralding a new age in photography and photographic processes. Thus, the Photobook Collection is not only an important historical repository of traditional photographic methods but, through collection development and continued acquisition of new materials, the Photobook Collection will also document the transition to, and uses of, emerging digital technologies as they appear in book format.

From an interdisciplinary standpoint, the CU Boulder Photobook Collection is a rich visual archive of images that encapsulate and bear witness to the peoples, events, places, cultures, sciences, technologies, and world views of the modern era. The collection is an integral tool in teaching visual literacy in the humanities and the sciences. From a purely artistic point of view, these books document 19th- and 20th-century photographic movements and contain the images of photography's formative years.

Future collection development plans include expanding holdings to include significant photo-illustrated works from the 19th century. Through additions such as these, CU Boulder's Photobook Collection will continue to provide researchers with an ever-broadening gateway to this vital and fascinating chapter in the history of books and printing.

(ABOVE)
"Fêng-Hsiang Hsia" [The Wind Box Gorge]. Plate XXV in *The Grandeur of the Gorges*. Donald Mennie. Shanghai: A.S. Watson and Company, 1926.

> Photos document areas to be impacted by Three Gorges Dam construction.

(OPPOSITE TOP LEFT)
Svítání. Emile Verhaeren. Prague: Odeon, 1925.

(OPPOSITE TOP RIGHT)
The Grandeur of the Gorges. Donald Mennie. Shanghai: A.S. Watson and Co., 1926. Silk cover.

(OPPOSITE BOTTOM LEFT)
Heart of the Rockies in Colorado. J. Douglas Crisp. Denver: Williamson-Haffner Engraving Co., 1906.

(OPPOSITE BOTTOM RIGHT)
La photographie française. George Besson. Cover image by Emmanuel Sougez. Paris: Editions Braun, 1936.

Colorado State University Libraries
Archives and Special Collections

Water Resources Archive

Wow! That's fascinating! Can I touch it? This is some really important stuff you have here.

COMMENTS such as these are overheard all night during the Water Resources Archive's annual fundraiser, Water Tables. A formal sit-down dinner, Water Tables begins with a cocktail hour in Colorado State University's Morgan Library. Guests enjoy hors d'oeuvres and drinks while mingling outside the Archives and Special Collections reading room. Inside the reading room, guests view dozens of items from Water Resources Archive collections on display, both in exhibit cases and on open tables.

Watching the guests—prominent professionals from Colorado's water community as well as budding graduate students—examine and marvel at historical documents, photographs, and artifacts highlights the significance of the archive's work. Newly established in 2001, the Water Resources Archive is the only repository in the state actively documenting the history of Colorado's most important resource. The Water Tables attendees know the importance of that history, but it is not every day that they experience it firsthand.

Today's water leaders become enchanted by yesterday's water pioneers when able to hold an 80-year-old diary, when allowed to turn pages of a century-old minute book, when able to examine a daguerreotype—a photographic format they may never have seen before. At the most recent fundraiser, a Colorado Supreme Court justice held a small, leather-bound diary from 1926 in his hands. This judge travels around the world to speak about the history of Colorado water law, and this was his first in-person encounter with a significant piece of that history. The diary was that of Delph Carpenter, a Colorado water lawyer who in the 1920s wrote and negotiated the Colorado River Compact, a treaty that still—despite drought and debate—governs the use of the West's most important river.

The Delph Carpenter Papers, containing the professional and personal materials of the state's most prominent water lawyer, give invaluable insight into early legal issues of western water. It is considered the cornerstone collection of the Water Resources Archive. Papers of water pioneers and records of water organizations comprise the archive and provide a unique resource for researchers as well as inspiration for today's leaders. The archive is particularly strong in its engineering collections, but it also documents policy, law, the environment, and water providers. Though perhaps not commonly known, names of engineers documented in the archive, such as Ralph Parshall and Robert Glover, are recognized by water experts around the world. The Parshall flume and the Glover equation are indispensable for irrigators and water managers.

With its broad range of subject coverage, the Water Resources Archive expertly aggregates collections and makes them available—onsite and online—so that all can learn from the past in order to improve the future.

http://lib.colostate.edu/archives/water/

(ABOVE TOP)
"Water Flowing through a Parshall Flume."
Lantern slide. Circa 1920s.

    The lantern slides in Parshall's collection were used to illustrate his publications and presentations.

(ABOVE CENTER)
"Ralph Parshall with One of His Flumes." 1932.

(ABOVE BOTTOM)
The Parshall Measuring Flume. Ralph Parshall. 1936.

    Parshall's own copy of his publication about the measuring flume.

(OPPOSITE)
Water-level recorder. Constructed by students at Colorado Agricultural College (now Colorado State University). 1900.

Columbia University Libraries
Rare Book and Manuscript Library

Joseph Urban Collection

ARL Maria Georg Joseph Urban (1872–1933) was one of the most significant stage designers of the early 20th century. Beginning with his work in Vienna, then in Boston, and later in New York, Urban's importance lay in his use of color, his introduction to American theater of many of the techniques and principles of the New Stagecraft, and his architectural sensibility.

Presented to Columbia University in 1955, the Joseph Urban Collection, with more than 135 linear feet of material, including 700 watercolor drawings, as well as architectural plans, elevations, scrapbooks, photographs, and 328 stage models, is the largest single holding of Urban's work. It covers a prolific and eclectic career encompassing not only his buildings and stage designs, but also his designs for films, exhibitions, interiors, automobiles, furniture, store windows, roof gardens, and ballrooms.

Grants from the National Endowment for the Humanities (NEH) and the Gladys Krieble Delmas Foundation provided for rehousing the collection and the creation of an archival finding aid. In 2002, the library received a grant from the NEH to preserve the three-dimensional stage models, and to support the creation of a digital archive. The Joseph Urban Stage Design Models and Documents Stabilization and Access Project Web site focuses on Urban's New York period (1914–33).

Researchers worldwide now have access to the work of one of the world's most creative designers. Equally at home in grand opera and more populist entertainments, Urban created over 50 productions for the Metropolitan Opera, including the US premier of *Turandot* (1926). For Florenz Ziegfeld, he designed 12 *Follies* and many other productions, including *Showboat* (1927). His New York City building designs included the Ziegfeld Theater, the New School for Social Research, and the interior of the Central Park Casino.

When William Randolph Hearst engaged him as art director for his movie studio (1919–25), Urban became one of the first artists to design for film. A chart showing how various colors appeared in black and white indicates how Urban used color for depth and texture.

During the past decade the collection has been cited in a number of books including: Robert Cole and Randolph Carter, *Joseph Urban: Architecture, Theatre, Opera, Film* (1992); Mary Henderson, *The New Amsterdam: The Biography of a Broadway Theatre* (1997); and Christopher Innes *Broadway to Main Street: Designing Modern America* (2005).

Works from the collection have been lent to exhibitions across the US and Europe; theater students have learned from the stage models; architects renovating Urban's buildings, such as Mar-a-Lago in Palm Beach, Florida, have studied his project files; color theorists have examined his drawings made as director of light for the Chicago World's Fair, A Century of Progress, 1933. Urban's work continues to delight and instruct. He was truly the "architect of dreams."

Urban Stage Design Models and Documents Stabilization and Access Project:

http://www.columbia.edu/cu/lweb/eresources/archives/rbml/urban/

Architect of Dreams: The Theatrical Vision of Joseph Urban

http://www.columbia.edu/cu/lweb/eresources/archives/rbml/urban/architectOfDreams/

Papers finding aid: http://www.columbia.edu/cu/libraries/indiv/rare/guides/Urban/

(ABOVE TOP)
Set model for *Flying High* (1930), act 1, scene 1, "Roof of apartment house in heart of Manhattan." Designed by Joseph Urban. Detail view.

(ABOVE BOTTOM)
"Flying High." Program. March 3, 1930.

(OPPOSITE)
Set model for *Flying High* (1930), act 1, scene 1, "Roof of apartment house in heart of Manhattan." Designed by Joseph Urban. Full view.

University of Connecticut Libraries
The Thomas J. Dodd Research Center

Alternative Press Collection

(ABOVE TOP)
Off Our Backs. June 26, 1970.

(ABOVE BOTTOM)
Berkeley Barb. March 22–28, 1968.

(OPPOSITE TOP LEFT)
Black Panther. December 6, 1969.

(OPPOSITE TOP RIGHT)
Black Panther. December 13, 1969.

(OPPOSITE BOTTOM LEFT)
Berkeley Barb. January 17–23, 1969.

(OPPOSITE BOTTOM RIGHT)
Berkeley Barb. August 16–22, 1968.

THE Alternative Press Collection at the University of Connecticut was founded in the late 1960s out of student participation in activist movements for social, cultural, and political change. Richard Akeroyd, a student assistant at the University of Connecticut Libraries, who later became curator of the collection and eventually the Connecticut State Librarian, built the collection along with then-director for Special Collections Richard Schimmelpfeng. The two collected fliers, handouts, and locally produced tabloids during the heyday of student demonstrations at the University of Connecticut and other New England campuses. In 1967, during the annual American Library Association conference in San Francisco, Schimmelpfeng collected posters and other materials scattered around the activist Haight-Ashbury district, adding to the geographic diversity of the collection. The library from the Radical Education Project of the Students for a Democratic Society (SDS) was added to the collection in 1972.

Today the collection extends beyond its humble origins to include thousands of national and international newspapers, serials, books, pamphlets, ephemera, and artifacts documenting activist themes and organizations, spanning the 1800s to the present. The bulk of the collection pertains to the Vietnam era. The collection contains more than 7,000 newspaper and magazine titles, 5,000 books and pamphlets, 1,800 files of ephemera from activist organizations throughout the country, plus miscellaneous posters, broadsides, buttons, calendars, and manuscripts. Alternative tabloids from the 1960s and early 1970s include *Georgia Straight,* the *Berkeley Barb,* and *Great Speckled Bird.* Contemporary peace movements regarding the US invasions of Iraq and Afghanistan, as well as materials pertaining to contemporary unrest in the Middle East, Central America, and Africa are also included.

An additional strength of the collection are liberation and civil rights movements, including a significant number of gay, lesbian, bisexual, and transgender materials and queer liberation publications. The collection also documents early feminist publications such as *Off Our Backs,* and contains materials pertaining to non-white racial and ethnic identities and power movements, including the Oakland-based *Black Panther* newspaper as well as flyers and ephemeral materials from demonstrations during the trial of Black Panther Bobby Seale. Asian, Latino, Native American, and interracial publications are all represented, as well as materials from organizations campaigning for the rights of children, the elderly, and people with physical and mental challenges.

The collection also includes a wide array of radical political materials, including approximately 3,000 books and pamphlets on socialism and communism, as well as anarchist materials and publications from the radical right.

Additionally, the Alternative Press Collection includes notable manuscript collections, including the Hoffman Family Papers, donated in 2000 by Jack Hoffman, the younger brother of activist Abbie Hoffman, the co-founder of the Yippie movement and co-defendant in the Chicago Seven Trial. Other manuscript materials include the Meyer Collection of Fat Liberation, the Connecticut Civil Liberties Union Records, and the Connecticut Citizens Action Group Records.

http://www.lib.uconn.edu/online/research/speclib/ASC/collections/apc/brochure.htm

THE BLACK PANTHER

Black Community News Service

25 cents

PUBLISHED WEEKLY — **THE BLACK PANTHER PARTY**

VOL. III NO. 1 — SATURDAY, DECEMBER 6, 1969

"THE ISSUE IS THE POLITICAL PRISONERS OF AMERICA. AND PEOPLE AS ONE TO STAND FOR THE RELEASE OF ALL POLITICAL PRISONERS."

HUEY P. NEWTON,
MINISTER OF DEFENSE
BLACK PANTHER PARTY
POLITICAL PRISONER

INSIDE THIS ISSUE..

HUEY P. NEWTON TO THE R.N.A.
ARTICLE FROM COMRADE KIM IL SUNG FROM THE D.P.R.K.

THE BLACK PANTHER

Black Community News Service

25 cents

PUBLISHED WEEKLY — **THE BLACK PANTHER PARTY**

VOL. III NO. 2 — SATURDAY, DECEMBER 13, 1969

He stood up in the midst of fascist gestapo forces and declared,

"I am a revolutionary."

Fred Hampton
Deputy Chairman
Illinois Chapter
BLACK PANTHER PARTY
MURDERED BY FASCIST PIGS
DEC. 4, 1969

INSIDE: • FRED HAMPTON MURDERED
• FASCIST PIGS ATTEMPT GENOCIDE ON B. P. P. — L.A.

Berkeley Barb

15¢ BAY AREA — 20¢ ELSEWHERE

"Seeds planted long ago are starting to bloom..." GOMEZ

NEWTON'S LAWYER--
'WE CAN'T LOSE'

story below

Berkeley Barb

15¢ BAY AREA — 20¢ ELSEWHERE

Yippie! CHICAGO AUG. 25-30

INSIDE:
¿BANDIDOS O GUERRILLEROS?

YIPPIE ALIVE!

COMMUNE FLASHES-- DID YOU SAY 'FLUSH'?

GIG-- JOB-- DIG?

TO SAVE TWO LIVES

by James A. Schreiber

After wading through eight days of contradictory, inconclusive testimony for the prosecution, we phoned Huey Newton's defense attorney, Charles Garry, Wednesday night.

It was startling to find him the most confident, cheerful person we'd talked with all week.

"I'm sure we're going to

THE TRIUMPH OF LOVE
IS A
HAPPY AND FRUITFUL MARRIAGE

THE
MARRIAGE GUIDE,

OR

NATURAL HISTORY OF GENERATION;

A PRIVATE INSTRUCTOR

FOR MARRIED PERSONS AND THOSE ABOUT TO MARRY,

BOTH MALE AND FEMALE;

IN EVERY THING CONCERNING THE PHYSIOLOGY AND RELATIONS OF THE SEXUAL SYSTEM, AND THE PRODUCTION OR REGULATION OF OFFSPRING; INCLUDING ALL NEW DISCOVERIES, NEVER BEFORE GIVEN IN THE ENGLISH LANGUAGE.

By DR. F. HOLLICK,

Author and Lecturer upon the Physiology and Diseases of the Generative Organs.

WITH NUMEROUS ENGRAVINGS AND COLORED PLATES.

309TH EDITION!!

MUCH ENLARGED AND IMPROVED, AND BROUGHT DOWN TO THE PRESENT DAY.

NEW YORK
THE AMERICAN NEWS COMPANY.

Cornell University Library
Division of Rare and Manuscript Collections

Human Sexuality Collection

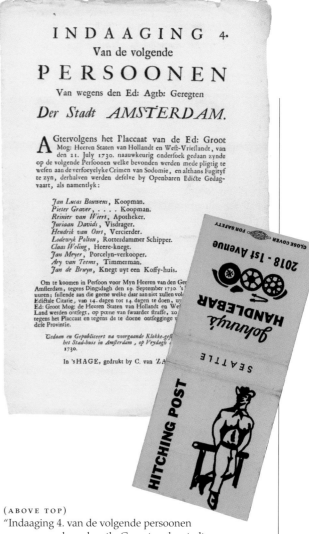

THANKS to the Human Sexuality Collection (HSC), people touring Cornell University Library's Division of Rare and Manuscript Collections may view Dutch wanted posters for sodomites issued in 1730, an 1826 letter from lesbian couple Eleanor Butler and Sarah Ponsonby, postcards of turn-of-the-century German transvestite performers, a 1930s photograph of two women in rural Michigan kissing, the diary of a gay man with AIDS, or contemporary trade cards advertising prostitutes in London.

Cornell University Library's Human Sexuality Collection was established with gifts from David B. Goodstein, longtime publisher of the *Advocate*, and Bruce Voeller, scientist and early leader of the National Gay Task Force. The two activists formed a friendship out of their mutual desire to combat misinformation and fears about sexuality. Both believed that society would benefit from increased research on sexuality's cultural and political contexts. Cornell embraced this mission with the establishment of the Human Sexuality Collection in 1988.

Voeller contributed the Mariposa Education and Research Foundation library. Founded to promote scholarship and public education about sexuality, one of Mariposa's contributions was its study of the effectiveness of various kinds of condoms in preventing the transmission of sexually transmitted diseases. Its library provided a tremendous collection of rare books going back to the sexologists of the 19th century and documenting the emergence of gay male erotica in the 1950s, nudism in the 1960s, and sexual liberation, gay liberation, and lesbian feminism in the 1970s. Its manuscript material traced the development of the gay rights movement in the United States and early responses to the AIDS epidemic.

An advisory committee of activists and scholars determined how Cornell could best help document important historical shifts in society's view of sexuality. These advisors recommended searching for topics that have stirred public controversy over time. Cornell has focused on issues and people that are outside the mainstream or not well represented in the historical record, including the voices of African-Americans and Latinos.

The Human Sexuality Collection is now especially strong on the US lesbian, gay, bisexual, and transgender rights (LGBT) movements, personal experiences of AIDS, lesbian and gay literature and publishing, transgender and intersex history, the politics of pornography and prostitution, and changing notions of proper courtship and deviant sexuality. HSC has collected and made accessible the records of most national LGBT organizations, including the largest, the Human Rights Campaign (HRC). In February 2007, Cornell opened to researchers the HRC records and an online exhibit highlighting 60 years of LGBT activism.

Carrying on Goodstein and Voeller's vision, HSC's ultimate goal is to encourage research on the many important and compelling topics related to sexuality. Tours, symposia, and frequent class presentations help bring the collection to the attention of potential users. Phil Zwickler Memorial Research Grants assist scholars traveling to use the collection.

Exhibition: http://rmc.library.cornell.edu/HRC/

Research Guide: http://www.library.cornell.edu/olinuris/ref/fgss.html

(ABOVE TOP)
"Indaaging 4. van de volgende persoonen van wegens den ed: agtb: Geregten der stadt Amsterdam." Amsterdam: C. van Zanten., [1730].
Wanted poster for sodomites.

(ABOVE BOTTOM)
Matchbook cover from Johnny's Handlebar, Seattle. From Larry Bragg's collection of matchbook covers. Circa 1980–89.

(OPPOSITE TOP)
The Marriage Guide, or Natural History of Generation: A Private Instructor for Married Persons and Those About to Marry, Both Male and Female…. Frederick Hollick. New York: American News Co., 1860.

(OPPOSITE BOTTOM LEFT)
"Till and Esther in a Field." Photograph from Michigan lesbian snapshot album. 1930s.

(OPPOSITE BOTTOM RIGHT)
Transvestite postcard. Hamburg and Altona, Germany: F. Heldberg and Hansa-Atelier, circa 1903–20.

Dartmouth College Library
Rauner Special Collections Library

The Stefansson Collection on Polar Exploration

To polar researchers around the world, Dartmouth is synonymous with the Stefansson Collection. Started as the private research library of Arctic explorer and Dartmouth faculty member Vilhjalmur Stefansson (1879–1962), the collection has become one of the largest of its kind in the world. Through extensive book, manuscript, and photographic collections, it documents exploration, social history, and scientific research related to the Arctic to 1930, and Antarctica to World War II.

Stefansson's career carried him into the Arctic early in his life. After several expeditions, including leading the Canadian Arctic Expedition (1913–1918), he became a tireless promoter of the North and his concept of the "Friendly Arctic." While many of his controversial theories, including the possible benefits of a high-protein diet, still have currency, his theories about settling northern regions were dealt a severe blow by the failed Wrangel Island experiment. In 1921, Stefansson sponsored a group consisting of three Americans, one Canadian, and one Inuit to establish a settlement on Wrangel Island. The expedition ended in death for four of the party. The only survivor was the hired native seamstress, Ada Blackjack. Her matter-of-fact, yet harrowing, 1923 diary from the expedition's final months is a centerpiece of the Stefansson Collection.

Generous endowments and the support of Stefansson's widow, Evelyn Stefansson Nef, have allowed the collection to continue to grow and "explore" new areas of research. The collection has recently purchased several children's books and popular publications related to the Arctic to provide cultural historians with another way to understand how the polar regions captured imaginations across Western Europe and North America. One of the most striking is Fridjof Nansen's *Farthest North* (1898) published in 20 parts. The original parts, issued fortnightly and luring readers with exciting cover images and the promise of "A Two Guinea Work for Ten Shillings," attest to the popularity of Nansen's adventures aboard the *Fram*. The parts' advertisements offer a fascinating glimpse into Nansen's audience: along with ads for Red, White & Blue French Coffee and Lyles Golden Syrup, is a plug for "Spratt's Patent Cod Liver Oil Dog Cakes" supplied to Nansen's expeditions. Readers who would never have the chance to visit the Arctic could vicariously experience the thrill of discovery each day while feeding their dogs—just as Americans served up Tang after the first Moon shot.

As global warming continues to make headlines, materials from the Stefansson collection are frequently featured in exhibitions around the world. With its online finding aids and international reputation, the collection attracts dozens of visiting researchers each year. Closer to home, the collection supports the research of the Institute of Arctic Studies within the Dickey Center for International Understanding at Dartmouth College. It has also become a prominent component of several popular courses taught at the college including the Department of Geography's Into the Wild and the Environmental Studies Program's Pole to Pole.

Wrangel, Island.

June. 23d. 1923.

The daid of Mr Knights death

He died on June 23d

I dont know what time he die though

Anyway I write the daid, Just to

let Mr Stefanssom know what month he

died And what daid of the month

writen by Mrs Ada B, Jack .

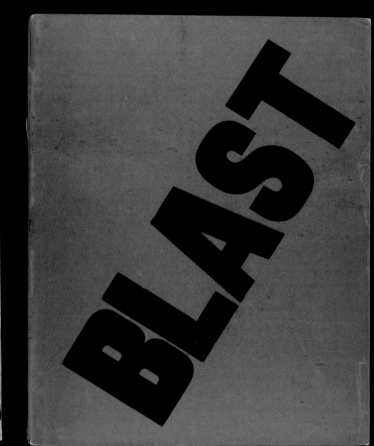

University of Delaware Library
Special Collections

Robert A. Wilson Ezra Pound Collection

IN June of 2004, the University of Delaware Library acquired through a combination of gift and purchase a major collection of works by and about the American poet Ezra Pound. The collection, which was acquired with the support of the Unidel Foundation, was assembled over several decades by the bookseller, collector, author, and bibliographer Robert A. Wilson. It comprises hundreds of books, including several of Pound's very rare first publications, manuscript material and correspondence, pamphlets, and other material related to Pound.

Born in 1885 in Hailey, Idaho, Ezra Pound became one of the leading proponents of Modernism. Equally a poet, translator, and critic, Pound was also a mentor and collaborator to many other writers, including Ernest Hemingway, Gertrude Stein, Robert Frost, H. D., Marianne Moore, William Butler Yeats, Wyndham Lewis, Ford Madox Ford, James Joyce, E. E. Cummings, William Carlos Williams, and perhaps most famously T. S. Eliot. Eliot acknowledged Pound's contribution and editing of *The Waste Land* by dedicating the poem to him as *il miglior fabbro*, the "better craftsman." In Italy, Pound became involved in fascist politics and did not return to the United States until 1945, when he was arrested on charges of treason for broadcasting fascist propaganda by radio to the United States during the Second World War. In 1946 he was acquitted but declared mentally ill and committed to St. Elizabeths Hospital in Washington, DC. During his confinement, the jury of the Bollingen-Library of Congress Award (which included a number of the most eminent writers of the time) decided to overlook Pound's political activities in the interest of recognizing his poetic achievements and awarded him the prize for *The Pisan Cantos* in 1948. After continuous appeals from writers won his release from the hospital in 1958, Pound returned to Italy and settled in Venice where he died in 1972.

Robert A. Wilson was born in Baltimore in 1922. Following service in the US Army and the diplomatic corps, he eventually became the fifth owner of the Phoenix Book Shop in Greenwich Village and ran the shop from 1962 to its closure in 1988. He is the bibliographer of Gertrude Stein, Gregory Corso, and Denise Levertov, and the author of a number of monographs, including *Modern Book Collecting* (1980) and the autobiographical *Seeing Shelley Plain* (2001). He is also one of the most important modern literature collectors of the 20th century.

The Robert A. Wilson collection of Ezra Pound comprises first editions of nearly all of Pound's published poetry, essays, and criticism, many in both the first British and American editions. The collection also includes manuscript material, including some correspondence with publisher Elkin Mathews, the original contract signed by Pound for the publication of *Provença* in 1910, and various other materials. The collection affirms and fixes Pound's place in 20th-century literature and complements the library's current collections. The collection also joins more than one thousand other books and manuscripts that the University of Delaware has acquired from Robert A. Wilson's collection and are now part of Special Collections.

(ABOVE)
"Ezra Pound at Rapallo." Photograph mounted by Glenway Wescott in his copy of *Poems 1918–21*.

(OPPOSITE TOP LEFT)
Blast 1, no. 2. London: John Lane, 1915.

(OPPOSITE TOP RIGHT)
Catholic Anthology 1914–1915. [Ezra Pound, ed.] London: Elkin Mathews, 1915.

(OPPOSITE BOTTOM LEFT)
Poems 1918–21. Ezra Pound. New York: Boni and Liveright, [1921].

This copy belonged to American writer Glenway Wescott.

(OPPOSITE BOTTOM RIGHT)
Blast 1, no.1. London: John Lane, 1914.

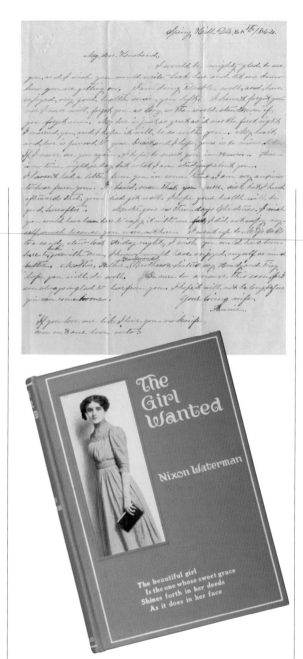

Duke University Libraries

Rare Book, Manuscript, and Special Collections Library

The Sallie Bingham Center for Women's History and Culture

FROM its beginnings soon after the founding of Duke University in 1924, the Rare Book, Manuscript, and Special Collections Library has been a repository for materials related to women. However, as in most libraries, these materials were collected inadvertently along with the papers of fathers, husbands, or other male relatives. In 1988, with support from writer and feminist Sallie Bingham, a women's archive was established to consolidate and build upon these holdings and to provide specialized reference, instruction, and outreach to researchers. Named the Sallie Bingham Center for Women's History and Culture in 1999, it has become a broad-based women's history library and archives whose main collecting areas include Southern and British women, feminist theory and activism, women authors and publishers, church women, girl culture, women artists, women's sexuality and gender expression, domestic culture, women's education, and women's work outside of the home.

The richness of women's experiences are reflected in the diversity of Bingham Center holdings, ranging from the diaries of plantation mistresses to the letters of enslaved women, from Victorian etiquette books to the papers of cyberpunk novelist Kathy Acker, and from the documents of suffragists to the manifestos of 1970s radical feminists. The center now actively collects in areas such as 19th- and 20th-century girls' literature, artists' books, and zines. The zines collection, one of the first and largest in the country, is made up of self-published works by women and girls that express the scope of interests and talents in this generation of women. This collection complements perfectly the letters, diaries, and literary and political writings that form the foundation of the Bingham Center's holdings.

In addition to building the library's holdings of women's materials, Bingham Center staff are constantly working to make these materials more accessible to potential researchers by creating subject guides highlighting collection strengths, collaborating with faculty to devise class projects that integrate the use of primary source materials, offering a research grant program, publishing a newsletter, and developing digital access projects. The Bingham Center mounts thematic exhibits and also regularly offers such innovative programming as dramatic readings, film festivals, artist demonstrations, and academic symposia that bring together donors, students, scholars, and the general public.

The symposia in particular, with themes ranging from abortion to artistic expression, spark discussion about issues central to scholarship and demonstrate the importance of the work of the Bingham Center, and of libraries and archives in general. This work promotes public conversation about these issues, addresses the relationship between academic institutions and social and cultural movements, and facilitates new collaborations amongst the center's diverse and expanding constituencies. The center's first director said that "developing an understanding of human experience requires access to historical documentation. And in order for women's roles and contributions to be fully recognized as a part of the human experience, our voices and writings must form a significant part of the historical record." The Sallie Bingham Center is dedicated to the work of giving voices and writings their rightful place so that the legacies of these women can be shared with future generations.

(ABOVE TOP)
Letter from Fannie Perry, a slave, to her husband Norfleet Perry. Louisburg, NC, December 28, 1862.

Perry was a personal servant to Theophilus Perry, who served in the Confederate Army. It is unclear if this letter was actually written by Fannie or dictated to her mistress. Fannie expresses her longing and love for her husband and refers to her extended family with whom she lives.

(ABOVE BOTTOM)
The Girl Wanted: A Book of Friendly Thoughts. Nixon Waterman. 1913.

(OPPOSITE)
Pink Corset Book. Tamar Stone. New York, 2000.

New York artist Tamar Stone creates one-of-a-kind Pink Corset Books, made from vintage corsets sewn together with text from corset advertisements and women's own experiences embroidered between the ribs of each garment. The act of opening and reading each layer simulates the process of unlacing and undressing.

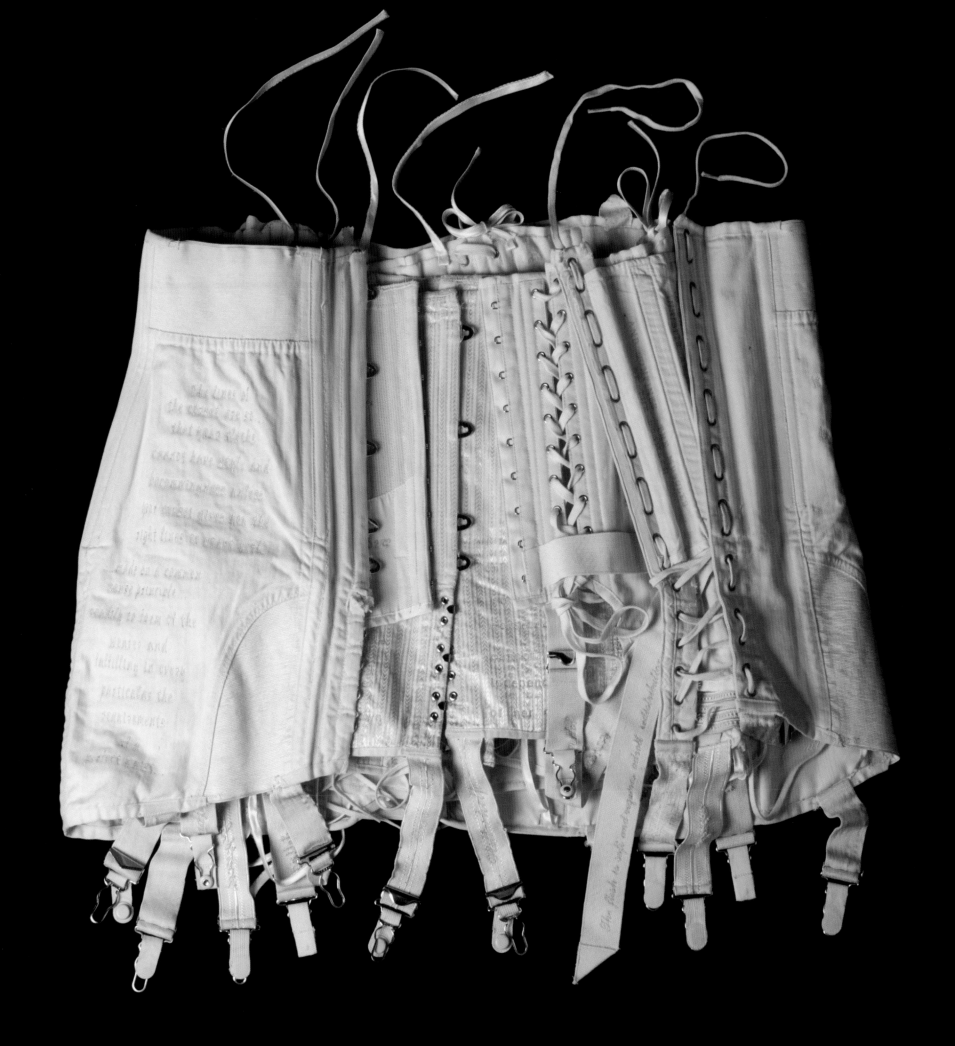

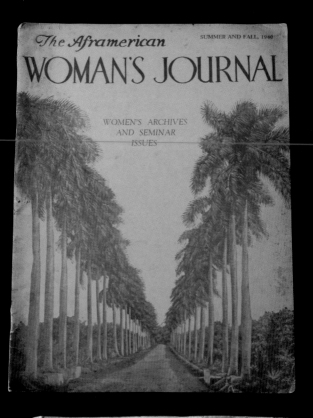

The Aframerican
WOMAN'S JOURNAL

SUMMER AND FALL, 1940

WOMEN'S ARCHIVES
AND SEMINAR
ISSUES

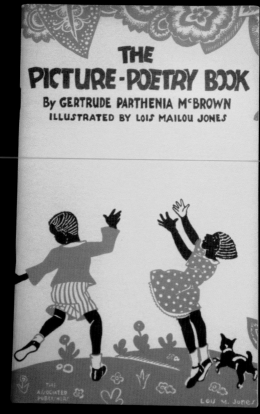

THE PICTURE-POETRY BOOK

By GERTRUDE PARTHENIA McBROWN

ILLUSTRATED BY LOIS MAILOU JONES

THE HINDERED HAND.

SUTTON E. GRIGGS.

THE RURAL NEGRO

CARTER GODWIN WOODSON

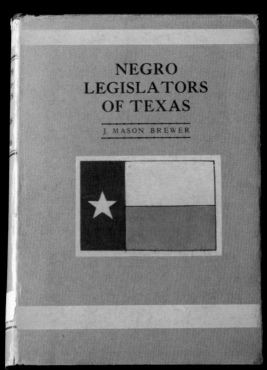

NEGRO LEGISLATORS OF TEXAS

J. MASON BREWER

THE NEGRO IN CHICAGO
1779 to 1927

Emory University Libraries
Manuscript, Archives, and Rare Book Library

The Carter G. Woodson Library

CARTER G. Woodson (1875–1950) was one of the foremost African-American intellectuals of the 20th century. Educated at Berea College and the University of Chicago, he was the second person of African descent to earn a PhD in history from Harvard University. Affectionately regarded as the "Father of Negro History," he founded the Association for the Study of Negro Life and History in 1915 and the *Journal of Negro History* in 1916. In 1921 he created Associated Publishers, which became the leading African-American–owned publishing firm producing scholarly books, novels, poetry, and children's and young adult books for the African-American community and the general public. He created Negro History Week in 1926 and the *Negro History Bulletin* in 1937 to promote the teaching of African-American history, the work to which he devoted his life.

By preserving and making the Carter G. Woodson library permanently available, Emory enables future scholars to understand the intellectual universe from which Woodson drew to produce the wealth of scholarship that is his legacy. His interests were wide-ranging: he gathered pro-slavery as well as anti-slavery texts; he acquired books about art, music, politics, economics, sociology, literature, philosophy, and religion; he was intensively interested in Africa and the Caribbean as well as Central and South America, Europe, and Asia. From a study of his library, scholars will find new sources for the intellectual biography of the man and of the institutions to which he devoted his life.

The Woodson Library is especially rich in African-American–authored and African-American–published books, pamphlets and periodicals, the world of literature created by and for the African-American community. Among the earliest African-American publishers represented in the collection is Annie Elizabeth Grey Brown, who published under the imprint A. G. Brown. Married to the noted historian William Wells Brown, she published the second edition of his *The Rising Son* (1882) and later editions of several of his other works. The Woodson Library also includes early and rare publications of the AME Church, the National Baptist Convention, and black colleges and universities as well as fraternal presses. Among the black newspapers that published books in the collection are the *Bystander*, the Baltimore *Afro-American*, and the *California Eagle*. Books of at least 69 African-American publishers are found in the Woodson Library.

The collection includes books inscribed to Woodson by Arthur A. Schomburg, W. C. Handy, Langston Hughes, Maggie Pogue Johnson, and dozens of other authors, both well known and obscure. It includes at least a half dozen titles not reported in any library, as well as rare books Woodson purchased on book-buying trips to Europe in the 1930s.

A catalog of the Woodson Library was published in September 2006 in conjunction with a major exhibition drawn from the library. The catalog includes essays by Emory's curator of African-American collections and two graduate students. Several hundred members of the Association for the Study of African American Life and History attended the exhibition opening. This popular exhibition was viewed by numerous high school and college classes and the general public.

University of Florida Libraries
Department of Special and Area Studies Collections

Baldwin Library of Historical Children's Literature

(ABOVE)
Paper doll with extra outfit included with *The History of Little Fanny, Exemplified in a Series of Figures.* Printed for S. & J. Fuller, 1810.

(OPPOSITE)
Pop-up illustration in *Little Red Riding Hood*. Anonymous. London: Dean & Son, circa 1856.

I N 1953, as a 35th-birthday present from her parents, Ruth M. Baldwin received 40 19th-century children's chapbooks. Baldwin had been a collector all her life, but within a year of receiving these 40 chapbooks, children's books became the focus of her collecting interest, resulting in what today is a collection of over 100,000 children's books published between 1668 and the present.

As a collector, Baldwin cast a wide net. Any English-language children's book published in the United States or Great Britain before 1900 was fair game. By the mid-1970s Baldwin had amassed a collection of over 35,000 pre-1900 children's books, all housed in her home in Baton Rouge, where she lived and worked as a professor at Louisiana State University. A series of negotiations brought the collection, and Baldwin as curator, to the University of Florida in 1977. After the move to Florida, Baldwin decided that a research library of historical children's literature should not end with the 19th century, so she began to collect 20th-century literature as well. Subsequent curators continue to fill in 19th-century gaps, to enhance the 20th-century holdings, and to update the collection with currently published books.

Baldwin's goal was not a collection of books deemed appropriate for children by adults or books in pristine condition, but rather a collection of books actually read and handled by children. This philosophy garnered many editions of popular and well known children's titles but also gathered in many unknown titles by anonymous authors that were read and loved by children over the years. These titles provide a cultural context for the well-known titles that have traditionally formed the accepted canon of children's literature. This array of unknown, uncelebrated authors and titles is one of the strengths of the collection, providing an opportunity for the scholar to explore the entire range of publishing for children.

The past 20 years has seen the growth of children's literature as an academic discipline, and the resources of the Baldwin Library have supported this growth and provided the material for a variety of papers, books, and dissertations from a cross section of disciplines, including the history of science, sociology, geography, music, American history, and English. A book on the history of American children's literature was based primarily on the holdings of the Baldwin Library. More recent projects have included papers by an undergraduate history class on publications during the American Civil War, the portrayal of fathers in the Little Golden Books, and an analysis of over 250 ABC books. These researchers have come from the University of Florida as well as from all parts of the United States and England. Now, through the efforts of the University of Florida Digital Library Center, with support of the National Endowment for the Humanities, selected books from the Baldwin Library are reaching a wider audience via the Internet and the collection Web site.

http://www.uflib.ufl.edu/spec/baldwin/baldwin.html
http://www.uflib.ufl.edu/UFDC/UFDC.aspx?m=hh

Away ran the Wolf at full speed, taking the nearest way; but the little girl amused herself with picking the wild flowers which grew in the wood, and making them up into a pretty nosegay for her dear grandmother, who was very fond of flowers.

The Wolf, who had run fast all the way, soon reached the cottage where Red Riding Hood's grandmother lived, and knocked at the door. Who is there? asked the grandmother. It is your grandchild, Red Riding Hood, said the Wolf, imitating her voice; Mother has sent me with some cheesecakes and a pot of fresh

Peuple! vois ton ami qui pour ta liberté,

Au peril de ses jours te dit la verité.

Se trouve a Paris chez Rochette rue St Jean de Beauvais N.º 38.

PLAN
DE
LÉGISLATION CRIMINELLE.

Ouvrage dans lequel on traite des délits et des peines, de la force des preuves et des présomptions, et de la manière d'acquérir ces preuves et ces présomptions durant l'instruction de la procédure, de manière à ne blesser ni la justice, ni la liberté, et à concilier la douceur avec la certitude des châtimens, et l'humanité avec la sûreté de la société civile;

Par M. MARAT,

Auteur de l'Ami du Peuple, du Junius Français, de l'Offrande à la Patrie, du Plan de Constitution, et de plusieurs autres ouvrages patriotiques.

Nolite, quitites, hanc sœvitiam diutius pati, qua non modo tot cives atrocissime sustelit, sed humanitatem ipsam ademit, consuetudine incomodorum. CICER.

A PARIS,
Chez ROCHETTE, Imprimeur, rue Saint-Jean-de-Beauvais, nᵒˢ 37 et 38.

1790.

Florida State University Libraries
Special Collections Department

Napoleon and the French Revolution Collection

DURING the 2002 ceremony naming history professor Donald D. Horward a Chevalier of the French Legion of Honor, several of his former students spoke about the importance of the Napoleon and the French Revolution Collection to their research. One hundred graduate students have received masters or doctoral degrees in French Revolutionary or Napoleonic era studies since Horward arrived at Florida State University in 1961 and began working with the University Libraries to build the collection into one of the finest in its field in the United States. In addition, more than 500 articles and scores of books have been based, at least in part, on research done in the collection.

Currently consisting of more than 20,000 volumes of published and unpublished material, the collection is strong in published memoirs, letters, serials, diaries, atlases, and government documents. In addition to standard resources such as the 32-volume *Correspondence de Napoleon Ier* (1858–1869) bound in red morocco and bearing the imperial crest of Napoleon III and the eight-volume *Dispatches of Field Marshall the Duke of Wellington* (1852), the collection includes many very rare items such as *Le Nain jaune réfugié* (1815–16); James Wyld's *Maps and Plans, Showing the Principal Movements, Battles & Sieges in Which the British Army Was Engaged during the War from 1808 to 1814, in the Spanish Peninsula and the South of France* (1840); and *Collection générale des décrets rendus par l'Assemblée nationale, avec la mention des sanctions et acceptations données par le roi* (1789–1791). Many volumes are held by no other library in an American university, and some are scarcely to be found in Europe.

Over the years, the collection has been enriched by purchases and generous gifts. Purchases include materials from the private collections of Ernest Augustus, King of Hanover, and of Phillipe Steenebrugen; from the collections of scholars of the period, including Octave Aubry, Jacques Arnna, Jean Regnault, and Marcel Dunan; and from the collection of Napoleonic bibliophile Marie-Antoinette Pardee. Among the gifts are 26 volumes of the French newspaper *Gazette nationale; ou, Le Moniteur universel* from Francois Ravidat, and from Dr. Ben Weider a complete set of the magnificent *Description de l'Égypte, ou, Recueil de observations et des recherches qui ont été faites en Égypte pendant l'expédition de l'armée française* (1808–1828), including the folio illustrations. In addition to printed and manuscript material, the collection contains several items of realia: a death mask of Napoleon cast from the mold created by Dr. Francis Burton who attended Napoleon on St. Helena; a set of 82 French medallions commemorating events from the Napoleonic era; and a facsimile of the Rosetta Stone. Materials acquired prior to 1973 are described in *The French Revolution and Napoleon Collection at Florida State University: A Bibliographical Guide* (1973), compiled by Horward and published by the Friends of the Florida State University Library. Bibliographic records for items in the collection are now searchable through the libraries' online catalog.

(ABOVE)
Death mask of Napoleon. 1821.

> This plaster death mask of Napoleon was acquired in 1984 from Dr. Edward Alderman Scott, who obtained it from the estate of Dr. David F. Sellers of Mobile, Alabama. Sellers acquired it from a family in New Orleans who claimed it had come from France with them. It is alleged to be a copy made from the original mold and cast created by physician, Dr. Francis Burton, on May 6, 1821, the day after Napoleon's death.

(OPPOSITE)
Plan de législation criminelle. Jean Paul Marat.
Paris: Chez Rochette, imprimeur, 1790.

> In this work, Marat expressed the need for enlightened reform of the penal system and advanced the view that the level of crime within a society may depend on the economic situation.

Westwood One Mutual Broadcasting System Records

(ABOVE)
Tape of *Tom Brokaw Reports*. NBC Radio Network. 1997–98.

(OPPOSITE TOP)
MCI JH110 two-track recording console.

(OPPOSITE BOTTOM)
Control buttons on MCI JH110 two-track recording console, including attached splice guide and marring on console cover caused by repeated splicings.

N 2001, Westwood One Radio Networks Inc. made a generous gift of nearly 900 cartons of audiocassettes and reel-to-reel tapes from the Mutual Broadcasting System to the George Washington University's Gelman Library System. Westwood One had purchased the Mutual Broadcasting System in 1985 but had ultimately decided to close its doors in 1999.

Founded in 1934, the Mutual Broadcasting System (MBS) ran continuously until 1999. Unlike the three other national networks of American radio's classic era, Mutual operated at first as a cooperative, which included more affiliates than any of the other big networks.

In 1953, eighteen years after its formation, the Mutual Broadcasting System became a wholly-owned subsidiary of General Tire when General Tire purchased the member stations in the cooperative. When General Tire sold the network five years later, Mutual lost its cooperative structure and adopted a more traditional, top-down management model. Over the years, Mutual changed ownership several times. When Westwood One purchased the network in 1985, it was the seventh owner in succession after General Tire.

Containing over 40,000 audiotapes from 1955 through 1999, the collection includes the recordings of well-known radio talk shows, such as the *Mike Walker Show*, 1990 to 1995; the *Jim Bohannon Show*, 1993 to 2000; and, perhaps most notably, the *Larry King Show*, 1970 into the 1990s. The collection also includes the Mutual Broadcasting System's various news programs, such as *America This Week*, 1990 to 2000; *First Light*, 1990 to 2000; *The Week in Review*, 1984 to 2000; *Seems Like Yesterday*, 1987 to 1989; *Weekend Headliners*, 1987 to 1999; *Newsbreakers*, 1985 to 1990; *America in the Morning*, 1984 to 2000; *The World This Morning*, 1978 to 1982; *The World Today*, 1958 to 1982; and *Reporter Roundup*, 1976 to 1988.

The collection also contains a treasure trove of recordings of prominent news stories including the first Persian Gulf War, 1991; the O.J. Simpson trial, 1994 to 1998; coverage of Ronald Reagan's presidency from 1981 to 1986, including the return of the Iran hostages in 1981 and the confirmation hearings of Reagan's cabinet nominees in 1981; coverage of George H. W. Bush's presidency from 1989 to 1992, including the Supreme Court Justice Clarence Thomas hearings, 1991; and coverage of Bill Clinton's presidency from 1993 to 1998.

At the time of the gift, this collection of recorded American radio shows threatened to overwhelm what was still a relatively young Special Collections program. By 2006, however, the department had built its staff and its professional capabilities to the point where it could handle such large collections of mixed-media formats, and Westwood One and the George Washington University began negotiations on a project to digitize the collection. As a result, the collection is being processed and each audio recording identified and described as part of what will be an ongoing effort to digitize and make available the contents of the entire collection to generations of scholars.

Joseph *Pleasant Rock*

THE
ALGERINE SPY
IN
PENNSYLVANIA:

OR,

LETTERS WRITTEN BY A NATIVE
OF *ALGIERS*

ON THE

AFFAIRS

OF THE

United States in America,

FROM THE CLOSE OF THE YEAR 1783 TO THE
MEETING OF THE CONVENTION.

—————————————————————————

——*Facto pius et sceleratus eodem.*
OVID.

—————————————————————————

PHILADELPHIA:

PRINTED AND SOLD BY *PRICHARD & HALL,* IN MAR-
KET BETWEEN FRONT AND SECOND STREETS.

M,DCC,LXXXVII.

Georgetown University Library
Special Collections Research Center

Russell J. Bowen Collection on Intelligence

AMONG the modern treasures of the Georgetown University Library is the remarkable collection of books on the subjects of intelligence, espionage, covert activities, and related fields assembled by the late Col. Russell J. Bowen, a chemical engineer and a technical intelligence analyst for many years with the Central Intelligence Agency. One of the largest collections of its kind in the country, it numbers more than 14,000 titles, many being scarce and some being rare, such as the first edition of Matthew Smith's *Memoirs of Secret Service* (1699). The collection includes works on cryptography, signals intelligence, tradecraft of all kinds, and the application of modern technology to intelligence gathering. Approximately 5,300 titles are listed in the 1983 bibliography of the collection as it then existed, *Scholars' Guide to Intelligence Literature*, with subject and title indices. Approximately 11,000 titles are more fully indexed in *The Electronic Database of the Russell J. Bowen Collection* published in 1991 by the National Intelligence Book Center and later updated. All the books are cataloged in the library's database.

The nonfiction collection is supplemented by the Bowen Spy Fiction Collection, another gift of Colonel Bowen, and is a separately maintained collection of more than 3,500 titles in the spy fiction genre. Largely English language in content, it includes such rarities as *The Algerine Spy* (1787). Its main value, however, lies in documenting the post–James Bond Anglo-American taste for espionage thrillers, although it includes a large number of earlier works and extends as well to encompass parodies and exploitative take-offs.

Colonel Bowen in his will left an endowment to the library, which has been used to enlarge the intelligence collection with both books and manuscripts, for example, the recent acquisition of the fascinating correspondence between novelist Graham Greene and spy Kim Philby. The presence of the Bowen Collection at the university has attracted other benefactors, one being former Director of Central Intelligence William E. Colby, who donated his intelligence library, containing many presentation copies, with the comment: "If Georgetown is good enough for Russ Bowen, it's good enough for me." Subsequently, other important collections have come to the library: the Howard Oakley collection of cryptography; papers of Martin S. Quigley concerning his work for the OSS in World War II; papers of the noted CIA counterintelligence figure Dr. Cleveland C. Cram, which deal in part with Kim Philby; archives of FBI special agent and spycatcher Robert J. Lamphere, who worked with the Venona intercepts and helped capture Klaus Fuchs; files of author and intelligence officer Edgar J. Applewhite, containing much about the CIA's James Jesus Angleton; and the vast archive of intelligence writer Anthony Cave Brown, who remarked, when finishing his Philby biography *Treason in the Blood* (1994), that if he had known earlier about the Bowen Collection, he could have saved two years of research time. Most recently, the library has been given the extensive papers of Richard Helms, Director of Central Intelligence under Presidents Johnson and Nixon.

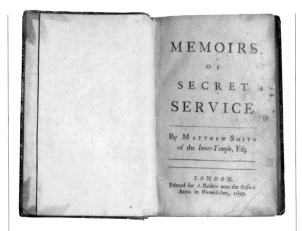

(ABOVE)
Memoirs of Secret Service. Matthew Smith.
First edition. 1699.

This work of intelligence and Jacobite intrigue created a sensation when published. The author purported to show a connection with the conspiracy of Charles Mordaunt, Earl of Monmouth, and complained of his treatment by Charles Talbot, Duke of Shrewsbury.

(OPPOSITE)
The Algerine Spy in Pennsylvania: Or, Letters Written by a Native of Algiers of the United States in America. Peter Markoe. First edition. 1787.

This fictional work attributed to the poet and dramatist, Peter Markoe, records the observations in America of Mehemet, the Algerine Spy.

University of Georgia Libraries
Hargrett Rare Book and Manuscript Library

DeRenne Library

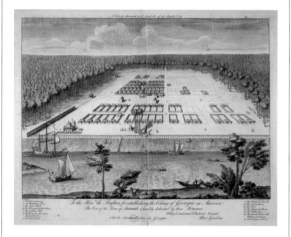

(ABOVE TOP)
"View of Savannah as It Stood the 29th of March, 1734."
Drawing by George Jones.

(ABOVE BOTTOM)
"View of Savannah as It Stood the 29th of March, 1734."
Peter Gordon after George Jones. Engraving by Fourdrinier.

(OPPOSITE)
"View of Savannah as It Stood the 29th of March, 1734."
Drawing by George Jones. Detail.

ACQUIRED by the university in 1938 from the De Renne family, the Wymberly Jones De Renne Georgia Library is the most complete collection of manuscript and printed materials relating to the early history of Georgia. The collection of 15,000 volumes and 35,000 manuscripts, once housed at Wormsloe plantation near Savannah, was begun in 1880 and consists of materials dating from Georgia's beginnings as a colony in 1732 into the 1930s. The library is an invaluable source for the study of Georgia's history. Primary source documents touching various aspects of the state's history are included. For example, the collection contains William B. Maxwell's *The Mysterious Father*, the first Georgia drama printed in Savannah in 1807.

One of a kind materials include the only known copy of the second Georgia Constitution of 1789, which includes the signatures of William Few, one of Georgia's two signers of the United States Constitution along with Governor Edward Telfair and other important historical figures. Other unique items include a 1780 *Royal Georgia Gazette* account of the siege of Savannah, a rare satin broadside of the Ordinance of Secession of the Republic of Georgia as passed in 1861, and the only extant copy of *The Death Song of the Cherokee Indian*, published in London in 1762.

The De Renne Library also has a rich map collection. John Mitchell's 1755 map of European dominions in North America and William Faden's 1783 map of North America are among the many notable cartographic treasures in the collection.

One of the rarest items in the collection is an original drawing of Savannah prepared by London draftsman George Jones in 1734. He prepared this image from a survey report by Noble Jones, ancestor of the DeRenne family, that was presented to the Trustees of the Colony of Georgia. The George Jones drawing became the basis of a famous engraving by P. Fourdrinier, and the image is commonly attributed to Peter Gordon, who delivered the report to the Trustees. The De Renne Library also owns a fine example of the Fourdrinier engraving.

The De Renne Library includes a wide variety of formats: books, manuscripts, engravings, newspapers, maps, broadsides, and photographs. The earliest book is dated 1700. This vast collection covers topics ranging from natural history of Georgia with original watercolors of Georgia birds by John Abbot, circa 1822, to Indian affairs in Georgia, to documents and books relating to the War between the States. The permanent Constitution of the Confederate States, engrossed on vellum 12 feet in length, is one of the rarest items and is viewed by hundreds of people when exhibited one day each year.

http://www.libs.uga.edu/hargrett/rarebook/derenne.html

http://www.libs.uga.edu/darchive/hargrett/maps/1734g6.jpg

http://www.libs.uga.edu/darchive/hargrett/maps/1734g6b.jpg

Georgia Tech Library and Information Center
Archives and Records Management Department

Fulton Bag and Cotton Mills Collection

I N 1985, the records of the Fulton Bag and Cotton Mills (FBCM) sat in the basement of the mill, never to see the light of day. The records would have been destroyed but for the efforts of the Georgia Institute of Technology's archivists and History, Technology, and Society (HTS) professors. They salvaged the materials and transported them to Georgia Tech's Archives. The institute's history with the textile industry made Georgia Tech a logical repository to house the materials.

The FBCM was a textile mill located just outside downtown Atlanta. Founded in 1868 by Jacob Elsas, a German-Jewish immigrant, the mill produced paper containers to house goods. In the mill's heyday, it had over 40,000 spindles operating and employed over 2,000 workers. Despite the early prosperity of the mill, the company was plagued by periods of labor disputes, most notably the 1914–15 strike, which focused on laborers' growing interest in unionization. After several months of unrest, the strike ended in failure in the spring 1915. By the 1960s, the mill had seen much change, including advancements in packaging and turnover in ownership. In 1968, the Elsas family sold the company to Allied Products Corporation. By 1978, the mill had closed its doors, and in 1997 Aederhold Properties redeveloped the historic mill into a mixed-income community of 182 loft apartments.

The rich contents of the FBCM records consist of architectural and mechanical drawings, photographs, business records, and executive correspondence that give a unique view of life inside a southern textile mill and mill community. In order to make the materials accessible, archivists processed the collection and in 2005 developed the finding aid available on the archives' Web site.

In order to provide a research experience for students in the use of primary sources and as a way to reach a larger audience, a portion of the collection was digitized in 2005. With assistance from the HTS professors, the digital collection was developed to promote research and scholarship through archival collections relating to the HTS academic curriculum. The mill's archival Web site offers researchers the opportunity to view and search digitized items, such as photographs of the mill workers and executive correspondence dealing with the 1914–15 strike.

http://www.library.gatech.edu/fulton_bag/

http://www.library.gatech.edu/archives/finding-aids/display/xsl/VAMD004

http://www.library.gatech.edu/archives/finding-aids/display/xsl/VAM004

http://www.library.gatech.edu/archives/finding-aids/display/xsl/MS004

(ABOVE TOP)
Striker ribbon. Circa 1914.

(ABOVE CENTER)
"Looms." Photograph by unknown artist. Circa 1910–30.

(ABOVE BOTTOM)
Threatening note to Mrs. Burdett. July 19, 1914.

(OPPOSITE)
"Female mill workers." Photograph by unknown artist. Circa 1915.

University of Guelph Library
Archival and Special Collections

Massey-Harris-Ferguson Collection

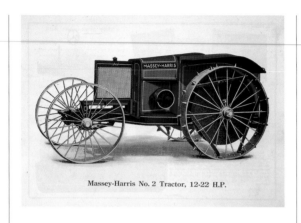

Massey-Harris No. 2 Tractor, 12-22 H.P.

(ABOVE)
Massey-Harris Farm Implements no. 2 tractor. N.d.

(OPPOSITE TOP LEFT)
"Around the World and around the Year."
Massey-Harris Poster. N.d.

(OPPOSITE TOP RIGHT)
"Monarchs of the World." Massey-Harris Poster. N.d.

(OPPOSITE BOTTOM LEFT)
"Loading with Massey-Harris Farm Implements."
Massey-Harris Poster. N.d.

(OPPOSITE BOTTOM RIGHT)
"Haymakers and Harvesters to the World."
Massey-Harris Poster. N.d.

BEGINNING with the early settlement of Upper Canada and for most of the 20th century, Massey-Harris, or as it was known after 1953, Massey-Ferguson, was one of the largest agricultural implement companies in the world. Farmers around the globe purchased Massey products and the Canadian company was an international leader in developing innovative farm machinery.

Daniel Massey (1798–1856) began manufacturing farm implements in 1847, and Alanson Harris (1816–94) established his own foundry in 1857. In 1891, Massey Manufacturing and A. Harris, Son & Co. merged to form Massey-Harris Company Ltd. By the mid-1890s, the company was the largest Canadian farm implement manufacturer, winning fame at international expositions, especially Paris in 1900. More mergers followed, especially with Johnston Harvester Company, located in Batavia, New York, in 1910, and J. I. Case Plow Works at Racine, Wisconsin, in 1928. Eventually the company became Massey-Harris-Ferguson Ltd. Massey-Ferguson prospered in the 1960s and 1970s with its tractor and combine production lines, but it declined rapidly in the changing farm equipment market during the 1980s.

The University of Guelph Library acquired the Massey-Harris-Ferguson Collection in 1999. The collection illustrates the growth of a large industrial corporation and serves as an essential resource for Canadian rural and agricultural history. The entire archive covers the period 1847 to 1986 and includes annual reports, administrative planning documents, financial records and statements for operations on four continents, posters, promotional catalogs and pamphlets, sales brochures and circulars, photographs, patent ledgers, exhibition medals and awards, speeches, price guides, repair manuals and parts catalogs, correspondence, marketing material, contractual agreements and deeds, legal records, company histories and biographies, 16mm films, and other company resources. It documents the company's production and history in Canada and overseas, including many firms that came to be part of Massey. In addition, there are important literary magazines encouraged by its most energetic president, Hart Massey (1823–96): *Trip Hammer*, *Massey's Illustrated*, and *Massey's Magazine*, plus many highly visual and posters and advertising sheets.

The majority of Massey items date to the 20th century, but the earliest items begin in the 1850s and extend until the company's merger with A. Harris, Son & Co. in 1891. Many archival series provide important details that mark the progress, success, and decline of the company. These include corporate mergers; records and decisions of the famous Harry Ferguson–Henry Ford lawsuit, 1947 to 1952; company submissions on Canadian government inquiries on farm machinery and on agricultural and rural life; and records relating to foreign branch operations in the United States, France, Germany, United Kingdom, Italy, South Africa, Australia, and other countries.

All materials are cataloged and more than 50 finding aids are available via the library's online catalog. As well, a Web site has been established to guide the public to more than 800 cubic feet of Massey records. It is anticipated that digitized images of machinery, company photographs, posters, and other historical documents will follow as the Web site is developed after 2007.

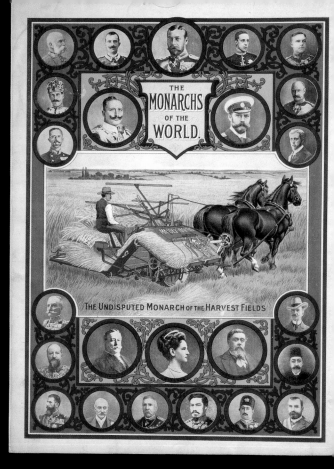

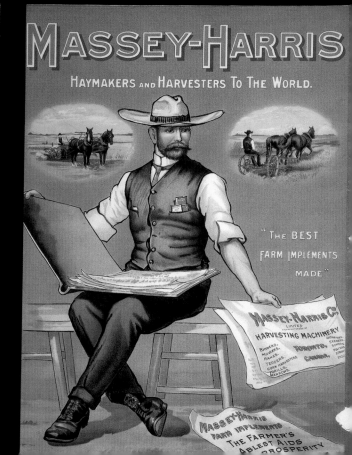

A poor — torn Heart — a tattered heart,
that sat it down to rest.
Nor noticed that the Ebbing Day
Flowed Silver to the West;
Nor noticed Night did soft descend,
Nor Constellation burn,
Intent upon a vision
Of Latitudes unknown.

The Angels, happening that way
this dusty heart Espied —
Tenderly took it up from toil,
And carried it to God —
there — Sandals for the Barefoot,
there — gathered from the gales
So the blue Havens by the hand
Lead the wandering Sails.

Harvard University Library

Harvard College Library, Houghton Library

Emily Dickinson Collection

EMILY Dickinson is one of America's most original poetic voices. Born in Amherst, Massachusetts, in 1830, she rarely ventured outside her father's grounds after the age of 23; she died there in 1886. These bare facts of a solitary and outwardly uneventful life do not explain how she produced such brilliant, startling poetry. She wrote that "Publication—is the Auction / Of the Mind of Man—" and presumably was content to be known locally for her gardening skills rather than her writing. Of the 1,789 poems that survive, only 10 were published in Dickinson's lifetime, all anonymously. While her family and friends knew that she wrote—she often enclosed poems in letters—it was not until after her death, and the discovery of hundreds of poems stuffed into the drawers of her bedroom bureau, that the extent of Dickinson's accomplishment was known.

It is this disjuncture between mundane life and sublime poetry that accounts for the continued fascination Dickinson holds for scholars and the general public. The Dickinson Collection attracts pilgrims from all over the world to work with the poet's manuscripts and letters, and to visit the Dickinson Room, which contains the family library and a selection of furniture (including the famous bureau, and the small bedroom table at which the poet wrote most of her poetry), paintings, and objects.

The Dickinson Collection came to Harvard in 1950, the gift of Gilbert H. Montague "in happy memory" of his wife, Amy Angell Collier Montague. Mr. Montague, a distant cousin of the Dickinsons, purchased the collection from Alfred Hampson, who inherited it from Martha Dickinson Bianchi, the poet's niece. Hampson was eager that the manuscripts be available for research at a major university, and Montague knew his alma mater would provide the proper environment to nurture the reputation of Emily Dickinson.

The Dickinson Collection is not a static memorial, but the center of an active research community. The collection has formed the basis for the standard publications in the field: Thomas Johnson, ed., *The Poems of Emily Dickinson* (1955); Thomas Johnson and Theodora Ward, eds., *The Letters of Emily Dickinson* (1958); Ralph Franklin, ed., *The Poems of Emily Dickinson: Variorum Edition* (1998); with an electronic *Poems and Letters* now in the planning stage. Harvard and Boston-area faculty use the Dickinson Collection regularly in teaching literary history and criticism, and creative writing. Visual artists incorporate manuscripts and objects into video, sculpture, and other art forms.

The library works closely with the Emily Dickinson Museum and the Emily Dickinson International Society to bring its collections to the public. Descriptive information about the family library and about Dickinson's manuscript books or fascicles, letters, herbarium, and family photographs are now on the Web, with a growing number of linked digital facsimiles.

http://nrs.harvard.edu/urn-3:FHCL.Hough:hou00321

http://nrs.harvard.edu/urn-3:FHCL.Hough:hou01457

http://nrs.harvard.edu/urn-3:FHCL.Hough:hou01525

http://nrs.harvard.edu/urn-3:FHCL.HOUGH:883158

http://nrs.harvard.edu/urn-3:FHCL.Hough:hou00049

http://www.emilydickinsonmuseum.org/

(ABOVE)
Herbarium. Emily Dickinson. Amherst, Massachusetts, circa 1829–30.
© The President and Fellows of Harvard College.

(OPPOSITE)
"A poor—torn Heart—a tattered heart."
Emily Dickinson. Circa 1859.
© The President and Fellows of Harvard College.

Autograph poem sent to Susan Huntington Dickinson. Attached with thread were two illustrations clipped from her father's copy of Charles Dickens's *Old Curiosity Shop*. Only one illustration remains attached, showing a young man in a graveyard kissing the hand of a young woman. The second illustration, now detached but with thread remaining attached to the poem, depicts four angels lifting a young girl up to heaven.

University of Hawaii at Manoa Library
Special Collections

Hawaiian Sugar Planters' Association (HSPA) Plantation Archives

(ABOVE TOP)
Wooden filing box of personnel cards. Lihue Plantation Company. 1930s.

These master personnel cards document each worker's name, "bango" number, nationality, sex, age, occupation, wage, dates of employment, and family members or dependents. Some cards include fingerprints.

(ABOVE BOTTOM)
"Sugar Worker Blas Erece and Family." Photograph by unknown artist, N.d.

This photograph accompanied Blas Erece's request to the Hawaiian Sugar Planters' Association (HSPA) that his family be brought to Hawaii from Ilocos Sur in the Philippines. The HSPA replied that their practice was to pay for the wife and up to two minor children of a worker. The price of passage for Erece's oldest daughter, according to the reply, was $33.40 and would be Erece's responsibility to pay.

(OPPOSITE)
"Hawi Mill and Plantation Co. Sprinkler System in Field 10I." Blueprint. Honokaa Sugar Company. 1939.

For the water-intensive sugar crop, planters went to great lengths to bring water to their fields, generally using irrigation or sprinkler systems such as this. In some cases more elaborate delivery systems channeled water through mountain tunnels and above-ground flumes.

The food that's sweet is hard to beat.
For weariness—eat Sugar

N 1929, when the trustees of the Hawaiian Sugar Planters' Association (HSPA) voted to use the first slogan shown above for their letterhead, and the second for their envelopes, they also recommended that various Hawaii sugar agencies and sugar companies do the same, to "assist in the campaign to encourage the use of sugar." A letter found in the HSPA Plantation Archives included additional suggested "Official Slogans and Lettering" such as "A bit of sweet makes the meal complete," and "Flavor with Sugar and you flavor with health." By the time these phrases were coined, they were the almost unnecessarily whimsical finishing touches to the development of the sugar industry in Hawaii, which by then had become a driving force in Hawaii's economy and had been a thriving commercial venture for nearly a century. From 1835, when the first successful commercial plantation was started at Koloa, Kauai, to 1999, when one of the last sugar plantations ceased operations, over 100 sugar plantations and mills played a major role in the economic and social history of Hawaii.

As plantations began, merged, and closed, the business records of these enterprises were often lost or placed in jeopardy. University of Hawaii labor history professor Edward Beechert found records in abandoned buildings, in bunkers left over from World War II, in attics, and under houses. In 1981, the HSPA created the Plantation Archives to serve as a repository for records of plantations that chose to donate their records. A collection of engineering drawings of the Honolulu Iron Works supplements the archives with drawings of sugar-growing and milling equipment. In 1995, the collection was donated to the University of Hawaii at Manoa Library.

The HSPA Plantation Archives is a rich and unique collection of records providing detailed insight into plantation life and the sugar industry in Hawaii spanning the years 1850 to 1991. Corporate records; correspondence; cultivation contacts; financial records; personnel and payroll records; production records; maps and blueprints; and records of plantation stores, hospitals, electric and ice companies, water and irrigation companies, and planters' associations are included, although not all kinds of records are present or complete for each company.

The Plantation Archives are of continuing personal and scholarly interest. Students seek information on all aspects of plantation life. For example, they research the evolution of ethnic relationships among the various peoples imported for plantation labor, and they study medical care provided on the plantations. Economists study wage questions and sugar technology, including the use of lumber, pesticides, water irrigation, power supplies, and sugar railroads. Information on genealogy is sought by community members and people with family ties to the plantations. While not every question can be answered, the Plantation Archives provide unique insights into the history of Hawaii.

http://www2.hawaii.edu/~speccoll/hawaiihspa.html

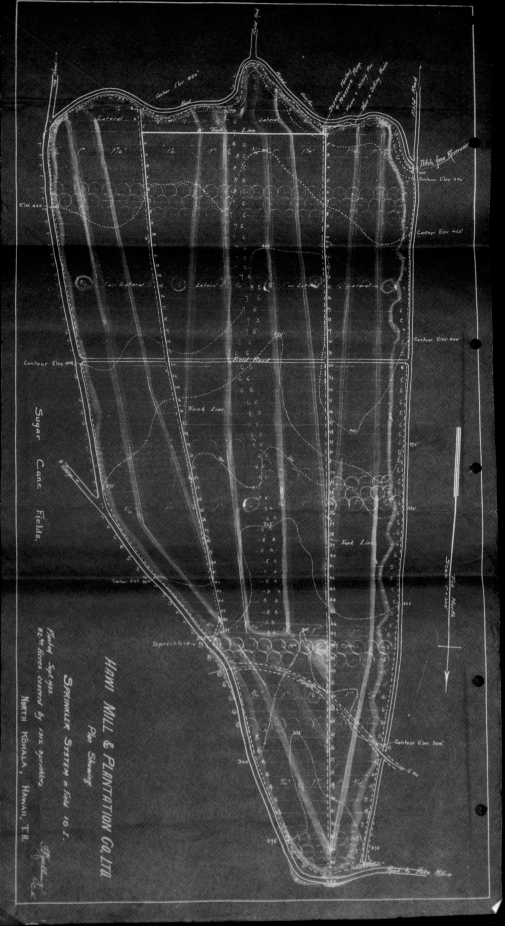

Domine labia mea aperies.
et os meum annunciabit
laudem tuam. Deus in
adiutorium meum intende.
Domine ad adiuuandum
me festina. Gloria patri et filio et spiritui sancto
sicut erat in principio et nunc et semper et in
secula seculorum amen. Alleluia. Inuitatorium
Aue maria gratia plena dominus tecum. ps.

Venite exultemus domino iubilemus
deo salutari nostro preoccupemus faciem
eius in confessione et in psalmis iubilemus
ei. Quoniam deus magnus dominus et rex
magnus super omnes deos qui non repellit
dominus plebem suam quia in manu eius
sunt omnes fines terre et altitudines montium
ipse conspicit. quoniam ipsius est mare et ipse fecit illud et aridam fun-
dauit manus eius venite adoremus et pro-
cidamus ante deum ploremus coram domino
qui fecit nos quia ipse est dominus deus noster
nos autem populus eius et oues pascue eius.

University of Houston Libraries
Special Collections

Medieval and Renaissance Manuscripts Collection

THE Medieval and Renaissance Manuscripts Collection includes a dozen manuscript books and eight manuscript leaves, dating from the 13th through the 16th centuries. The earliest book, a 13th-century Paris Bible filled with historiated, zoomorphic, and decorated initials, is known as the "Gwysaney Bible." The collection also includes three illuminated books of hours: a 14th-century manuscript (use of Sarum) from northern France or Flanders, a 15th-century northern French manuscript (use of Reims), and a 15th-century Dutch manuscript (use of Utrecht). It also contains a 15th-century choral service book from Italy.

Faculty from the departments of art, art history, English, history, modern and classical languages, and music seek out this collection to introduce graduate and undergraduate students to these beautiful books. Courses include: Medieval Art; Artist Workshop; Patron in the Middle Ages; The Book and Beyond; Medieval Latin; and Introduction to Musicology, among others. Assignments are not uncommon, students often being asked to write an impressionistic paper about one of the manuscripts. These manuscripts are a key component of a cross-disciplinary distance learning course, The Flowering of the Middle Ages, which features 16 lecturers who address various aspects of the Middle Ages; the course also includes a discussion with Special Collections staff about the production of medieval manuscripts.

Students from the art history graduate course Medieval Illuminated Manuscripts curated the exhibit "Lustre: Spiritual Treasures, Sensory Pleasures: Medieval Texts & Images from Houston Collections" in 2005, using items drawn from this collection. They were involved in most aspects of production: selecting materials, conducting research, planning the display, writing label text, and producing a catalog and Web site. Students also created artworks based on medieval manuscripts. One produced a large folio detailing the Martha Stewart trial and another constructed a full-scale scribe's desk and bench. Additional manuscript books were borrowed from local public and private collections to enhance community interest in the exhibition.

Earlier exhibitions also have drawn heavily on this collection, including "Incunabula, 1455–1500: The Cradle Years of Book Printing" (1995), co-curated with John Lienhard, host of *Engines of Our Ingenuity*, heard on many public radio stations. A printed catalog also accompanied this exhibition. "Glorious Works: Manuscript Books from the University of Houston Libraries" (1996), was curated by Special Collections and exhibited at Trinity Episcopal Church, Houston. It was presented in conjunction with a concert by the internationally renowned vocal ensemble Gothic Voices, who sang a chant from the Italian choral service book as part of their concert.

The Medieval and Renaissance Manuscripts Collection proves that manuscript books need not languish in darkened stacks, but can be learning tools for students and the public, and may even be brought to life through performance. Web exhibits include: "Stultifera Navis; The Ship of Fools" and "Topsell's The History of Four-footed Beasts and Serpents."

http://info.lib.uh.edu/sca/digital/ship/

http://info.lib.uh.edu/sca/digital/beast/

(ABOVE)
"Annunciation" and "Office of the Blessed Virgin Mary." In *Book of Hours (Use of Sarum)*. [Northern France or Flanders, 1350–1425]. Detail of illuminated initial "D".

(OPPOSITE)
"Annunciation" and "Office of the Blessed Virgin Mary." In *Book of Hours (Use of Sarum)*. [Northern France or Flanders, 1350–1425]. Leaves.

Howard University Libraries
Founders Library

Moorland-Spingarn Research Center

(ABOVE)
"$2,500 Reward!" Runaway slave reward poster.
August 23, 1852.

(ABOVE)
"$2,500 Reward!" Runaway slave reward poster.
August 23, 1852.

(OPPOSITE TOP)
"Caroline, a Slave for Life." Deed of sale.
April 21, 1844.

(OPPOSITE BOTTOM)
"Der Neger in Westindien." Hand-colored lithograph
by Friedrich Campe. N.d.

THE Moorland-Spingarn Research Center (MSRC) is a special *collection* because it covers a specific subject—African and African-American materials; but it is also a special *library* because of the depth and scope of this coverage and because it operates independently. After Howard University was established in 1867, MSRC began as a collection of reference books for students. MSRC was formally established in 1914, and its collections now include over 200,000 books on the African diaspora. The center is named for two of its earliest mega-donors, Jesse E. Moorland and Arthur B. Spingarn, both well-known bibliophiles, who worked with the NAACP during its inception and development. The three directors of MSRC have all been historians, scholars, and bibliophiles: Dorothy Porter Wesley served from 1930 to 1973; Michael Winston served from 1973 to 1983; and Thomas C. Battle has served from 1986 to the present.

Seminal books for the MSRC came from the university's principal founder, Gen. O. O. Howard and others. However, the earliest sizeable donation was the bequest of abolitionist Lewis Tappan, who was instrumental in the story of the freedom-seeking Africans aboard the 1839 slave ship *Amistad*. These books, and other secondary source materials, such as newspapers, periodicals, dissertations, news clippings, and microforms, are housed in the center's Library Division, where there is also a special collection of rare books. The oldest book in the center's holdings, de Villegagnon's *Caroli V Imperatioris Expeditio in African and Argieram* (1542), is from Moorland's gift of 1,400 books in 1914, and the second oldest book in the center's holdings, Juan Latino's *Ad Catholicum Pariter et Invictissimum Phillippum dei Gratia Hispaniarum Regum* (1573), is from the purchase of 3,000 books from Spingarn in 1946. The Manuscript Division houses the center's primary source materials and original documents, such as oral history recordings and transcriptions, personal and organizational papers, photographs and other images, sheet music and recordings. The Howard University Archives houses the records and archives of the university, and the Howard University Museum houses the center's artifacts. A more detailed description of individual collections, materials, and artifacts appears in the recently published book about the center, *Legacy: Treasures of Black History*, edited by Thomas C. Battle and Donna M. Wells (2006).

The resources of the MSRC include materials in the humanities and social sciences primarily. Titles cataloged since 2003 appear in the Howard University Libraries' online catalog; however, the bulk of the book collection is not yet in this catalog. Many subject lists and finding aids are available, and the collection guides for manuscripts have been digitized and indexed. The MSRC's collection development policy is not limited in scope but generally excludes children's books and cookbooks, unless they are significant or contain a considerable amount of cultural or historical information. The center enjoys an international reputation and attracts an international clientele of students, faculty, novelists, poets, historians, playwrights, journalists, actors and directors, musicians, dancers, publishers, government officials, photographers, inventors, scholars, and knowledge-seeking groups and individuals. Users often report that they can locate material at MSRC that they cannot find elsewhere.

...ived April 25th 1844 of Artaxerxes F. Offut
...Hundred and seventy five dollars payment
...o Girl named Caroline which I Sold the
a slave from Life and against the cla...
...persons whatsoever — Given under my han...

...mas Knowles

Thomas B. G...

Weit von meinem Vaterlande
Muß ich hier verschmachten und vergehn,
Ohne Trost, in Müh' und Schande;
O, die weißen Männer klug und schön!!

Der Neger in Westindien.

Und ich hab den Männern ein Erbarmen
Nichts gethan!
Du im Himmel, ach hilf du mir armen
Schwarzen Mann!

Nürnberg bei Friedrich Campe.

WORLD'S FAIR
CHICAGO
1934

Tour the World at the Fair
SEE FIFTEEN FOREIGN VILLAGES

University of Illinois at Chicago Library
Special Collections Department

A Century of Progress Records

A Century of Progress International Exposition, held in Chicago during the summers of 1933 and 1934, gave the nation an exciting diversion from the difficulties of the Great Depression. The success of the first summer of the fair led President Roosevelt to urge planners to continue the exposition for a second summer. The fair commemorated the incorporation of Chicago in 1833, dramatizing, according to fair boosters, the progress of civilization during the hundred years of Chicago's existence and highlighting the century's spectacular advances of science and technology. Chicago was the only city of major importance whose entire life had been passed within this remarkable century, one in which the application of science to industry had brought profound changes in both the economic and cultural structure.

The Century of Progress collection tells the story of the exposition and of the historical moment. The collection contains unique materials that provide insights into the nation's economic conditions, America's popular culture during the Great Depression, and life in the 1930s. There are over 16,000 files of individuals, companies, and organizations from across the United States and around the world that contacted or were contacted by the exposition's management. The records provide unique, behind-the-scenes, well-organized, and detailed documentation about this important, modern American exposition and its geographical and historical context.

The records document the fair's relationship to participating businesses and industries, modern architecture, design and graphics, mural arts, entertainment, food, culture, popular culture, corporate sponsorship, political figures, and celebrity visitors. The fair also focused on transportation, music, local immigrant groups, the economic crisis and political changes in Europe, religion in American life, women's history, participation of ethnic and minority groups, particularly African-Americans and Native Americans, the growth of modern advertising and promotion, American handicrafts, graphic art, and fine art.

UIC's collection places the fair in the context of the history and politics of Chicago. Its topics include science as presented to the public, the history of modern architecture, international affairs, American studies, engineering, race relations, employment practices, public parks, urban planning, and large civic projects. The design of the exposition was innovative: never before had color and architectural illumination been used for decorative effects, building identification, and crowd control.

The Special Collections Department acquired the official records of the Century of Progress in 1968 with the papers of Lenox Riley Lohr, the fair's general manager. The records include reports, correspondence, memoranda, corporate and exhibitor publications, posters, and phonograph records. The collection also contains architectural blueprints, employee records, photographic items, newspapers clippings, and artwork. The collection consists of 555 linear feet of corporate records divided into 17 series. The Special Collections department has an active outreach program that includes working with Chicago Public Schools through the Chicago Metro History Fair project and other organizations in Chicago, and teaching on campus to introduce students to conducting research using primary sources.

http://www.uic.edu/depts/lib/specialcoll/services/rjd/findingaids/COP1f.html

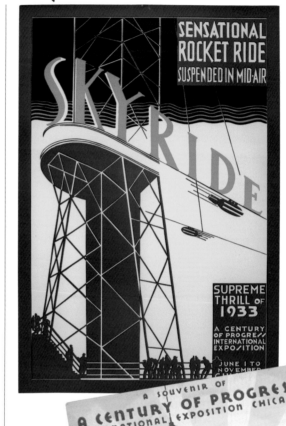

(ABOVE TOP)
"1933 World's Fair: I Was There." Lapel button. [1933.]

(ABOVE CENTER)
"Sky Ride: Sensational Rocket Ride Suspended in Mid-Air." Poster. 1933.

(ABOVE BOTTOM)
"A Century of Progress, International Exposition Chicago, 1934." Admission ticket. 1934.

(OPPOSITE)
"World's Fair Chicago, 1934: Tour the World at the Fair: See Fifteen Foreign Villages." Poster by Weimer Pursell. Chicago: Neely Printing Company, n.d.

University of Illinois at Urbana-Champaign Library
The Rare Book & Manuscript Library

Thomas W. Baldwin Collection

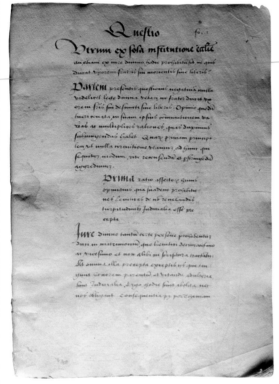

THE Thomas W. Baldwin Collection is a centerpiece of the University of Illinois at Urbana-Champaign's extensive holdings of imprints from the age of Shakespeare. Baldwin, a distinguished Professor of English at the University of Illinois from 1925 to 1958, assembled the collection to support his research relating to the education of Shakespeare and his contemporaries. Consequently, the collection is strong in Renaissance rhetoric, pedagogy, religion, and history, and in editions of classical texts taught in English schools.

In the early 20th century, the University of Illinois began to build its collections in earnest in order to support faculty in conducting primary research far removed from major urban centers. Professor Harris F. Fletcher, a member of the English faculty from 1926 to 1962, amassed a collection of books by and about John Milton which, in 1937, was housed in the Seventeenth Century Room on the fourth floor of the University Library. Likewise, Professor Baldwin was gathering books in his study on behalf of the library, "assembled by long search in second-hand catalogues and in English book-stalls," as the annual report for 1941 records. By 1943, Baldwin's cache of library books had joined Fletcher's to form the core of what is now the Rare Book & Manuscript Library.

Through the years, Professor Baldwin also built a personal collection, using it as a supplement to the books that the university had purchased on his recommendation. From these resources, Baldwin produced dozens of studies and editions of Shakespeare's works. In his *William Shakespere's Small Latine & Lesse Greeke* (1944), Baldwin pays tribute to the library for allowing him to acquire thousands of volumes pertinent to his research. Baldwin's personal library, consisting of some 5,800 volumes, was acquired by the library in 1966.

Although books from the Baldwin Collection have been featured in exhibitions, exposing the public to their richness, and have been used by scholars who visit the University of Illinois Library, online access to the collection remains limited; this situation will be remedied with the help of an Andrew W. Mellon Foundation cataloging grant.

In sum, the Baldwin Collection, along with the Milton and Miltoniana books gathered by Harris F. Fletcher, forms the core around which the strengths of the University of Illinois's collections have been built. In 1950, University of Illinois alumnus Ernest Ingold donated a set of the four Shakespeare folios, followed over the years by a substantial number of other Shakespeare items, such as a set of eight Pavier quartos (1619). Subsequently, the University of Illinois has become one of the most important repositories of pre-1801 English imprints in the world. In addition, the library holds more than 1,100 incunabula, making it one the premier collections in North America, and significant collections of 16th- and 17th-century Continental books. Manuscript collections range from Elizabethan legal documents to a commonplace book in the hand of Gabriel Harvey and the papers of Sir Robert Clayton, banker and Lord Mayor of London in 1679. The scholarly enterprise embodied by the Thomas W. Baldwin Collection continues to flourish at the University of Illinois.

(ABOVE)
Elizabethan manuscript. Circa 1550.
This is a treatise on why a man should not marry his dead brother's widow (a topic of interest to Queen Elizabeth).

(OPPOSITE TOP)
Imperatorum et caesarum vitae: cum imaginibus ad vivam effigiem expressis. Johann Huttich. Borders and portraits by Hans Weiditz. Argentorati [Strassburg]: Wolfgang Capito, 1534.

(OPPOSITE BOTTOM)
Elizabethan schooltexts. [16th century.]

DOMITIVS NERO, XVIII Cal.Ianuarias, ex Gn.Domitio Nerone patre & Agripp:na Germanici filia procreatus. Quo ædito, statim prodigiosa uox patris, gratulātibus amicis excepta, nihil ex se & Agrippina, nisi detestabile & malo publico nasci potuisse. Trimulus patre āmisit: mox matre relegata inops apud amitā sub duobus pædagogis, saltatore & tonsore nutritus. Seneca præceptore usus græcā & latinā edoctus linguas, ad necem eū cōpulit. Christiani sub eo primū afflicti suppliciis. Expeditiōes duas tantummodo suscepit. Musica & cantu mirum inmodum delectabatur, & adeo ut etiam de his triumphæret. Aurigandi & cythariz andi studiosus. Et in tantum libidini deditus, ut puerum exectis testibus in muliebrem transformaret naturam, seq; ipsum prostitueret. Sacrilegus & parricida, ut nec hominibus, ita nec mœnibus patriæ pepercit, quam in multis incendit locis. Sic omnibus uitæ probris contaminatus seipsum interfecit, & Domitiorū monumento conditus. Anno XXXII ætatis. XIIII Inperij. In eoq; Cæsarum progenies defecit.

Gn.Domitius Nero ex Antonia maiore genitus, pater Neronis: omni parte uitæ detestabilis, homicida, perfidus, maiestatis, adulteriorum, incestiq; cum sorore Læpida reus factus, tandem morbo aquæ intercutis decessit, sublato prius filio Nerone ex Agrippina.

Agrippina Germanici & Iuliæ filia, non illa M. Agrippæ, ut falso quidam scripserunt, facem humani generis Neronē procreauit ex Domitio.

D,

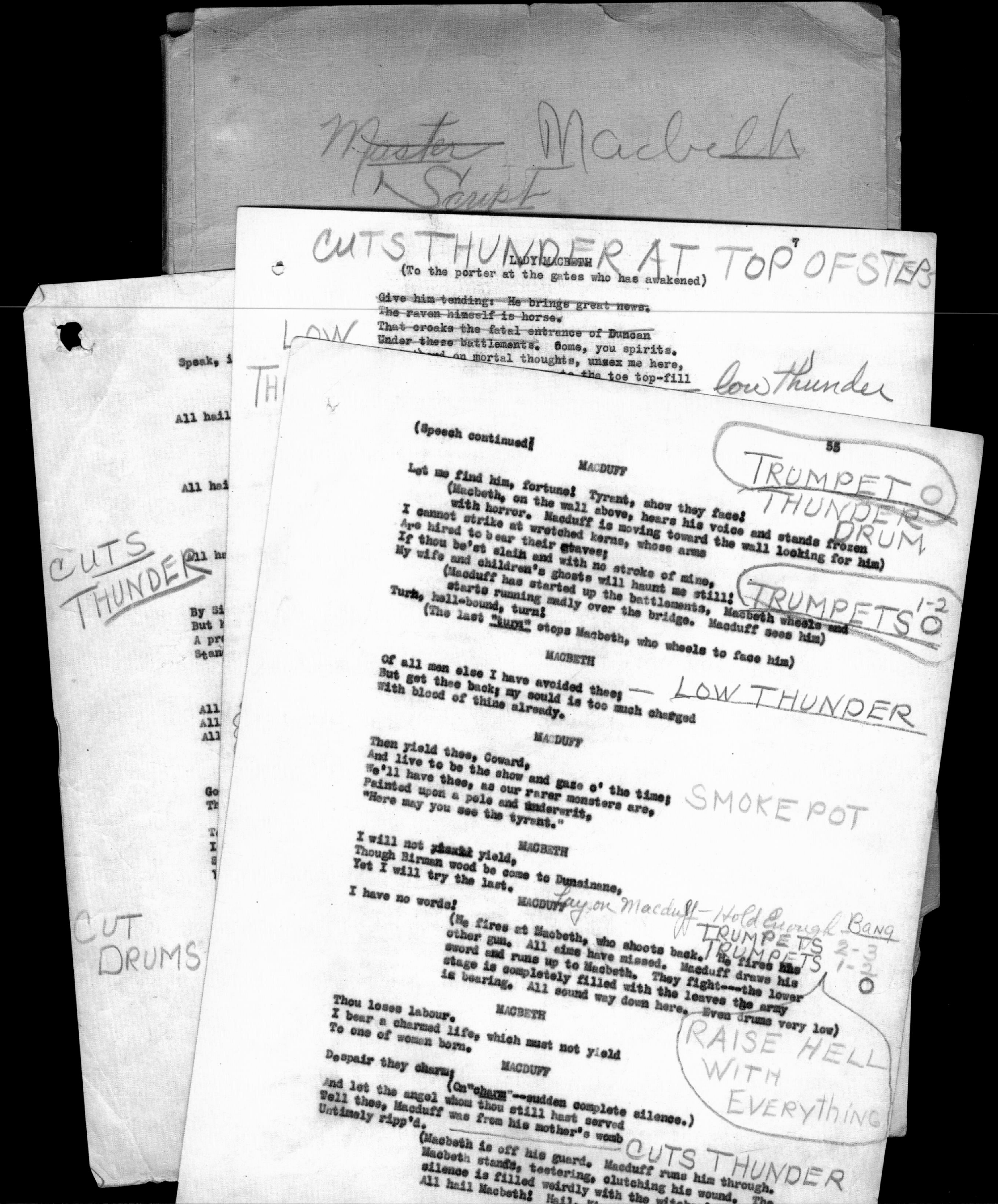

CUTS THUNDER AT TOP OF STEPS

(handwritten annotations:) low thunder

LADY MACBETH
(To the porter at the gates who has awakened)

Give him tending: He brings great news.
The raven himself is horse,
That croaks the fatal entrance of Duncan
Under these battlements. Come, you spirits,
~~...~~ on mortal thoughts, unsex me here,
~~...~~ the toe top-fill

(Speech continued)

MACDUFF

Let me find him, fortune! Tyrant, show thy face!
(Macbeth, on the wall above, hears his voice and stands frozen
with horror. Macduff is moving toward the wall looking for him)
I cannot strike at wretched kerns, whose arms
Are hired to bear their staves;
If thou be'st slain and with no stroke of mine,
My wife and children's ghosts will haunt me still!
(Macduff has started up the battlements. Macbeth wheels and
starts running madly over the bridge. Macduff sees him)
Turn, hell-bound, turn!
(The last "turn" stops Macbeth, who wheels to face him)

MACBETH

Of all men else I have avoided thee;
But get thee back; my soul is too much charged
With blood of thine already.

— LOW THUNDER

MACDUFF

Then yield thee, Coward,
And live to be the show and gaze o' the time;
We'll have thee, as our rarer monsters are,
Painted upon a pole and underwrit,
"Here may you see the tyrant."

SMOKE POT

MACBETH

I will not ~~fight~~ yield,
Though Birnam wood be come to Dunsinane,
Yet I will try the last.

I have no words!   **MACDUFF** Lay on Macduff—Hold enough Bang
(He fires at Macbeth, who shoots back.   TRUMPETS 2-3
He fires his
other gun. All aims have missed. Macduff draws his   TRUMPETS 1-2
sword and runs up to Macbeth. They fight—the lower
stage is completely filled with the leaves the army
is bearing. All sound way down here. Even drums very low)

MACBETH
Thou losest labour.
I bear a charmed life, which must not yield
To one of woman born.

Despair thy charm;   **MACDUFF**
(On "charm"—sudden complete silence.)
And let the angel whom thou still hast served
Tell thee, Macduff was from his mother's womb
Untimely ripp'd.

(Macbeth is off his guard. Macduff runs him through.
Macbeth stands, teetering, clutching his wound. The
silence is filled weirdly with the witches.
All hail Macbeth! Hail...

CUTS THUNDER

(circled handwritten annotations, right margin:)
TRUMPET 0
THUNDER
DRUM

TRUMPETS 0   1-2

RAISE HELL WITH EVERYTHING

(left side pages, handwritten:)
CUTS THUNDER

CUT DRUMS

Indiana University Libraries Bloomington
The Lilly Library

Orson Welles

ACTOR, writer, producer, and director Orson Welles is widely recognized as one of the most significant figures in 20th-century dramatic arts. His 1938 radio broadcast of H. G. Wells's *The War of the Worlds* and his film *Citizen Kane* (1941), often cited as the most innovative film ever made, are only two of the works that have helped make him an almost legendary figure. Welles acted and directed on stage, radio, film, and television, made numerous recordings, and authored plays, film scripts, and a newspaper column. As a political activist, he devoted considerable energy to the 1944 presidential campaign in support of Franklin Roosevelt. His work is of deep interest to students and scholars in a broad variety of disciplines, both here and abroad.

The Orson Welles materials in the Lilly Library at Indiana University can be found in a number of collections. The largest of these, the Wells mss., numbers about 20,000 items and pertains to Welles's activities on radio, stage, and film as well as to his personal and political life. Covering principally the years 1936–47, they include extensive documentation of his stage and radio careers, as well as voluminous materials for the films he planned and produced. The Fanto manuscripts consist of correspondence, film and theater production materials, photographs, and clippings pertaining to the work of Welles and his cameraman George Fanto. Correspondence and legal papers relating to the financial affairs of Welles and Mercury Theatre Inc., as handled by Welles's personal attorney, L. Arnold Weissberger, may be found in the Weissberger manuscripts. The Pauline Kael manuscripts add substantial information about his career as a film director. Film scripts and press kits for several of the films in which Welles acted as well as directed may be found in the printed collections of the Lilly Library. A detailed guide and inventory to the Orson Welles collection is available on the Lilly Library's Web site.

The Orson Welles materials have been used steadily for numerous published articles and books, including most recently Simon Callow's definitive biography, the second volume of which, *Hello Americans*, appeared in 2006. In addition, the materials have served for both study and inspiration in a number of graduate and undergraduate courses at the university in the departments of English, film studies, and telecommunications, among others.

New material continues to be added to the Lilly's Welles holdings. The library recently acquired a third copy of one of Welles's earliest publications, *Everybody's Shakespeare: Three Plays* (1938), edited for reading and arranged for staging by Welles and Roger Hill, this one with the young writer's extensive pencil annotations and revisions for radio production. An even more surprising acquisition came this past year with a series of love letters and whimsical self-portraits from Welles to his wife Rita Hayworth, preserved for years in her traveling cosmetics case.

http://www.indiana.edu/~liblilly/guides/welles/orsonwelles.html

(ABOVE TOP)
"Citizen Kane." Souvenir Program. 1941.

(ABOVE BOTTOM)
Rita Hayworth's makeup case. 1940s.

(OPPOSITE)
Voodoo Macbeth. Orson Welles.
Annotated typescript. 1936.

University of Iowa Libraries
Special Collections & University Archives

The Redpath Chautauqua Records, 1890–1944

(ABOVE TOP)
Redpath Agency postcard. 1913. Detail.

(ABOVE BOTTOM)
"Chautauqua, Iowa City, Iowa." Program. 1916.

(OPPOSITE)
"Chautauqua Storyteller Surrounded by Crowd."
Photograph by unknown artist. N.d. Detail.

AT its peak in the mid-1920s, circuit Chautauqua performers and lecturers appeared in more than 10,000 towns and small cities in 45 states before audiences totaling 45 million people. Big city lyceums brought similar "talent" before urban dwellers all year round, and few thought much about it; but rural people were keenly aware of what was showcased in the course of highly orchestrated three-, five-, or seven-day summer events brought to their community by town boosters. These tent performances drew friends and relatives from miles around, and they were memorable, often claimed as transforming. Today a fading memory of Chautauqua resides primarily with the descendents of those who trod the circuits or sat under canvas on folding chairs to be both instructed and entertained.

Chautauqua first appeared in 1874 in the upstate New York town now of that name. Founded by two Methodists, its primary goal was better training for Sunday School teachers. The idea of a summer "retreat" for spiritual and cultural renewal spread quickly, however, and similar programs were created near other cities. Soon competition for talent made booking difficult, while talent found itself with downtime and burdensome travel schedules. In 1904, Keith Vawter, a Redpath Lyceum Bureau manager in Cedar Rapids, Iowa, rationalized supply and demand, creating the first "circuit" by organizing talent to appear serially in 15 towns across Iowa, supplying tent, chairs, stage, and tickets while securing financial underwriting from a sponsoring committee in each town. The first season required a large investment in equipment and the enterprise lost money, but circuits quickly turned profits and spread like wildfire. They quieted in the late 1920s and died in the early 1930s, victim to the Depression, movies with sound, and network radio.

In 1906, Theodore Roosevelt declared Chautauqua "the most American thing in America" and, confirming his assertion, students and scholars have repeatedly found in the Redpath Records persuasive, multi-faceted evidence of the forces and values that underpin life as we know it in the 21st century. Circuit Chautauqua was situated squarely atop key transitions that still reverberate: a rural population becoming urban, an economy moving from agrarian to post-industrial, racial and ethnic uniformities confronting diversity, conservative values clashing with emerging liberalism.

Bureaus, basically, were communication centers matching the needs of towns to available performers. They lived by their files and on letters, thereby documenting in extraordinary detail an exceedingly complex phenomenon, a cultural dance that blossomed rapidly and disappeared quickly but exhibited amazing vitality in between. Vawter left his personal papers to Harrison John Thornton, professor of history at Iowa from 1929 to 1952, who willed them to the university. The Redpath-Chicago Bureau office files came to Iowa City in 1951. With continuing additions, the still-growing collection runs to over 650 linear feet.

A related Web site, "Traveling Culture," contains 7,949 publicity brochures representing 4,545 individual and group performers. A detailed inventory of the records, with bibliography and suggestions for further study, can be found at:

http://sdrc.lib.uiowa.edu/traveling-culture/inventory/MSC150.html

http://memory.loc.gov/ammem/collections/chautauqua/

Constitution

of the American Statistical Society.

Article I. This Society shall be denominated the American Statistical Society.

Art. II. The objects of the Society shall be to collect, preserve, & diffuse statistical information in the different departments of human knowledge.

Art. III. The Society shall be composed of Fellows, Corresponding Members, Honorary Members, & Foreign Members.

Art. IV. The Fellows shall be chosen by ballot, having been previously nominated by the Board of Directors — the affirmative votes of four fifths of those Fellows present being necessary to a choice; & no balloting shall take place unless ten Fellows be present. Corresponding, Honorary, & Foreign Members shall be nominated & elected, in the same manner. Each Fellow, on admission to the Society shall pay into the treasury five Dollars, & an annually afterwards, two Dollars, or, thirty Dollars at one time. Corresponding, Honorary & Foreign

Art. V. Fellows only shall be entitled to v but Corresponding, Honorary & Foreign

Samuel Shattuck
Secretary pro

Iowa State University Library
Special Collections Department

American Statistical Association Records

FOUNDED on an 1839 wintry morning in Boston, the American Statistical Association was organized to "collect, preserve, and diffuse statistical information in the different departments of human knowledge." The American Statistical Society (Association as of 1840) was chartered by the Commonwealth of Massachusetts, and by 1841 its membership of 109 individuals included President Martin Van Buren. Other early members included Florence Nightingale, Andrew Carnegie, Herman Hollerith, and Alexander Graham Bell. Now known as one of the oldest professional organizations in the United States, the American Statistical Association (ASA) numbers nearly 18,000 members in the United States, Canada, and internationally. As noted in a recent history of the ASA, the organization continues "a tradition of promoting excellence in statistics in its application to the frontiers of science, from biological to socio-economic to the physical sciences."

Iowa State University, founded in 1858 as the Iowa Agricultural College and Model Farm, became a land-grant university in 1862. Its early coursework utilized statistics in several fields, but the university truly came of age when mathematics professor George Snedecor arrived in 1913 and began teaching courses with statistical content. He was a pioneer in the area of applying statistical methods to agricultural research and worked with Henry A. Wallace, editor of *Wallace's Farmer*, in this area in the 1920s. In 1933 Professor Snedecor established and became the first director of the Statistical Laboratory at Iowa State, the first institute of its kind in the United States; he served as its director until 1947. He remained in the Statistics Department until his retirement in 1958. He also served as president of the American Statistical Association in 1948.

Due to these close relationships, the ASA collection was donated to Iowa State in 1984. It documents the ASA from its beginning to the present. The records include the original constitution, correspondence, committee files, financial records, publications, indexes to journals, conference proceedings, news clippings, and research proposals. The collection contains some records dealing with international programs as well as the organization of the Institute of Mathematical Statistics. In addition, the Special Collections Department houses collections documenting the editorial activities of the *Journal of the American Statistical Association*, published by ASA, and the *Annals of Statistics*, published by the Institute of Mathematical Statistics (IMS). There are also collections of personal papers of notable statisticians in the United States, many of them former officers and fellows of the ASA or the IMS, including Joseph Berkson, Raj C. Bose, Ralph Bradley, Dorothy St. John Cooke, Jerome Cornfield, William C. Guenther, H. O. Hartley, Oscar Kempthorne, C. Frederick Mosteller, and George Snedecor.

Thanks to ongoing support from the ASA, the department has been able to preserve and provide online access to the collection guide and make it available to scholars. The department also works collaboratively with the ASA Archives Committee to ensure better documentation of the statistics field and also provides assistance and advice for ASA members interested in locating a repository for their papers. The finding aid for the American Statistical Association is available online:

http://www.lib.iastate.edu/spcl/manuscripts/MS349.html

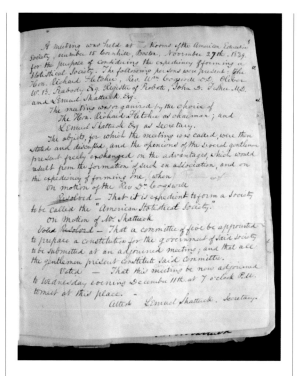

(ABOVE)
Minutes of the first meeting of the American Statistical Society [now American Statistical Association]. [Boston, 1840.]

(OPPOSITE)
"Constitution of the American Statistical Society [now American Statistical Association]." N.d.

Lester S. Levy Collection of Sheet Music

(ABOVE)
"Pork and Beans." C. Luckyth Roberts.
New York: Jos. W. Stern & Co., 1913.

(OPPOSITE TOP LEFT)
"Petroleum Court Dance." H.C. Watson & Charles
Fradel. New York: Wm. Hall & Son, 1865.

(OPPOSITE TOP RIGHT)
"Get Your Lamps Lit!" Theo. A. Metz.
New York: Theo. A. Metz, 1895.

(OPPOSITE BOTTOM LEFT)
"Lily Redowa." Chas. D. Blake. Chicago: White,
Smith & Company, 1882.

(OPPOSITE BOTTOM RIGHT)
"The Klondike March of the Gold Miners."
Theo. A. Metz. New York: Willis Woodward & Co.,
1897.

LESTER Levy, a Baltimore businessman and philanthropist, began collecting sheet music in 1929. His first acquisition was a dozen song sheets from the 1850s and 1860s, purchased for fifty cents each. It was six dollars wisely spent, and this modest investment marked the beginning of a lifelong passion for sheet music. As his collection grew, it quickly became more than a hobby; Levy recognized the significance of his collection as a window into the past. In his book *Grace Notes in American History: Popular Sheet Music from 1820–1900* (1967), he wrote: "Everywhere, and especially in this exuberant young country of ours, the song after the event has been the reporter and interpreter of history, free to describe and to criticize, to praise and to scoff, and to retell events in his own particular way."

By 1976 when Mr. Levy began donating the music to his alma mater, Johns Hopkins University, the collection had grown to over 29,000 pieces of sheet music. The collection was small but focused. According to one authority: "Among the major collections that were assembled in and just before Levy's day, his is one of the smallest, mainly because it perhaps reflects the best taste of any of them. He was not interested in 'junk' (of which there is an appalling lot)."

As he collected, Lester Levy selected music that could tell a story with lyrics and illustrated covers. Among the pieces in his collection are those that vividly record momentous milestones like the California Gold Rush and the discovery of oil in Pennsylvania. Wars are commemorated from the Revolutionary War to World War I. Inventions that altered the course of history are celebrated in song, such as the automobile, airplane, telephone, and telegraph as well as those destined for obscurity like the pathephone and velocipede. Fleeting fashions and fads like bloomers and the "Grecian Bend" are illustrated, as are those that have become a way of life such as the bicycle and cigarette smoking. There are pieces recounting disasters, natural and manmade, and praising triumphant successes.

The collection is one of the most actively used in Special Collections—consulted for dissertations, teaching materials, books, scholarly and popular articles, television programs, and exhibits, both museum-based and virtual. A Peabody Conservatory student, who learned of the collection through a musicology course, wrote and produced a chamber opera based on a song from the collection.

Mr. Levy enjoyed sharing his collection with others, and the Sheridan Libraries continue that tradition. The Levy sheet music was one of the first collections to be searchable online. In 1992, before the advent of graphical Web interfaces, patrons could search the Levy database and view scanned images. Today the Sheridan Libraries continue to take advantage of new technologies to improve access to this remarkable collection.

http://levysheetmusic.mse.jhu.edu/

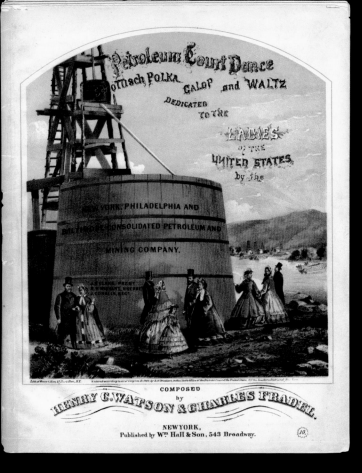

Petroleum Court Dance
Schottisch, Polka, Galop and Waltz

DEDICATED TO THE

LADIES
OF THE
UNITED STATES
by the

NEW YORK, PHILADELPHIA AND
BALTIMORE CONSOLIDATED PETROLEUM AND
MINING COMPANY.

COMPOSED
by
HENRY C. WATSON & CHARLES FRADEL.

NEW YORK,
Published by Wm. Hall & Son, 543 Broadway.

DEDICATED TO THE "SEARCH-LIGHT LANTERN."
THE HIT OF THE SEASON!

"GET YOUR
LAMPS LIT!"

Published by
THEO. A. METZ

SONG
POLKA

BY PERMISSION OF NEW YORK HERALD.

NEW YORK.
REMOVED 51¼ NEAR BROADWAY
1335 Broadway.

LONDON.
192 HIGH HOLBORN, W.C.

Copyright 1895 by THEO. A. METZ. Entered Stationers Hall.

TO
OSCAR WILDE

SUNFLOWER WALTZ
DAISY POLKA

VIOLET MARCH
LILY REDOWA

BY

CHAS. D. BLAKE.

White, Smith & Company,
PUBLISHERS OF SHEET MUSIC AND MUSIC BOOKS.

CHICAGO, ILL.
188 & 190 STATE ST.

BOSTON, MASS.
516 WASHINGTON ST.

OTTAWA, ILL.
SIMON BROS.

PROVIDENCE, R.I.
N. DARLING & CO.

NEW YORK
SPEAR & DEHNHOFF.

DETROIT, MICH.
C.J. WHITNEY.

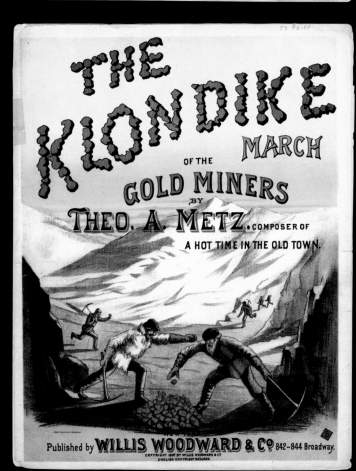

THE
KLONDIKE
MARCH
OF THE
GOLD MINERS
BY
THEO. A. METZ. COMPOSER OF
A HOT TIME IN THE OLD TOWN.

Published by WILLIS WOODWARD & Co. 842-844 Broadway.

COPYRIGHT 1897 BY WILLIS WOODWARD & Co.
ENGLISH COPYRIGHT SECURED.

University of Kansas Libraries
Kenneth Spencer Research Library

Joseph J. Pennell Collection

THE Kansas Collection, housed at the Kenneth Spencer Research Library at the University of Kansas (KU), is home to more than 30,000 glass plate negatives that represent the life work of Joseph J. Pennell, a successful commercial studio photographer who worked in Junction City, Kansas, from the early 1890s to the early 1920s. It provides a comprehensive view of life in a moderately-sized midwestern army-post town on the Great Plains at the turn of the last century.

The Pennell Collection, compelling because of its scope, depth, and the very high quality of Pennell's photographic skill, provides the researcher with an opportunity to view life at a time of great change in the United States. Included in the collection, in addition to many studio portraits of residents of the town and officers and enlisted men from Fort Riley, are images documenting businesses, from laundries to brothels and saloons; military life at Fort Riley, including examples of the kinds of training provided for the US Cavalry; and the town's and post's social life and customs, from weddings to funerals. The photographs provide important documentation of the African-American experience in mid-America during this time period.

The University of Kansas acquired the collection of glass plate negatives, along with 10 ledgers of business records, in 1950. Pennell's novelist son, Joseph Stanley Pennell, was persuaded to donate them to the university by Robert Taft, a KU faculty member. Taft culled what he judged the most significant images, printed them, and prepared a traveling exhibition, which generated a great deal of interest, especially in Kansas. In 1983, the University of Kansas Libraries gained funding from the National Endowment for the Humanities to preserve and provide increased intellectual access to the collection.

Today, the Pennell Collection is recognized as an important source for researchers in many fields, especially history of the American West, the US Army, the changing role of women, and the African-American experience. All who are interested in learning more about the period following the end of the western frontier will find much here to discover. The collection often is used to teach students about the use of photographs as primary sources, and hundreds of KU students interact with the collections each year.

Publishers have used images from the collection in many books about American life. Documentary features created by Ken Burns on baseball and the American West also have included Pennell images. The Pennell Collection has been at once a source for a war exhibition mounted at the Corcoran Gallery and a source for saloon images used in the opening title screen for the television show *Cheers!*

A 1983 exhibition of Pennell prints, "Frozen in Time," curated by Thomas Southall and funded by the Mid-America Arts Alliance, traveled throughout the Midwest. The collection was the subject of the well-received scholarly book *Our Town on the Plains* (2000) by James R. Shortridge, a KU professor of geography, with a long essay by John Pultz, curator of photography at KU's Spencer Museum of Art and a KU professor of art history.

(ABOVE TOP)
"Charles Bumstead's Ford." Photograph by Joseph J. Pennell. Junction City, Kansas, 1906. Glass plate. Negative image.

(ABOVE CENTER)
"Miss Crook and Miss Mickey at the Wareham-Dewey Switchboard." Photograph by Joseph J. Pennell. Junction City, Kansas, 1915.

(ABOVE BOTTOM)
"Rudy Sohn's Barbershop." Photograph by Joseph J. Pennell. Junction City, Kansas, 1903.

(OPPOSITE)
"Charles Bumstead's Ford." Photograph by Joseph J. Pennell. Junction City, Kansas, 1906.

The Borowitz True Crime Collection

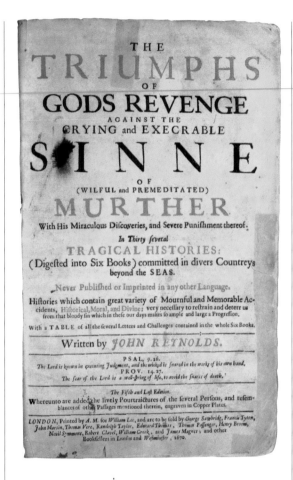

(ABOVE)

The Triumphs of Gods Revenge against the Crying and Execrable Sinne of (Wilful and Premeditated) Murther. John Reynolds. 1670.

This illustrated volume of various crimes and punishments is asserted by its author to be based on "continental records," but almost certainly consists entirely of fictional accounts. A series of "cautionary tales" in which heinous murders are punished by "divine retribution," this work enjoyed wide popularity and was published in multiple editions.

(OPPOSITE)

"God's Revenge against the Crying and Execrable Sin of Murther." From *The Triumphs of Gods Revenge against the Crying and Execrable Sinne of (Wilful and Premeditated) Murther.* John Reynolds. 1670.

One of Reynolds's murder "histories" is the story of Don Juan and Marsillia, which involves adultery, poisoning, a duel, a beheading, and the burning of two murder victims.

ALBERT Borowitz started collecting at the age of 12 when he asked his father to buy an edition of the complete Sherlock Holmes stories for him. Later, as a student at Harvard Law School, his experiences in a criminal law course that required readings of case narratives increased his interest in true crime texts. Though Borowitz went on to practice corporate—not criminal—law as a partner in an international firm, he devoted much of his personal life to scholarly exploration of true crime literature. By the time of his retirement from law practice in 1983, he had amassed a library of over 12,000 volumes on the subject. The Borowitz True Crime Collection reflects the multidisciplinary expertise of Borowitz, a Harvard graduate with degrees in classics and Chinese regional studies as well as law, and his wife, Helen Osterman Borowitz, a Radcliffe-educated art historian with literary interests. In addition to collecting, Albert Borowitz is himself a scholar of true crime, having published over 10 books and dozens of articles on the topic, most notably his masterwork, *Blood & Ink: An International Guide to Fact-Based Crime Literature* (2002).

The Borowitz Collection includes both primary and secondary sources on crime as well as literary works based on true crime incidents. The collection documents the history of crime internationally, with primary emphasis on the United States, England, France, and Germany, from ancient times to the present day. It includes materials on specific criminal cases which have had notable impacts on art, literature, and social attitudes, providing researchers with a wealth of material on those cases and their cultural effects. Special areas of note include an excellent collection of Sherlock Holmes and other Arthur Conan Doyle early editions; nonfiction and fiction works related to Jack the Ripper; 19th- and 20th-century British and American crime pamphlets and broadsides; a Wild West collection; crime-related photographs, playbills, postcards, and other ephemera; a vast collection of popular sheet music that includes a fascinating subset of crime-related and crime-themed music; and artifacts, graphics, and memorabilia related to crime.

Almost as fascinating as the collection itself is the wide array of researchers who utilize its contents in a variety of scholarly endeavors. The collection provides rich sources to users as diverse as crime historians, film documentarians, museum curators, television and radio producers, antiquarian book dealers, and faculty and students in history, American studies, women's studies, and criminal justice. Additionally, materials are routinely loaned for exhibit by other cultural heritage institutions, such as the National Library of Medicine, which recently made use of several items in an exhibition on the history of forensic medicine.

The Department of Special Collections has taken particular care to document the complex and often subtle relationships among items in the collection. Highly detailed catalog records and finding aids are available online through the library catalog and Borowitz Collection Web site. The department has also showcased the collection in multiple exhibitions and publications.

http://speccoll.library.kent.edu/truecrime/borogateway.html

Idiaques   Marsillia   Idiaques   Don Iuan   Don Iuan   Marsillia   Marsillia   Idiaques

Honoria poysond   Marsillia   Mathurina   De Perez   Mathurina

Don Iuan De Perez   Marsillia killd   a letter found   Marsillia afterburnt   Idiaques executed

16

GOD's Revenge against the Crying and Execrable Sin of Murther.

HISTORY XVI.

Idiaques *causeth his Son* Don Juan *to marry* Marsillia, *and then commits Adultery and Incest with her. She makes her Father in Law* Idiaques *to poyson his own old wife* Honoria; *and likewise makes her own brother* De Perez *to kill her Chamber-maid* Mathurina: Don Juan *afterwards kill* De Perez *in a Duel:* Marsillia *hath her brains dasht out by a horse, and her body is afterward condemned to be burnt:* Idiaques *is beheaded, his body likewise consumed to ashes, and thrown into the air.*

Mr Coleridge presents his respectful
Compliments to Mr Kirkland, or the
Gentleman, his assistant — requests, that
there may be sent by the Bearer three
ounces of Laudanum (in the accompanying
bottle — or whatever quantity it may hold) half an
oz of crude opium (if there be none purified) — &
two ounces of the Tincture of Cardomum. As
soon as the weather relaxes, Mr Coleridge
will call in on Mr Kirkland, and
settle his general account.

        Sunday Morning.

AA
54

University of Kentucky Libraries
Special Collections and Digital Programs

W. Hugh Peal Collection

WHEN W. Hugh Peal was given a copy of Charles and Mary Lamb's *Tales from Shakespeare* (1807) as a child, to keep him occupied and away from horses, little did anyone realize the gift's consequences. Peal's acquisition developed into a lifelong interest in Charles Lamb and the English Romantics. A native of rural Ballard County, Kentucky, Peal graduated from the University of Kentucky where he learned to read German, French, and Latin—skills that earned him a Rhodes scholarship to Oxford, where he received a law degree. Returning to the United States, Peal embarked in the 1920s on what became a distinguished legal career in New York, where he frequented the city's bookshops and eventually turned to auction houses and dealers who purchased materials for his growing collection of British and American literature. Retiring to a large country estate near Leesburg, Virginia, in the 1960s, Mr. Peal considered himself "a gentleman farmer." Although he sent portions of the collection to the University of Kentucky beginning in the early 1950s, it was not until 1981 when the Peals moved to Leesburg proper that the bulk of the collection came to the university.

Hugh Peal's collection of over 12,000 volumes and 7,000 manuscripts and letters represents one of the most significant holdings of 19th-century literary material in the United States. The heart of the collection is the papers and books of the English romantics Lamb, Coleridge, Southey, and Wordsworth. The collection contains a number of association copies, such as Lamb's copy of *Album Verses* (1830), inscribed to his publisher Edward Moxon. Beyond the holdings of early Romantics is a distinguished collection of the second generation—writers such as Byron, Shelley, Campbell, Crabbe, Cunningham, De Quincy, Edgeworth, Hunt, Moore, Scott, and Mary Shelley.

Beyond these holdings are the Victorians, well-represented by works and letters of Charles Dickens. Also represented are primary source materials generated by such authors as Elizabeth Barrett and Robert Browning, Robert Burns, Lewis Carroll, Willkie Collins, Thomas Hardy, the Rossettis, Robert Louis Stevenson, William Makepeace Thackeray, Oscar Wilde, and many more. Other "high spots" in the collection are no less spectacular and include an Isaac Newton manuscript, letters from Charles Darwin, Michael Faraday, Alexis de Tocqueville, Randolph Churchill, Harriet Beecher Stowe, Mark Twain, Edmund Burke, and Voltaire, to name a few. The Peal Collection also includes several incunabula, printer John Baskerville's *Paradise Lost* (1757) and his Bible (1763), Gibbon's *Decline and Fall of the Roman Empire* (1776–1778), and numerous extra-illustrated works including a copy of the *Life of Sir Robert Walpole* (1798) containing a group of 105 letters written to him or his contemporaries.

In recent years the Peal Collection has been the object of numerous exhibitions, class assignments, and visits by researchers and scholars. In particular, the collection has received the attention of numerous inquirers, researchers, and editorial projects from the British Isles. An extensive exhibition catalog was published at the time of the collection's dedication in 1982.

http://www.uky.edu/Libraries/libpage.php?lweb_id=470&llib_id=13

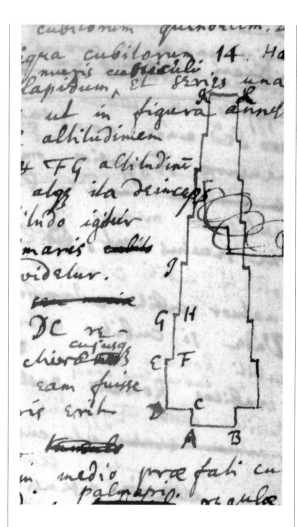

(ABOVE)
Autograph manuscript in Latin. Sir Isaac Newton. Detail.
  Notes on the mensuration of ancient monuments, believed to be for Newton's book *The Chronology of Ancient Kingdoms,* Amended.

(OPPOSITE)
Letter from Samuel Taylor Coleridge to Mr. Kirkland. [Late December 1815?]
  Coleridge requests that Kirkland "send three ounces of Laudanum…& half an ounce of crude opium…."

(ABOVE TOP)
"Shamanic Cure." Steatite sculpture by Lukie Airut. N.d.
> This sculpture depicts an unusual scene in Inuit art of a teenager being treated by a shaman.

(ABOVE BOTTOM)
"Touladi." Photograph by Arthur Lamothe. N.d.
> Image from the Culture Amérindienne Collection dedicated to the ethnographic illustration of Innu culture.

(OPPOSITE)
"Greenland Aboriginals." From *Historie von Grönland, enthaltend die beschriebung des landes und der einwohner….* David Cranz. 1765.

Bibliothèque de l'Université Laval
Collections Spéciales

Nordicity and Ethnology Collection

THERE is much more to the North than the location of Santa Claus's workshop! The Library of Université Laval may not be able to shed much light on this enigma, but it is a great place to find answers about the North and its people.

The French word *nordicité* was coined, in the early '60s, by L.-E. Hamelin, a professor of geography at Université Laval and the founder the *Centre d'études nordiques.* The term refers to high-latitude regions and takes the North as an object of study in its entirety, encompassing geological, geographical, botanical, biological, and human aspects. This interdisciplinary view also applies to the library's Nordicity and Ethnology Collection.

Long before the current rise in interest in the North because of climatic change, the library started to collect texts relating to Europeans' experience in the polar regions. These documents constitute the historical nucleus of the Nordicity Collection. Most of the books are accounts and journals by explorers, notably Sir John Franklin and, ironically, those who participated in the search for the missing ships of Franklin's expedition, and by later Arctic and Antarctic explorers such as Amundsen, Nansen, Fiala, Sverdrup, Mikkelsen, Stefansson, and Shackleton, as well as more exotic explorers such as Léonie d'Aunet and Luigi, duc des Abruzzes. These books date from the mid-17th century to the early 20th century. The collection also includes memoirs of Arctic missionaries in the late 19th and early 20th centuries as well as compilations of narratives and books on polar exploration, generally from the 18th and 19th centuries, in English, French, and German. The oldest book is *Relation du Groenland* (1647) by Isaac de La Peyrère. Several others date from the 18th century, including *Considérations Géographiques et Physiques sur les Nouvelles Découvertes au Nord de la Grande Mer: Appellée Vulgairement la Mer du Sud: avec des Cartes qui y sont Relatives* (1753). Among the more remarkable but recent volumes is a deluxe limited edition of Robert Peary's *The North Pole* (1910) signed by Peary, and *Seven Log-books Concerning the Arctic Voyages of Captain William Scoresby, Senior, of Whitby, England* (1917).

The Film Library possesses an impressive array of ethnographic archives focusing on Inuit culture, the core of this collection being the complete filmography of Arthur Lamothe. This important and quasi-exclusive holding constitutes a vivid testimony dedicated to the vanishing traditions and customs of northern aboriginal nations and shows performances of some ancient ceremonies and rituals now abandoned. The Geospatial and Statistical Center also holds important documents. Besides many maps of the Northwest Territories and the Nunavik, a few maps drawn in the early 20th century are of special interest. These document explorations led by J.-E. Bernier between 1904 and 1911, and are of special political significance because they support Canada's territorial claims to the Arctic Archipelago. The Nordicity Collection includes even more unusual holdings such as 1,451 artifacts and archaeological pieces—mainly tools and clothes—found in diverse regions of northern Quebec.

THE OLD FLAG.
THE OLD POLICY,
THE OLD LEADER.

Library and Archives Canada
Canadian Archives and Special Collections

The Prime Ministers Collection

SINCE Canadian Confederation in 1867, twenty-one men and one woman have served as Prime Minister of Canada, assuming the ultimate challenge of political leadership in Canada's federal parliamentary system. They successfully battled both party rivals and opposition parties to gain, and hold, the office that has been called "the apex of power" in Canada. And they left an extraordinary documentary record.

Library and Archives Canada (LAC) was founded in 1872 by Canada's first prime minister, Sir John A. Macdonald. Fittingly, Macdonald's papers (125 linear feet) were LAC's first prime ministerial acquisition, in 1914. The Prime Ministers Collection has subsequently grown to include approximately 12,700 linear feet of textual records, 18.9 gigabytes of electronic records, 700 reels of microfilm, and over one million photographs, as well as numerous paintings, caricatures, posters, films, videocassettes, audio cassettes, philatelic items, medals, and political buttons.

The collection held at LAC encompasses the original textual records of eighteen prime ministers, with microfilm copies of the papers of another two. These extensive holdings comprise not only official and political documents, but also personal and family papers, constituting an invaluable source that is regularly consulted by students, scholars, journalists, and other researchers. The historian John English, who recently worked on the early papers of Pierre Elliott Trudeau at LAC, underscored the importance of such holdings: "Trudeau's private papers are an exceptionally rich lode for a biographer to mine, and valuable nuggets appear in virtually every box."

The collection includes many such treasures, but arguably the most remarkable is the diary kept by Canada's longest-serving prime minister, William Lyon Mackenzie King. This document, which King began in 1893 when he was an undergraduate student, ended in 1950, a few days before his death. It comprises nearly 30,000 pages and more than 7,500,000 words. Not only is it a remarkable political record, but it is also one of Canada's greatest literary achievements. According to the critic Robert Fulford, it "might turn out to be the only Canadian work of our century that someone will look at in 500 years." In 2003, LAC made the entire diary available on its Web site under the title: *A Real Companion and Friend*.

King's diary is only one of many significant prime ministerial items now available on the LAC Web site. Most of the prime ministers' finding aids are online, as are detailed correspondence indexes and databases relating to art and photos. In addition, LAC has created "First among Equals," a massive Web exhibition that draws upon a wide variety of records to explore the role of the prime minister in Canadian life and politics.

The Prime Ministers Collection is a crucial part of LAC's mandate to preserve and make known Canada's documentary heritage. As one former National Archivist observed: "It is obvious that if we forget our prime ministers, we lose an important part of our heritage; for these are…individuals who have made a difference, shaping Canada's identity, often in profound ways."

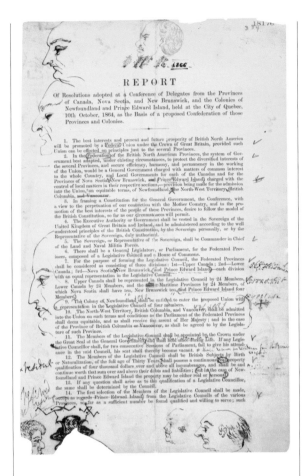

(ABOVE)
"Report of Resolutions Adopted at a Conference of Delegates from the Provinces of Canada, Nova Scotia, and New Brunswick, and the Colonies of Newfoundland and Prince Edward Island, Held at the City of Québec, 10th October, 1864, as the Basis of a Proposed Confederation of Those Provinces and Colonies."

Doodles attributed to the Right Honourable Sir John A. Macdonald. Circa 1866.

(OPPOSITE)
"The Old Flag, the Old Policy, the Old Leader." Poster by unknown artist. Published by the Industrial League, printed by the Toronto Litho. Co., 1891.

This poster depicts the first Prime Minister of Canada, the Right Honourable Sir John A. Macdonald (in office 1867–73 and 1878–91).

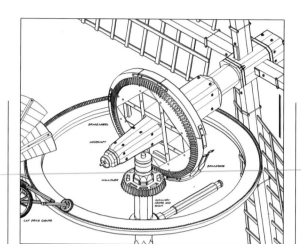

Library of Congress
Prints and Photographs Division

Historic American Buildings Survey, Historic American Engineering Record, and Historic American Landscapes Survey Collection

HISTORIANS, secondary school teachers, architects, homeowners, and set designers are some of the many people who turn daily for both information and inspiration to the HABS/HAER/HALS collection—the records of the Historic American Buildings Survey (HABS), Historic American Engineering Record (HAER), and Historic American Landscapes Survey (HALS). They benefit from viewing images of national landmarks along with technical drawings and photographs that explain the construction of sites ranging from houses, churches, and jails to metal foundries, railroad stations, and cranberry bogs. Insights into family, cultural, and architectural history also come from ready access to documentation of structures as diverse as Indian pueblos, Spanish missions, sod houses, kitchens, and the Rose Bowl Stadium.

Charles E. Peterson conceived the Historic American Buildings Survey (HABS) while working for the National Park Service (NPS) during the Great Depression. In late 1933, Peterson proposed a project to employ 1,000 out-of-work architects and draftsmen for 10 weeks to document "America's antique buildings" systematically before they vanished. That special project soon expanded into an ongoing program through a cooperative agreement among the Library of Congress, the American Institute of Architects, and NPS. HABS has also inspired two companion programs called the Historic American Engineering Record (HAER, formed in 1969) and the Historic American Landscapes Survey (HALS, formed in 2000). All three NPS initiatives continue to document new sites each year. The Library of Congress Prints and Photographs Division provides public access services as well as archival preservation for the resulting records.

The collection is one of the most heavily used special collections in the Library of Congress. The encyclopedic coverage of America's built environment, the exceptional clarity of the visual materials, and the general lack of copyright restrictions account for thousands of online catalog searches each month. In more than 35,000 surveys, researchers can discover a comprehensive range of building types, engineering technologies, and landscape features dating from pre-Columbian times to the present day and located throughout the United States and its territories. The multiformat surveys total more than 60,000 measured drawings, 250,000 large-format black-and-white and color photographs, and numerous written historical reports. A major digital conversion initiative at the library has helped researchers explore this rich visual collection through an online catalog.

Books based on HABS/HAER/HALS already fill several library shelves. The new W. W. Norton/Library of Congress Visual Sourcebooks for barns, canals, lighthouses, and bridges show hundreds of HABS/HAER/HALS images. At least one murder mystery, *Artifacts*, uses HABS records in its plot. The library's Learning Page provides activity ideas related to gold rush and missile defense sites, motion picture palaces, and authors' homes to encourage educators and students to delve into United States history, critical thinking, and the arts and humanities. Like the Association of Research Libraries, HABS is reaching its own 75th anniversary and can look forward to a long future of stimulating exploration and discovery with new generations of researchers.

http://lcweb2.loc.gov/pp/hhhtml/hhabt.html

(ABOVE TOP)
"Isometric of Machinery, Beebe Windmill, Bridgehampton, New York." Measured drawing delineated by Kathleen S. Hoeft and Chalmers G. Long Jr. 1976. (HAER.)

(ABOVE BOTTOM)
"Section of Beebe Windmill, Bridgehampton, New York." Measured drawing delineated by Chalmers G. Long Jr. 1976. (HAER.)

(OPPOSITE)
"Cap, Rafters for Ogee Cap, Brake Wheel, and Windshaft of Beebe Windmill, Bridgehampton, New York." Photograph by Jet Lowe. 1978. (HAER.)

Louisiana State University Libraries
Special Collections

Louisiana and Lower Mississippi Valley Collections

I T is ironic that the Great Depression, which brought hardship and long-lasting poverty to Louisiana, also provided opportunities that led to the creation of the state's greatest collection of research materials devoted to its history and culture. The Works Progress Administration's Louisiana Historical Records Survey employed more than 300 workers, including LSU history instructor Edwin Adams Davis. A tenacious and persuasive advocate for archives, Davis convinced the LSU Department of History that it should establish and support a separate Department of Manuscripts and Archives at the university. Davis headed the new department from 1935 until 1946, systematically collecting historical records and family papers in the lower Mississippi Valley. While Davis built the archives, librarians followed a parallel track within LSU's library, amassing published materials about the state. Five decades later, the two collections were united in 1985 to form the Louisiana and Lower Mississippi Valley Collections (LLMVC).

Recognized as one of the nation's premier collections of regional history materials, LLMVC includes not only personal and family papers but also records of plantations, merchants, financial institutions, and political, social, and labor organizations. The collections cover the lower Mississippi Valley, from Memphis to New Orleans, with special strength in the Natchez, St. Francisville, and Baton Rouge areas. LLMVC continues to acquire 18th- and 19th-century manuscripts, as well as substantial collections of 20th-century materials and oral histories relating to the region.

In addition to its manuscript collections, LLMVC includes more than 120,000 volumes of books and periodicals, as well as maps and other published material, and a comprehensive collection of Louisiana newspapers on microfilm. There are also more than 200,000 historic photographs, offering fascinating glimpses of the past.

On a typical day, users might include genealogists, a lawyer, a marine biologist, a Civil War re-enactor, and students. Scholars have used LLMVC to produce award-winning books, such as Richard Follett's *The Sugar Masters: Planters and Slaves in Louisiana's Cane World, 1820–1860* (a 2005 *Choice* Outstanding Academic Title, winner of the Gulf South History Book Award and the Louisiana Literary Award) and Craig Colten's *Unnatural Metropolis: Wresting New Orleans from Nature* (2006 winner of the Association of American Geographers' John Brinkerhoff Jackson Prize).

LLMVC staff provide presentations, exhibitions, online subject guides, finding aids, and one-on-one help. Special Collections microfilms 90 Louisiana newspapers, supplying film to parish (Louisiana's equivalent of county) libraries and individuals. The digital collection The Louisiana Purchase: A Heritage Explored, partially funded by the Institute of Museum and Library Services, presents some 20,000 pages of materials from LLMVC. Digital exhibitions include the bilingual "Creole Echoes / Résonances Créoles," a collaboration of LSU's Center for French and Francophone Studies and the LSU Libraries, which won a Certificate of Commendation from the American Association of State and Local History. LLMVC looks forward to a rich future of collaboration with its users as it strengthens its collections and adds digital access.

http://www.lib.lsu.edu/special/llmvc.html

http://www.lib.lsu.edu/special/exhibits/elecex.html

(ABOVE)
William F. Tunnard Carriage and Harness Factory. Ambrotype by unknown artist. N.d.

In 1845, William F. Tunnard (1809–71) purchased a lot on the corner of Church and Main Streets in Baton Rouge, where he built his carriage and harness factory. Ambrotypes—made by creating a negative image on glass and displaying it, backed with black, in a decorative case—were made from 1851 until the 1890s.

(OPPOSITE)
"Mother and Child." Photograph by Henry Norman. Circa 1890.

The Norman Studio operated in Natchez, Mississippi, from the 1870s until the 1950s, serving both the white and African-American communities, despite the Jim Crow laws in effect at the time.

University of Louisville Libraries

University Archives and Records Center; Photographic Archives

Louisville and Nashville Railroad Collection

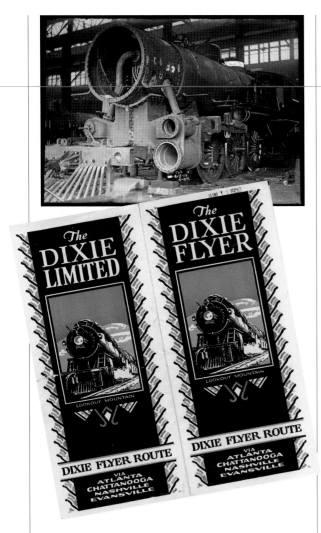

(ABOVE TOP)
"Locomotive under Construction in L&N Railroad's South Louisville Shops." Photograph by L&N Railroad. 1918.

This was one of over 400 engines built in the L&N's South Louisville Shops, which operated as a construction and repair facility between 1905 and 1990.

(ABOVE BOTTOM)
"The Dixie Flyer." Brochure. L&N Railroad, 1930.

This brochure contains the timetable and route map for a "luxurious" train running between Chicago and Miami and featuring glass-enclosed observation cars and "Special Dixie Dishes on Dixie Diners."

(OPPOSITE)
"Locomotive under Construction in L&N Railroad's South Louisville Shops." Original glass plate. Photograph by L&N Railroad. 1918.

THE archive of the Louisville and Nashville Railroad (L&N), with 255 linear feet in the University of Louisville University Archives and Records Center and an additional 600 vintage prints and original glass negatives in the Photographic Archives, yields information as broad as the industrialization of the New South and as specific as the shape of an inner bolt on the wheel assembly of a particular freight car. Each year hundreds of researchers, including historians, journalists, editors, museum curators, railroad enthusiasts, authors, and students, comb through minute books, financial records, annual reports, timetables, station lists, maps, architectural drawings, and much more. The documents and photographs provide a comprehensive record of the L&N Railroad, a transportation giant that positioned Louisville, Kentucky, at the center of North/South commerce in the decades following the Civil War.

Within the records of the L&N, the collection also offers annual reports and other historical evidence of numerous predecessor and subsidiary lines operating at various times beginning in 1836. These include the Atlanta and West Point Railroad Company; the Carolina, Clinchfield, and Ohio Railway; the Chicago and Eastern Illinois Railroad; and the Monon Railroad. These smaller regional railroads, built before the concept of a national railroad system was even imagined, sometimes used distinctive track sizes. The L&N's annual reports document such historic actions as the 1886 decision of southern railroads to switch to the standard gauge track already used in the North.

The L&N archive has supported the work of scholars, including research on the roles of African-American railroad workers, relationships with shippers, suppliers and financiers, and economic development initiatives throughout the South. The rich files have offered detailed evidence for curators restoring historic rolling stock: locomotives, Pullman cars, and diesel engines. They have provided documentation for group projects such as the centennial celebration of Cornersville, Tennessee. The town, on the border with Kentucky, is one of many communities throughout the South that were founded or grew because of the L&N Railroad. From the 1920s through the 1970s the *L&N Magazine*, which is indexed by an in-house topical card file begun in the offices of the L&N and maintained in University Archives, included a 16-page section of employee news. Genealogists and scholars alike find such details invaluable, particularly since the collection does not include personnel records. More than 50 oral histories, recorded in the 1980s, include interviews of a range of employees, speaking from their perspectives as dining car waiters, telephone operators, or company president.

University of Louisville archivists are quick to mention their ongoing collaboration with volunteer Charles Castner, a former L&N Railroad public relations official. Castner, who even has a stretch of train track belonging to L&N's successor CSX bearing his name, is a local legend who is generous with his knowledge of the railroad and its archive. He is one of countless special collections volunteers whose significant expertise sometimes accompanies an archive or collection. An online finding aid to the L&N archive is available through the Kentuckiana Digital Library.

http://kdl.kyvl.org/

but which, in point of fashion, are generally a few years behind those of Europe. The elderly women still adhere to long waists, full caps, and large clubs of hair behind. Some of the younger branches of the countrywomen are becoming more modern, having imbibed a spirit for dress from the French girls who live in the towns as servants.

The Habitans have almost every resource within their own families. They cultivate flax, which they manufacture into linen; and their sheep supply them with the wool of which their garments are formed. They tan the hides of their cattle, and make them into moccasins and boots. From woollen yarn they knit their own stockings and *bonnets rouges;* and from straw they make their summer hats and bonnets. Besides articles of wearing apparel, they make their own bread, butter, and cheese; their soap, candles, and sugar; all which are supplied from the productions of their farm. They build their own houses, barns, stables, and ovens; make their own carts, wheels, ploughs, harrows, and canoes. In short, their ingenuity, prompted as much by parsimony as the isolated situation in which they live, has provided them with every article of utility and every necessary of life. A Canadian will seldom or never purchase that which he can make himself; and I am of opinion that it is this saving

J. Lambert delt.

Habitans in their Summer dress

McGill University Library
Rare Books and Special Collections Division

Lawrence Lande Collection of Canadiana

L AWRENCE M. Lande (1906–1998) was a consummate collector of Canadiana in all its aspects—political, economic, cultural, and historical—and has left a legacy that continues to benefit and inspire his university and his country. Born in Ottawa, Ontario, Lande graduated with a BA from McGill in 1928 and was awarded an honorary DLitt (1969). He was made a member of the Order of Canada in 1967. A bibliophile, compiler of bibliographies, poet, and composer, Lande had wide-ranging interests that included the poet William Blake and the Book of Job in addition to Canadiana. In 1996 the library published *Bibliotheca Canadiana: A Historical Survey of Canadian Bibliography: Catalogue of an Exhibition in Honour of the Ninetieth Birthday of Dr. Lawrence M. Lande*, a suitable way indeed to celebrate Lande's central place in the bibliographic world of Canadiana.

Inspired by a love of Canadian history, Lande had long collected Canadian materials, and in 1965 the first part of the Lande Canadiana Collection was acquired from its creator. It comprised some 2,300 items, and this original nucleus has since grown to some 12,000 items, including pamphlets, maps, prints (among them over 50 early views of Montreal), periodicals, government documents, and broadsides, as well as books. The original gift is recorded in *The Lawrence Lande Collection of Canadiana in the Redpath Library of McGill University* (1965), and this volume is still cited as one of the standard references for Canadian material.

Lande was interested in all aspects of Canadian history from its discovery and exploration to its historical development to the end of the 19th century. Outstanding among the descriptions of early discoveries are André Thevet's *Les singularitez de la France antarctique, autrement nommée amerique* (1558) and Wytfliet's *Histoire universelle des Indes orientales et occidentals* (1605), which has some of the earliest maps of Canada. The Jesuit Relations are an invaluable primary source for the study of the early French Regime in Canada and the Jesuit's missionary efforts. Among other areas of concentration are the search for the Northwest Passage and Arctic exploration, the controversy over Confederation, and early Canadian imprints. An insight into early Canadian social history is provided by the personal narratives of such travellers as Kalm, Lambert, Weld, Heriot, and Bonnycastle, and by ephemeral items which include broadsides, circulars, and sheet music.

Three other significant collections were added over the years. The Arkin Collection was assembled by the Winnipeg collector Nathan Arkin and purchased with Dr. Lande's assistance in 1966. This material concentrates on the development of the Prairie Provinces and British Columbia during the late 19th and early 20th centuries, with special emphasis on the Northwest Rebellions, the Manitoba School Question, and immigration literature. The two other collections center upon First Nations peoples and the work of the Moravian missionaries among the Inuit of Labrador.

Not only has this rich assemblage of documentation and iconography provided generations of students and researchers with essential texts and unexpected discoveries, it has also played a much larger role. The Lande Canadiana Collection at McGill with the Lande Collection at Library and Archives Canada and the many published bibliographies are repositories of the Canadian historical memory.

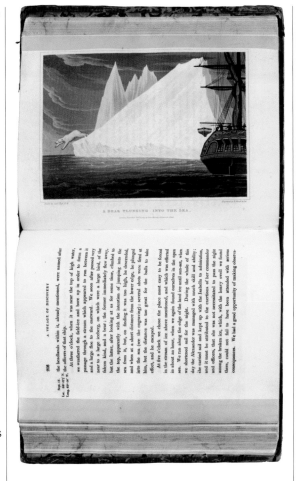

(ABOVE)
"A Bear Plunging into the Sea." Colored plate drawn by Capt. Ross., engraved by R. Havell & Son. In *A Voyage of Discovery,…for the Purpose of Exploring Baffin's Bay, and Inquiring into the Probability of a North-West Passage.* John Ross. First edition. London: 1819.

(OPPOSITE)
"Habitans in Their Summer Dress." Hand-colored plate after drawing by John Lambert. In *Travels through Canada, and the United States of North America in the Years 1806, 1807 & 1808.* John Lambert. Second ed. corrected. London, 1813.

This is an important and "true" account of the economic and social situation in Canada at this early phase of its development.

McMaster University Libraries
William Ready Division of Archives and Research Collections

The Bertrand Russell Archives

(ABOVE)
Letter from Bertrand Russell to Frank Russell (his
brother, second Earl Russell). Written from Brixton
Prison. May 6, 1918.

> Bertrand Russell tells his brother of his plans to return
> to writing philosophical works and that the only real
> hardship of prison is not seeing friends—"Prison has
> some of the advantages of the Catholic Church."

(OPPOSITE)
"Points about Denoting." Manuscript notes
by Bertrand Russell. Circa 1905.

> Russell made these notes around the time when he
> wrote "On Denoting," his famous paper about the
> theory of descriptions that was published in *Mind*.

I N 1967 Bertrand Russell (1872–1970), the philosopher, mathematician, Nobel Prize winner, and social reformer, put up his archives for auction to raise money for his peace campaigns. An unlikely buyer emerged in the person of William Ready, the University Librarian at McMaster University Libraries. From the Victorian era of Lord John Russell to the troublesome decade of the 1960s ending with the Vietnam War, Russell's archives span more than a century of activity on many fronts in diverse fields, such as analytic philosophy, the foundations of mathematics, nationalism, imperialism, and war and peace in the 20th century.

In the Health Sciences Centre at McMaster University one can find slices of Albert Einstein's brain, but in the Russell archives there is all of Russell's mind, including his correspondence with Einstein and the last letter that Einstein wrote, dated April 11, 1955, in which Einstein agrees to sign a document, the Russell-Einstein Manifesto, with other notable scientists against the proliferation of nuclear arms. Another slogan about the Russell archives is that they cover from Lenin to Lennon—that is to say, Russell's diary notes in May 1920 of his interview with Lenin in the Soviet Union to the card of thanks written by John Lennon and Yoko Ono sent to Russell just a few weeks before his death. Practically every facet of Russell's life and times is represented in his rich archives. In many cases the correspondence is voluminous and in-depth. He wrote, for example, 1,900 love letters to Lady Ottoline Morrell, the doyenne of the Garsington circle; her epistolary enthusiasm by comparison flagged with merely 1,200 letters in return.

Russell's archives contain his fascinating library of 3,600 volumes, his manuscripts, correspondence, periodicals, offprints, leaflets, photographs, audio discs and reels, films, videocassettes, microfilms, news clippings, posters, some furniture, artwork (including a bust by Jacob Epstein), awards and medals. The first and second accruals of Russell's archives came to the McMaster University Libraries in 1968 and 1972, respectively. Russell's personal library arrived at McMaster in 1978. More than 1,500 "recent acquisitions" of various documents have been obtained from various sources outside of the Russell estate. The archives are supplemented by a supporting research library of 3,200 books, theses, and periodicals pertaining to Russell and his circle. There are also the archives of Russell's parents, cognate archives of two of his wives, and those of Lady Constance Malleson, Rupert Crawshay-Williams, and Anton Felton, his literary agent.

The Bertrand Russell archives are used and consulted on a daily basis by researchers and the public from around the world. Scores of articles and books have been published as a result of this constant research. Although the archives are accessible through two printed guides and card catalogs, correspondence can also be searched through BRACERS, an online database describing some 108,000 letters. The Bertrand Russell Research Centre at McMaster University functions as the scholarly buttress of Russell's historical legacy with a focus on *The Collected Papers of Bertrand Russell* (1983–) and the projected online edition of his letters. The Russell Centre also publishes *Russell: The Journal of Bertrand Russell Studies* (1971–) edited by Dr. Kenneth Blackwell, the honorary Russell archivist, and sponsors Russell-l, the Russell electronic mailing list.

http://www.mcmaster.ca/russdocs/russell.htm

Points about Denoting.

1). That sometimes we know that something is denoted, without knowing what.

This occurs in obvious instances, as e.g. if I ask: Is Smith married? & the answer is affirmative, I then know that "Smith's wife" is a denoting phrase, although I don't know who Smith's wife is. We may distinguish the terms with which we are *acquainted* from others which are merely *denoted*. E.g. in the above case, I am supposed to be acquainted with the term Smith & the relation *marriage*, & thence to be able to conceive a term having this relation to Smith, although I am not acquainted with any such term.

So again in other cases. It is known that every class of material points has a centre of mass: this is demonstrated without reference to particular classes of material points. Thence, given a particular class, e.g. the Solar System, we infer that it has a centre of mass; thus we can denote the centre of mass in question, without being acquainted with it.

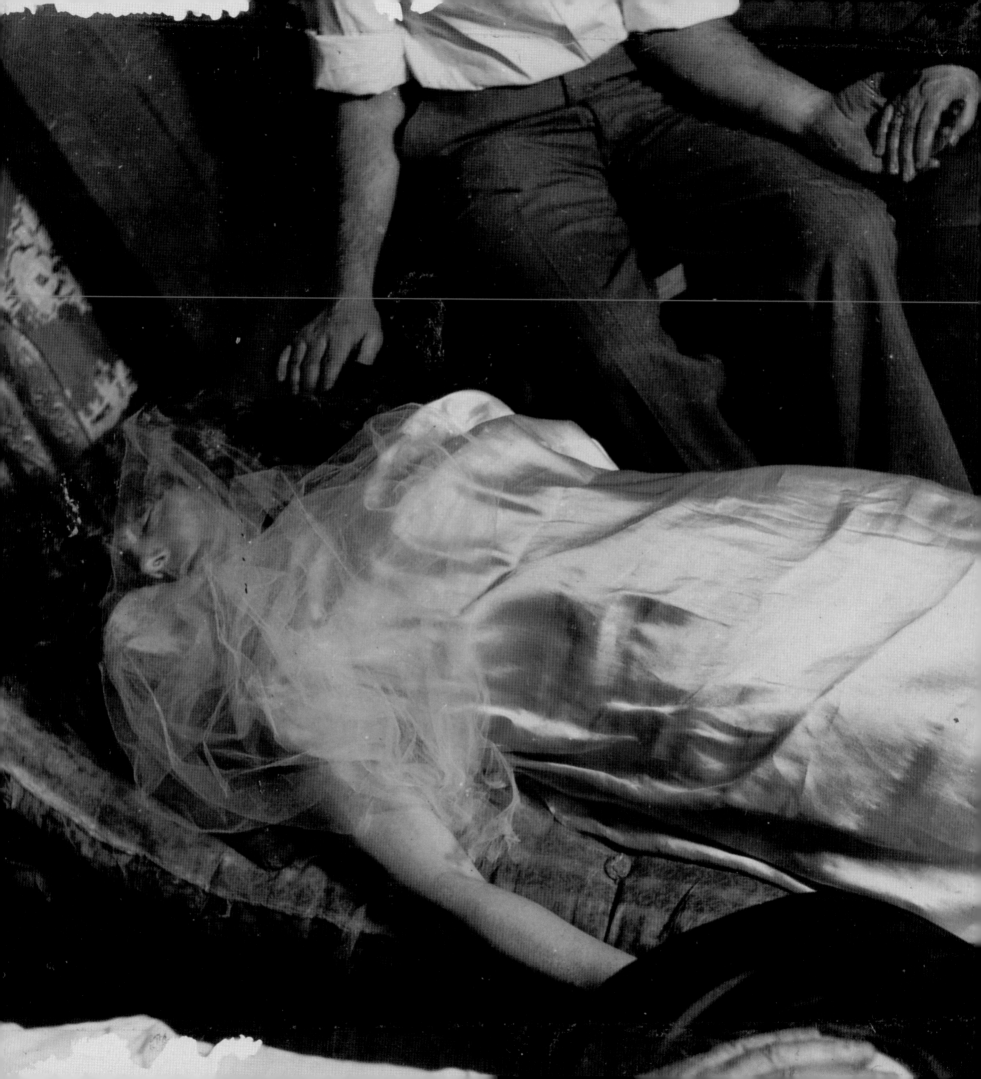

University of Manitoba Libraries
Archives & Special Collections

Hamilton Family fonds

ECTOPLASMS, table tiltings, rappings, and spiritual manifestations—this likely was not what Winnipeg physician T. G. Hamilton expected when he first was drawn to psychic inquiry by his friend W. T. Allison in 1913. The heartbreak of the death of his three-year-old son in 1918, however, likely inspired first his wife Lillian, then T. G. himself, to begin their secret investigations into the paranormal. From 1918 to 1923, Hamilton and his wife searched for the physical proof of life after death. What came next, however, would produce the amazing but eerie archives of the Hamilton Family: the development in 1923 of the "home circle." With unpaid mediums, respected fellow doctors, and his wife by his side, T. G. set up a room in his house, boarded up the windows, bolted the door, and lit the room "by a single ruby photographic lamp attached to an electric cord." A bank of eleven cameras, three flash-light boxes, and three push-button controls allowed Hamilton to take periodic photographs of what happened in that little room.

From 1923 to 1945, first T. G., then after his untimely death in 1935, Lillian, conducted séances. The Hamiltons began by inviting a neighbor, Mrs. Elizabeth Poole, to join the circle. Medium Mrs. Mary Marshall joined them in 1925, because it was "suspected that she had psychic faculties worth investigating." The first table rappings of "Elizabeth M" were followed by clairvoyance, trance states, table tilting, automatic writing, visions, then the manifestations of materializations, wax molds, bell ringing, and finally in 1928, ectoplasms. Hamilton controlled the conditions of the séances as closely as possible to validate his experiments scientifically.

When the news about these circles finally came out, the Hamilton family's work became known in the United Kingdom, Europe, and the United States. Canadian Prime Minister William Lyon MacKenzie King, Sherlock Holmes author Sir Arthur Conan Doyle and later his widow Lady Jean Conan Doyle, and Americans Mina Crandon, the medium known as "Margery," and her husband, Dr. L. R. G. Crandon, all traveled to Winnipeg to participate in the Hamiltons' circles. Between 1926 and 1934 T. G. Hamilton presented 86 lectures and wrote numerous articles.

Scrapbooks, seance attendance records and registers, affidavits, automatic writings, correspondence, speeches and lectures, news clippings, journal articles, photographs, glass plate negatives and positives, prints, slides, tapes, manuscripts, and promotional materials related to major publications make up the records of this strangely intriguing collection.

The Hamilton fonds has been used in many art exhibitions, including ones recently held in Paris and at the Metropolitan Museum of Art in New York, in books, plays, lectures, and scholarly articles, and is the frequent subject of television and radio documentaries. Many members of the public have employed the collection. In 2001, a small virtual exhibit of photos from this collection was created on Archives & Special Collections' Web site. These were joined in 2006 by over 700 images from the Hamilton Family fonds. The T. Glendenning Hamilton grant program provides funds for researchers to come to Winnipeg to study the collection and has supported lectures. This collection has also become the foundation for the acquisition of other spiritualist materials. If there is no life after death, at least T. G. Hamilton's work lives on.

http://www.umanitoba.ca/libraries/archives/hamilton.shtml

I came away with the conclusion that Winnipeg stands very high among the places we have visited for its psychic possibilities.

— Sir Arthur Conan Doyle,
  Our Second American Adventure (1921)

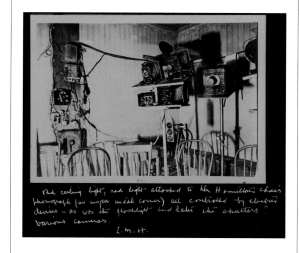

(ABOVE)
"Photographic Equipment Used by Dr. Thomas Glendenning Hamilton." Photograph by T. G. Hamilton. Winnipeg, Manitoba, n.d.

(OPPOSITE)
"The Medium, Mercedes, Enveloped in a Teleplasmic Materialization of a Shining Garment and Veil that Belonged to the Spirit, Katie King, during a Séance Held at the Home of Dr. Thomas Glendenning Hamilton." Photograph by T.G. Hamilton. Winnipeg, Manitoba, February 25, 1931. Detail.

University of Maryland Libraries

Collection Management and Special Collections Division

Gordon W. Prange Collection

I N the fall of 1949, and for several months thereafter, 540 large wooden crates containing 20 tons of Japanese books, magazines, newspapers, and other ephemera arrived at the University of Maryland. Now known as the Gordon W. Prange Collection, these materials represent the nearly complete publishing output of Japan for the early years of the occupation, 1945 to 1949. Originally file copies of the Civil Censorship Detachment (CCD) established by General MacArthur's General Headquarters, the collection contains everything from newsletters of farm cooperatives, labor unions, and stamp collecting clubs to children's comics and first editions of well-known authors such as Nobel Laureate Yasunari Kawabata and Junichiro Tanizaki. Many of these materials are unique and exist nowhere else, not even in Japan.

Japanese agencies and private individuals were required to submit their publications to the CCD, which then determined whether they contained violations of the Code for the Japanese Press. Censorship action, when it occurred, involved additions to or deletions from texts, suppressions of materials, disapprovals, publishing delays, and changes. The code included such directives as: news must adhere strictly to the truth; nothing should be printed which might, directly or indirectly, disturb the public tranquility; and there shall be no destructive criticism of the Allied Occupation and nothing that might invite mistrust or resentment of those troops. Approximately 600,000 censorship documents are contained in the Prange Collection.

The collection is vast—18,047 newspaper titles, 13,799 magazine titles, 71,000 books and pamphlets, 640 maps, 10,000 news agency photographs, and miscellaneous ephemera. Treasures have been unearthed by happenstance, such as a poem by Nobel Laureate Kenzaburo Oe written at age 15 and a short story by Tanazaki suppressed by the CCD. Most recently, five missing works by Osamu Tezuka, creator of *Astro Boy* and the original *Lion King*, were discovered by a scholar compiling a database for the Prange magazine collection. Tezuka is known as the godfather of postwar *manga* (Japanese comics) and a pioneer in television animation in Japan. These five cartoon strips may fill the last remaining gaps in the Tezuka opus.

The UM Libraries have worked closely with the National Diet Library of Japan to process, preserve, and provide access to the collection. Six million pages of magazines and newspapers have been microfilmed. Currently, the 8,000-title children's book collection is being digitized.

Materials from the Prange Collection have been exhibited throughout Japan, from Sapporo to Okinawa. The 10th in a series of such exhibits took place at the Osaka Museum of History in summer 2006. Tens of thousands of people have viewed these exhibits, including the Empress of Japan.

The collection is named in honor of Gordon W. Prange, Professor of History at the University of Maryland and Chief Historian for General MacArthur during the occupation of Japan. He was responsible for the transfer of the CCD file copies to the University of Maryland. Prange is known today for major works on the war in the Pacific, particularly *Tora! Tora! Tora!*

http://www.lib.umd.edu/prange/

(ABOVE TOP)
Kindai Nippon no seiji. Galley proof marked "suppressed." Ikujiro Watanabe. [Pre-1948.]

This work deals with the politics in modern Japan and discusses the reign of Emperors. The reason for suppression may have been nationalistic propaganda.

(ABOVE BOTTOM)
Kobito no kuni no Gariba. Juro Fujii and Seichi Takehara. 1949.

This pop-up book for young children was based on *Gulliver's Travels* by Jonathan Swift.

(OPPOSITE)
Dowa kyoshitsu. (Photographed on top of stack of books.) Nihon Dowa Kyokai [Association for Japanese Children's Stories], ed. 1947.

"The Star of Ethiopia"

A History of the Negro Race

Portrayed by

1010 Actors in Costume

PHILADELPHIA, 1916

May

Tuesday
16

Thursday
18

Saturday
20

8 P.M.

May

Tuesday
16

Thursday
18

Saturday
20

8 P.M.

Chorus of 200 - 53 Musical Numbers - Full Brass Band

To Celebrate the

100th General Conference of the A.M.E. Church

CONVENTION HALL

BROAD & ALLEGHANY AVENUE

University of Massachusetts Amherst Libraries
Special Collections and University Archives

W.E.B. Du Bois Papers

THE library at UMass stands out, quite literally. As one of the tallest library buildings in the world, it might get noticed on its own, but its 26 floors of bricks and books are towered over by its namesake, W.E.B. Du Bois, one of the most influential African-American intellectuals and activists of the 20th century. Summarizing the life and career of a man like Du Bois is no easy task. As a person who confronted injustice wherever he saw it, whenever he saw it, he lent his name and talents to dozens of causes and organizations. Born in the early days of Reconstruction, he witnessed many of the major events that shaped America over nearly a century, from *Plessy v. Ferguson* to *Brown v. Board of Education*, from the onset of Jim Crow to the March on Washington.

As the first African-American to receive a doctorate from Harvard, Du Bois originally planned upon an academic life, and he made important scholarly contributions to history and sociology, among other disciplines. Having witnessed the effects of racial violence and repression first hand, however, as well as the vibrancy and resilience of African-American culture, Du Bois left the academy to dedicate himself to challenging the status quo. Never the leader of a mass movement, he was nevertheless an inveterate organizer, helping to found the Niagara Movement in 1904 and its successor the NAACP in 1909, becoming a key theorist of the Pan-African Movement, and a significant supporter of African-American literary and artistic production. A theorist of social justice, editor, agitator, essayist, poet, and novelist, he famously observed that "the problem of the Twentieth Century is the problem of the color line," but he came increasingly to recognize that racial justice could not be won without also addressing the entrenched problems of educational and economic inequality, women's rights, and the struggle for peace, and without opposing colonial domination of the Third World.

The Du Bois Papers arrived at the Department of Special Collections in 1973 through the efforts of Randolph W. Bromery and Du Bois's widow, Shirley Graham Du Bois. Having been spread out at locations from New York to Accra, Ghana, they contain over 165 linear feet of manuscript material representing the bulk of Du Bois's personal papers. The collection is an invaluable resource for examining the history of the civil rights movement in the United States, and thanks to Du Bois's stunning breadth of vision, it offers insight into topics ranging from urban sociology to the history of education, African-American religion, the Harlem Renaissance, American political culture, and international relations.

To promote use of the collection, the Department of Special Collections has built a substantial and rapidly growing Web site featuring digitized versions of over 15 books by Du Bois, numerous articles and documents, over 850 photographs, an extensive finding aid, and virtual exhibits. Annually on about February 23, Du Bois's birthday, the department sponsors a physical exhibit of materials from the collection and an invited lecture by a prominent African-American historian on Du Bois's life and legacy.

http://www.library.umass.edu/spcoll/collections/dubois/

(ABOVE)
Flier for the *Crisis*. December 1910. W.E.B. Du Bois Papers (MS 312).

> W.E.B. Du Bois founded the *Crisis*, magazine of the NAACP, in 1910, and served as Editor-in-Chief for 25 years.

(OPPOSITE)
"The Star of Ethiopia." Poster by unknown artist. 1916. W.E.B. Du Bois Papers (MS 312).

> This pageant by W.E.B. Du Bois commemorated the 50th anniversary of the Thirteenth Amendment to the US Constitution, which abolished slavery.

Massachusetts Institute of Technology Libraries
Institute Archives and Special Collections

DSpace@MIT

(ABOVE)
"Communities in DSpace@MIT." Home page.

(OPPOSITE: LEFT TO RIGHT; TOP TO BOTTOM)
"Richard P. Feynman, 1965 Nobel Laureate—Physics. Thesis (BS)—Physics." Item record.

"Kofi A. Annan, 2001 Nobel Laureate—Peace. Thesis (MS)—Management." Item record.

"Oldest issue dates—1873." Search results screen.

"Newest issue dates—2007." Search results screen.

"Gareth H. McKinley, Hatsopoulos Microfluids Laboratory (HML). Preprint." Item record and content.

"Alexander Mitsos, Thesis (PhD)—Chemical Engineering." Item record and content.

"Hal Abelson, Computer Science and Artificial Intelligence Lab (CSAIL). Preprint." Item record and content.

"MIT OpenCourseWare—Physics 8.02." Archived course content. Item record and content.

FOR centuries the primary format for communicating and preserving knowledge was paper-based print. Within the past century and a half, new technologies conveyed information through photographic images, sound recordings, and moving images, and libraries readily adapted their practices to accommodate each new format. In the 21st century, computer-based digital information is becoming pervasive and is increasingly the format of record. While other formats have not disappeared, the amount of digital content has increased exponentially.

Several challenges are presented by this change. The use of this information, which exists only as bits and bytes, relies on ever-changing hardware or software-based intermediaries for interpretation. Research materials, cultural artifacts, creative works, and scholarly publications are created in increasingly complex digital formats, and are in danger of being lost to posterity as successive computing platforms are adopted. Despite technological improvements, capturing and maintaining digital special collections in a coordinated, systematic way remains problematic.

MIT's answer to these challenges was the creation of DSpace, an open source digital repository platform, jointly developed by the MIT Libraries and Hewlett-Packard, that enables libraries to capture, store, index, preserve, and redistribute digital assets. Many research libraries have collected in printed form the working papers, creative works, reports, theses, research notes, and manuscripts produced by their institutions. Much of this output is now created only in electronic form. DSpace bridges the special collections digital divide, providing a platform for digitized traditional assets as well as the 21st-century output that has never been presented in print, such as moving images and sound, 3-D simulations, hyper-linked objects, and datasets. DSpace facilitates the acquisition and long-term curation of such previously "unsaveable" special collections.

DSpace@MIT is MIT's own installation of the DSpace platform. It is MIT's institutional repository for capturing and curating the research and teaching output of MIT, in digital form. Coming online in November 2002, DSpace@MIT now consists of over 50 research communities and contains over 24,000 items, ranging from singular files such as a scientific technical report or thesis to complex objects such as multi-file Web sites in the archived Web pages of MIT's OpenCourseWare. DSpace@MIT is accessible over the World Wide Web to researchers around the globe.

The DSpace platform is freely available to institutions as an open source system that can be customized and extended. Research institutions worldwide use DSpace for a variety of digital archiving. Critically, it has prompted wide debate and deliberation on fundamental ideas about how an institution thinks of its intellectual output. The DSpace Federation Inc. coordinates the planning, research, development, and distribution of the software.

Increasingly, DSpace is used beyond its academic institution roots, providing opportunities for libraries and historical and cultural institutions to collaborate in addressing the challenges of promoting and curating digital collections. As digital collections grow, commercial providers are offering DSpace set-up, consultation, customization, and hosting for smaller institutions.

http://dspace.mit.edu/

http://dspace.org/

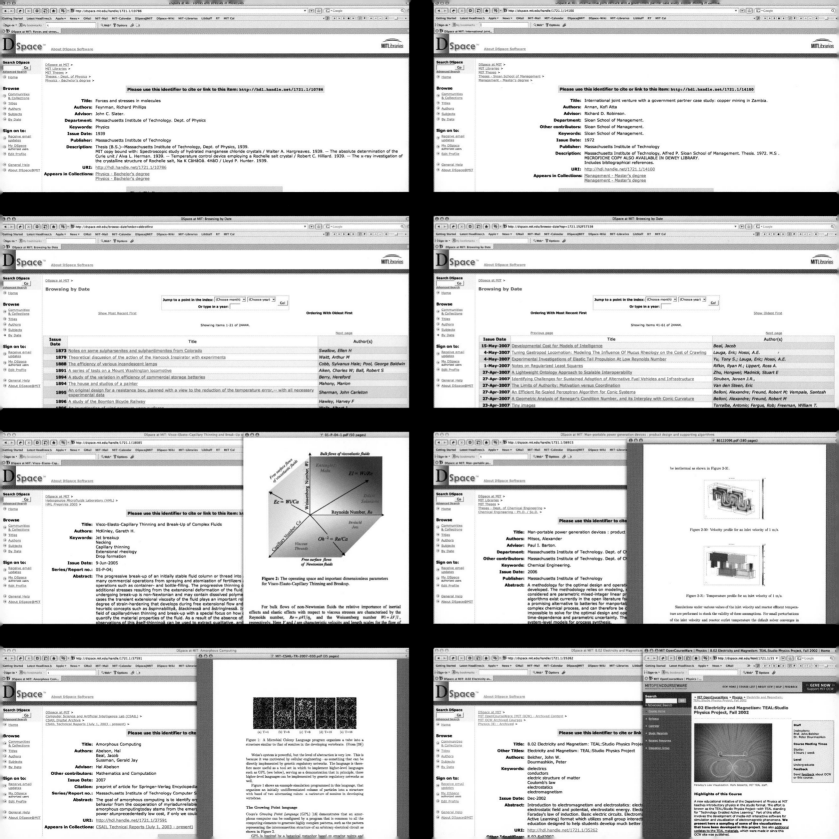

and the end is the future and the unknown. What we can know lies somewhere there between. The course only along which for a little way once proceeds, the changing life, the varying light, must somehow be fixed in a moment clearly, from which one may look before and after and try to comprehend wholeness.

So it is with the Everglades, which have that quality about them, of long existence in their own nature. They were changeless. They are changed.

They were complete before men came to them, and for centuries afterward, when ~~man was only one of those forms knew~~ he himself as only one of those forms which shared, in a finely balanced harmony, the forces and the ancient nature of the place. ~~itself. Then~~ they were ~~most~~ truly themselves.

~~That is the time when I have chosen to begin at which I have chosen to begin with the Everglades.~~ *Then, when The Everglades were most truly Themselves, is the Time to begin with them.*

Transfiguration of them by poetry. The weak artist shirks the truth by a feeble idealism; the prosaic artist fails to transfigure it."

17 March.
Back from Key West with Ruth.
Amphibians from Ft. Lauderdale with Von Paulsen.
Idea for first k.

West, by gum. The great man of words to that effect. The Island could be done I think, well. Must know the town a heap better. But gosh, what material. What chance to do the kind of stuff I must go down. Eats.

University of Miami Libraries
Special Collections

Marjory Stoneman Douglas Papers

IN the early 1940s, Hervey Allen was editor of Rinehart and Company's Rivers of America series. Visiting his aunt who lived in Miami, Allen stopped by Marjory Stoneman Douglas's house to see if she might write a book about the Miami River. She thought that there was not much to say about the Miami River and that maybe she should write about the Everglades instead. Allen agreed, and so did Douglas embark on an adventure that would consume the rest of her life. Her seminal book *The Everglades: River of Grass* was published in 1947.

As historian Robin Faith Bachin notes, "The Everglades are the ecological heart of Florida." Stretching 100 miles from Lake Okeechobee to Florida Bay, this unique ecosystem is home to a wide variety of wildlife, ranging from the Great Blue Heron to the endangered Florida panther. It was the historic home of several Native American tribes and today includes part of the Seminole tribal lands. Although the Everglades were named a national park in 1947, the encroachments of civilization continue to this day.

From the publication of her first book until her death in 1998 at the age of 108, Marjory Stoneman Douglas eloquently celebrated the mysteries of South Florida's wilderness and championed the preservation of South Florida's River of Grass. A writer and environmentalist, Douglas came to Florida in 1915 at the age of 25, fleeing a failed marriage. She joined her father Frank Bryan Stoneman as a writer at the *Miami Herald*. A few years later, Douglas started writing short stories for the *Saturday Evening Post* and other national publications.

Douglas joined the faculty of the University of Miami only a year after its founding and went on to direct its Winter Institute of Literature and serve as editor for the University of Miami Press. In 1960, she founded the University's Friends of the Library. Perhaps her most valuable expression of friendship to the library was her donation of her personal papers in 1987.

The Marjory Stoneman Douglas Papers are today one of the most vital research collections at the University of Miami Libraries. The papers contain extensive material for historians and students of the Everglades and South Florida's environmental history. Douglas also wrote prolifically about Miami and its culture, politics, and social conditions. These writings and her vast correspondence are valuable sources for the study of Miami, its development, and its history. The collection has served a major role in two digital library projects. Reclaiming the Everglades: South Florida's Natural History, 1884 to 1934 is the result of a collaboration among the University of Miami Libraries, Florida International University, and the Historical Museum of Southern Florida. Most recently, Dr. Bachin included materials from the Douglas Papers in her Travel, Tourism, and Urban Growth in Greater Miami digital archive.

http://everglades.fiu.edu/reclaim/

http://scholar.library.miami.edu/miamidigital/

There are no other Everglades in the world….
—Marjory Stoneman Douglas

(ABOVE)
"Marjory Stoneman Douglas Touring the Fakahatchee Strand on the Southern End of the Big Cypress Swamp in South Florida." Photograph by unknown artist. Circa 1946.

This photo was taken while Douglas was researching her book, *The Everglades: River of Grass*.

(OPPOSITE TOP)
Typescript with holograph notations of first chapter of *The Everglades: River of Grass*. Marjory Stoneman Douglas. N.d.

(OPPOSITE BOTTOM)
Diary entry. Marjory Stoneman Douglas. March 1928.

University of Michigan Library
Special Collections Library

The University of Michigan Papyrus Collection

ROOM 807 of the Graduate Library at the University of Michigan houses a very prestigious collection of ancient manuscripts. With over 12,000 papyri and hundreds of texts on ostraca (potsherds), wood, wax tablets, parchment, and lead, dating from around 1,000 BCE to 1,000 CE, this is the largest research and teaching collection of its kind in North America. Most of the papyri are in Greek (the *lingua franca* of the eastern Mediterranean after the conquests of Alexander the Great), but there are also many in Egyptian hieroglyphic, demotic, and Coptic, and some in Arabic and Latin.

The collection was founded in 1920 with papyri acquired both through purchases and in the pioneering University of Michigan scientific excavations at the ancient Egyptian town of Karanis (1924–1935). Its contents include fragments of works by classical authors, with rare texts of writers such as Aristophanes, Euripides, Menander, Callimachus, Dioscorides, and Seneca, and copies of known works by Homer, Xenophon, Demosthenes, Isocrates, Aristotle, and Euclid. Important religious papyri include 30 leaves from the earliest known copy of the biblical letters from Saint Paul to the early churches from the second century CE and one of the earliest copies of the Christian text "The Shepherd of Hermas." There are also magical texts, scientific writings (astronomy, mathematics, medicine) and rare examples of musical notation. Most of the papyri are public and private documents such as imperial decrees, administrative and taxation records, letters, accounts, wills, and marriage agreements.

The University of Michigan has long been recognized as an international leader in editing papyri texts and promoting interdisciplinarity. The rich evidence of the papyri from Karanis in combination with the artifacts found there provides a unique opportunity for the study of this ancient community across several disciplines.

The papyrus collection has also led the way in bringing the past into the future through digital technologies. Efforts in the 1990s to catalog and digitize the papyri at Michigan became the foundation for a national consortium project in 1996 known as the Advanced Papyrological Information System (APIS). The aim of APIS is to unify the collections of its now over 25 partners into a global virtual papyri library, freely accessible throughout the world. The project consists of cataloging, translating, conserving, and digitizing the original artifacts. Thousands of Michigan's papyri have been conserved and made available through the APIS project. Funded largely by the National Endowment for the Humanities (NEH), APIS contains overall more than 25,000 records and 15,000 images.

The papyrus collection not only provides rich sources for study by advanced papyrologists and Egyptologists from around the world, but also serves as a teaching tool for undergraduate courses on Egypt and as a laboratory in training graduate students in the study, publication, and collection management of papyri. The collection has also engaged actively in outreach to students and teachers in K–12 education, in part through exhibits on its Web site. All of these efforts focus on how exposure to this collection can lead to a richer understanding of the ancient world.

http://www.lib.umich.edu/pap/

http://www.lib.umich.edu/pap/apis/apis.html

http://www.lib.umich.edu/pap/exhibits/exhibits.html

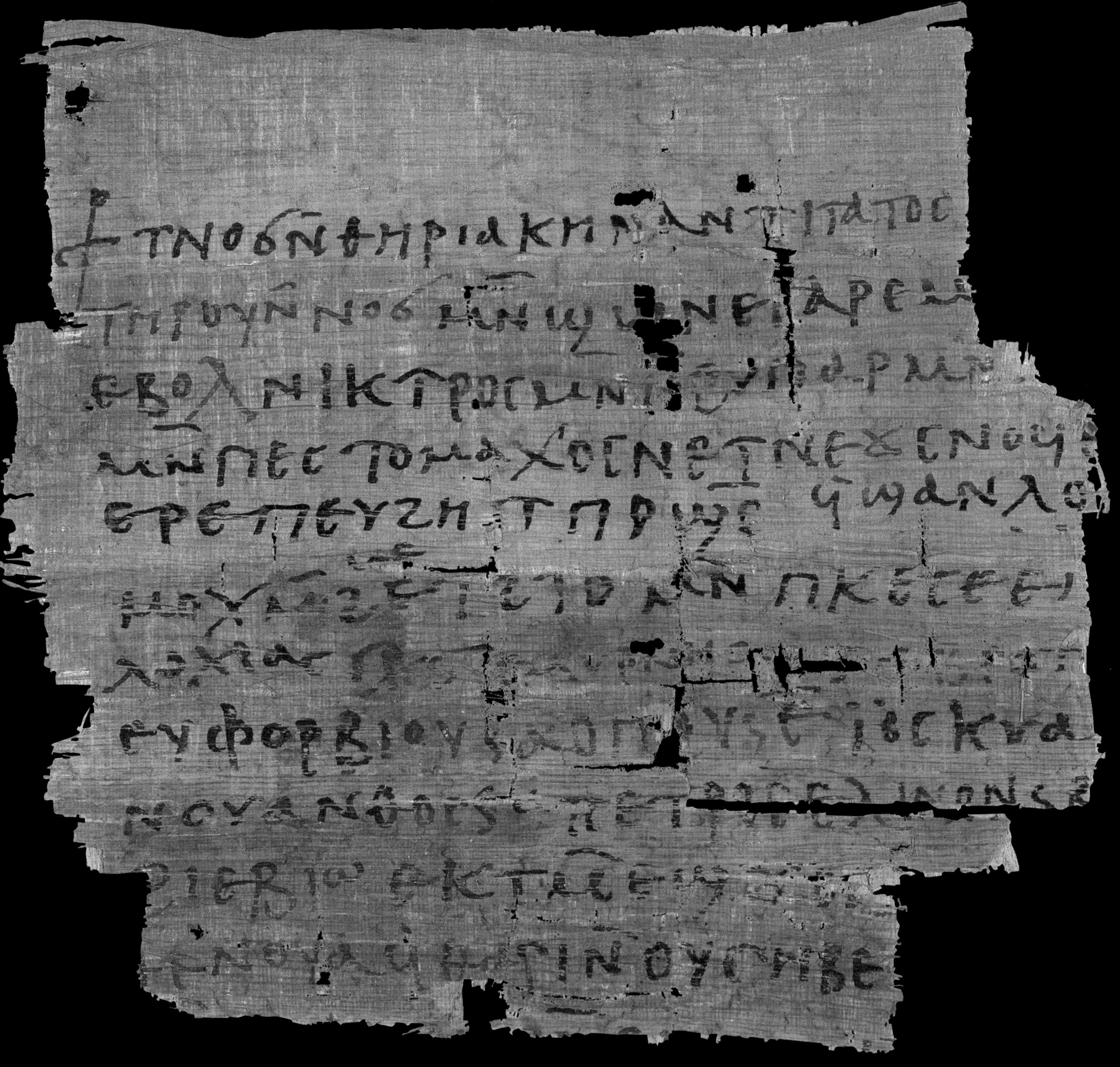

✝ ΤΝΟΟΠΝΘΗΡΙΑΚΗΝ ΑΝΤΙΠΑΤΟΟ
ΤΗΓΟΥΝΝΟΟ ΑΝ ΙΩ ΩΝ ΕΙ ΑΡΕΙ
ΕΒΟΛ ΝΙΚ ΤΡΟΟ ΛΙΝΙΟ ϩⲀΡΜ
ΛΗ ΠΕΟ ΤΟΜΑΧΟΟ ΝΕ ΤΝΕΧΕΝΟΥ
ΕΡΕ ΠΕΥΓΗ ΤΠΡΩϢ ϤϢΑΛΛΟ
ΜΟΥΛΑϨ ΕΤΟ ΤΟ ΑΝ ΠΚΕΤΕΕϤ
ΛΑΧΑ ... ...
ΕΥΦΟΡΒΙΟΥ ... ... ιϲ ⲃ ⲕ ⲣ Δ
ΝΟΥΑΝΘΟΙΟ ... ... ⲱ ⲛ ⲥ
ΒΙΕΒΙΟ ΕΚΤΑϹΕ ...
ΝΕΝⲞⲨ ⲀⲨ ... ⲅ Ν ΟΥ Ο ΝⲂⲈ

Little Joseph having become an orphan was chased from his paternal home by unmerciful creditors.

As he was sadly going along, he met with an elegant hunter who allowed him to carry his bag.

The hunter finding that Joseph was intelligent took him home to his country-house and engaged him as a servant.

One day Joseph found a letter without any address and read it.

Joseph gave the letter to his master and told him he had read it to know to whom it belonged.

The same night the son of his master offered him money to know what the letter contained.

Joseph refused to speak. The son ill-treated and chased him out of the house.

The little boy went along and being fatigued, he sat down by the side of the road. A rich lady passed in a carriage.

The lady proposed to take him in her carriage if he would reveal the contents of the letter.

Joseph continued his way. He met a traveller who was dining on the grass; the child asked him for a piece of bread.

All is for you said the traveller, if you will tell me the secret of the letter. Joseph went away without saying anything.

Exhausted with fatigue and dying of hunger, the little boy fell on the grass and went to sleep.

When he woke he found himself in a soft bed. A lady was sitting at his bed-side.

A comfortable dinner was brought. Joseph recognized the traveller and the lady whom he had met.

The master of the house appeared, he kissed the child for his discretion, and promised to look to his future.

Joseph is now a farmer; he often relates to his family the origin of his success, and says :

CHILDREN BE DISCREET.

Imagerie d'Epinal. — PELLERIN, imp.-édit.

Michigan State University Libraries
Special Collections Division

Comic Art Collection

THE Comic Art Collection in the Michigan State University (MSU) Libraries has grown constantly since the 1970s to become North America's premier research destination for the study of the comic book. Currently the collection holds 180,000 American comic books, plus 40,000 foreign comic books and 20,000 volumes of history, criticism, and related material. A steady stream of local students and visiting researchers uses the collection, and the collection regularly supplies material for museum exhibits. Interlibrary loan requests are received regularly, and are filled using scans whenever appropriate in legal and preservation terms.

In 1970, according to the Michigan State University Libraries' newsletter the *University Library* (January 1971), the Rhode Island School of Design requested the loan, for exhibit, of our first edition of Rodolphe Töpffer's *L'Histoire de Monsieur Crépin* (1837). This note is the first formal mention in our records of what was to become the Comic Art Collection, and is auspicious in two ways. Töpffer's stories in narrative art are consistently argued to be the very first comic books. A complete set of first or very early editions of Töpffer, donated by a faculty member in the 1960s, was an appropriate beginning for a collection defined not around newspaper comics or magazine cartoons, but around pictorial narratives intended for separate publication, in other words, comic *books*. The 1971 evocation of Töpffer is also important in that it declared from the beginning that our collection was international, and retrospective.

The contemporary "popular culture" aspect of the collection began when Russel B. Nye, a professor of English at MSU, was finishing his book *The Unembarrassed Muse* (1970). Nye's intent was to inaugurate academic discussion of the "arts of commercial entertainment," and the book was indeed widely read. In the course of this writing, he discovered that academic libraries could not support his chapter on the comics. Nye was a persuasive man. He talked two of his students into donating their comic book collections to the MSU Library, and he talked the library into accepting them, all 6,000 of them. The American comic books are still the central part of the collection, which is now the largest in any library in the world. The collection does not begin and end with Superman, though superheroes are the salient American genre. Romances, westerns, funny animals, science fiction, detectives, and every other imaginable genre of comic book sit on our shelves. We have moved beyond popular culture to document comics as a literary form, so every kind of anti-generic underground, new wave, and alternative comic is present from all over the world. We collect modern graphic novels globally, and we continue to accumulate mass-produced North American, European, and Latin American comic books retrospectively.

Cataloging and indexing of the Comic Art Collection are high-priority activities, and there is no backlog of uncataloged material. Catalog records for all titles appear in WorldCat and in the local online catalog, and indexing of serials and other multi-part items, including indexing of most critical books and journals, can be found in the Reading Room Index on our Web site.

http://www.lib.msu.edu/comics/

(ABOVE)
Imagerie d'Epinal: Album d'Images: Textes en Anglais.
Kansas City, circa 1888. Cover.

This was the first color comic book in America.

(OPPOSITE)
Imagerie d'Epinal: Album d'Images: Textes en Anglais.
Kansas City, circa 1888. Pages.

University of Minnesota Libraries
Archives and Special Collections

James Ford Bell Library

(ABOVE)
[*Reysen und Wanderschafften durch das gelobte Land.*]
Sir John Mandeville. 1481. Detail.

    This was the first German and the first illustrated edition of Mandeville's travels, supposedly undertaken in 1322–56, originally written in French. The fanciful illustrations, drawn from the text, are based on the writings of Pliny the Elder (1st century CE) and Solinus (3rd century CE).

(OPPOSITE)
[*Reysen und Wanderschafften durch das gelobte Land.*]
Sir John Mandeville. 1481. Leaves.

A GREAT library should tell a great story. This sentiment was expressed often by Minnesota industrialist James Ford Bell as he contemplated the development of his library. It was not the story of acquiring books and manuscripts that he was anticipating, rather the story in their contents—the record of human experience committed to paper and ink. "Bound fragments of time," he called them in his address on October 30, 1953, when he entrusted his personal library to the University of Minnesota, where he envisioned its continued growth and the opportunity to tell its story.

The James Ford Bell Library has indeed grown in the more than 50 years it has been a part of the university, from Mr. Bell's original contribution of 600 items focused on European expansion to approximately 30,000 rare books, maps, and manuscripts that tell the story of international trade and its impact around the world. The collection ranges from handwritten invoices for goods dated as early as 400 CE to early 19th-century accounts of expeditions into the North American wilderness. Merchants, explorers, colonists, missionaries, and other travelers recorded their experiences in the books and manuscripts that form the heart of the collection. Treaties, account books, insurance contracts, navigational tools, and textbooks illuminate the practical aspects of their adventures, while the library's many geographies, atlases, and maps provide a physical representation of their dreams and achievements.

The great story of human global interaction before the modern age is enjoyed, investigated, and retold by the hundreds of students and researchers who use the collection each year. The Bell Library inspires visits and class projects by students in courses as varied as Revolutions in Science: The Babylonians to Newton, Visual Culture in the Atlantic World, and Middle Eastern Geographies. Dissertation research in the Bell collection is currently focused on accounts of 16th-century earthquakes in Peru, the failed attempt to develop a Dutch West Indies trading company, and the cultural construction of Africa by 18th-century Europeans, among others. A recent visiting scholar investigated the treatment of Jews in 18th-century Surinam.

Recently, a post-graduate volunteer has been working on a detailed collection description of the family and business papers of a 17th-century English diplomat and merchant, Sir Thomas Bendish. The student's excitement and enthusiasm for the project has led to her decision to pursue graduate studies in the correlation between diplomacy and trade in the early modern world—a decision that would have warmed the heart of the library's founder, a merchant and book collector who saw in global commerce the best long-range hope for friendship among nations.

The James Ford Bell Library enjoys support from both the University of Minnesota and the wider community that enables it to add to the collection, and to reach out to both the scholarly and general communities through lectures, exhibitions, special events, and publications. The James Ford Bell Library, its premier collection, and its innovative programs support scholarship and education at all levels, enriching the community by helping to make the world more meaningful.

Do ist ein ande-
re insel do seid vn-
sauber leüt jnnen
die habent nit häu-
pter· vñ steend jne
die augē an de ach-
selen· vñ der mund
steet in mitten an
der prust· vnd ist in
krum als ein hüff-
eÿsen· vnd habend
gar grosse augen·

Hye merckt von wunderlichen leüten den ist das
antlicz flach als ein deller·

Aber ist ein ande-
re insel da sind leü-
te jnnen den ist das
antlücz aller ding
flach als ein deller
vnd habend keinē
munde dann do in
der mund soll steen
do habent sy zwey
kleine löchlin vnd
sind gar ser zornig
leüt·

In der insel do seind leüt die habend vnsauber
groß lebsen vñ deckent jr antlicz damit wenn
sy an der sumen ligen·

Hie komt man
aber in ein andere
insel do sind auch
vnsauber leüt jm
die habent als gar
groß lebsen wann
sy an der sumen li-
gen so bedeckent sy
jr antlücz darmit
wann die sunn do
selben gar ser sche-
net vnnd heyß ist

In dem land do seind mann die habend har in dem
bart als die katzen vnd seind lange har·

Do ist ein ande-
re jnsel do seind
leüt jm die seind
gar schön· vñ die
mann habē kaum
ly har in dem bart
die seind lang als
einer katzen· Vñ
die frawen do sel-
ben die seind gar
schön vnd hübsch
Vñ do ist ein stat
in dem lannd die

heyßt latorij· vnd ist nun ein leg von dem mör· vnnd
die hat ein schifreychs waffer vñ hat als vil schif als
ein statt die man vinden mag·

Do wil ich eüch sagen von schauffen die seind
zweymal als groß als vnsere schaf·

Annunciat
rex Adolphus
siderauerunt

101.

University of Missouri–Columbia Libraries
Elmer Ellis Library

Fragmenta Manuscripta Collection

I N 1968, the University of Missouri–Columbia Libraries purchased a 217-piece collection of manuscript leaves dating from the 8th to the 15th centuries. The origin of the *Fragmenta Manuscripta* Collection is somewhat enigmatic. The respected bookseller William Salloch who sold the collection to the university thought that the collection was started by Anglican Archbishop Thomas Tenison (1636–1715), who founded the first public library in London. After Tenison sold the books and manuscripts belonging to this library in 1861, the collection came into the possession of the manuscript collector Sir Thomas Phillipps. Compilation of the collection may in actuality have been done by the London bookseller John Bagford (1650–1716).

The earliest piece in this collection is from *De Orthographia* of the Venerable Bede, probably dating from the 8th century. It is an extremely interesting piece, its script being very close to that of the manuscript of the *Magna Moralia* of St. Gregory the Great, written by the Anglo-Saxon monk Peregrinus working in Freising.

One of the most beautiful pieces of this collection is a page of the Acts of the Apostles from the Canterbury Bible. It has very fine initials, one in blue and gold depicting two birds; the other on the verso has a very delicate illustration of the subject with the large initial "P" of the first chapter of the Acts narrating Christ's ascension into the heavens. Disciples flank the empty central space from which Christ ascends, and only his feet and ankles are visible below the frame around the initial.

Though the emphasis of the collection is on the development of the English manuscript hand—fragments can be attributed to the schools of Peterborough, Canterbury, and Bury—there are also specimens of continental origin.

A miniature painting of the early 14th century is most probably Italian. It depicts a very unusual group of four people: an older man sitting, a couple, and a young man with a sword. It is thought the subject is an allegory of the story of the expulsion from Paradise. This illustration is strongly influenced in style by Byzantine iconography.

The *Roman de la Rose* is a French manuscript of the second half of the 13th century. One of the finest leaves in the collection, it is from a codex on parchment, with three pen drawings. The delicately drawn figures and faces resemble the style of the great French miniaturists who illustrated *L'Histoire du Graal* in the Bibliothèque Nationale.

The Division of Special Collections, Archives, and Rare Books of the Ellis Library is a participant in the Digital Scriptorium project coordinated by Columbia University. The Digital Scriptorium is a searchable database for the manuscript holdings of 29 cultural institutions across the United States and includes all 217 leaves in the *Fragmenta Manuscripta* Collection. Participants contribute research and images of their items in order to provide access via the Internet to these rare and fragile materials; all at no cost to the user. The Digital Scriptorium fosters scholarship and enriches the growing corpus of information about medieval and Renaissance manuscripts.

http://mulibraries.missouri.edu/specialcollections/digital.htm

http://www.scriptorium.columbia.edu

(ABOVE TOP)
Paper sundial circle by unknown artist. N.d.

(ABOVE BOTTOM)
"St. Jerome Writing at His Desk." Miniature painting by unknown artist. N.d.

(OPPOSITE)
Miniature painting of group of four people by unknown artist. Text from a book of law. Italian, early 14th century.

Pomological Watercolor Collection

DURING the mid-19th century, Americans embraced new and exotic varieties of fruits and nuts with increased fervor. Farmers were expanding orchards in response to growing markets, while horticulturists and explorers were importing new plant species from foreign expeditions and developing them for introduction into American agriculture. In response to this increased interest and activity, the United States Department of Agriculture (USDA) in 1886 established the Division of Pomology. The mission of the division was to document new varieties, publish illustrations, and disseminate research findings to fruit growers and breeders through specialized publications. Scientifically precise representations of the fruits were critical in enabling farmers to understand and apply the information covered in agricultural publications. Since photography had not yet developed to the point where it could meet these needs, the USDA recruited artists to create technically accurate illustrations of newly introduced fruits and nuts.

William Henry Prestele was the first artist appointed to the Division of Pomology in 1887. Many other artists, including a significant number of women, joined him over the next four decades. The USDA Pomological Watercolor Collection is the fruit of their labors.

Chadwick-Healey and other publishers indexed the collection of approximately 7,700 watercolors created from 1888 to the 1930s. Building on those indexes, NAL developed a Web database which contains additional details of each watercolor and links to the images. The database includes information handwritten by the artist giving the plant species and variety; name of the property owner; the county, city, and state where the subject specimen was grown; and the date that the watercolor was painted. The collection also includes 90 wax models of fruit that reproduce the exact weight, color, and texture as well as appearance of the specimens. NAL has photographed the models and has developed a conservation plan to ensure their availability into the future. The annual reports of the *Pomologist* and other publications featuring lithographs produced from the original watercolors are also part of this collection and can be accessed on the NAL Web site.

Unique to NAL, the USDA Pomological Watercolor Collection is a major historic and botanic resource for horticulturists, historians, artists, and publishers. Drawn from nature, the paintings serve as the basis for exhibits at NAL and in collaboration with other institutions, and they are one of NAL's most popular collections. The primary research use is to trace the characteristics of early fruit varieties and analyze introductions from early plant exploration expeditions. This research informs horticulturists and can influence the direction of breeding programs. The collection is increasingly appreciated for its aesthetic value; therefore reprints of images are frequently requested. To increase access to the collection for both the research community and the public, over 300 watercolors have been scanned and are available on the Special Collections Web site. Digitized images and newly discovered facts about the artists and their work are added regularly.

http://www.nal.usda.gov/speccoll/collectionsguide/mssindex/pomology/pomology.shtml

National Library of Medicine
History of Medicine Division

Public Health Films Collection

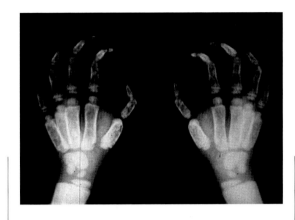

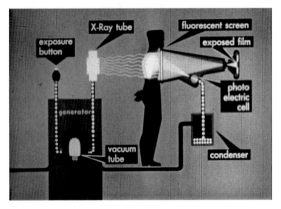

NEW technologies open up the world in new and unexpected ways. So it was with films—a technology of the end of the 19th century that became a defining mark of the 20th. The ability of movies to entertain and to instruct was clear. Over the course of the century filmmakers grasped the ability of film to persuade and to motivate. The rhetorical force of films, and the connection between entertainment and public service, were new things to the medium's new masters.

The National Library of Medicine (NLM) holds the country's largest collection of historical medical films, numbering about 14,000. At the center of the collection are public health films, dating from the 1910s to the present. The collection comes from many sources, including government agencies—notably the Public Health Service, and especially the Center for Disease Control and Prevention (CDC). Other films come from private health organizations, and from groups such as the American Dental Association. As these institutions move their productions from film to video and digital, they often offer NLM their older collections, and thus the holdings continue to grow.

Throughout the 20th century the rhetorical power of the cinema was formed and developed, and in these films that power was marshaled for public health. Indeed, one of the division's manuscript collections, the Adolf Nichtenhauser collection, chronicles the efforts of Navy medicine to study and to harness the potential of medical films. Public health films provided the opportunity to change people's attitudes and behaviors. Movies showed them how to do new things, such as going in for a physical, and celebrated heroic efforts, such as pushing back yellow fever in the tropics. In the war, these films were produced and promoted to keep both troops and the home front ready to work and to serve. Films connected medical research with better health, and asked people to be generous with their support. The medium also provided other, more subtle messages about American society: assumptions about gender, status, and race helped structure the way that public health was "done" in the past, as these films manifestly show.

The library is using this collection in new ways, for new audiences. Documentary filmmakers—producing for PBS, BBC, Discovery Channel, and others—have long come to the library, and recently film scholars and medical historians have as well. The library has a program to bring university teachers to the library to study films, obtain reference copies, work them into and use them in their courses, and have their course syllabi posted on the NLM Web site. The films are rich resources for the classroom, helping students learn about modern medicine, American and global societies, and cultural communication in the 20th century. As part of interpretive programs on medicine and society, the library is screening these films at the National Academy of Sciences and the College of Physicians in Philadelphia, at meetings of the American Association for the History of Medicine, as well as at the library. They show up in NLM's exhibits. To bring the collection to wider audiences, the History of Medicine Division is selecting some of its films for a prototype for a new DVD series—the first offering will be "The Public Health Film Goes to War."

(ABOVE GROUP)
Routine Admission Chest X-Ray in General Hospitals. US Public Health Service. Graphic Films Corp. for Division of Visual Education, US Office of Education, producer, 1946.

X-ray of hands with tuberculosis.

Animation of the working of the X-ray.

This film demonstrated how to set up X-ray units for screening incoming hospital patients.

(OPPOSITE LEFT GROUP)
The Work of the Public Health Service. US Public Health Service. Bray Studios Inc., producer, 1936.

Fumigating clothing.

Title frame.

Newly arriving immigrants.

Pasteurizing milk.

This film describes the US Public Health Service (USPHS), the agency charged with promoting America's health. The USPHS inspected immigrants for disease, ensured the purity of the nation's food, and conducted medical research.

(OPPOSITE RIGHT GROUP)
The Fight against the Communicable Diseases. Federal Security Agency, Public Health Service, Communicable Disease Center. 1950.

Spraying for insects from an airplane.

Technicians in research lab.

Title frame.

In this film, the Communicable Disease Center showcased its research work, as well as its service to state and local health departments.

Philip L. and Helen Cather Southwick Collection

(ABOVE)
"Willa Cather in French Countryside." Photograph
by unknown artist. 1920.

(OPPOSITE)
"Willa Cather Writing [in Jaffrey, New Hampshire?]."
Photograph by unknown artist. Mid-1920s.

I N 1902, Willa Cather, who would become one of America's most acclaimed authors, went to Europe for the first time. Long a lover of European culture, her tour of Great Britain and France at age 29 was a momentous event for her. So when Cather scholars first looked at the Philip L. and Helen Cather Southwick Collection and saw a detailed scrapbook of that journey, they knew they were looking at something special. There, pasted onto gray paper, was photograph after photograph of Willa Cather and her companions on the ship, in England, and in France, accompanied by newspaper clippings, postcards, and other mementos. Long recognized as an important moment in her biography, Cather scholars could now sense, for the first time, the details and texture of that tour.

The European scrapbook of the 1902 and 1908 trips is, however, only one of the astounding artifacts that make up the Southwick Collection. The life and works of Willa Cather, the aunt of the donor, Helen Cather Southwick, is documented extensively in both texts and images. Hundreds of snapshots of Cather and her environs, probably taken by her companion Edith Lewis, are an intimate counterpoint to the typical, more formal photographs of her. Also included are dozens of letters written by Cather to her family, letters written by others to Cather, and letters exchanged by Cather's friends and family. Of particular interest are the manuscripts and corrected typescripts of a dozen novels, short stories, and essays, including her celebrated works *The Professor's House* (1925), *Shadows on the Rock* (1931), *Lucy Gayheart* (1935), and *Obscure Destinies* (1932). For decades, scholars assumed that no manuscript material survived, and this collection significantly altered the historical understanding of many of her works.

Since Willa Cather was an author who based many of her works on people and places she knew well, some artifacts within the collection feel like they have fallen out of the pages of her novels. For example, in *My Ántonia*, the narrator Jim Burden describes his modest room and includes this detail: "On the blank wall at my left the dark, old-fashioned wall-paper was covered by a large map of ancient Rome, the work of some German scholar." The Southwick collection includes a map of ancient Rome owned by Willa Cather and created by "C. Hoffmann." In looking over the photographs in the collection, one can see snapshots of Willa Cather standing next to a statue of Archbishop Lamy in Santa Fe, New Mexico, the same Lamy who became the prototype of Father Latour in *Death Comes for the Archbishop* (1927).

The value of the Southwick Collection is enhanced through the context of other holdings on Willa Cather at the University of Nebraska, which include 14 different collections of letters, books, manuscripts, and other research materials. Finding aids for these collections are available online, and many of the materials, particularly the photographs, are accessible to people around the world on the Willa Cather Archive.

http://cather.unl.edu/

University of New Mexico Libraries
Center for Southwest Research

Tony Hillerman Papers

TONY Hillerman, writer and teacher, was born May 27, 1925, in Sacred Heart, Oklahoma. He grew up in the rural community and attended the only local grade school, a Catholic school for girls. When the United States entered World War II, Hillerman joined the army and served for two years in Europe. He returned to Oklahoma and received a BA from the University of Oklahoma in 1946. He worked as a newspaper reporter in Texas and Oklahoma until he became UPI's Santa Fe Bureau Manager in 1952. In 1954 he joined the staff of the *New Mexican* as a political reporter and later became an editor. He came to the University of New Mexico as a graduate student in English in 1962. Hillerman received his MA in 1966 and became a professor of journalism, serving as department chair. He retired from teaching in 1986.

Hillerman's journalism career influenced his later writing. His style, clear and direct, produced beautiful and vivid descriptions of the stark Southwestern landscape. His first novel, *The Blessing Way,* was published by Harper & Row in 1970. The University of New Mexico Press published a collection of stories, five of them from Hillerman's master's thesis, under the title, *The Great Taos Bank Robbery* (1972). In addition to the popular and successful Navajo mystery series of novels, Hillerman has written texts for photography and travel books on New Mexico and the Southwest. Articles by Hillerman have appeared in *New Mexico Quarterly, New Mexico Magazine, National Geographic Traveler, Arizona Highways,* and other magazines.

The Tony Hillerman Papers consist of literary manuscripts, correspondence, published materials, and lecture notes. His literary manuscripts include drafts, revisions, and edited manuscripts for all of Hillerman's published novels, as well as page proofs and screenplays for some titles. Related research materials and correspondence with agents and publishers regarding revisions and editing are located with the respective manuscripts. The collection also contains letters from agents and publishers concerning contracts and various publishing projects; requests for appearances, book signings, conference participation, and lectures; and a considerable amount of fan mail. Tony Hillerman continues to add materials to his collection. These additional materials reflect his changing writing interests.

A finding aid to the Hillerman Papers is available online as part of the On-Line Archives of New Mexico. Tony Hillerman's collection is used extensively by students and researchers in creative writing, Southwest studies, history, and anthropology. On occasion Tony will visit the Center for Southwest Research and informally talk with students using his papers, sharing advice and stories. Each year many fans come to Special Collections during the Tony Hillerman Mystery Writers Conference held in Albuquerque.

Tony Hillerman's Papers, much like Tony himself, are Southwest treasures to be researched and enjoyed by anyone interested in good storytelling.

http://rmoa.unm.edu/docviewer.php?docId=nmu1mss501bc.xml

...the details must be exactly accurate—from the way a Hogan is built, to the way a sweat bath is taken to the way it looks, and sounds, and smells at an Enemy Way Ceremonial at 2 am on a wintry morning.

—Tony Hillerman

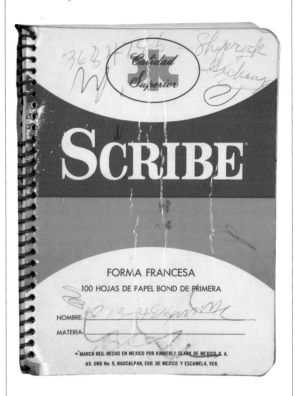

(ABOVE)
Tony Hillerman's story-idea notebook.

(OPPOSITE)
"Tony Hillerman Fishing in New Mexico."
Photograph by unknown artist. Circa 1959.

The New York Public Library, Astor, Lenox, and Tilden Foundations
The Research Libraries, Humanities and Social Sciences Library

Spencer Collection

THE Spencer Collection was established with a bequest from William Augustus Spencer, a native New Yorker living in Paris, who was lost in the *Titanic* disaster in April 1912. Spencer's will stipulated that the library receive his collection of turn-of-the-century French illustrated books in fine bindings, and a portion of his estate. The gift provided for an endowment to acquire "the finest illustrated books that can be procured of any country and in any language…thus constituting a collection representative of the arts of illustration and bookbinding."

The provisions of the bequest offered curators wide latitude in developing a collection, beginning as early as 1918 with the acquisition of exceptional Western manuscripts, among them the *Tickhill Psalter*. These early acquisitions also included great monuments of the Western printed book, such as the Aldine *Hypnerotomachia Poliphili* on vellum, the 1481 copperplate edition of Dante's *Divina Commedia*, and Dürer's three great woodcut albums. Curators, beginning with Karl Kup in 1934, have continued to acquire the finest illustrated books of numerous varieties, from festival books, emblem books, and architectural treatises to novels, poetry anthologies, and *livres d'artistes*, and they have expanded the scope of the collection to encompass illustrated and illuminated books and scrolls from China, Japan, India, Indonesia, Malaysia, and Thailand. With the recent acquisition of the Elaine Lustig Cohen Dada Collection, the Spencer Collection now can document that 20th-century art movement through illustrated books, periodicals, posters, prints, drawings, and related ephemera.

The Spencer Collection has been featured in numerous library exhibitions, beginning in 1914 with "The Spencer Collection of Modern Book Bindings." In recent years these shows have included "Tales of Japan: Scrolls and Prints from The New York Public Library"; "The Splendor of the Word: Medieval and Renaissance Illuminated Manuscripts at The New York Public Library"; and "Ehon: The Artist and the Book in Japan." These recent exhibitions were accompanied by major catalogs, which join another scholarly publication documenting primarily Spencer holdings, *Islamic Manuscripts in The New York Public Library* (1992). Other exhibitions, drawn extensively from Spencer, have featured artists' books and *livres d'artistes* by contemporary artists, including Christian Boltanski, Richard Long, Richard Tuttle, Jim Dine, and Lawrence Weiner.

The Spencer Collection is also increasingly visible and accessible through digital projects. The Spencer Collection, with the library's Manuscripts and Archives Division, participated in Digital Scriptorium. The more than 2,000 medieval and Renaissance manuscript pages and associated illuminations are on the library's NYPL Digital Gallery Web site with 3,900 other images from the Spencer Collection. Present also are digital images of the Japanese printed books and scrolls, many in their entirety, that are reproduced in the catalog for *Ehon: The Artist and the Book in Japan* (2006).

Two all-day symposiums have been hosted by the Spencer Collection in conjunction with its exhibitions, and a video of the "Ehon" symposium has been posted on the NYPL Web site. Both attracted large audiences including the general public, scholars, and graduate students. School groups, focusing on K–12, were invited to attend special classes and tours for the "Ehon" exhibition, and teachers have continued to bring their classes to learn about other collections.

http://digitalgallery.nypl.org/nypldigital/

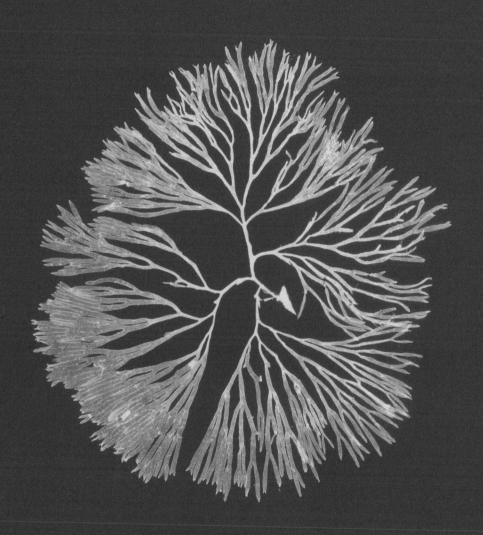

Halymenia furcellata.

Aegst E den 21 July 1654

Ick dog geuen aen Messieurs mijn
cosijns Cornelis van de gol_ En Ferdinand
van wou Haert in compaignie, dese naer
volgende gooderen in de Kipper sijn Jn
Jan der graft, ther gonaract
de gelders Blom. de gooderen sijn
gouenbroot en den prijs als volght
om te vercopen tot onser meeste profijt

E W	12 Elle		a 26 L de	15 : 12	
	25 Elle kant — W D	a 2¼ L de	2 : 16 : 4	
	1 ring a du 1 gael	a	3 :	
B	1 stuc nopen kost		10 : 5	
A	1 stuc ditto kost		12 :	
C	3 Elle fijne galon a 50 L de		7 : 10	

Aen boecken — gf — 51 : 3 : 4

Elenden En bedruf van Frederick
gendrick prince van oranye — f 1 : 10
Elenden En bedruf van gendrick
de groote — f : 14
gel frans En duijts testament f 1 : 10
gel indruct Elde En der saliegheijt f : 12
vondels Joseph f : 14
den ander boeck Spooeckade
van gel gelous f : 6 : 12

Somma f — 56 : 10 : 0

Gerrit Lambertse koecken
Jan van Welij

13-140

Van Rensselaer Manor Papers

SHOES, stockings, shirts, linen pants, blankets, brandy, cloth, cheese, vinegar, merchandise, brown medicinal beer, a suit of clothes, an English hat, a Rouen hat, oil lamps, a gun and baldric, powder and lead, cordage, grain scythes—these are some of the goods that two of America's early Dutch farmers, Brant Peelen and Cornelis Theunisen, must have been happy to receive from the ship *Eendracht* in 1634. They had lived in the wilderness at the upper Hudson for three years during which they lived off whatever they produced themselves, whatever they could trade with the Indians, and whatever was being sent to them by their employer, Kiliaen van Rensselaer from the Dutch Republic. Just four years earlier this wealthy Amsterdam jewelry trader had established the patroonship of Rensselaerswijck in New Netherland, which would remain in the hands of his descendants until about 1860.

Together, the heavily damaged letters, contracts, bonds, accounts, maps, ledgers and other documents that are left of the manuscripts of Van Rensselaer's patroonship are almost like a movie account of the development of one of America's earliest European settlements. Mere fragments of manuscripts provide images of how a settlement of not even 10 farmers in 1634 grew in 18 years to a community of more than 200 colonists who practiced law, religion, and poor relief, and became a full-grown society.

How contacts between colonists and Indians in those years took place is revealed in detail by letters, accounts, and various treaties of land transactions. Numerous accounts provide insights into various religious celebrations and customs as well as the routines of daily life. This collection contains an abundance of details about 17th-century material culture such as food, clothing, jewelry, furniture, and house and barn plans and descriptions. From one blacksmith's account we learn that cows were wearing bells that were produced and sold in Rensselaerswijck for a certain price. From tailors' accounts we learn about the products they made, materials they used, and prices, as well as the manner in which they worked; a tailor would often work for days and sometimes weeks at the Van Rensselaer's house. The records show that certain Dutch customs were kept long after the English had taken over New Netherland; a 1675 baker's account mentions that Maria van Rensselaer bought *Sinterklaas* [Santa Claus] goods illustrating that the feast of Saint Nicolas was celebrated in Albany at that time. In addition to business information, letters written between family members and friends reveal personal matters, such as relations with friends and other inhabitants of the village, raising children, illness, and death.

The Van Rensselaer Manor Papers reveal the successes and hardships of ordinary people, men, women, and children, wealthy and poor, masters and slaves, from the earliest years of America's written history into the 19th century. The users of this collection include historians, genealogists, archaeologists, and lawyers researching land titles and Indian rights. A finding aid is available on the New York State Library's Web site:

http://www.nysl.nysed.gov/msscfa/sc7079.htm

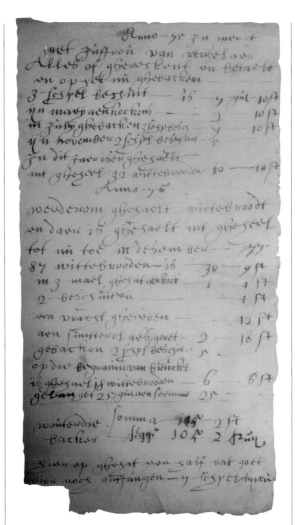

(ABOVE)
Baker's account from Wouter de backer (Wouter Albertsz). March 1675.

This document mentions that Maria van Rensselaer fetched rusks, cookies, whitebread, etc. This is the first reference to the celebration of *Sinterklaas* [Saint Nicholas] in New Netherland, recording that she spent ƒ2:10 on *Sinterklaas* goodies: "…aen suntterclaesgoet ƒ2:10."

(OPPOSITE)
Invoice of goods shipped to New Netherland. July 1654.

This is a detailed account of books, lace, and other textiles sent with Cornelis van Schel and Jeremias van Rensselaer from Amsterdam via the ship *De Gelderse Blom* to New Netherland to be sold on behalf of Gerrit Lambertse Kock and Jan van Wely.

The Downtown Collection

"Poodle with a Mohawk." Poster (silkscreen and
felt tip pen) by Lydia Barry. 1982.

Barry's poster—proposing that the most effete of
dogs could don the most outrageous hairstyle of the
era and release the inner punk—became an instant
punk classic.

"Untitled [Wolf's Head]." Mixed-media mask by
David Wojnarowicz. 1989.

Wojnarowicz made this mask for Rosa von
Praunheim's film, *Silence = Death*, in which he
appeared along with Keith Haring.

LAST March a master's candidate from London spent a week doing research in the Fales
Library at New York University. Her thesis was on David Wojnarowicz, the New York
artist who died at 37 in 1992. In England 15 years after his death, she had been finding
Wojnarowicz a fascinating if somewhat remote figure. In the Fales, she found a sense of
immediacy that brought her research alive. "I didn't realize everyone in the library would
know who he is," she told a librarian. "His friends, like Dennis Cooper, have actually been
here. Dennis was looking in the archive and actually found a letter David had written to him
but he never received!" The student said that her research in Fales's Downtown Collection
would form the central focus of her thesis.

The Downtown Collection is the largest collection of printed and archival materials related
to the Downtown New York art scene anywhere and the only one in an academic library. What
better place? Fales is located in NYU's Bobst Library on Washington Square in Greenwich
Village, one of the pulse points of downtown Manhattan. Its always-growing Downtown
Collection contains 12,000 printed items (monographs, periodical titles, zines, posters,
invitations) and works in film, video, and audio. Fales's archival holdings include the papers
of Richard Hell, the man for whom the term "punk rock" was coined; Richard Foreman, a leader
of avant-garde theater; Dennis Cooper, the poet, novelist, and editor; as well as Jacki Apple,
Eric Bogosian, Laura Foreman, Gary Indiana, Lynne Tillman, Martha Wilson, and others.
Fales holds the archives of its neighbor, Judson Memorial Church, a major center for avant-garde
performance in the 1960s; Fashion Moda, the Bronx outsider gallery that promoted graffiti art;
AIR Gallery, the first women's art collective gallery in New York City; Godzilla, the Asian-
American art network; the Postal Art Network, one of NYC's preeminent mail art collections;
the avant-garde theater company Mabou Mines; and Creative Time, one of the first organizations
to foster large-scale public art, among others. The collection is heavily used by scholars and the
art community and was the central focus of "The Downtown Show: The New York Art Scene
1974–1984," which was named best thematic show of 2006 by the US chapter of the International
Association of Art Critics. *The Downtown Book: The New York Art Scene 1974–1984* (2006) won an
Association of American Museums award for design in 2006.

University of North Carolina at Chapel Hill Libraries
Louis Round Wilson Library

Documenting the American South

WHEN the University of North Carolina at Chapel Hill's University Library debuted Documenting the American South (DocSouth) in 1996, it was envisioned as a modest effort to digitize a few fragile and frequently consulted slave narratives. DocSouth has since blossomed into a comprehensive digital publishing initiative that provides free access to a growing record of southern history, literature, and culture. DocSouth comprises thousands of books, manuscript materials, images, posters, artifacts, oral history interviews, recorded songs, and scholarly essays. DocSouth digitized materials are arranged as 10 thematic collections, with new collections being developed:

"The First Century of the First State University" presents hundreds of primary documents about the creation and development of the University of North Carolina, from 1776 to 1875.

"Oral Histories of the American South" will ultimately collect 500 oral history interviews about civil rights, politics, women's issues, and other topics in recent North Carolina history.

"True and Candid Compositions: The Lives and Writings of Antebellum Students at the University of North Carolina" presents edited and transcribed letters and other documents written by UNC students from 1795 to 1868.

"First-Person Narratives of the American South" offers letters, memoirs, and autobiographies by slaves, laborers, women, aristocrats, soldiers, and officers.

"Library of Southern Literature" includes the most important Southern literary works from the colonial period to the beginning of the 20th century.

"North American Slave Narratives" documents a unique genre of the 18th, 19th and early 20th centuries.

"The Southern Homefront, 1861–1865" presents materials related to life during the Civil War.

"The Church in the Southern Black Community" traces the role of Protestant Christianity in the life of Southern African Americans.

"The North Carolina Experience" tells a story about North Carolina, its people, and its history.

"North Carolinians and the Great War" examines how World War I shaped the lives of North Carolinians on the battlefield and the homefront.

From the very beginning, DocSouth has been guided by a formally-constituted editorial board composed of faculty, librarians, and partners from the UNC Press. DocSouth uses open-source technology and protocols, all digital texts are encoded according to the Text Encoding Initiative Guidelines, and each receives full-level cataloging records available through OCLC's WorldCat service.

Digital collections draw a wide range of readers including scholars, teachers, students from the elementary to the doctoral level, genealogists, novelists, and members of the general public. They come from as close as the UNC–Chapel Hill campus and as far away as Russia and Japan. The comments and questions that readers send to us reveal that they are engaged in all types of research and learning activities.

The library makes special efforts to facilitate and enhance the use of DocSouth for K–12 education. The "Classroom" section of the site includes sample lesson plans and additional resources. In partnership with UNC's School for Education, the library has also conducted four Teachers' Summer Institutes to help integrate DocSouth resources into K–12 classrooms.

http://docsouth.unc.edu/

(ABOVE)
"Mico Chlucco the Long Warrior." Drawing by William Bartram. From *Travels through North & South Carolina, Georgia, East & West Florida, the Cherokee Country, the Extensive Territories of the Muscogulges, or Creek Confederacy, and the Country of the Chactaws*. William Bartram. Circa 1790.

(OPPOSITE)
"Their Danses Vvhich They Vse att Their Hyghe Feastes." Drawing by John White. From *A Briefe and True Report of the New Found Land of Virginia*. Thomas Hariot. Late 1500s.

North Carolina State University Libraries
Special Collections Research Center

The Entomological Archive

THE NCSU Libraries' Entomological Archive is a world-class research collection that began close to home. North Carolina State University faculty were not only the primary creators but also the initial patrons of this major collection of rare books, manuscripts, and drawings related to the study of entomology. Over several generations, donations of papers, research materials, significant personal libraries, and funds have contributed to this unique resource.

The archive originated with Zeno Payne Metcalf, professor of entomology and zoology at NC State from 1912 to 1950. Dr. Metcalf devoted his life to the study of *Homoptera*, a group of insects now known as *Auchenorrhyncha*. He amassed a collection that contained virtually every word published on *Homoptera* from 1771 through 1955. Metcalf worked on an index to his collection, the extraordinary 42-volume *General Catalogue of the Homoptera of the World* (1927–1971), until his death in early 1956. This crucial foundation for further research was completed by Metcalf's assistant, Virginia Wade Burnside, and Metcalf's successor, David A. Young. The Zeno P. Metcalf Entomology Research Collection contains this collection of some 1,150 rare books and 11,000 monographs, journals, and papers.

Additional important collections of faculty research materials include the Clyde F. Smith papers, an extension of the Metcalf collection primarily pertaining to the insect family *Aphididae*, with more than 1,400 papers, pamphlets, and books dating from 1758, and two bibliographies that serve as indexes to the papers. Also faculty-built is the Maurice Hugh Farrier Collection, a comprehensive compilation of publications on mites by scientists from all over the world.

Two additional collections were acquired with faculty collaboration. David A. Young, who helped finish Metcalf's magnum opus, alerted the libraries to the sale of the Friedrich F. Tippmann Collection. The personal library of a Viennese engineer and amateur entomologist, the Tippmann collection is comprised of 975 monographic titles and periodicals; it contains some of the rarest entomological works in the world, including Ulisse Aldrovandi's *De animalibvs insectis libri septem cvm singvlorvm iconibvs ad viuum expressis* (1602) and Charles De Geer's *Mémoires pour servir à l'histoire des insectes* (1752–1778). It also includes classics in the history of science such as the 10th edition of Carolus Linnaeus's *Systema Naturae*, the work that established the use of binomial taxonomy in zoology.

Two rare works by Eugène Alain Séguy, portfolios of prints called *Papillons* and *Insectes*, were added to the archive through joint fundraising between the NCSU Libraries and entomology faculty. Published in the 1920s, they portray butterflies, beetles, grasshoppers, and cicadas in gorgeous color, using the pochoir technique, which requires hand coloring each plate through stencils.

These collections are heavily used not only by students and faculty in the NCSU Colleges of Agriculture and Life Sciences, Design, and Veterinary Medicine, but also by researchers from around the world. Web access to the majority of this collection will soon be available, thanks to a grant from the National Science Foundation. The Séguy portfolios are available digitally and the libraries plan to digitize the majority of the Metcalf and Tippmann rare book collections— connecting the digital future of special collections with the impressive past of this collection.

The East African Railway - On the Mau Escarpment

A Woman at Nairobi

A Wahikuyu Woman

Streets at Nairobi

A Woman at Nairobi

Men at Nairobi

Northwestern University Library

Melville J. Herskovits Library of African Studies

The Winterton Collection of East African Photographs

ACCESS to historical photographs of Africa is essential to successful understanding of African life and culture. Collecting such photographs has always been an integral component of collection building for the Melville J. Herskovits Library of African Studies at Northwestern University. But many collections of African photographs primarily document European life and work in Africa, and aspects of African life perceived as "exotic" by European photographers.

The Winterton Collection of East African Photographs, acquired by the Herskovits Library in December 2002, is distinctive for its comprehensiveness of scope and its emphasis on the more prosaic matters of daily African life and culture. Assembled over a 30-year period by British collector Humphrey Winterton, it is comprised of 7,610 images taken primarily in East Africa between about 1860 and 1960, organized in 75 separate albums, scrapbooks, or loose collections. The earliest photographs in the collection were taken in 1860 inside the Zanzibar slave market by the Scottish explorer James Augustus Grant, whose best-selling work *A Walk across Africa* was published in 1864. The latest were taken during the pre-independence election in Kenya and depict Jomo Kenyatta, Kenya's first president, addressing a campaign rally.

The Winterton Collection documents street scenes in emerging urban areas as well as the less-than-glamorous aspects of colonial life. It also chronicles remarkable changes to the East African landscape. It depicts the building of East Africa's railways, the growth of its urban centers, and the development of colonial administration. It preserves a record of rural life as well as of the travels and work of European colonial officials and private businessmen. There are outstanding examples of portraiture, especially from emerging commercial studios in Nairobi and Zanzibar. The Winterton Collection also constitutes an unsurpassed resource for the study of the history of photography in East Africa. An existing inventory to the collection enhances its accessibility.

Research and teaching about Africa has a long history at Northwestern, where the Program of African Studies, established in 1948, was the first of its kind at a major research institution in the United States. Since its arrival at Northwestern, the Winterton Collection has had a significant impact on both undergraduate teaching and on the research of graduate students and faculty. Images from the collection are used in classroom lectures and discussion, undergraduates are assigned research that makes use of them, and an art history seminar was focused solely on the Winterton Collection for an entire quarter. The photographs have also been used in documenting faculty research and graduate student dissertations. Beyond Northwestern, the collection has been used to document research in monographs, dissertations, and journal articles; accompany text in popular historical magazines; and provide images for a major motion picture and an educational DVD.

The initial Winterton Web site, created in 2004, has generated a great deal of interest in using the collection. This interest will expand greatly as a result of an Institute of Museum and Library Services National Leadership grant (2006–08), which makes possible the digitization, cataloging, and creation of an inventory that will be accessible through a new Web site.

(ABOVE)
"An Officer and Chimpanzee." Photograph by unknown artist. Page from photo album, *Zur Erinnerung an Deutsch Ost Afrika. S.M.S. "Bussard" 1906–1908.* 1906–08. Detail.

The album contains 113 captioned silver prints, a mixture of professionally-taken images and snapshots, recording a voyage to Dar es Salaam, Tanga, Zanzibar, the Seychelles, Durban, Madagascar, and Mozambique.

(OPPOSITE)
Page from photo and souvenir album. Photographs by Susan Hicks-Beach. November 1907–June 1908.

The album records Susan Hicks-Beach's trip to eastern Africa in the company of H.R.H. Elene, Duchess of Aosta. They visited Egypt, Sudan, the Congo, Uganda, Kenya, German East Africa, Zanzibar, Djibouti, and Eritrea. As well as sightseeing, they hunted in Sudan, Congo, and Uganda, and paid official visits to the local rulers—kabakas—of the kingdoms that today are the country of Uganda.

University Libraries of Notre Dame

University Libraries, Department of Special Collections

The Rev. Edmund P. Joyce, CSC, Sports Research Collection

(ABOVE TOP)

The Football Calendar 1917. Walter Camp. [1917.]

Football-shaped printed ephemera, often "bound" with lacing, were popular in the early 20th century. This calendar contains a coaching bromide for each week of the year.

(ABOVE BOTTOM)

South Bend Blue Sox 1946 Year Book. [South Bend, Indiana, 1946.]

The Joyce Collection includes a notable body of materials from the All-American Girls Professional Baseball League of 1943–54.

(OPPOSITE)

"Wladek Zbyszko." Poster (color lithograph). 1921.

This poster of professional wrestler Wladek Zbyszko is part of the Jack Pfefer Collection—more than 100 cubic feet of materials accumulated by Pfefer over a 45-year promotional career in professional wrestling.

THE University Libraries' Joyce Sports Research Collection is an extensive body of books, periodicals, printed ephemera, and other formats dedicated to American sports and physical culture, and their antecedents abroad. Most materials pre-date the mid-20th century. The book collection, numbering upwards of 3,000 volumes, includes many of the field's scarce and seminal titles, from the physician Girolamo Mercuriale's treatise on physical culture in classical antiquity (*De arte gymnastica,* 1573) to Walter Camp's introduction to a game newly popular on the campuses of the Northeast (*American Football,* 1892). The collection's hundreds of periodical titles range from the earliest of all sports journals (the *Sporting Magazine,* published in London from 1792 to 1871) to the four mid-20th-century American magazines named, confusingly, *Sports Illustrated* (three of which were short-lived, and are today quite scarce). But perhaps the greatest strength of the Joyce Collection lies in its tens of thousands of pieces of printed ephemera—record books, rulebooks, media guides, yearbooks, programs, scorecards, catalogs, and the like. Many of these items were published by colleges and universities, or by franchises in the professional sports leagues that flourished in the United States from the late 19th century. There are, for example, more than 18,000 college football game programs pre-dating 1970, and more than 3,500 professional football programs from the same era. The Joyce Collection also comprises a smaller, but substantial, amount of non-printed matter, including several significant manuscript collections and an important collection of boxing photographs. It should be added that the collection as a whole is notable not just for its breadth but for its depth; several of the sport-specific sub-collections that make up the Joyce are of national stature, including those dedicated to boxing, wrestling, American football, billiards, and golf.

The Joyce Collection has been assembled over the last 40 years, the product of dozens of important donations as well as purchases large and small. Much of the present collection was culled from the purchase, in 1977, of the full inventory of the Los Angeles sports publications dealer Goodwin Goldfaden, which totaled around 30,000 books and 300,000 additional pieces of printed matter. In 1987 the university endowed the collection in honor of Rev. Edmund P. Joyce, CSC, Notre Dame's longtime executive vice president. This endowment, and another funded by John and Dessa Campbell, allows for the collection's continued growth and development.

The idea, in the 1960s, to develop a general sports collection at Notre Dame was in several ways prescient. For one thing, it anticipated the subsequent decade's new interest in the application of scholarly methodologies to the study of sports. And the collectors' market for sports-related publications boomed in the 1980s, after the greater part of the existing collection had been acquired. Today, the Joyce Collection stands as an important resource for scholars, journalists, filmmakers, and collectors researching the history, sociology, economics, and culture of American sports. Those interested in learning more of the collection may consult the finding aids and exhibits located on the Web at:

http://www.library.nd.edu/rarebooks/collections/sports/index.shtml

FRANCES Theatre DYERSBURG

Coming Direct From Princess Theatre, Nashville --- 2 Days Com.

FRIDAY - FEB. - 24

Paul Reno
············ Offers ············

MAXINE'S BALLYHOO REVUE

9 Vodvil Acts
Girls ▾ Gowns ▾ Dancers
Comedians

Memphis Syncopaters
STAGE BAND

What A Show!

Ohio State University Libraries
Jerome Lawrence and Robert E. Lee Theatre Research Institute

The Curtiss Show Print Collection

DONATED by Nyle Stateler to the Ohio State University Libraries' Jerome Lawrence and Robert E. Lee Theatre Research Institute, the Curtiss Show Print Collection is a remarkable record documenting the beautiful letterpress work done by the company for its show business clients. Curtiss Show Print began in Kalida, Ohio, in 1905, but founder Bill Curtiss moved his printing business to nearby Continental, Ohio, to take advantage of its location and access to the railroad. The shop specialized in turning orders around very quickly and gained a reputation among its show business clients for fast and excellent work. The more than 1,200 printing blocks, as well as photographs, correspondence, job tickets, ledgers, and colorful print materials including posters, window cards, heralds, tickets, ads, and letterhead stationery, tell not only the story of the show printer, but also the history and legacy of traveling companies in the early to mid-20th century. Vaudeville and tent repertoire companies including the Ohio-based Kinsey Komedy Kompany, minstrel shows such as Shufflin' Sam From Alabam', *Uncle Tom's Cabin* companies, Mysterious Brown and other magicians, numerous circuses, and other touring companies took Curtiss printing around the country. Today that printing provides a visual glimpse of what entertained America.

A young Nyle Stateler took a job at Curtiss Show Print in 1941, learning to do setup, layout, and printing. With a brief hiatus for military service during World War II, he has spent his entire career working for, and later owning, Curtiss Show Print. He and his wife Helen continue to keep the shop and all its presses, including a linotype machine, running and busy.

The Curtiss Show Print Collection was given to the Ohio State University in the summer of 2006 and immediately began to receive significant attention and use. In fall 2006, the printing blocks and posters formed the core hands-on project for a class of theater graduate students who created catalog records, selected pieces, and wrote captions for an exhibition on display at the Lawrence and Lee Institute in 2007. The final class meeting for this project was held in the Ohio State University Libraries' Center for Book Arts/Logan Elm Press where book arts specialist Robert Tauber demonstrated the printing process by printing on hand presses from selected Curtiss blocks. While collection processing is still underway, the Curtiss Show Print Collection has already been used by theater and dance students for research on minstrel shows and show girls. The Curtiss Show Print Web page highlights examples of the rich holdings of the collection, documents collection processing work, and will be joined by a digital video story of the business and the collection.

In 2005, Nyle Stateler and Curtiss Show Print were the focus of an award-winning documentary, *Continental, Ohio*, produced by Murphy & Associates Inc. and WOSU-TV. *Continental, Ohio*, received the 2005 Midwestern Regional Emmy Award for a documentary program. The Curtiss Show Print Collection was the subject of a January 2007 article in *OnCampus*, the university-wide newspaper.

http://library.osu.edu/sites/tri/exhibits/Curtiss.php

(ABOVE TOP)
"Dancing Girl and Stage Band in Silhouette."
Printing block. N.d.

 This printing block was used in Curtiss Show Print printed materials, including Maxine's Ballyhoo Revue.

(ABOVE BOTTOM LEFT)
"Female Performer in Polka Dots and Umbrella."
Photograph by unknown artist. N.d.

(ABOVE BOTTOM RIGHT)
"Female Performer in Polka Dots and Umbrella."
Original artwork by unknown artist for use in Curtiss Show Print printed materials. N.d.

(OPPOSITE)
"Paul Reno Offers Maxine's Ballyhoo Revue…[and] Memphis Syncopaters Stage Band, Frances Theatre, Dyersburg." Window card printed by Curtiss Show Print. N.d.

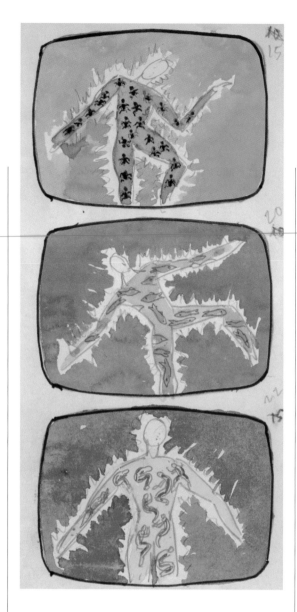

Ohio University Libraries

The Robert E. and Jean R. Mahn Center for Archives and Special Collections

The Alwin Nikolais and Murray Louis Dance Collection

THE Alwin Nikolais and Murray Louis Dance Collection, a dazzling multimedia collection, illustrates 80 years of modern dance in the United States and chronicles the careers of two modern dance icons. Alwin Nikolais (1910–1993), often referred to as the "father of multimedia theater," choreographed dance, composed electronic music, and integrated sets, lighting, slide projections, and costumes for "total theater" dance performances. Murray Louis (1926–), a successful and multi-talented choreographer, dancer, teacher, and writer, collaborated with the National Endowment for the Arts in bringing dance to public school children, and was an innovator in university artists-in-residence programs. Together and separately, the nationally and internationally acclaimed Nikolais and Louis created over 250 choreographic works, as they developed a philosophy of dance and a method of teaching it.

According to the PBS *American Masters* series, "Through their constant experimentation, Alwin Nikolais and Murray Louis have inspired generations of young choreographers to move beyond the limits of contemporary dance…. Among [Nikolais's] many great honors were the 1987 National Medal of Arts awarded by President Ronald Reagan, and the French Ministry of Culture's subsidizing of a school dedicated to his teachings. It is through [the school] and the continued work of Murray Louis that the experimentation of both men remains a challenge to new generations."

Ohio University Libraries' Nikolais and Louis collection contains over 400 cubic feet of primary source materials, extending chronologically from the 1920s through 2006. It includes manuscripts, sound scores, dance notation, photographs, video and audio, posters, programs, and reviews—virtually every artifact produced during the careers of Nikolais and Louis. An openly accessible university Web site dedicated to the collection includes the finding aid and sample images from each of the collection series. Sixteen innovative dances—over five hours of performance—are viewable in streaming video on the Web site.

Murray Louis donated the collection to Ohio University in the late 1990s as a result of his lifelong friendship and artistic collaboration with Gladys Bailin, who danced with Nikolais and Louis and subsequently directed Ohio University's School of Dance.

The collection quickly became a valuable research tool and an inspiration for performers, which is exactly what Murray Louis had in mind when he chose an academic setting for it.

Each year students from Ohio University's History of Dance classes research the collection as a required component of their class projects. Meanwhile, students and faculty from the University's School of Dance, along with researchers and professional dancers from outside of the university, continue to review the collection for both scholarship and performance. Scholarly journals, dance history books, university publications and dance magazines include research from—and reference to—the Alwin Nikolais and Murray Louis Dance Collection. Claudia Gitelman's *The Returns of Alwin Nikolais,* to be published in the spring of 2007, includes essays based on material gleaned from the collection by dance historians.

http://www.library.ohiou.edu/archives/dance/

(ABOVE TOP)
"Performance on the *Steve Allen Show*." Storyboard by Alwin Nikolais. September 28, 1959. Detail.

This storyboard demonstrates the elements that Nikolais incorporated in his "Total Dance Theater."

(OPPOSITE LEFT)
"Girls Trio" from *Vaudeville of the Elements*. Figurine by Nikolais/Louis Foundation for Dance. 1996.

This 3-D costumed figurine from "Girls Trio," from the full-length performance of *Vaudeville of the Elements*, was used in the opening sequence of the five-part video series, *The World of Alwin Nikolais*.

(OPPOSITE RIGHT)
"Girls Trio" from *Vaudeville of the Elements*. Photograph by Milt Oleaga. 1965. Detail.

The Galileo Collection

IN 1949, oil magnate and bibliophile Everette Lee DeGolyer loaned 129 of the landmark volumes that he had collected in the history of science to his alma mater, the University of Oklahoma. He promised to give these books and others to the university only if it would agree to establish a program in the history of science. He insisted that he wanted the books to be used by students, scholars, and all who appreciated the importance of these books to our cultural heritage. In 1949, there were only three programs in the history of science in the United States— at Harvard, Cornell, and Wisconsin. The University of Oklahoma hired a young Harvard PhD, Duane Roller, to establish its program in 1954. Under his watch, a Department of the History of Science was initiated and the History of Science Collections grew rapidly.

The first book DeGolyer gave the University of Oklahoma was a first edition of Galileo's *Dialogo*, a copy which Galileo himself corrected. The corrections were incorporated in the second edition, also owned by the collections. Upon arriving at the university, Duane Roller wrote a letter to Mr. DeGolyer asking about the provenance of the *Dialogo*. DeGolyer replied that he had purchased it in Rome from a bookseller whom he did not trust. He paid $1,000 for the book. The only way of assuring the authenticity of the handwriting was to ask an expert to validate it. Galileo scholar Stillman Drake was invited to the university and validated the handwriting.

The *Dialogo* is one of four of the collections' twelve first editions of Galileo's works. Galileo's first book, *Le operazioni del compasso geometrico* (1606), and his second, *Difesa di Galileo Galilei Lettore delle matematiche nello studio di Padoua* (1607), also contain his handwriting, as does the presentation copy of *Sidereus nuncius* (1610).

The Galileo Collection includes more than 470 books by or about Galileo as well as about 60 items associated with the *Accademia dei Lincei,* an early scientific society that claimed Galileo as one of its most notable members. The Galileo Collection has played a prominent role in the library's research and public service activities, including its support of the research and teaching mission of the Department of the History of Science. Visiting scholars from four continents have taken advantage of Mellon Travel Fellowships to visit the collections. The Galileo Collection was placed on special exhibit in the History of Science Collections during the autumn of 2002.

The collections' curator and librarian illustrate their classes and tours with items from the Galileo Collection several times each week. They provide numerous presentations about the collection both nationally and internationally. The librarian developed a teaching Web site showing a concise overview of Galileo's life and the significance of the *Accademia dei Lincei.* The *Lynx*, newsletter of the History of Science Collections, described the *Accademia dei Lincei* and the Galileo Collection in its first issue (2002).

http://libraries.ou.edu/hsci/

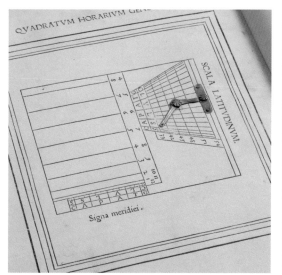

(ABOVE TOP)
"Volvelle." In *Kalendarium.* Johannes Mueller (Regiomontanus). 1476.

The position of the Moon could be determined using this volvelle, a circular calculating device.

(ABOVE BOTTOM)
"Sundial." In *Kalendarium.* Johannes Mueller (Regiomontanus). 1476.

A miniature sundial with a moveable brass pointer adorns this page.

(OPPOSITE)
"Volvelle." In *Kalendarium.* Johannes Mueller (Regiomontanus). 1476. Detail.

Angie Debo Papers

When I start on a research project I have no idea how it will turn out. I simply want to dig out the truth and record it…. Once I felt that when this truth was uncovered and made known, my job was done. Later I came to see that after my findings were published I had the same obligation to correct abuses as any other citizen.

—Angie Debo

I N 1976, when historian Angie Debo set these words to paper in her essay, "To Establish Justice," she was 86 years old. Grandmotherly in appearance, she spoke not just from the wisdom of age but from the position of a "scholar warrior," someone who uses their immense intelligence to secure justice. Debo's 11th and last book, *Geronimo: The Man, His Time, His Place* (1976) had also been published that year. Her national network of over 250 groups and individuals had, in the years immediately preceding this time, successfully secured water rights for Arizona's Havasupai Indians and title rights for Alaska Natives.

Debo's career as a scholar warrior and as a pioneering ethno-historian is remarkable not just for its outstanding scholarship and its attempt to right injustices, but for having flourished at all in an environment in which women historians were systematically ignored or pushed aside. The winner of the 1934 Dunning Prize of the American Historical Association for her outstanding dissertation, and later first book: *The Rise and Fall of the Choctaw Republic* (1934), Debo could not find stable employment until 1947 when she was hired as curator of maps at the Oklahoma State University Library. By this time she had written a number of other books including *And Still the Waters Run* (1940), documenting the "criminal conspiracy [by whites in Oklahoma] to cheat these Indians out of their land," and *The Road to Disappearance* (1941), a history of the Creek Nation. Both works are considered so authoritative that the federal courts have repeatedly called them the "pre-eminent works in the field" and have used them with the agreement of all parties involved in numerous cases involving American Indian peoples. Repeatedly passed over for jobs that went to less talented men, Debo received many awards and recognitions throughout her career, culminating in the American Historical Association's Award for Scholarly Distinction just before her death at age 98 in 1988. In receiving this award, she became the first woman historian and still the only independent scholar to be so honored.

Since the opening of the Angie Debo Papers in the early 1990s, scholars from around the world have utilized the collection. It consists of the unexpurgated manuscripts and research notes from all of Debo's books and journal articles as well as many of the speeches and papers she presented, extensive personal and business correspondence with a wide array of private citizens and public figures on numerous issues, photographs, personal diaries, newspaper clippings with marginalia, her personal library, and other personal papers including genealogical research on the Debo family.

(ABOVE)
"Final Rolls 1907." Notes by Angie Debo for "The White Man's Land System," chapter 2 of *And Still the Waters Run* (1940).

These handwritten notes are part of the extensive collection of Debo's research for *And Still the Waters Run*. The unexpurgated manuscript was placed with the Oklahoma State University Libraries, not to be read until after Debo's death.

(OPPOSITE)
"Angie Debo in Canyon, Texas." Photograph by unknown artist. 1930s.

Debo used her car to travel throughout Oklahoma and Texas collecting information for her research.

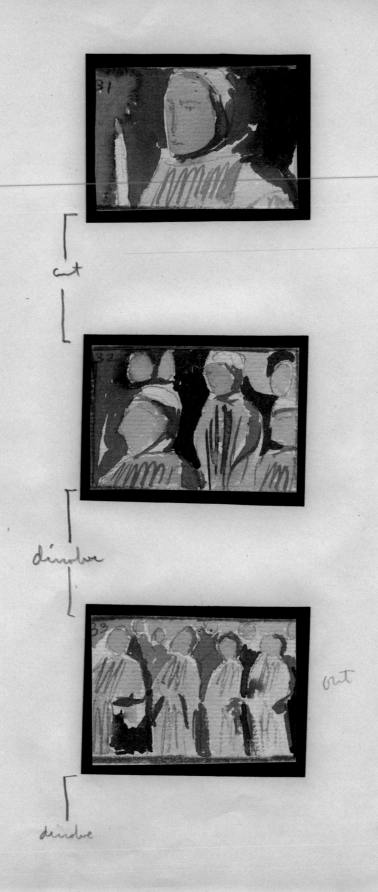

cut

dissolve

dissolve

cut

University of Oregon Libraries
Special Collections and University Archives

James Ivory Papers

IN 2003, film director James Ivory met with a class of aspiring filmmakers at the University of Oregon. "Get the best possible cameraman you can afford," he told them, and "Always try to get your own way." Once a student himself at the UO, graduating in 1951, James Ivory went on to become a major figure in contemporary cinema, establishing a partnership with well-known producer Ismail Merchant and novelist-screenwriter Ruth Prawer Jhabvala, which led to the formation of Merchant Ivory Productions.

The James Ivory Papers in Special Collections and University Archives at the University of Oregon provide a unique through-the-lens look at contemporary filmmaking, the career of a prominent working filmmaker, and the artistic development and process of a creative mind. In 1999, Ivory was formally asked by the library to donate his papers to the University of Oregon. He organized and identified material to fill some 26 boxes that he shipped to the library. His personal remarks, on Post-It notes on many of the papers, give insight and background to many of the documents and will in themselves be of interest to researchers and students of film. The library has a continuing commitment to collect, process, and preserve future materials from James Ivory as he pursues new films and projects.

The James Ivory Papers constitute a remarkable collection of primary source material that documents over 40 years of filmmaking by one of the film industry's oldest and most prestigious companies. Ivory's feature films are lauded for their elegance, beautiful visual imagery, and award-winning actors. Hallmarks too of Ivory films are finely-honed historical detail and extraordinary foreign locations. Actor Christopher Reeve stated simply about Ivory, "He's a terrific judge of what's good and what isn't."

Merchant Ivory Productions include Academy Award winners *A Room with a View, Howards End,* and *Remains of the Day.* For each of his films, every aspect of filmmaking is represented in this collection: location scouting, set design, script writing, actor selection, direction, filming, editing, and publicity. Researchers will find correspondence, notes, sketches, call sheets, original screenplays, photographs, and artifacts. The collection is particularly rich in correspondence between Ivory and major film stars with whom he has worked, including Tom Cruise, Judi Dench, Emma Thompson, John Lithgow, and Vanessa Redgrave.

The James Ivory Papers offer scholars and students a remarkable resource for research in numerous fields of study, including filmmaking, writing, set design, and film production. The Film Studies faculty at the University of Oregon have used the James Ivory Papers as a teaching collection that offers an abundance of primary source material. Film scholars and film buffs alike can search the online finding aid through Northwest Digital Archives and use the collection on site.

To celebrate the acquisition of the James Ivory Papers in 2003, the library mounted an exhibit from the collection. At the opening reception Ivory remarked to a local reporter, "It's good to hear that I wasn't just saving all these things in vain."

(ABOVE)
"Maggie Smith, James Ivory, and Ismail Merchant on the Set of *A Room with a View.*" Photograph by Sarah Quill. 1985.

(OPPOSITE)
Storyboard for *Venice: Theme and Variations.* James Ivory. University of Southern California thesis documentary film. 1953.

University of Pennsylvania Library
Rare Book and Manuscript Library

The Horace Howard Furness Memorial

A UNIVERSITY library collects William Shakespeare? No surprise. But that the main entry for Shakespeare in Penn's catalog gets well over five thousand hits may seem a bit of overkill. Shabby old Milton gets under eight hundred, Dickens six, Chaucer four, Austen two. The Bard appears in industrial strength. Everyone else makes a cameo.

Of course, Penn acquired Shakespeare for years. The Furness Memorial, however, its Shakespeare collection, only arrived in 1931. Horace Howard Furness Jr. gave Penn the library begun by his father. Son and epigone of the Furness who began the New Variorum Shakespeare, Junior had continued the collection and wanted it kept intact, nurtured, and used. He got his wish. Ably curated by several generations of scholars—Matthew W. Black, Matthias A. Shaaber, Roland M. Frye, and Georgianna Ziegler, all assisted by William E. Miller—the collection actively supports in-house study, teaching, and use by Shakespearian students and scholars and, in a digital environment, work independent of physical location. The Furnesses might be surprised. They would not be disappointed.

Currently, a gaggle of Shakespearians and book historians make Furness their laboratory. Advanced study and textual work adjoin teaching. Students, asked to describe 16th-, 17th-, or 18th-century Shakespearian or related texts, learn to recognize kinds of information contained in original and early editions that later, modern editions or facsimiles, however good they may be for Shakespeare's text, cannot provide. Confronting the protean variability of "the text" in edition after edition, they grasp the constructed nature of all mediated texts—of every text with which editors, proofreaders, typesetters, and printers have interfered. Examining how individual words are used in the polyglot resources of Furness and its surrounding rare book and manuscript library, together with the digitized materials that modern research libraries provide their users, students find rich contexts for understanding early modern English, using sources not always themselves in English. Wherever they live, off-site users freely access Penn's Schoenberg Center for Electronic Text and Image. It presents Shakespeare's texts, including various quartos and the 1623 folio; Restoration, 18th-century, and later adaptations or editions; texts from neighboring libraries (such as Marlowe's *Jew of Malta*, 1633); promptbooks; 16th-century anti-theatrical texts; ancillary texts from Ovid and the Bible through the present; costumes; and masses of illustration.

Growth continues, as does use. Keeping current with critical and historical scholarship benefits both students and senior scholars. Nineteenth-century German-language translations, French opera posters, comic books, *manga* Shakespeare, juveniles and novels: all document reception. Sixteenth-century editions—Saxo Grammaticus, Latin school drama—document sources and context. Theatrical posters, playbills from the present as well as previous centuries, various forms of realia—a skull used for Yorick and signed by noted actors, a recently-donated second pair of "Shakespeare's gloves"—all support a collection built not for envious show but for use. Even the skull gets use, recently appearing as Vindice's murdered mistress in a student production of Tourneur's *The Revenger's Tragedy*. Shakespeare lives. So does the Furness Memorial Library.

(ABOVE TOP)
Skull. [Philadelphia, 19th century?]
This skull was used for many years at Philadelphia's Walnut Street Theatre to represent Yorick in productions of *Hamlet*.

(ABOVE BOTTOM)
"Hamlet." Poster by unknown artist. N.d. Gift of Mrs. Edward J. Parker.
This poster advertises Ambroise Thomas's *Hamlet*, an opera in five acts based on Shakespeare's play.

(OPPOSITE)
[William Shakespeare's gloves?] N.d.
Purportedly Shakespeare's gloves—Furness owns two pairs—this pair surfaced at David Garrick's Stratford 1769 Shakespeare Jubilee. Actress Fanny Kemble gave them to Horace Howard Furness Sr. in 1874.

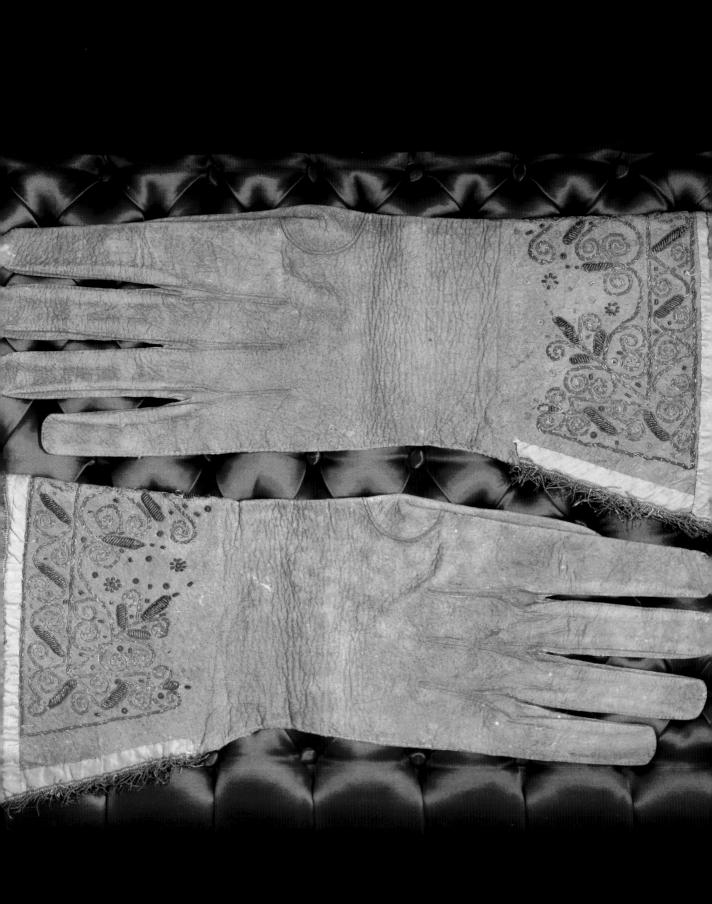

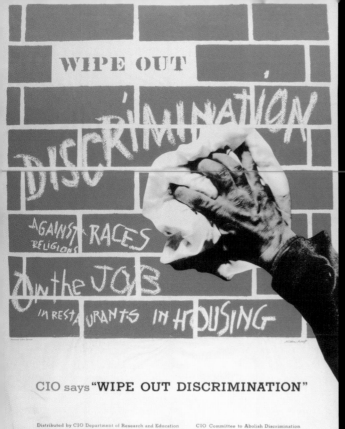

WIPE OUT DISCRIMINATION

DISCRIMINATION

AGAINST RACES RELIGIONS ON the JOB IN RESTAURANTS IN HOUSING

CIO says "WIPE OUT DISCRIMINATION"

Distributed by CIO Department of Research and Education   CIO Committee to Abolish Discrimination

SPEAKING FOR AMERICA

"Sticks and stones can break your bones — and *names* can hurt you, too. The Nazis called names to stir up racial and religious hatred. That was part of their 'divide and conquer' racket. Right now, political gangsters in America are pulling the same trick. We've got to stop them. That's the biggest job ahead of us today."

Frank Sinatra

CIO COMMITTEE TO ABOLISH RACIAL DISCRIMINATION   DISTRIBUTED BY CIO DEPARTMENT OF RESEARCH AND EDUCATION

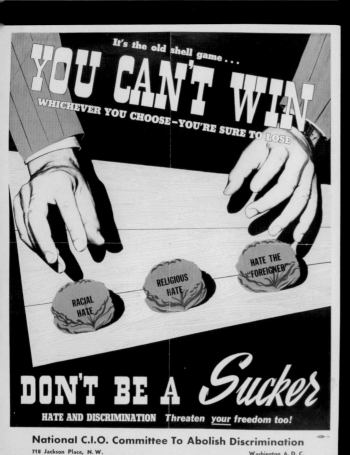

It's the old shell game . . .

YOU CAN'T WIN

WHICHEVER YOU CHOOSE—YOU'RE SURE TO LOSE

RACIAL HATE   RELIGIOUS HATE   HATE THE "FOREIGNER"

DON'T BE A *Sucker*

HATE AND DISCRIMINATION *Threaten your freedom too!*

National C.I.O. Committee To Abolish Discrimination
718 Jackson Place, N. W.   Washington 6, D. C.

KNOCK HIM OUT!

LABOR

DISCRIMINATION

LABOR CAN DO IT

CIO COMMITTEE TO ABOLISH RACIAL DISCRIMINATION   DISTRIBUTED BY CIO DEPARTMENT OF RESEARCH AND EDUCATION

Pennsylvania State University Libraries
Special Collections Library, Historical Collections and Labor Archives

United Steelworkers of America Archive and Oral History Collection

ORIGINATING in a long-standing tradition of service to the education and training of future labor leaders, the Pennsylvania State University and the United Steelworkers of America (USWA) have enjoyed a strong and unique partnership. Since the 1940s, the Steelworkers' presence on campus has been evident in the yearly Summer Labor Institutes and Union Leadership Academies attended by rank-and-file members and prospective union leaders in training. In 1967, the Penn State University Libraries' Historical Collections and Labor Archives (HCLA) became the official repository for the historical records of the USWA. A dedicated Steelworkers' Room was established to feature selections from the union's trove of historical photographic images and memorabilia. From modest beginnings the USWA Archive has become a pre-eminent institutional labor collection for research, attracting national and international scholars from a variety of academic disciplines. The USWA Archive has served as a foundation for HCLA's acquisition of other significant labor holdings to support the academic program of the University's Labor Studies and Industrial Relations Department, among other constituencies.

Dating from the establishment of its predecessor—the Steel Workers Organizing Committee in 1936—the USWA Archive comprises nearly 3,000 cubic feet of records, 554 reels of microfilm, over 150 oral history interviews, and 7,500 items including photographs, film and videos, sound recordings, publications, original graphic art, and a variety of union memorabilia. The most important USWA record groups are the International Executive Board Proceedings and the papers of USWA presidents David J. McDonald, I. W. Abel, and Lloyd McBride. Records of the district and local offices contain valuable documents on organizing, contract negotiations, grievances, and political action at the regional and local levels. The roles played by the USWA professional staff emerge fully from the files of key departments: Arbitration, Civil Rights, Contracts, Education, Housing, International Affairs, Legal, Legislative, Communications, Research, and Health and Safety. The archive also includes a variety of the personal papers of significant figures in steel organizing and the industrial union movement.

The USWA Oral History Collection, which captures the rich collective historical perspectives of former union officers, staff members, and rank-and-file activists, complements the Steelworkers' official records. Researchers have mined the USWA Photograph Archive to illustrate books and other publications, and to incorporate images in exhibitions and documentary projects. The USWA's voluminous film and video collection has also been drawn upon for numerous documentary film productions. The Steelworkers have accessed a variety of media in producing educational and training materials for its own membership.

The USWA Archive has been an invaluable resource for documenting the history of the industrial union movement and the complex issues facing steelworkers and their communities following the decline of steel manufacturing. Researchers have used the collection to study how important social issues such as civil rights, gender equity, and health care continue to shape the workplace. Another prominent theme is union political action activity and its impact upon American politics.

http://www.libraries.psu.edu/speccolls/hcla/steel.html

(ABOVE TOP)
"United Steelworkers of America-CLC-CIO." Lapel pin by unknown artist. From William Garvey Collection. 1952.

(ABOVE BOTTOM)
"Steelworkers Observe Operations of Blast Furnace." Photograph by unknown artist. Pittsburgh, circa early 1960s.

(OPPOSITE TOP LEFT)
"Wipe Out Discrimination." Poster by Milton Ackoff. CIO Committee to Abolish Discrimination, 1949.

(OPPOSITE TOP RIGHT)
"Frank Sinatra, Speaking for America." Poster by unknown artist. CIO Committee to Abolish Racial Discrimination, 1946.

(OPPOSITE BOTTOM LEFT)
"You Can't Win…Don't Be a Sucker." Poster by unknown artist. CIO Committee to Abolish Discrimination, 1949.

(OPPOSITE BOTTOM RIGHT)
"Knock Him Out! Labor Can Do It." Poster by Bernard Seaman. CIO Committee to Abolish Discrimination, 1951.

University of Pittsburgh Libraries
Special Collections Department

Archives of Scientific Philosophy

PHILOSOPHY has long been influenced by scientific research and studies, and its deliberations have frequently followed scientific models. The University of Pittsburgh established itself as a leader in scientific philosophy during the last decades of the 20th century. It was only natural, then, that the university acquire and build resources to support the faculty and students who were committed to scholarly investigations of intellectual currents. So in 1979, the University Library System (ULS) began to acquire traditional research materials, along the lines of personal papers, archives, microfilm, and books that, collectively, became known as the Archives of Scientific Philosophy.

The Rudolf Carnap Collection is perhaps the most widely known collection in the Archives of Scientific Philosophy. Born in 1891, Carnap held positions in Vienna and Prague where he developed the groundwork for his own logical empiricism and where he was an active participant in the Vienna Circle. After he came to the US in 1935, he taught at the University of Chicago and later at UCLA from 1954 until 1970. Carnap made significant contributions in the epistemological foundations of physics and mathematics, the syntactical structure of language, semantics, modal logic, and probability theory. His collection includes over 10,000 pages of letters, much of it with some of the most prominent scholars of his generation, and more than 2,000 books.

The papers of Wilfred Sellars, Carl Gustav Hempel, Frank Ramsey, Rose Rand, Hans Reichenbach, and Bruno de Finetti are also central to the growing body of original materials that comprise the Archives of Scientific Philosophy. Supplementing these resources are microfilm copies of the Ludwig Wittgenstein Collection, Herbert Feigl Collection, and the Archives for the History of Quantum Physics. In addition, the University of Pittsburgh has established a partnership with the University of Konstanz to share copies of key archival materials.

In the fall of 2000, the ULS was instrumental in the development of PhilSci Archive, an open access online archive for more current resources. PhilSci Archive primarily serves as an archive for preprints. It promotes communication in the field of philosophy of science through the quick dissemination of new studies. As the first electronic self-publishing initiative undertaken by the ULS, PhilSci Archive includes nearly 1,300 documents and has branched out to include out-of-print texts in the public domain that are deemed of central importance to the philosophy of science and are actively sought by today's scholars.

Researchers learn about the Archives of Scientific Philosophy through finding aids available through the Web site of the Special Collections Department. Researchers have used the collections for scholarly investigations associated with philosophy, history of science, literature, political science, history, sociology, economics, and educational theory. Their research has led to the publication of books, chapters in books, journal articles, papers delivered at professional meetings, and class papers. Indeed, a "Bibliography of Works Publishing or Citing Material from the Archives of Scientific Philosophy" presently includes over 260 citations, attesting to the strong interest that these materials are to the research community.

Entwicklung der Thesen des "Wiener Kreises"

bearbeitet von Rose Rand, Nov. 1932 bis März 1933.

blau: ja, rot: nein, grün: sinnlos, O: fehlt, ?: unbestimmt.
S.: Schlick, W.: Waismann, C.: Carnap, N.: Neurath, H.: Hahn, K.: Kaufmann.

Thesen		S.W.C.N.H.K
1. Die Philosophie will durch Aufstellung von Regeln die Begriffe und Regeln der Wissenschaft klären.	vor Tract. Tractatus nach Tract.	O O O O O
2. Die Philosophie will die Begriffe und Sätze der Wissenschaft und des täglichen Lebens klären, indem sie zwar keine Regeln des Gebrauchs der Worte vorschreibt, doch die Regeln des Gebrauchs eines Wortes ausbreitet und auf die logischen Folgen einer Regel aufmerksam macht. Schärfer: Die Philosophie gebietet nicht einen bestimmten Gebrauch eines Wortes, doch verbietet sie es die Folgerungen der angenommenen Regeln zu vermischen oder sie nicht zu halten.		
3. Die Sprache bildet die Wi		
4. Die Sprache ist ein Sys verglichen wird. Von e darf nicht gesprochen physischer Begriff ei		
5. Der Satz ist eine Kon ihre Syntax bestimmt		
6. Der Satz bildet den		
7. Der Sinn eines Sat		
8. Die Methode der der Worte, die i werden weiter de		
9. Die Verifikati den Definition das Gegebene d		
1o. Es gibt nur nition durch Erlebnisse i sprechen da		
11. Die Definit		

قوله قولا لذر ابيض شبه زهر الزعفران
واوراق شبه ورق بصل

الزيزوقيل

انه بصل الزيت البري
مشابهه الاوراق لكنه ادهن وقضيبه
طوله شبرا واكثر وفي رأسه ثمرة ات سواد على اصله قشورا كله الى الصابض عضو
حلو مملكه لبناقرثوب هوعته بشبه الخبث ويعلوكذراع وينبت في المواضع الصخره
على جابة البحر والاوراق دهن ما كله الى البياض ما شبه ورق البقل لكنه اعرض منها
واطول وطعمها
مالح ولها زهر ابيض

وله ثمر كالباقلويي
مدور نطيب للرايحه
لينه ويابسه يتلقى واصله هذه الثمرت بذر كالخط واصول عليظ ثلثه او اربع
اصبع وطبى للراحه وثمره قوة
ينفع عصر ابول والبرقان ويدر
الحيض قوله مينى له اوراق
شبه الدلاويه قضبان ذا كهلمنه
على الاعضان لنعا وليهم زهر سفى طيب الرأ
وله ثمر كالعنب لينه حريفة الطعم نوم وصل
هذا يكنو لاستعمله وينبت في اماكن الخل

Princeton University Library
Department of Rare Books and Special Collections

Islamic Manuscripts

AMONG the greatest treasures of the Princeton University Library are some 9,500 Islamic manuscripts, chiefly bound paper codices containing more than 20,000 texts. Princeton's rich holdings constitute the premier collection of Islamic manuscripts in the Western Hemisphere and are among the finest in the world. The collection is located in the Manuscripts Division of the Department of Rare Books and Special Collections, and housed at the Harvey S. Firestone Memorial Library. Robert Garrett collected approximately two-thirds of these manuscripts and donated them to the library in 1942. Since then, the library has continued to acquire manuscripts by gift and purchase. The manuscripts are chiefly in Arabic but also include Persian, Ottoman Turkish, and other languages of the Islamic world. They date from the early centuries of Islam through the fall of the Ottoman Empire. Most of the manuscripts originated in Arabia, Egypt, Syria, Iraq, Iran, and other main centers of Islamic civilization. But there are examples from Moorish Spain and the Maghreb in the West, from the Indian subcontinent and the Indonesian archipelago in the East, and even from sub-Saharan Africa.

Subject coverage is broad and comprehensive, including theology based both on Quran and tradition (*hadith*); Islamic law (*fiqh*); history and biography, especially of the Prophet and other religious leaders; book arts and illustration; language and literature; science; magic and the occult; and other aspects of the intellectual and spiritual life of the Islamic world and its diverse peoples. Representative works of virtually every important Muslim thinker are present. Although textual manuscripts are predominant, there are also illuminated Qurans and Persian literary works, including five Safavid and Qajar manuscripts of Firdawsi's *Shahnamah*, the Persian national epic. The Manuscripts Division also holds Arabic papyri and documents, calligraphy collections, and modern personal papers relating to the Near East. Supporting research in this area are some 300,000 printed volumes in the library's Near Eastern Studies circulating collections.

The Princeton Library has long been committed to making these collections available to researchers worldwide, with access provided by published catalogs, principally those compiled by Philip K. Hitti (1938), Mohammed E. Moghadam and Yahya Armajani (1939), Rudolf Mach (1977), and Rudolf Mach and Eric L. Ormsby (1987). Thousands of additional manuscripts, including most of the Persian and Ottoman Turkish holdings, are described briefly in an online checklist. In order to improve access to these rich collections and share them worldwide through digital technology, the library has recently embarked on a four-year project under the overall direction of Don C. Skemer, the library's Curator of Manuscripts, made possible by generous support from the David A. Gardner '69 Magic Project. The project will produce accurate and consistent cataloging, searchable through Web-based bibliographic utilities, to replace the existing patchwork of printed catalogs. Two full-time Near Eastern Studies project catalogers are already at work. The library has also begun digitizing an initial group of 200 manuscripts, with more to follow, and will make them accessible on the Internet.

http://www.princeton.edu/rbsc/department/manuscripts/islamic.html

(ABOVE)
"Astronomical Work on the Constellations." Manuscript by unknown author. 18th century.

(OPPOSITE)
Botanical manuscript by unknown author. 15th century.

William Freeman Myrick Goss Library of the History of Engineering

Learning to look backward with reverence and to benefit from the successes and failures of the past should enable the engineer to build better today and tomorrow.

— A.A. Potter, Dean of Engineering,
Purdue University, 1947

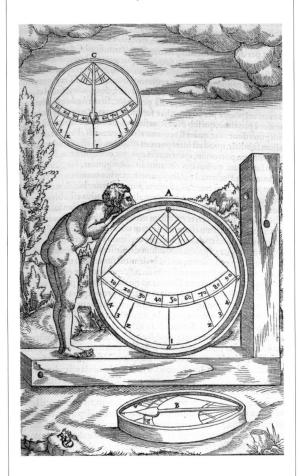

(ABOVE)
"Man Using Carpenter's or Mason's Level." Engraving from *De Re Metallica*. Georg Agricola. 1556. Detail.

(OPPOSITE)
"Whitworths Patent Duplex Lathe for Turning Railway Wheels." Illustration from *The Imperial Cyclopedia of Machinery, Being a Series of Plans, Sections and Elevations of Stationary, Marine and Locomotive Engines, Spinning Machinery, Grinding Mills, Tools &c….* William Johnson. Circa 1852. Detail.

IN 1928 Purdue University received the personal library of former Dean of Engineering William F. M. Goss. The Goss Library comprised approximately 900 volumes related primarily to the history of engineering, with particular emphasis placed on Goss's research on locomotives and the railroads. Soon, the library received an addition of approximately 200 volumes from the collection of former Purdue Professor Michael J. Golden. With the combined libraries of these two former colleagues and friends, the university began to focus on building a major resource on the history of engineering.

In 1930, Mrs. William Goss established an endowment for the Goss Library that ensured its permanence and provided ongoing funds for purchases over time. The Goss Library has also benefited from substantial contributions of books from Purdue alumni, engineers, and friends of the university. By the late 1940s, the collection had grown to 3,500 volumes.

Reflecting the land grant nature of Purdue University, the Goss Library's strengths lie in documenting the history of science, engineering, and technology. From the beginning, emphasis was placed on acquiring items that students and faculty would use to complement the university's curricular interests. The purpose of the Goss Library remains much the same today—to promote a broader interest in the progressive engineering sciences by preserving their early history and present development. The history of transportation is well documented in the collection, particularly the history of railroads, but also canal navigation, hot air balloons, and aviation. Electrical engineering, hydraulics, bridges, metallurgy, mathematics, chemistry, physics, and scientific inventions represent additional subject strengths in the Goss Library.

Items from the collection were featured in the 2004 Purdue exhibition, "Voices That Changed the World." University of Arizona chemistry professor Wayne E. Wesolowski has used the Goss Library for various publications over the years, including several videos for PBS on model railroading. Professor John H. Lienhard has also published using the Goss Collection; his *Engines of Our Ingenuity* (2000) offers an engineer's perspective on technology and culture. Graduate-level English courses at Purdue have studied volumes in the collection, working to translate 16th- to early 20th-century texts in Spanish, Latin, and English, and striving to clarify the relationships between engineering and the liberal arts.

The Goss Library is fully cataloged and can be searched within the Purdue University Libraries online catalog. The collection has been featured in newsletters and brochures, and will be included in an upcoming series of note cards highlighting treasures of the Purdue University Libraries. Select highlights of the Goss Library include: Copernicus's *De Revolutionibus Orbium Caelestium* (1617); Newton's *Philosophiae Naturalis Principia Mathematica* (1714); Descartes' *Geometria* (1659–1661); Euclid's *Opera* [*Megarensis*] (1509); Agricola's *De Re Metallica* (1556); Hero of Alexandria's *Spiritali di Herone Alessandrino* (1592); and Agostino Ramelli's *Le Diverse et Artificiose Machine del Capitano Agostino Ramelli* (1588).

– 2 –

Those for IF I WERE PAN.

The outward feature of the haunting soul,
If I were Pan upon a day in spring,
The yeil that hides the mystery, --
In some remote ravi...ls,
The fragrant ...
When th... spring.
...the sky
...
... rainy
...ire,
...
...mould.
...ks

If I were Pan.

I.

If I were Pan upon a day in spring,
e morning when the gold was in the Sky,
a remote ravine among the hills,
Slowly as the purple of the peaks
issolved before the footfall of the Sun,
I would emerge and take on form and voice
...myself the dreamer and the dream.

Edith and Lorne Pierce Canadiana Collection and
Lorne and Edith Pierce Collection of Canadian Manuscripts

LORNE Pierce (1890–1961) devoted his life to the promotion of Canadian literature. As an ordained minister; founding member of the Canadian Authors Association, the Bibliographical Society of Canada, and the Art Gallery of Ontario; member of the Champlain Society and the Arts and Letters Club; Fellow of the Royal Society of Canada; literary executor for the poet Bliss Carman; private book collector and editor of the Ryerson Press from 1920 to 1960, Dr. Pierce had a broad knowledge of Canadian history, culture and the book industry. He knew many of the early Canadian poets and novelists and was eager to build a strong Canadian collection at his alma mater.

Pierce began to donate books to Queen's in 1928, established an endowed fund for the future development of holdings, and bequeathed his personal library and papers—including his correspondence as editor of Ryerson Press—to the university. Since then, Queen's curators, archivists, and faculty working in the area of Canadian Studies have built on this strong base.

When Special Collections was established, Dr. Pierce's gifts formed the nucleus of what became known as the Edith and Lorne Pierce Collection of Canadiana. The literary component of the collection includes the works of poets and authors Bliss Carman, Major John Richardson, Charles G. D. Roberts, William Kirby, Archibald Lampman, Thomas Chandler Haliburton, and F. P. Grove and incorporates a number of literary sub-collections including the libraries of writers John Glassco, George Whalley, Mazo de la Roche, and F .R. Scott.

Over the same period, one of the largest collections of literary papers in Canada has been developed by Queen's University Archives, beginning with the gift of the Lorne Pierce Papers. Nearly every Canadian literary figure of note for the period 1920 to 1960 is represented by at least some manuscript material in the collection. Highlights include the letters and manuscripts of William Wilfred Campbell, John Richardson, William Kirby, Wilson Macdonald, Charles G. D. Roberts, and Marjorie Pickthall. Also represented are the papers of Raymond Knister, Duncan Campbell Scott, Archibald Lampman, Camille Roy, Stephen Leacock, Marius Barbeau, Earle Birney, A. J. Pratt, and Al Purdy along with some papers of the artists J. E. H. Macdonald, A. Y. Jackson, C. W. Jeffreys, and Thoreau Macdonald. This invaluable resource for the study of Canadian literature has been supplemented with numerous collections in recent years— including George Woodcock, Al Purdy, Hugh Garner, Dorothy Livesay, Ralph Gustafson, the Oberon Press fonds, and a large portion of the Bliss Carman fonds. The collection was enriched in 1989 when Beth Pierce Robinson, Lorne Pierce's daughter, donated a collection of correspondence, subject files, material relating to Canadian writers, photographs, and writings of her father.

The Canadiana collections held in the Jordan Library and the University Archives have been recognized as among the best in the world. These collections support and stimulate research to the post-doctoral level, as well as garnering interest from other parts of Canada and abroad.

(ABOVE)
"Bliss Carman." Photograph by unknown artist. Late 19th–early 20th century.

(OPPOSITE)
"If I Were Pan." Holographic manuscript and typescript of unpublished poem by Bliss Carman. N.d. Detail.

University of Rochester Libraries

Department of Rare Books, Special Collections and Preservation

William Henry Seward Papers

THE size and scope of the William Henry Seward Papers, along with the quality of the materials it contains, not only makes it the crown jewel in the special collections at the University of Rochester but also places it in the top rank of major historical 19th-century manuscript collections in this country. The collection, the largest extant Seward archive, documents Seward's career over a 50-year period and constitutes an invaluable resource for the study of mid-19th-century American political, diplomatic, and social history. Containing over 160,000 items with more than 60,000 pieces of correspondence, the collection was given to the library by the Seward family starting in 1945, and then, in 1951, by the bequest of William Henry Seward III, Seward's grandson. In addition to the public, private, and family correspondence of William Henry Seward and his immediate family, the collection is comprised of files from Seward's term as governor of New York State (1839–1842); as Senator from New York (1849–1861); as Secretary of State under Presidents Lincoln and Johnson (1861–1869); personal financial and legal records; speeches, proclamations, diaries, and secondary printed material and memorabilia relating to his life and career.

The collection also contains the personal papers of Seward's wife Frances Adeline (Miller) Seward, a Quaker, abolitionist, and major influence on Seward's political and social beliefs. The correspondence of his three sons, Augustus, Frederick, and William Henry Jr., his daughter, Frances (Fanny) Adeline, and his daughter-in-law Janet McNeil (Watson) Seward can also be found here.

As can be expected with a collection of this size and historical importance, within the papers there exist several "special" special collections. Most notably: 80 letters, notes, memoranda, and documents from Abraham Lincoln to Seward, added to the collection in 1987; the diaries of daughter Fanny Seward, started at the age of 14 and continued until her death at the age of 22, which include her impressions of Washington political life during the war years as well as her personal account of the attempted assassination of her father as part of the Lincoln assassination conspiracy; a collection of over 1,000 letters exchanged between the Seward and Miller families that provide a fascinating glimpse into mid-late 19th-century family life; and a collection of over 3,000 rare pamphlets dealing with the controversial issues of the day—slavery, abolitionism, foreign policy, and so forth.

In addition to being the focus of exhibits and presentations to undergraduates, the William Henry Seward Papers continue to provide primary source material for books, doctoral dissertations, master's theses, and scholarly articles. Doris Kearns Goodwin recently used the collection while researching her book, *Team of Rivals: The Political Genius of Abraham Lincoln* (2005).

The collection is featured in the department's online exhibit "150 Years, 150 Treasures: An Exhibit in Honor of the University's Sesquicentennial." In 2007, the library began its Lincoln Letters Online Project, which will include digital facsimiles and transcriptions of Seward letters and documents selected from the collection. Both print and online finding aids are available:

http://www.library.rochester.edu/index.cfm?page=1136

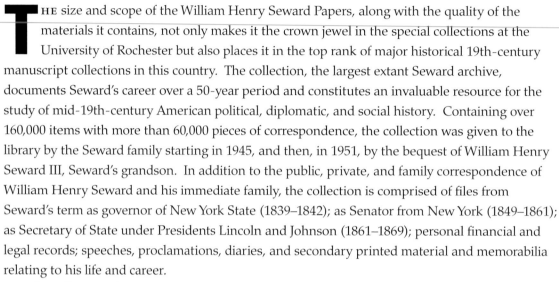

(ABOVE TOP)
Engraved gold cigar box with views of Alaska. Unknown artist. N.d.

In 1869 Seward stopped in San Francisco, where the Pioneer Society of California presented him with this cigar box.

(ABOVE BOTTOM)
"William Henry Seward." Portrait by unknown artist. N.d.

(OPPOSITE LEFT)
Letter from Abraham Lincoln to William Henry Seward. December 8, 1860.

In this formal letter, Lincoln offers Seward the position of Secretary of State.

(OPPOSITE RIGHT)
Letter from Abraham Lincoln to William Henry Seward. April 14, 1865.

Lincoln was assassinated later that day.

Springfield, Ills. Dec. 8. 1860

My dear Sir:

With your permission, I shall, at the proper time, nominate you to the Senate, for confirmation, as Secretary of State, for the United States.

Please let me hear from you at your own earliest convenience—

Your friend, and obedient servant

A. Lincoln.

Hon. William H. Seward.
Washington
D. C.

Washington, April 14. 1865.

Hon. Sec. of State
Sir:

Please assemble the Cabinet at 11. A.M. to-day, Gen. Grant will meet with us.

Yours truly

A. Lincoln

Rutgers University Libraries
Institute of Jazz Studies

Jazz Oral History Project Collection

I N praising a jazz performance, musicians often use the phrase "telling a story," or playing a solo that has a narrative or vocal quality. The Jazz Oral History Project Collection of the Institute of Jazz Studies is where 120 leading jazz artists literally "told their stories," not in music but in words. Over the past two decades, this collection has been used by countless media productions both in the US and abroad—from Ken Burns's *Jazz* to National Public Radio's *Jazz Profiles*, Public Radio International's *Riverwalk Jazz*, BBC radio and television, and Japanese television. It is the most comprehensive and widely consulted body of jazz oral histories extant.

The Jazz Oral History Project (JOHP) was initiated in 1972 by the Jazz Advisory Panel of the Music Program of the National Endowment for the Arts. Musicians 60 years and older (as well as several younger artists in poor health) were interviewed in depth about their lives and careers. The taped interviews range in length from five to thirty-five hours and are accompanied by typed transcripts. The Institute of Jazz Studies assumed administration and archiving of the JOHP in 1979 and conducted further interviews, as well as editing transcripts of prior interviews.

Participants included not only such luminaries as Roy Eldridge, Teddy Wilson, Count Basie, Mary Lou Williams, and Charles Mingus, but also many significant if lesser-known figures, whose stories exist only here. Beyond their obvious value in tracing the history of jazz, the interviews offer insights into many other aspects of 20th-century American life, race relations and the struggle for civil rights, the vagaries of the music business, the Great Depression, Prohibition and other aspects of social history, as well as life "on the road."

Some subjects were quite advanced in age at the time of their interviews and represent a direct link to the music's often obscure origins. Of special interest are such pioneers as Arthur Briggs, who went to Europe with Will Marion Cook in 1919 and remained active there for seven decades; Sam Wooding, whose band made history in Europe from 1924 to 1934; Reb Spikes (90 when interviewed), a close associate of Jelly Roll Morton and among the first to bring jazz to California in the first decade of the 20th century; and veteran New Orleans bassist Ed Garland, also a nonagenarian when interviewed.

By the late 1990s, the condition of the original reel-to-reel and cassette tapes and even of some of the service copies had deteriorated to the point where it was no longer possible to offer access to large parts of the collection. With NEH funding, a project to digitize all the interviews for both preservation and access was completed in 2006.

Of the 120 seminal pre-Swing and Swing Era artists interviewed between 1972 and 1983, only two survive as of 2007. Through the collection, however, they all continue to tell their stories.

http://newarkwww.rutgers.edu/IJS/OralHistory.html

(ABOVE)
"Mary Lou Williams." Photograph by unknown artist. Circa early 1930s.

(OPPOSITE)
"Count Basie Meets and Signs Autographs for Fans." Photograph by unknown artist. Early to mid-1940s.

University of Saskatchewan Library
Veterinary Medicine Library

Rosen Collection of Veterinary Medicine History

A BEAUTIFUL oak box with a brass stomach pump and accompanying parts, including an ebony mouth gag, in an antique store window caught the attention of Dr. Jack Rosen, and subsequently launched for him a 30-year adventure collecting veterinary medicine books and memorabilia. Dr. Rosen first became interested in history as a student while attending the Ontario Veterinary College; this interest naturally developed into a desire to learn more about the history of his own profession. When the time was right to transfer his private collection to a public venue, Dr. Rosen sought out a library attached to a Canadian veterinary college that would keep the collection together and make it available for study by interested patrons: his search ultimately led him to the University of Saskatchewan's Western College of Veterinary Medicine Library, which became the home of his specialized collection in 2004.

The Rosen Collection of Veterinary Medicine History consists of approximately 500 books, journals, newsletters, family records, offprints, pamphlets, clippings, certificates, and awards reflecting the history of veterinary medicine and agriculture from the early 16th to the mid-20th centuries, both in North America and Europe. The oldest book in the collection is a 1528 printing of *Libri de re rustica*, an anthology of ancient Greek and Roman agricultural manuscripts. This copy has been re-bound and is in perfect condition.

Dr Rosen's particular interest in the history of veterinary medicine lies in the use of the existing store of knowledge as one means to improve modern professional practice, an approach exemplified in the following item in the collection, *A Treatise on the Prevention of Diseases Incidental to Horses*, written in 1788 by J. Clark, who proposes a paradigm linking good hygiene and animal health.

The Rosen Collection also provides a glimpse of the birth pangs of the profession of veterinary medicine in Canada in the form of a diploma and textbook, *Veterinary Science: The Anatomy, Diseases and Treatment of Domestic Animals*, both of which were issued by a diploma mill that operated from 1896 to 1921 in London, Ontario. Although the American Veterinary Medical Association (AVMA) had already been formed in 1863 in the United States, specialized training for veterinary personnel was not available in Canada until 1862 when Andrew Smith, a graduate of the University of Edinburgh's College of Veterinary Medicine, established a two-year training course in Toronto to counteract the trend of farriers in Canada providing veterinary services without specialized training.

Interested patrons may view the Rosen Collection either in a rare books room at the Veterinary Medicine Library or at a rotating display in the Veterinary College. It is the library's intention to fill in the gaps that exist in the veterinary history collection, although, according to an independent evaluator, the collection is focused and nearly complete. Because the collection is new to the library, plans are also in development to publicize its existence beyond the veterinary college and hopefully attract scholars and interested users from other disciplines on campus and abroad.

71.—Laagers in Open Country.

1. The best formation for this purpose is that of a hollow square, animals inwards, the wagons arranged axletree to axletree as closely as possible, the corners of the laager being protected by drawing up the corner wagons obliquely so as to round off the angle.

2. There are various methods by means of which laagers may be formed, the details of which depend on the configuration of the ground, march formation, &c. Plates X, XI, and XII are examples for guidance.

The formation of laagers in open country is to be frequently practised where suitable ground exists.

72.—Protection that can be Obtained on Roads.

A convoy confined to the road is peculiarly liable to confusion and disaster in case of attack, as a few horses killed may seriously hamper the advance or retreat. The chief object is to protect the horses from fire, which is most easily done by using the wagons as a screen.

Fig. 4 represents a convoy moving along a road in column of route. In case of sudden attack the wagons are inclined across the road, and closed up as much as possible, thus affording fairly good cover to the horses. This plan is very simple and easy to carry out, but requires with pairs a road 20 feet wide, and, of course, more with teams.

Fig. 5 represents a convoy advancing in double column on a wide road and attacked on both flanks. In this case the wagons incline inwards, till the horses' heads meet, and cover is thus given to both teams and drivers by the loaded wagons. A road 35 feet wide is wanted for this formation, and a corresponding increase with teams. This plan is very handy for two-wheeled carts, as they can form up on a much

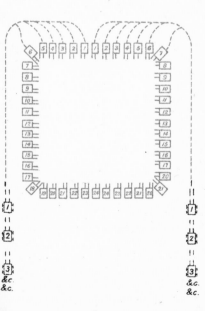

PLATE X.

EVOLUTION IN BATHS.

A & O. "VEDORA" BATH.

The Super Elto 1927

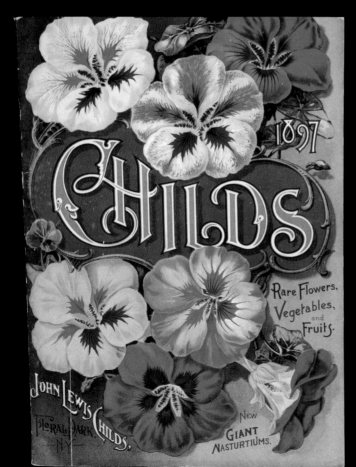

1897

CHILDS

Rare Flowers, Vegetables, and Fruits.

JOHN LEWIS CHILDS.
Floral Park. N.Y.

New GIANT NASTURTIUMS.

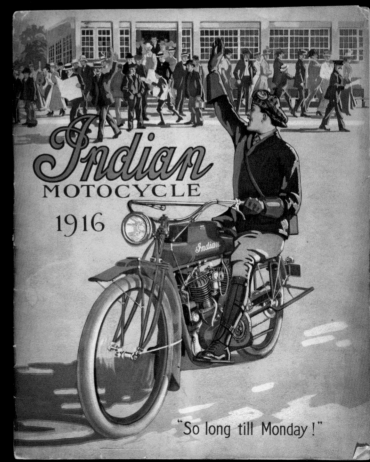

Indian MOTOCYCLE 1916

"So long till Monday!"

The Trade Literature Collection

WHAT did assembly lines look like before Henry Ford's methods standardized them? As the United States underwent intense industrialization in the period 1870 to 1930, how were women workers portrayed in industry literature? You have acquired a very old foot-operated treadmill sewing machine with the words "Domestic Sewing Machine Co." on it. As a curator, you would like to refurbish it, but what parts are missing? Are there seed/nursery catalogs from around 1910 that would verify the original layout of the Biltmore Estate gardens?

The Smithsonian Institution Libraries curates one of the most unusual collections, trade literature: the trade catalogs and books that were part of the merchandising of American business. There are trade catalogs throughout the Smithsonian's libraries; a substantial collection is at the Cooper Hewitt National Design Museum library in New York City but most are housed in Washington, DC, at the National Museum of American History, Kenneth E. Behring Center. A Smithsonian curator estimates that fully half the information in this collection is unavailable elsewhere.

"Trade catalog" derives from the expression "to the trade," and the materials were originally produced by manufacturers and wholesalers for their salesmen to market to retailers. The Trade Literature Collection is internationally known as an extraordinary source for the history of American business, technology, marketing, consumption, and design. Trade literature includes printed or handwritten documents, usually illustrated, of items offered for sale, ranging in size from small pamphlets to oversized folios of several hundred pages. The Smithsonian collection contains more than 500,000 catalogs, technical manuals, advertising brochures, price lists, company histories, and related materials, representing more than 30,000 companies. The largest single component, primarily dealing with engineering and industry, was a gift from Columbia University. Other large collections came from the US Patent Office, Harvard University, and the Center for Research Libraries and were augmented with private collections, such as the Mel Heinz collection on machine tools and metal working and the W. Atlee Burpee and the J. Horace McFarland Collections of seed and nursery catalogs. In the early 1990s, the libraries purchased over 56,000 catalogs that had been originally owned by Philadelphia's Franklin Institute.

Researchers use the trade literature collection to determine the history of companies or individual industries, identify design styles from furniture to machinery, analyze marketing and management techniques, learn how products operated, and study their impacts on society. Since the trade literature collection covers a wide variety of American manufactured goods, it is invaluable in documenting objects in museum collections. Historians, collectors, historical preservationists, authors, industrial designers, home renovators, and patent lawyers are among the most frequent users.

Whereas contemporary catalogs are printed in the millions and distributed to consumers through the mail, early trade literature exists only in libraries. The Smithsonian Libraries is committed to cataloging and digitizing this priceless collection. Two substantial collections of sewing machine and scientific instrument catalogs are available online:

http://www.sil.si.edu/DigitalCollections/Trade-Literature/Sewing-Machines/

http://www.sil.si.edu/DigitalCollections/Trade-Literature/Scientific-instruments/

(ABOVE)
Burpee's Farm Annual [seed catalog].
W. Atlee Burpee & Co., 1908.

(OPPOSITE TOP LEFT)
Evolution in Baths [trade catalog].
Ahrens & Ott Manufacturing Co., 1896.

(OPPOSITE TOP RIGHT)
The Super Elto 1927 [trade catalog]. Milwaukee:
Elto Outboard Motor Company, 1927.

(OPPOSITE BOTTOM LEFT)
Childs Rare Flowers, Vegetables, and Fruits [seed catalog].
John Lewis Childs (lithography by H.M. Wall).
Floral Park, New York: Mayflower Presses, 1897.

(OPPOSITE BOTTOM RIGHT)
Indian Motocycle 1916. Springfield, Massachusetts:
Hendee Manufacturing Co., 1916.

University of South Carolina Libraries
Department of Rare Books and Special Collections

Audubon's *Birds of America*

(ABOVE)
"Snowy Heron or White Egret." Painted in Charleston
in 1832 by John James Audubon and George Lehman.
Engraved by Havell. From *Birds of America*, v. 3. 1835.

> Lehman's background depicts a South Carolina
> low-country plantation.

(OPPOSITE)
"Bachman's Warbler." Painted in Charleston in 1833 by
John James Audubon and Maria Martin. From *Birds of
America*, v. 2. 1833.

> Both Audubon's painting of the bird (not sighted
> again in South Carolina until 1901) and Maria Martin's
> painting of the plant Franklinia (long believed extinct
> in the wild) preserve unique scientific evidence.

I N October 1831, William Campbell Preston, a graduate and trustee of South Carolina College, was traveling south by coach from Richmond. Among his fellow-passengers was a tall bearded artist, hunting subscribers for a massive new publishing project. It was John James Audubon, who wrote to his wife, "Col. Preston thinks that the College at least will subscribe." On December 17, 1831, lobbied hard by Audubon's Charleston ally John Bachman, the South Carolina House narrowly agreed (Yeas 51, Nays 50) to purchase Audubon's Birds of America, for $800 (the final cost was $925.50). It was an act of faith, as only 125 of an eventual 435 plates were yet available, and it was the first definite commitment by any American state to purchase the greatest of American illustrated books. The final numbers arrived from Charleston by ox-cart in 1838.

Audubon's *Birds of America* was originally a work of science. Bachman wrote that it "will be a standard work for centuries; ere then, we will be among the planets studying something else." It remains distinctive in four ways: its ambition, because it aimed to provide life-size engravings of all known North American bird species; the quality of its hand-colored engravings (for the engravings, Audubon went to Britain, first to Lizars of Edinburgh and then Havell in London); its size, "double-elephant folio," about 28 by 40 inches; and the extraordinary price that sets have commanded at auction. Of fewer than 200 sets produced, 120 survive complete, 33 are in ARL libraries, though only three ARL universities (South Carolina, Harvard, and Columbia) were among the original subscribers.

Libraries differ from museums in providing a research context for their treasures. The 1831 legislative committee asserted that "the College library already contains all other works on American ornithology," so that Audubon's work "is necessary to perfect the class of work on that subject." The college did purchase many of the relevant contemporary books and journals, and others have been added since. Ornithological holdings range from Belon, Aldrovandi, and Jonston in the Renaissance, through Willughby, Catesby, and Edwards, to such contemporaries as Wilson, Selby, and Gould. The collection includes Audubon's other works including his *Ornithological Biography*, his *Synopsis*, the *Vivaparous Quadrupeds* donated by Governor Adams in the 1850s, and a variety of octavo editions, as well as books about him. Additional individual engravings, including examples by Lizars, Havells, and Biens, were donated in the 1970s by Jennie Haddock Feagle. Related recent gifts have included the Emily Pope Brown collection of natural history watercolors, the C. Warren Irvin Jr. Collection of Charles Darwin, and Bachman and Audubon manuscripts donated by James P. Barrow. Other natural history collections include botanical books from the Richard Wingate Lloyd and Phelps Memorial Collections and watercolors by the lepidopeterist John Abbot.

The Havell Audubon is now valued and studied, not as science, but as art. Recent growth in South Carolina's special collections has focused on other areas, notably literature and history. Nonetheless, the landmark acquisition of 1831 resonates as a continual reminder that a single major purchase can have a lasting influence in the development of a library and the university it serves.

PLATE. CLXXXV.

Drawn from Nature by J.J.Audubon. F.R.S.F.L.S.   *Bachmans Warbler.* SYLVIA BACHMANII. *And. Male. 1. Female. 2.   Gordonia pubescens.*   Engraved, Printed, & Coloured by R.Havell. 1833.

University of Southern California Libraries
Special Collections

Shoah Foundation Institute Visual History Archive

I N 1994, after completing the film Schindler's List, Steven Spielberg established the Survivors of the Shoah Visual History Foundation to document the experiences of survivors and other witnesses of the Holocaust. From 56 countries and in 32 languages, men and women recounted their life histories, including the suffering and horrors they witnessed and experienced during the Holocaust between 1933 and 1945. Videotaped testimonies from every corner of the world streamed into the foundation's Los Angeles office, where they were digitized and indexed.

In total, the Shoah Foundation collected nearly 52,000 video interviews, creating the largest archive of its kind and preserving a vast well of primary research material. In January 2006, the foundation and its archive became part of the University of Southern California.

The testimonies contained in the Visual History Archive represent a diversity of experiences and perspectives. Interviewees include Jewish survivors, rescuers, liberators, political prisoners, Sinti and Roma survivors, Jehovah's Witness survivors, participants in war crimes trials, survivors of eugenics policies, and homosexual survivors.

In their interviews, survivors and witnesses speak about their lives before, during, and after the Holocaust. At the conclusion of their interviews, they show photographs, documents, and artifacts on camera. Several hundred interviews contain literary and musical performances or displays of artwork. More than 150 interviews were given by survivors and witnesses at sites of former concentration camps, ghettos, and mass graves.

The archive is international in scope. Nearly 20,000 interviews were conducted in the United States, 8,500 in Israel, and more than 3,000 in Ukraine. Other interview locations included Canada, Australia, South Africa, and countries in South and Central America and in western, central, and eastern Europe. Almost 25,000 interviews were conducted in English, while more than 7,000 were given in Russian, and over 6,000 in Hebrew, among other languages.

The testimonies were indexed such that users can search the more than 50,000 subject keywords and one million personal name records that are linked to time codes in the video. This creates rich and varied avenues of electronic access, allowing researchers to find, for example, specific geographical locations; descriptions of prewar education and religious observance; eye-witness accounts of camps, ghettos, mass executions, and resistance groups; personal experiences of postwar immigration; and the names of family members, friends, victims, or perpetrators.

In addition to USC students and faculty, scholars, genealogists, documentary film makers, exhibition organizers, writers, journalists, and the public regularly use the archive for research purposes. With its partners worldwide, the USC Shoah Foundation Institute for Visual History and Education utilizes the archive to develop educational programs for use in secondary schools in many countries and languages. USC Libraries Special Collections and the institute share resources to maintain, develop, and promote public access to the Visual History Archive.

http://www.usc.edu/libraries/vha/

(ABOVE)
"Aaron Rosenzweig [center] Introducing Family Members." Frame from video by unknown artist. N.d.
  Rosenzweig survived the Piotrków ghetto in Poland and several camps.

(OPPOSITE: LEFT TO RIGHT; TOP TO BOTTOM)
"Boris Brauer." Frame from video by unknown artist. N.d.
  Brauer, who was deported by the Soviets to Siberia, was released to join the Soviet Army and liberated the Stutthof concentration camp.
"Halyna Chernii." Frame from video by unknown artist. N.d.
  Chernii's family hid Jews in the village of Novaia Tsybulevka in Ukraine.
"Edith Coliver." Frame from video by unknown artist. N.d.
  Coliver, a refugee from Nazi Germany, later worked for the prosecution in the Nuremberg Trials.
"Floyd Dade." Frame from video by unknown artist. N.d.
  Dade liberated the Gunskirchen concentration camp with the US Army.
"Mara D'iakova's Parents." Fragment of last surviving photograph. Frame from video by unknown artist. N.d.
"Kamil Fischl." Frame from video by unknown artist. N.d.
  Fischl, one of the oldest interviewees in the archive (born 1894), fled from Czechoslovakia to Palestine after the German invasion.
"Dina Gottliebova-Babbitt." Frame from video by unknown artist. N.d.
  Gottliebova-Babbitt, who survived the Auschwitz-Birkenau death camp, was assigned by Josef Mengele to paint portraits of Sinti and Roma prisoners.
"Siegfried Kersten." Frame from video by unknown artist. N.d.
  Kersten survived Nazi eugenics policies.
"Lutsiah Kornhauzer." Frame from video by unknown artist. N.d.
  Kornhauzer escaped from the Bochnia ghetto in Poland and fled to Slovakia.
"Friderika Krasznai." Frame from video by unknown artist. N.d.
  Krasznai, a Sinti and Roma, survived the Zalaegerszeg ghetto in Hungary.
"Stella Rosenak's Family before the War." Photograph by unknown artist. Frame from video by unknown artist. N.d.
"Henry Rosmarin." Frame from video by unknown artist. N.d.
  Rosmarin's harmonica playing helped him survive the concentration camps.

All images courtesy of the USC Shoah Foundation Institute for Visual History and Education, University of Southern California.

Southern Illinois University Carbondale Library
Special Collections Research Center

Katherine M. Dunham Papers

I N February 1965, the culmination of Katherine Dunham's 11-week period as an Artist-in-Residence at Southern Illinois University Carbondale was a stage performance of Gounod's opera *Faust*. Dunham staged and choreographed the production herself and gave it a unique twist by setting it in World War I Germany. Over the next few years, Dunham would continue to teach as an Artist-in-Residence at Southern Illinois University Carbondale and Southern Illinois University Edwardsville. By September 1965, she would honor Morris Library's Special Collections Research Center (SCRC) by donating her personal and faculty papers highlighting her career through the period of her association with Southern Illinois University Carbondale ending in the late 1960s.

The Katherine Dunham Papers consists of correspondence, writings, scripts, notes on dance techniques, and musical scores that illuminate the extraordinary journey of a woman who changed the face of American modern dance. Her collection documents all aspects of her varied experience as an African-American anthropologist, dancer, choreographer, and educator. Her personal correspondence makes up the bulk of this collection. Among others, notable correspondents include Josephine Baker, Harry Belafonte, Doris Duke, W. C. Handy, Langston Hughes, Eartha Kitt, Butterfly McQueen, Anthony Quinn, and Paul Robeson.

This collection also highlights Dunham's early explorations as an anthropologist in the 1930s when she studied a multitude of movement types and dance forms. However, it is Dunham's focus on the movements and dances of the African diaspora that so influenced her development as a performer, choreographer, and teacher. Her papers also contain examples of music from her field research from Haiti, recorded by Dunham and others. Additionally, the collection consists of photographs documenting Dunham's remarkable career as a performer and choreographer for her company, which introduced African and Caribbean dance movement to the American public, as well as her manuscripts related to her published works *The Dances of Haiti* (1938), *Journey to Accompong* (1946), *Island Possessed* (1969), and *The Negro Dance*.

Dunham's papers provide direct support for teaching and research at SIUC while also serving a larger research community around the world. These papers are recognized as a leading source of biographical information about the artist herself, in addition to supporting research by national and international scholars of dance. Also, Dunham's papers serve the Southern Illinois University Carbondale community as a foundation for research and exhibitions, as it contains extensive material, including early sound recordings of Haitian music, for historians and students of African-American dance and dance anthropology. More information about Dunham's collection is available on SCRC's Web site. Other institutions that have some holdings related to Dunham and her work include the Library of Congress and the Missouri Historical Society.

(ABOVE TOP)
"Dance Practice." Photograph by unknown artist. Circa 1945.

Katherine Dunham opened Dunham's School of Dance and Theater, Manhattan, in 1945.

(ABOVE BOTTOM)
Katherine Dunham's high school scrapbook. Joliet, Illinois. 1920s.

(OPPOSITE)
"Costume Design for Katherine Dunham." R.P.B. 1963.

satin Lastex

Fruit in Horsehair,
Rhine Stars ect.

Pleating, shirring,
rucking, ect in
different diapten
metalic gauze.

R.P.B. 63

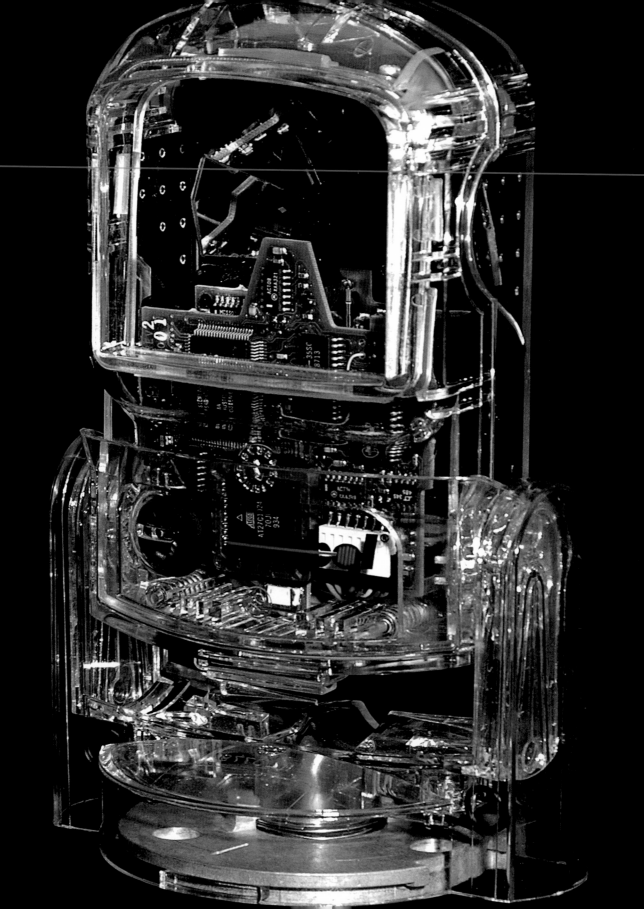

Stony Brook University, State University of New York, Libraries
Special Collections and University Archives

The AIDC 100 Archives: Automatic Identification and Data Capture

BARCODES, smart cards, radio frequency identification (RFID), biometrics, and magnetic stripe are technologies that encompass the rapidly evolving science and industry of Automatic Identification and Data Capture (AIDC). This field of high technology uses the latest advances in scanning and computer processes to capture information quickly and accurately in an automated manner. AIDC technology is ubiquitous, from driver's licenses to credit cards, and it is revolutionizing the way we live.

But who is recording the history and documenting the work of the scientists, businesses, and organizations that are developing these technologies? That was the concern of George and Teddy Goldberg when they approached Stony Brook University in the late 1990s about establishing an archive. As pioneers in the field of AIDC and publishers of *SCAN Newsletter*, the industry's first trade publication, the couple wanted to ensure that the past and the future of AIDC would be documented and preserved.

Stony Brook University Libraries understood the need to collect, catalog, and make this unique history accessible and entered into a partnership with AIDC 100, a nonprofit organization comprised of the top 100 automatic information and data capture professionals. In 2000, Special Collections established an archive of record for Automatic Identification and Data Capture and is one of only a few institutions in the United States that is actively acquiring materials pertaining to this field.

The AIDC 100 Archives now provides the university community and the public with a comprehensive record of the history and current state of AIDC. The collection is comprised of the personal papers of leaders in the industry, trade publications, journals, books, and artifacts. All formats, including print, microform, audio, visual, and digital, are accepted into the archive. Engineers, computer scientists, and visiting scholars regularly consult the documents located within the personal papers of George Goldberg, Richard Meyers, Allan Gilligan, and Paul Bergé. Special Collections anticipates receiving approximately 100 cubic feet of new material per year over the course of the next five years.

The AIDC 100 has established a $200,000 endowment fund for the support of the archive and event programming. Stony Brook University Libraries hosts the AIDC 100's annual national conference titled "Truth in Technologies." Membership in the AIDC 100 is by invitation-only; its primary goal is to facilitate the business community's knowledge and understanding of AIDC technologies.

In 2006, Special Collections digitized and published the electronic versions of the national and international editions of *SCAN Newsletter*, founded in 1977 by George and Teddy Goldberg. Detailed finding aids and an AIDC resource page can be accessed from a Web site that provides researchers with comprehensive information about the collections comprising the AIDC 100 Archives at Stony Brook University:

http://www.stonybrook.edu/libspecial/collections/manuscripts/aidc/

(ABOVE)
Bar-coded batteries. From the Robert La Moreaux Collection. Radio Shack, n.d.

(OPPOSITE)
LS 9100 Omni-Directional Scanner. From the Paul Bergé Collection. Symbol Technologies, 1994.
This hands-free, stationary scanner allows for scanning from any angle or direction.

Cartoons and Cartoonists

THE Special Collections Research Center (SCRC) at Syracuse University is home to one of America's most complete collections of original cartoon art. It includes original work by approximately 173 artists (20,000 items) and comprises more than 1,000 linear feet of material. The origins of this collection date to the 1960s when library curators like Martin H. Bush solicited the papers of many progenitors of popular culture, including contemporary cartoonists. Today—more than ever—the collection resonates with students and scholars of American culture.

SCRC's cartoonist collection spans the course of the 20th century. It includes the work of Bud Fisher (1885–1954), whose *Mutt and Jeff* (1907) was the earliest successful daily comic strip; William Gropper (1897–1977), whose leftist political cartoons in the *Daily Worker* sought to raise working-class consciousness during World War II; Mort Walker (1923–), whose *Beetle Bailey* (1950) anticipated the changing notions of American masculinity and militarism during the Cold War; Hal Foster (1892–1982), whose lavishly illustrated *Prince Valiant* (1937) elevated the artistic ambitions of the genre; and Morrie Turner (1923–), whose *Wee Pals* (1965) was the first comic strip to chronicle the lives of racial and ethnic minorities in American life.

As jazz is to American music, so too are cartoons to American popular culture: a vernacular art form that expresses the ambitions and anxieties of everyday people. Upwards of 100 million people read the daily comic strips or "funnies." It would, however, be unfair to dismiss comic art as solely a "low-brow" or "mass" phenomenon. SCRC is home to the personal papers of Boris Drucker (1920–), who in 1966 was hired as a staff cartoonist by the "high-brow" *New Yorker*. Other *New Yorker* alumni represented in the collections include Gluyas Williams (1888–1982), Otto Soglow (1900–1975), Robert Kraus (1925–2001), Alan Dunn (1900–1974), and Mary Petty (1889–1976).

Original drawings by Thomas Nast (1840–1902) and the records of dime-novel publisher Street and Smith (1855–1960) complement the 20th-century focus of this collection. During the latter half of the 19th century, Street and Smith's editorial board anticipated the popular appeal and commercial potential of illustrated fiction. Accordingly, they employed writers like Upton Sinclair, Horatio Alger, and Theodore Dreiser, as well as artists like N. C. Wyeth, to compose tales of romance and adventure for mass consumption. This collection totals more than 400 linear feet of material and includes the editorial files for serials like *Buffalo Bill Picture Stories*, *Crime Busters*, *Doc Savage Comics*, *FBI Comics*, the *Shadow*, and the *Yellow Kid*.

Historically, industry insiders and textbook publishers have made heaviest use of the cartoons and cartoonists collection. More recently, SCRC is actively seeking to draw scholarly attention to this long under-publicized collection. Searchable online finding aids to the papers and drawings of nearly 70 cartoon artists are currently available via our Web site. There, virtual patrons can also consult portions of the Street and Smith ("Street and Smith Publishers' Archive and Dime Novel Cover Art") and William Gropper ("People are My Landscape: Social Struggle in the Art of William Gropper") collections, as well as a selection of political cartoons ("Draw Your Own Conclusions: Political Cartooning Then and ?").

http://scrc.syr.edu/

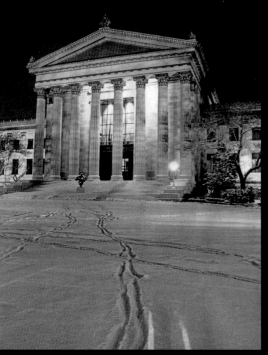

Temple University Libraries
Urban Archives

Philadelphia Evening Bulletin Collection

THERE is a reason why the *Philadelphia Evening Bulletin*'s slogan was "Nearly Everybody Reads the Bulletin." From the late 19th century until 1982, the *Bulletin* was a staple of daily life in the city of Philadelphia. Reading it was as much a part of its citizens' daily routine as was going to work or school. At the height of its popularity in the 1950s and 1960s, the *Philadelphia Bulletin* was the largest-circulation afternoon daily in the country.

But cultural and societal change rang the death knell for the afternoon paper. A dramatic increase in suburban sprawl and traffic-clogged roads contributed to the *Bulletin*'s demise. And just as the Internet today challenges all print newspapers, it was then another disruptive technology—television and the evening news—that made afternoon papers of less interest to the *Bulletin*'s long time readers.

Though the last issue rolled off the printing press on January 29, 1982, the *Philadelphia Bulletin* lives on in all its glory at Temple University Libraries. The *Philadelphia Evening Bulletin* Collection is the most comprehensive collection documenting the social, cultural, economic, political, and physical development of the Philadelphia region. The collection consists of the *Bulletin*'s clipping files, or what the journalists of the day sentimentally referred to as the "morgue," and over two million original photographs and negatives that accompanied those articles.

The *Bulletin* collection, which is the centerpiece of Temple Libraries' Urban Archives, tells of the city's life and its stories. Consider the adversarial relations that defined the political careers of Austin Meehan (1897–1961) and Richardson Dilworth (1898–1974). Their battles over the running of the city government are well documented in nearly 30 packets of clippings. Those studying the roots of the city's contemporary political tension or corruption can discover that local government has perhaps remained the same the more it has changed. The economic changes that resulted in the eastern "Rust Belt"; the cause and effect of the population shifts from the great eastern cities that began with such classic developments as Levittown, Pennsylvania, a model for the large-scale planned suburb; and the impact of the construction of the Interstate Highway System on city neighborhoods and public transportation were also well documented. The clippings, photographs, negatives, and internal index form a related system from which information about almost any aspect of Philadelphia and east coast life can be extracted.

To date, over 30,000 images have been preserved, cataloged and digitized for Internet access. The libraries hold an annual signature exhibit featuring photographs and newspaper clippings from the *Philadelphia Evening Bulletin* Collection. The event draws attendees from Temple University as well as area universities, historical groups, and the community at large. A McDowell Family Foundation fellowship provides stipends to visiting scholars to use the *Philadelphia Evening Bulletin* Collection to produce a dissertation, article, book, or similar scholarly work. More recently, the McLean Contributionship established an endowment for the purpose of further digitizing and expanding access to the libraries' *Philadelphia Evening Bulletin* and *Sunday Bulletin* archives.

The Temple University Libraries' Urban Archives allow scholarly researcher and local citizen alike the opportunity to access the rich history of America's first great city.

(ABOVE)
"*Philadelphia Evening Bulletin* Library." Photograph by staff photographer. For *Philadelphia Evening Bulletin*, circa 1930s.

(OPPOSITE TOP LEFT)
"Gallagher Club Mummers." Photograph by staff photographer. For *Philadelphia Evening Bulletin*, 1946.

(OPPOSITE TOP CENTER)
"Campaign to Raise $1 million for Philadelphia Orchestra." Photograph by staff photographer. For *Philadelphia Evening Bulletin*, 1919.

(OPPOSITE TOP RIGHT)
"Pretzel Vendor." Photograph by staff photographer. For *Philadelphia Evening Bulletin*, July 28, 1940.

(OPPOSITE BOTTOM LEFT)
"Philadelphia Art Museum." Photograph by staff photographer. For *Philadelphia Evening Bulletin*, January 21, 1970.

(OPPOSITE BOTTOM CENTER)
"Flower Mart in Rittenhouse." Photograph by staff photographer. For *Philadelphia Evening Bulletin*, May 22, 1930.

(OPPOSITE BOTTOM RIGHT)
"Italian Market." Photograph by staff photographer. For *Philadelphia Evening Bulletin*, May 24, 1952.

William C. Cook Jacksonian America Collection

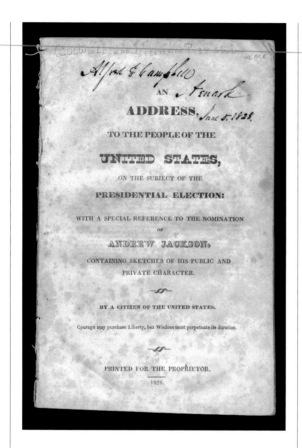

DURING 2006, William C. Cook of Nashville donated to the University of Tennessee Special Collections Library his collection of nearly 1,000 rare books and imprints related to the life and presidency of Andrew Jackson (1767–1845). Among the materials are numerous first editions and autographed texts, as well as biographies of Jackson, children's literature from the period, and many pamphlets that reflect both the pro- and anti-Jackson political rhetoric of the day. Controversial aspects of Jackson's presidency, including his opposition to a national bank, tariff legislation, and the Indian Removal Act of 1830, appear frequently within these rare texts.

Numerous copies of James Parton's multivolume work *Life of Andrew Jackson*, one of the most famous biographies of the seventh President, are contained in the Cook Collection. Additionally, one of two extant printings of Parton's abridged *Life*, which was never commercially issued, is included. Other biographies, including F. J. Dreer's unique edition of W. J. Snellings's *A Brief and Impartial History of the Life and Actions of Andrew Jackson* (1831), constitute a valuable resource for scholars interested in the life and career of Jackson.

The Cook Collection also contains over 30 children's biographies of Andrew and Rachel Jackson, representing the works of several of America's leading children's authors. Published in 1845, John Frost's *The Life of Andrew Jackson* is the oldest children's title in the collection. Also of interest are *Andrew Jackson, The Fighting President* (1929) by Helen Nicolay, *Rachel Jackson: Tennessee Girl* (1955) by Christine Noble Govan, and *A Cannon for General Marion: A Story of Young Andrew Jackson* (1975) by Alfred Leland Crabb. These volumes, intended to foster patriotism and establish character models for young Americans, provide an excellent resource for understanding Jackson as a source for the "great American hero" myth.

In documenting the dynamism of Jacksonian politics, the collection contains abundant texts and pamphlets relating both pro-Jackson polemics and anti-Jackson invectives. Included in the pro-Jackson pieces are several campaign biographies written by Robert Walsh and a New England biography of Jackson, printed for Isaac Hill, a New Hampshire Jacksonian Democrat and editor of the *New England Patriot*. An interesting anti-Jackson piece found in the collection is "The Wise Sayings of the Honorable Isaac Hill," printed by the *Patriot's* competitor, the *New Hampshire Journal*. Personal attacks against Jackson are recorded in a complete bound collection of *Truth's Advocate and Monthly Anti-Jackson Expositor*.

The Cook Collection builds upon the Special Collections Library's impressive holdings of materials related to the three United States presidents from Tennessee: Jackson, James K. Polk, and Andrew Johnson. During the fall 2006 semester, an exhibit of some of the most significant pieces from the Cook Collection was displayed in the library. Additionally, in October 2006, the library teamed with the Center for Jacksonian America to present a lecture by renowned Jackson scholar Harry L. Watson on "Freedom and Majority Rule: Andrew Jackson's Complex Legacy." As the premier location for research on Jackson and the Jacksonian period, the library looks forward to making this important collection and others like it available to scholars.

University of Texas Libraries

The Nettie Lee Benson Latin American Collection

THE Nettie Lee Benson Latin American Collection is a research library on the campus of the University of Texas at Austin whose mission is to acquire and provide access to materials on Mexico, Central and South America, the Caribbean, and the Hispanic presence in the United States. Works, dating from the 15th century to the present, may be in any language including indigenous languages.

In 1920, representatives of the University of Texas attending President Álvaro Obregón's inauguration in Mexico City were surprised to find for sale the first edition of Bernal Díaz del Castillo's *True History of the Conquest of New Spain* (1632). That purchase led the university to buy the Genaro García library, an exquisite collection for the study of Mexico, the Americas, the West Indies, and Spain. Building on this extraordinary resource, the University Library decided to form a Latin American Collection in 1926. Its first librarian, Carlos E. Castañeda, laid a foundation upon which Nettie Lee Benson, his successor after 1943, was able to construct one of the world's most important libraries of Latin Americana. The collection grew by purchase, gifts, and exchange agreements with Latin American governments, academic societies, and cultural organizations. Whole libraries were added on: Mexico and the Spanish Southwest, Guatemala and Central America, and Chile and the countries of the Río de la Plata including Brazil. The Mexican American Library Program, established in 1974, now includes all ethnic groups with roots in Latin America living in North America. It has amassed both a superior print collection as well as archival collections related to organizations, political and civil rights activists, educators, artists, and literary authors.

Foremost among the library's collections are the 247 volumes selected in 1937 from the Joaquín García Icazbalceta library. Among its treasures are a priceless series of original 16th-century reports and maps relating to Mexico and Guatemala known as the *relaciones geográficas*; and a large body of the first books published in the New World, those published in Mexico City from 1543 to 1600. Among the unique donations to the Benson was that by former university faculty member Dorothy Schons, who bequeathed first editions by the 17th-century luminary Sor Juana Inés de la Cruz along with the *Libro de profesiones* with the nun's religious vows signed in her blood.

While the Benson Collection is heralded for its unparalleled historical collections, its principal area of growth for the last half-century has been contemporary information in all formats. This pattern of growth is exemplified by its volume count: from 30,000 in 1943, to 305,000 in 1975, to 960,000 today. In the past, the Benson has received numerous federal grants to take the lead in creating automated library records and to microfilm books and newspapers. Today's technology has prompted the partnership of the University of Texas Libraries and Google Books to ensure that Latin American publications are represented in the digital age. Outreach also includes exhibitions, symposia, specialized reference service, and in-house publications.

http://www.lib.utexas.edu/benson/

(ABOVE TOP)
"Elisa García López." Photograph by unknown artist. From Carlos Villalongín Dramatic Company Collection. 1848–1945.

(ABOVE BOTTOM)
"Molina's Parrot." Lithograph from *Argentine Ornithology*. Philip Lutley Sclater. London: R. H. Porter, 1888–89.

(OPPOSITE)
"Ordaz Mendoza and María Magiscatzin Genealogy." Unknown author. From Joaquín García Icazbalceta Manuscript Collection. [1500]–1887.

Texas A&M University Libraries
Cushing Memorial Library and Archives

Cervantes Collection

(ABOVE TOP)
Vida y hechos del ingenioso cavallero Don Quixote de la Mancha. Miguel de Cervantes Saavedra. Bruselas: Juan Mommarte, 1662. Book binding.

(ABOVE BOTTOM)
Vida y hechos del ingenioso cavallero Don Quixote de la Mancha. Miguel de Cervantes Saavedra. Bruselas: Juan Mommarte, 1662. Detail of text.

(OPPOSITE: LEFT TO RIGHT; TOP TO BOTTOM)
The History of the Most Renowned Don Quixote of Mancha [sic]. Miguel de Cervantes Saavedra. Translated into English by John Philips. London: T. Hodgkin, 1687.

Vida y hechos del ingenioso cavallero Don Quixote de la Mancha. Miguel de Cervantes Saavedra. Madrid: A. Sanz, 1735.

Vida y hechos del ingenioso hidalgo Don Quixote de la Mancha. Miguel de Cervantes Saavedra. Londres: J. y R. Tonson, 1738.

Leben und Thaten des weisen Junkers Don Quixote von la Mancha. Miguel de Cervantes Saavedra. Translated into German by F. J. Bertuch. Leipzig: Caspar Fritsch, 1780–81.

Don Quixote de la Mancha. Miguel de Cervantes Saavedra. Translated into English by M. Smirke. London: C. Daly, 1842.

Don Quixote of the Mancha. Retold by Edward Abbot Parry. London: Blackie & Son; Manchester: Sherratt & Hughes, 1900.

Don Quichotte en estampes: mis a la portée des enfants. By Mme. Wetzell. Paris: Langlumé et Peltier, [1845].

F**ROM** text to icon to myth, thousands of illustrations comprise the textual iconography of the *Quixote*. They represent a key element of its printing history and have played a crucial role in making it both a popular book and a classic novel. Charles-Antoine Coypel, John Vanderbank, William Hogarth, Francis Hayman, Antonio Carnicero, Daniel Chodowiecki, Robert Smirke, George Cruikshank, Tony Johannot, Gustave Doré, Adolphe Lalauze, William Crane, Daniel Urrabieta Vierge, Berthold Mahn, and Salvador Dalí are some of the artists that have illustrated the *Quixote*, the seminal work by Miguel de Cervantes Saavedra. The corpus of these illustrations is best exemplified in the over 700 editions of *Don Quixote* that comprise the Eduardo Urbina Cervantes Project Collection at the Cushing Memorial Library and Archives at Texas A&M University.

Founded in 1995, the online Cervantes Project, led by Eduardo Urbina, is the definitive resource for the study of the life and works of Cervantes. The book collection we celebrate serves as the basis for the study of the textual iconography of *Don Quixote*. The collection began in 2001 when Urbina proposed a collaborative project with the Cushing Library to collect illustrated editions of the *Quixote*. In 2006, the project was awarded a National Endowment for the Humanities grant to fund the digitization of editions and the creation of a hypertextual archive. This grant built on an earlier National Science Foundation award to support the creation of an electronic variorum edition.

With renewed scholarly interest in visual culture, the collection provides an important research archive for not only scholarship on the *Quixote* but also for the study of artists, illustrators, and engravers who have interpreted Cervantes's classic novel over the centuries, as well as for the study of the illustrated book.

Since its inception, the Cervantes collection has grown to over 1,200 volumes and 15,000 engravings, drawings, and vignettes. It includes both the classical, canonical illustrated editions as well as unique extra-illustrated editions, with many very rare items for which few copies are known and available to scholars in public libraries, some 130 of them unique items found only at the Cushing. Editions in the collection run the gamut from the most popular such as the iconic edition illustrated by Gustave Doré, one of the most prolific artists of the 19th century, to rare early editions, to versions for children, to modern artistic interpretations, such as those with illustrations by Gregorio Prieto and Salvador Dalí. The earliest *Quixote* in the collection is Thomas Shelton's English translation of 1620; the oldest item in the collection dates from 1573; one of the more recent editions is the Chinese translation from 2001. The countries represented in the collection include Spain, France, Germany, Italy, England, the United States, Belgium, Scotland, Norway, Turkey, Argentina, Poland, Mexico, Russia, China, Sweden, Denmark, Australia, the Netherlands, and Canada. Together the Cervantes collection and archive of images and metadata provide research resources to students and scholars from around the world for the study of the material culture, critical reception, and textual iconography of the *Quixote*.

http://cervantes.tamu.edu/
http://dqi.tamu.edu/

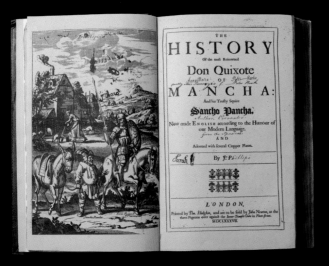

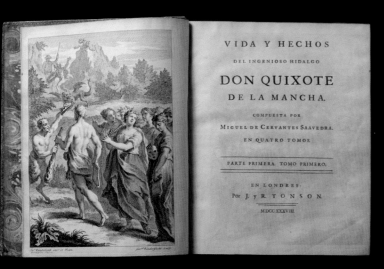

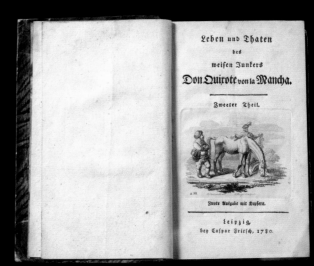

W. Hollar fecit 1643

4

The cold, not cruelty makes her wear   Winter   For a smoother skinn at night.
In Winter, furrs and Wild beasts haire   Embraceth her with more delight.

University of Toronto Libraries
Thomas Fisher Rare Book Library

Wenceslaus Hollar Collection

THE Fisher Library at the University of Toronto is privileged to be one of the largest repositories for the artistic works of Wenceslaus Hollar, along with Windsor Castle and the National Gallery Collection of Prints and Drawings in the artist's native Prague. The library's Hollar collection was donated by Dr. Sidney Fisher of Montreal, who had begun assembling the etchings in order to reconstruct the London of Shakespeare's day. Along with Fisher's Shakespeare collection, which includes all four folios, the Hollar collection was one of the foundation collections which came to the Department of Special Collections upon the opening of the new library in 1972. A great strength of the Fisher Hollar collection is the presence of multiple states of many of the images, which provides a unique opportunity to study the alterations to the plates and the transmission and distribution of the etchings, both during and after Hollar's lifetime.

Hollar was born in Prague in 1607, and his earliest etchings date from 1625. Very little is known of his early life and artistic training, but in 1636 he came to the attention of a renowned art collector, the Earl of Arundel, who was making an official visit to the continent; Hollar subsequently became a part of the Arundel household, settling in England in 1637. He remained there during the beginning of the English Civil War period, but moved to Antwerp in 1642. Ten years later he returned to London, working on a number of major projects for the publisher John Ogilby and the antiquary Sir William Dugdale. Hollar died in London in 1677, one of the most skilled etchers of his or any other time.

Hollar's oeuvre is remarkable for its great range and for its sophisticated technique. The majority of Hollar's work was produced in and about his adopted England, and famously includes 45 plates detailing the interior of old St. Paul's Cathedral just before its destruction in the Great Fire of 1666, as well as general views of London before and after the fire. His artistic output also includes religious and historical prints, maps and views, portraits, costume studies, and natural history. Hollar exploited the technique of etching to its fullest, recording even the tiniest details with great economy and clarity. He was able to portray complicated and massive architectural compositions such as Strasbourg Cathedral as readily as the whorls in a seashell. He was a master at conveying the textural complexity of a lace collar, or the tactile qualities of a feather fan or a fur muff. Over the course of his lifetime he produced some 2,700 separate etchings, and he was still at work when he died at age 70.

The Hollar collection has been known and consulted since it came to the library. Individual works have often been exhibited in Toronto and elsewhere, and reproduced in scholarly articles as well as in their own right as works of art. This year, with support from the Delmas Foundation, the entire collection has been digitized and can now be freely consulted by users everywhere, in high resolution form and with supporting material on Hollar's life and work.

http://link.library.utoronto.ca/hollar/

(ABOVE)
"Spring." Etching by Wenceslaus Hollar. From *The Seasons* (three-quarter-length figures). 1641.

(OPPOSITE)
"Winter." Etching by Wenceslaus Hollar. From *The Seasons* (full-length figures). 1643.

Tulane University Library

Howard-Tilton Memorial Library Special Collections

William Ransom Hogan Archive of New Orleans Jazz

THE Hogan Jazz Archive at Tulane University was established with Ford Foundation funding in 1958 as the Archive of New Orleans Jazz and was posthumously renamed in honor of William Ransom Hogan, the chair of the Department of History who wrote the initial grant proposal. Ford funding enabled an oral history fieldwork project with pioneers of New Orleans jazz under the direction of William Russell, the archive's first curator, and his successor, Richard B. Allen. This generated nearly 2,000 reels of taped interviews with written transcripts, which is the largest collection of jazz oral history extant.

In addition to the interviews, the archive hosts a full range of bibliographic materials on jazz, 11,000 photographs, 65,000 recorded sound items, 55,000 sheet music titles, 350 films, 225 linear feet of manuscripts and vertical files, and artifacts such as vintage phonographs and cylinder players, art works, and a select assortment of musical instruments. Although the collection development policy of the Hogan Jazz Archive began with a very tight focus on traditional New Orleans jazz, it has been expanded in recent years to include a multiplicity of New Orleans-related genres, such as ragtime, blues, gospel, rhythm and blues, Mardi Gras Indian chants, rock and roll, and non-indigenous variants, such as zydeco.

Among the significant personal collections of musicians held by the archive are those of Dominic "Nick" LaRocca, leader of the Original Dixieland Jazz Band, which made the first jazz record in 1917; the sheet music library of John Robichaux's orchestra, the main competition to Charles "Buddy" Bolden, the celebrated ur-jazz avatar; the papers of guitarist and writer Danny Barker, including materials belonging to his uncle, drummer Paul Barbarin; photographs collected and taken by drummer Ray Bauduc (Bob Crosby Orchestra); and the papers of trumpeter Max Kaminsky, including original scores from his State Department tour of Asia with Jack Teagarden in 1958. The Ralston Crawford New Orleans Jazz Collection is comprised of 840 photographic prints made by the Canadian artist from 1949 through 1961, comprising a unique vision of that era. Much of the photography and sheet music was donated by musical producer and caricaturist Al Rose, who discovered a Buddy Bolden invitation, the only original document deriving from that musician's career, at a flea market. Recently, the rock critic Robert Palmer's papers have taken the collection in some new and surprising directions.

Patrons using the Hogan Jazz Archive represent the interdisciplinary nature of jazz studies and the international appeal of jazz as an exemplary American vernacular music. Among the scholarly publications reflecting research at the archive are Thomas Brothers, *Louis Armstrong's New Orleans* (2006) and Lawrence Gushee, *Pioneers of Jazz: The Story of the Original Creole Band* (2005). Documentary filmmakers such as Ken Burns (*Jazz*) and Don McGlyn (*Louis Prima: The Wildest*) have also made intensive use of its resources, but the collection is open to anyone who loves jazz, whether teacher, student, or aficionado.

(ABOVE TOP)
New Orleans musicians' business cards. Circa 1908/1918.

Musicians such as clarinetist "Big Eye" Louis Nelson Delille and violinist/saxophonist James Palao used business cards to find work. Besides noting accomplishments, cards often expressed a willingness to adapt to the customer's needs, reading "music for all occasions" or "what it takes to suit you I got."

(ABOVE BOTTOM)
"Dansante: A Grand Soiree, Economy Hall."
Poster by unknown author/designer. 1909.

Band leader John Robichaux wrapped orchestrations in this poster, thus the center crease. Such artifacts yield a wealth of information, including performers, membership of sponsoring organizations, purpose of the event, and duration of the ball—eight hours!

(OPPOSITE)
"Piron-Williams Orchestra." Photograph by Arthur P. Bedou. 1915.

Bedou's portrait of this band organized for a vaudeville tour that never materialized included such future jazz stars as Clarence Williams (top left), Jimmie Noone (clarinet), Oscar Celestin (cornet), Armand Piron (violin), and Johnny St. Cyr (lower right). Bedou had a studio in Tremé and toured as a staff photographer with Booker T. Washington.

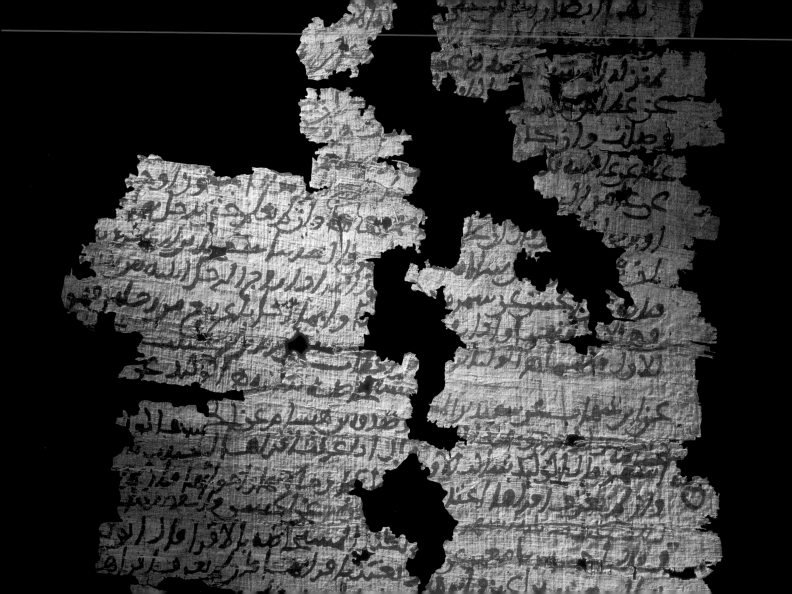

University of Utah Library
Special Collections

Aziz S. Atiya Arabic Papyrus and Paper Collection

MATT Malczycki pored over ancient papyri in the University of Utah's J. Willard Marriott Library. The pieces intrigued and excited the graduate student completing his doctoral dissertation. He spoke earnestly about the Arabic collection at seminars around the country. The experts chided him. No such collection existed, they said. But it does: Eight centuries of rich Muslim history and lore, stories of life under many caliphs gathered over several years by Professor Aziz S. Atiya, founder of the university's Middle East Center. Atiya acquired the fragments of papyrus, paper, parchment, and cloth in Beirut, Cairo, London, and from the University of Chicago. The majority of the fragments originated in Egypt. Dr. Atiya and his wife Lola donated the collection to the J. Willard Marriott Library in 1975.

The Aziz S. Atiya Arabic Papyrus and Paper Collection consists of nearly 1,700 pieces—more than 800 papyrus fragments, nearly 900 paper fragments, 10 parchment fragments, and 4 cloth fragments. The fragments date from the eighth century CE through the Fatimid, Ayyubid, Mamluk, and Ottoman eras (922 AH/1517 CE). It is the largest collection of its kind in North America. And it is one of the richest. The fragments include legal, literary, and magical texts; administrative records, tax receipts, contracts, private letters, official business correspondence, sections from the Quran, and several bilingual documents.

Professor Donald P. Little of McGill University, with a grant from the Fuqan Foundation, surveyed the collection. In his report to the foundation he wrote, "[The collection is] an extremely important segment of the medieval Arabic heritage and an invaluable resource for scholars interested in the history and culture of Islamic Egypt." Still, until just recently the collection was practically unknown.

Malczycki became instrumental in bringing awareness of the collection's existence to scholars throughout the world. One of the scholars Malczycki contacted was papyrologist Dr. Gladys Frantz-Murphy. Frantz-Murphy visited the library and was astounded by what she saw. In a letter she said, "[It is] by far the largest collection of pre-modern Arabic documents in the United States, and therefore, the Americas…it is also the most diverse…distinguished…also by the time span that it covers."

The collection is open for study to all researchers and is presented state-wide to students and the community through lectures, presentations, exhibitions, and workshops. A plan to digitize the collection and place the images on the Web will help make the antique pieces accessible to the global community, adding primary source materials to scholastic work the world over.

The early Arabic world reveals itself to its future through the abundant materials in this collection. The study of Arabic papyrus is of immeasurable value in enhancing understanding of the history of the Middle East. The collection helps give insight into the political and social history, finance and taxation, trade and commerce, topography, religion, and law—in short, the development of Islamic civilization.

(ABOVE)
Arabic calligraphic manuscript on paper.
Anonymous author. Circa 11th–12th century.
    This piece shows a highly simplified ornamental form of Arabic script, arranged to form a geometric design.

(OPPOSITE)
Collection of Hadith. Anonymous author.
Circa 10th century.
    This collection of traditions of the Prophet Muhammad includes chains of transmitters.

Vanderbilt University Library

W.T. Bandy Center for Baudelaire and Modern French Studies

Gilbert Sigaux Collection

VANDERBILT acquired the Gilbert Sigaux Collection of 20th-century French theater material in 1986 through the generosity of the Friends of the Library. The former W.T. Bandy Center director and other members of the French faculty were acquainted with Sigaux and his family and suggested that his collected materials would complement and enhance Vanderbilt's French collections.

Gilbert Sigaux (1918–1982) was an editor, critic, and author of books on topics ranging from tourism to vaudeville, the French Resistance, and 19th- and 20th-century theater. He was a professor of theater history at the Conservatoire National d'Art Dramatique in Paris and secretary of the Société des auteurs et compositeurs dramatiques. He edited over 100 literary and dramatic texts for publication and served as literary editor and consultant for several French publishing companies. His prefaces, critical notes, and other editorial additions appear in works by Alexandre Dumas, Georges Simenon, and Henrik Ibsen, among others. He collaborated on anthologies, composed entries for reference works, contributed articles to journals and newspapers, wrote essays, and published four novels. A colleague wrote of Sigaux, "A day in the life of Gilbert Sigaux was a frightening thing. Frightening for someone who cannot sustain such a rhythm, accomplish so much work, such varied work. In a single day, Gilbert wrote (original fiction, articles, erudite texts, not to mention the correspondence), telephoned, traveled, edited, taught, ran, negotiated, read, cut out printed materials, filed, and helped others. His days were too short and his nights even shorter."

Sigaux gathered an enormous personal library of play texts, books, and documents in various media on French theater. Complementary topics include architecture, painting, philosophy, ballet, opera, cinema, and the circus. The Sigaux Collection contains approximately 6,000 volumes, including monographs, theater journals, and over 75,000 items in the dossier files on authors, directors, actors, and theaters. The range of materials in each category is wide enough to encompass, for instance, Sarah Bernhardt and Bridgette Bardot in the actors' files.

With the establishment of the Sigaux Collection, Jacques Sigaux lectured at Vanderbilt on his father's life and his legacy in contemporary French theater. The lectures added a personal dimension to the importance of the collection. Interestingly, "Jacky" Sigaux is a producer at the Café Théâtre de la Gare in Paris.

Gilbert Sigaux participated in the intellectual life of his time with a scope and depth that make him a key chronicler of 20th-century French arts and letters. According to Dan M. Church, Emeritus Professor of French at Vanderbilt, "The collection represents the single most valuable resource for research on theater in France in the 20th century."

http://www.library.vanderbilt.edu/bandy/

http://www.library.vanderbilt.edu/bandy/collections.shtml#sig/

http://www.library.vanderbilt.edu/central/sigaux/html/boxindex_p1.htm

http://www.library.vanderbilt.edu/central/sigaux/exhibit/

~~American songs~~ ~~Those~~
~~Mouth = ~~Those~~ of mechanics—
each (sings his own) one, as it should be,
blithe and strong,
The carpenter singing his, as
he measures his plank
or beam,
The mason singing his, as
he makes ready for work,
or leaves off work
The boatman singing what belongs to him in his
boat — The deck=hand
singing on the steamboat
deck,
The shoemaker singing as he sits on
his bench — The hatter
singing as he stands,

The delicious singing of the
mother or of the young
wife (or of the girl sewing or washing-) at work, — each
sings what belongs to
her, and to none else,
The day what belongs to the
Day — At night the party
of young fellows, ~~rot~~
robust, friendly, clean=blooded,
singing with melodious
voices, melodious thoughts—

Come! some of young write ~~true~~
American ~~mouth=songs,~~
~~And come~~ still be flooding the
States with hundreds ~~of~~
and thousands of mouth=songs, fit for the
States only. —

University of Virginia Library
The Albert and Shirley Small Special Collections Library

The Clifton Waller Barrett Library of American Literature

SHIPPING magnate Clifton Waller Barrett (1901–1991) was set upon his collecting course in 1940 by collector and bibliographer Carroll Atwood Wilson, who convinced him to stop "dallying with high spots…and become a dedicated collector of American literature."

Around this time, Barrett received an encouraging letter from James Southall Wilson, chair of the English Department at his alma mater, the University of Virginia. Alderman Library had just been built, and it boasted a stately paneled room housing a remarkable collection of primary and reference sources on early American history bequeathed by Detroit philanthropist Tracy W. McGregor. Barrett seized upon the idea of furnishing a room opposite with an equally worthy collection of American literature. "I had a plan influenced by one Wilson and a purpose inspired by another," he later remarked.

The original Barrett Room was dedicated in 1960 at a ceremony attended by poet Robert Frost, whom Barrett had befriended and collected assiduously. By the time of Barrett's death in 1991, his overall collection had grown to approximately 35,000 volumes and 112,000 manuscripts. With the opening of the Albert and Shirley Small Special Collections Library in 2004, the contents of the Barrett Library were moved and the new reading room was fittingly named in Barrett's honor.

Taking Lyle Wright's bibliographies of American fiction as a guidebook, Barrett collected all fiction, poetry, drama, and essays published by an American author in book form from the American Revolution through 1875. For the period 1875–1950, he gathered first and important editions of every major American writer and hundreds of lesser ones. To complement the printed works, he added stores of literary manuscripts and correspondence.

The Barrett Library includes many outstanding features, among them an inscribed presentation copy of William Hill Brown's *Power of Sympathy* (1789) that establishes the authorship of what is widely regarded the first American novel, scarce copies of the earliest known novels by African-Americans, the earliest surviving manuscripts of Walt Whitman's *Leaves of Grass*, and the original manuscripts of Stephen Crane's *Red Badge of Courage* and John Steinbeck's *The Grapes of Wrath*. The library continues to grow though ongoing acquisitions. All printed items are cataloged, and finding aids for manuscript and archival materials have been published for dozens of significant authors, including Susanna (Haswell) Rowson, Louisa May Alcott, Mark Twain, Henry James, Willa Cather, and others, with more guides in preparation.

The subject of several exhibitions and catalogs, the Barrett Library has provided the substance for many more. Barrett items are featured regularly in instructional presentations and Web projects, such as the *Uncle Tom's Cabin & American Culture* multimedia archive. The Barrett Library has also supplied the raw materials for numerous critical works, bibliographies, and dissertations. Visiting fellowships are now available for short-term research residencies. With support from The Andrew W. Mellon Foundation, some 444 titles from the Barrett Library have been fully digitized and made available through ProQuest's *Early American Fiction 1789–1875*.

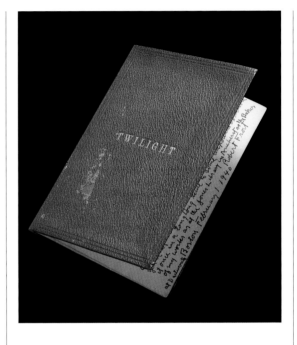

(ABOVE)
Twilight. Robert Frost. [Lawrence, Massachusetts: self-published, 1894.]

This is the sole surviving copy of Frost's first book of poetry. He privately printed two copies and then destroyed one of them. Clifton Waller Barrett successfully acquired this copy after 10 years of trying.

(OPPOSITE)
"Mouth Songs" [later reworked and retitled "I Hear America Singing"]. Walt Whitman. From surviving manuscripts of *Leaves of Grass*. Circa 1860.

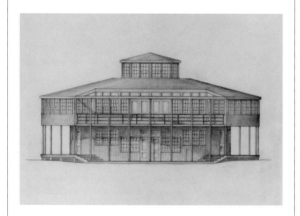

International Archive of Women in Architecture

THE record of women who have contributed to the design of our built environment is being gathered and preserved in the International Archive of Women in Architecture (IAWA) at Virginia Tech. Special Collections houses 1,200 cubic feet of primary sources documenting over 300 women, and its biographical database chronicles 650 women from 51 countries. The online guide includes links to rich details in over 125 inventories, and the VT ImageBase provides over 1,200 digital images from the IAWA. Two traveling exhibitions were donated by the American Institute of Architects. The American Architectural Foundation of the AIA, on the centenary of the induction of women, created "That Exceptional One: Women in American Architecture, 1888–1988." The AIA's Women in Architecture Committee created "Many More: Women in Architecture."

The IAWA relies on donations but this has not limited the variety, breadth, and depth of careers preserved and available to the public. Eleanore Pettersen, Jane Duncombe, and Lois Davidson Gottlieb represent Frank Lloyd Wright's apprentices. Architect, artist, and educator Beverly Willis donated over 150 projects documenting the application of computers to architectural design and land analysis. Rosaria Piomelli was the first woman dean of any school of architecture in the United States and her collection details many facets of her career. Interests beyond their careers are also demonstrated in the artwork of Anne Tyng, Sharon Sutton, and Martha Crawford; the illustrated travel diaries of Sigrid Rupp; and the writings of Susana Torre, among others.

Founded in 1985 by Milka Bliznakov, the IAWA is a collaboration between the College of Architecture and Urban Studies and the University Libraries at Virginia Tech. While Bliznakov was already concerned that local faculty and students were unaware of women's contributions, as she neared retirement she envisioned the potential loss of the record of her contemporaries' work.

Because women who initially practiced architecture and related design fields were often not allowed formally into the professions, "women *in* architecture" includes those who designed without formal training, registration, or licensure. Women in architecture includes all the designers of our built environment, including landscape architects, interior designers, industrial designers, and urban planners. The IAWA is full of stories waiting to be told about those who persevered in the face of veiled and blatant discouragement, including those who survived the long educational preparation and the rigorous registration process in spite of isolation and marginalization when they were, indeed, allowed to participate.

Annually, scholars and researchers vie for the Bliznakov Prize that rewards original research illuminating women's professional achievements. The first prize winner was Claire Bonney of Basel, Switzerland, for her research on Adrienne Gorska. The Bliznakov Honorarium rewards projects that specifically draw on the IAWA. Professor Joseph Chuo Wang, the first Honorarium winner, prepared the Chinese language article "The International Archive of Women in Architecture is Alive and Thriving at Virginia Tech," targeted for a national professional journal.

http://spec.lib.vt.edu/iawa/

http://lumiere.lib.vt.edu/iawa_db/

http://imagebase.lib.vt.edu/browse.php?folio_ID=/iawa

(ABOVE)
Garvey House, Amagansett, New York.
Architectural design by Susana Torre. 1984–87.
　Model.
　　North façade (front) elevation.
　　South façade (garden) elevation.

(OPPOSITE)
Garvey House, Amagansett, New York.
Architectural design by Susana Torre. 1984–87.
　　Upper-floor plan.
　　Overhead site plan.

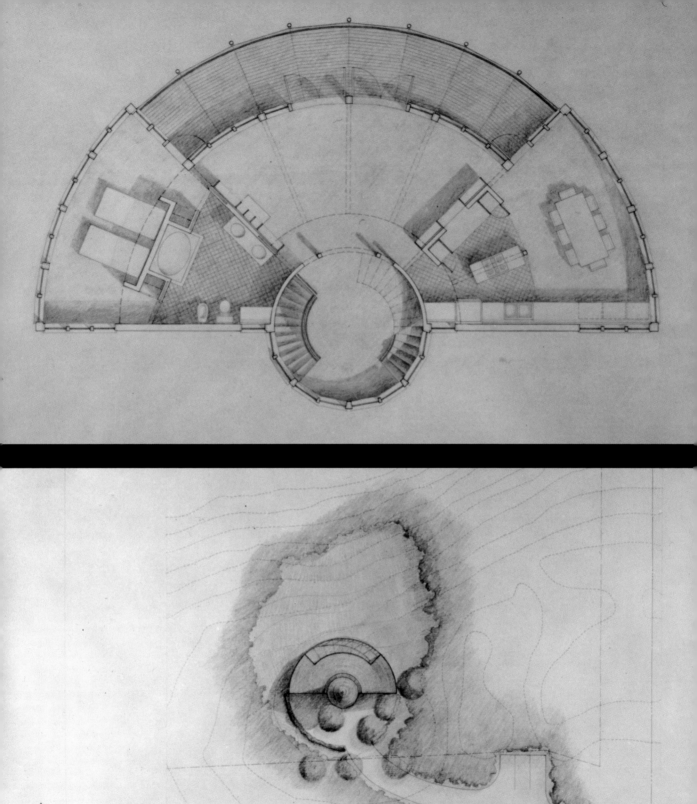

Dear Miss Evanson

I am writing to you today because I am expecting to move away with in a very short time. As you always know the Japanese people has been asked by our goverment to evacuate. I do not know yet where we will go. I hope there will be some good school in which I can continual, my school work. I am very sorry to leave Seattle

University of Washington Libraries
Special Collections Division

Japanese American Evacuation and Internment Collections

A LARGELY overlooked chapter in United States history concerns the forced internment of Japanese-Americans (Nikkei) from the west coast into euphemistically named "relocation centers" during World War II. Collections at the University of Washington Libraries provide glimpses into this history, the saga that followed the attack on Pearl Harbor, the "Day of Infamy," December 7, 1941. There are many stories of incarceration of the Nikkei. As the drama and controversy around the imprisonment unfolded after the war, members of the Japanese-American community brought their memories and materials to the University Libraries for safekeeping.

Some of the stories that are documented in our collection had national impact—well known is Gordon Hirabayashi's stand against the curfew and evacuation, his subsequent arrest, and his Supreme Court challenge to the incarceration in *Hirabayashi v. United States*. But it is in the lesser known stories of children, students, and ordinary folk where the incarceration comes to life. Kenji Okuda's story is told through letters found in Special Collections. Kenji, a friend of Gordon Hirabayashi's, was an undergraduate majoring in economics when the United States declared war on Japan. Through his letters, we follow Kenji's journey to the Puyallup Assembly Center, where he was deemed a troublemaker by the Army, then to the Granada Relocation Center in Colorado ("a paradise for insect hunters"). Kenji's frustrations, anger, and hopes echo through the years:

> When am I going to get out of this hell hole? I certainly don't know—I wish I did— but it isn't even certain that we students will be permitted to leave. The picture now is black, but the situation changes from day to day. …hell, we aren't saboteurs or spies!!

Other voices can be heard through the collections. The students in Ella Evanson's class write letters to her depicting the conditions in the camp and plead, "Please write to me…because it is lonely here." Eddie Sato expressed himself through his drawings of everyday of camp life—old men playing mahjong, the ramshackle buildings, a sumo tournament. The love story of a young couple separated by the incarceration—she white, he Nikkei—can be heard in the love letters between Betty Adkins and her fiancé Tom Fukuyama.

The Evacuation and Internment Collection is supplemented by collections in other formats— microfilmed War Relocation Authority records, camp newspapers, University Archives, moving image materials, and a strong selection of secondary sources detailing the history of the incarceration. Online exhibits and digitization projects highlight the collections and provide access to students, scholars, and community members. Many of these resources have been used by scholars, writing about the internment experience. The results include works ranging from a child's story about baseball in the camps to one of family life interrupted by separation during imprisonment. Special Collections' partnerships with Seattle organizations such as Densho (the Japanese American Legacy Project), the Wing Luke Asian Museum, and the Nikkei Alumni Association strengthen community ties and bring new opportunities for collaboration and collection building.

http://www.lib.washington.edu/exhibits/harmony/

(ABOVE TOP)
Identification tag with *Challenge to Democracy*. War Relocation Authority. May 14, 1942.

Japanese-Americans were issued identification tags as they reported for evacuation. The publication *Challenge to Democracy* shows a grandfather and grandson wearing their tags as they wait for the evacuation bus.

(ABOVE BOTTOM)
"Japanese-American Family in 'Apartment' Created for Them from Converted Livestock Stall at Puyallup, Washington, Assembly Center." Photograph by Howard Clifford. 1942.

(OPPOSITE TOP)
Album of notes and photographs from students evacuated to the Puyallup, Washington, Assembly Center. Collected by Ella C. Evanson. Seattle, 1942.

Evanson, a teacher in Seattle, asked her students to write in her autograph book before they left for Camp Harmony in Puyallup, Washington. Shown here are photographs and one of the notes from her students. Evanson continued to receive letters from many of her students when they went on to the Minidoka Internment Camp in Idaho.

(OPPOSITE BOTTOM)
"Camp Minidoka Internment Camp, Hunt, Idaho." Watercolor by unknown artist. [1940s.]

Washington State University Libraries
Manuscripts, Archives, and Special Collections

Lucullus Virgil McWhorter Papers, 1848–1945

Lucullus McWhorter (1860–1944), a rancher in the Yakima River valley of Washington State, was deeply and significantly involved in preserving the cultural heritage of the first peoples of the Columbia Plateau, particularly the Yakama and Nez Perce peoples. As an author, amateur historian, linguist, and anthropologist, McWhorter collected stories, artifacts, drawings, maps, photographs, and printed materials in an effort to preserve the history and culture of these indigenous peoples. He captured photographic images of individuals and landscapes, including battle sites; he documented Indian-government relations in Eastern Washington; and he preserved evidence, including individual recollections, of Indian wars such as the Nez Perce War of 1877 and the Yakima Indian War of 1855–1858. McWhorter's published works include *Yellow Wolf: His Own Story* (1940), *Tragedy of the Wahk-Shum: Prelude to the Yakima Indian War, 1855–56* (1937), *Hear Me, My Chiefs! Nez Perce History and Legend* (published posthumously, 1952), and *The Crime against the Yakimas* (1913). McWhorter himself is the subject of Steven Ross Evans's book, *Voice of the Old Wolf: Lucullus Virgil McWhorter and the Nez Perce Indians* (1991).

The McWhorter papers are an essential and valued resource for tribal communities of the Columbia Plateau, for the scholarly community at Washington State University, and for researchers anywhere in the world investigating questions about the heritage and history of Columbia Plateau peoples. The papers consist of approximately 26 linear feet of material. In conjunction with McWhorter's photographs (the L.V. McWhorter Photograph Collection) and his collection of books and other printed materials (the McWhorter Collection), also held by Manuscripts, Archives, and Special Collections (MASC), as well as his artifact collection, held by the Museum of Anthropology at WSU, these papers preserve rare and unique evidence of lives, lifeways, and "lost" history. The collection is widely and intensively used.

The importance of Washington State University's McWhorter collections, as well as their direct connection to the university's geographical location, makes them extremely valuable for outreach and teaching purposes. For example, they were connected directly to the WSU curriculum during 2005–2006, when graduate students in the public history program curated an exhibit in MASC featuring items from all of the McWhorter collections, "Learning Each Other's Language: L.V. McWhorter and the Columbia Plateau Tribes." They were responsible for selecting the items and used the papers, photographs, and printed materials to conduct research for their interpretive texts. After this exhibit, images of items from the McWhorter artifact collection were added to MASC's digital collections, helping to re-establish and preserve connections to the papers and photographs.

http://www.wsulibs.wsu.edu/holland/masc/McWhortr/Mcwh1.htm

http://www.wsulibs.wsu.edu/holland/masc/McWhortr/photographs.htm

http://www.wsulibs.wsu.edu/holland/masc/xmcw_artifacts.html

(ABOVE TOP)
Silver medal given by Lucullus V. McWhorter to Yellow Wolf. Circa 1909.

The medal's verso bears a quotation from Yellow Wolf's narrative in *Yellow Wolf: His Own Story* by L. V. McWhorter.

(ABOVE BOTTOM)
"Peopeo Tholekt and Lucullus V. McWhorter." Photographic postcard by unknown artist. Photograph circa 1911; postcard n.d.

(OPPOSITE)
"Peopeo's Fight with a Grizzly Bear." Pencil and crayon drawing by Peopeo Tholekt. Circa 1926.

In an accompanying account of the fight, Tholekt described the attack and how he was saved when two Sioux friends shot and killed the bear.

An Index to the following Alphabet of Action, or Table of Rhetoricall INDIGITATIONS.

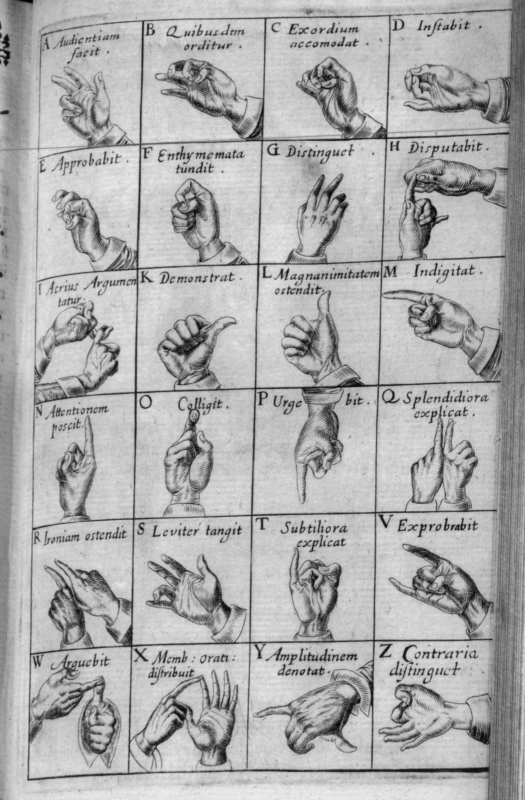

† The verball periphrasis of the gesture F, by accident hath been overslipped: but the *Plate* speakes Canonically for it selfe. It is one of *Quintilians* Gestures, which he observes the Greekes much to use (even with both Hands) in their Enthymemes, when they chop, as it were, their Logick, and inculcate and knock it down, as with a horne.

This following Table doth not onely serve to expresse the Rhetoricall postures of the *Fingers*; but may be used as Cyphers for private wayes of Discourse or Intelligence.

Washington University in St. Louis Libraries
Department of Special Collections

Philip Mills Arnold Semeiology Collection

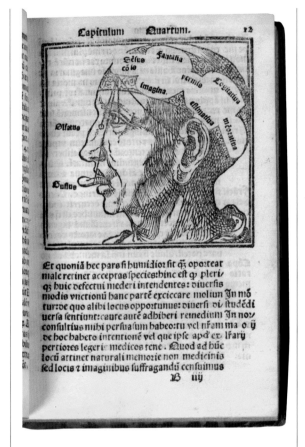

Pʜɪʟɪᴘ Mills Arnold (1911–1994) began collecting books while a student at Washington University. After receiving his undergraduate degree and a master's degree in chemical engineering, he worked for nearly 40 years at Phillips Petroleum Company, retiring as vice president for research and development in 1976. Throughout his professional career and into retirement, Mr. Arnold continued to develop his remarkable collection of books and manuscripts in the specialized field of semeiology, often called semiotics. He donated his collection to the libraries in 1969, and subsequent purchases were sent directly to the Department of Special Collections. The collection currently numbers some 1,600 items, and new materials are added through a sizeable endowment left to the libraries upon Mr. Arnold's death.

The American philosopher Charles W. Morris has defined semeiology as "a theory of signs in all their forms and manifestations, whether in animals or men, whether normal or pathological, whether linguistic or nonlinguistic, whether personal or social." Signs might include an actor's gestures, a writer's alphabet, a stenographer's notations, or images used to convey ideas or emotions, such as a nation's flag. Mr. Arnold identified important developments in the field of semeiology and collected landmark works in its major areas of enquiry: cryptography, the decipherment of ancient writing systems, languages for the blind and deaf, memory and mnemonics, palaeography, the philosophy of language, shorthand, signs and symbols, telegraphy, and universal writing. Notable among a collection rich in imagery and striking design elements are a rare 1591 broadside illustrating the organization of universal knowledge, and the first printed edition of Rabanus Maurus's magnificent series of pattern poems, *De Laudibus Sancte Crucis Opus* (1503).

Reflecting Mr. Arnold's interest in the non-verbal aspects of signs and their relationship to written and verbal expression, the collection is especially strong in works that explain a given system's theoretical underpinnings. In a 1989 letter to the department he writes that "in the field of communication for the blind and deaf, I excluded books printed in Braille or other raised letters that do not explain the system used; in shorthand and cryptography I excluded books written by such methods that do not explain the methods." Included, then, are works on cryptography such as Blaise de Vigenère's *Traicté des Chiffres* (1586) and John Falconer's *Cryptomenysis Patefacta* (1685), both of which describe methods for conveying concealed messages. In *Chironomia: or, The Art of Manuall Rhetorique* (1644), the 17th-century physician John Bulwer admonishes speakers against gesturing with the left hand alone, explaining that the right hand is "planted neerer the fountain of the blood. And verily, the Left Hand seems to be born to an obsequious compliance with the Right."

This emphasis on description and explanation by contemporary theorists makes the Arnold Semeiology Collection particularly valuable for researchers studying semiotics and, more broadly, the history of ideas, philosophy, and human expression. But the collection is equally valuable for practitioners—artists, graphic designers, performers, cryptographers, and others—who seek to inform their work through a greater understanding of the nature of communication in its many forms.

http://www.library.wustl.edu/units/spec/rarebooks/semeiology/

(ABOVE)
Congestorium artificiose memorie.
Johann Horst von Romberch. 1533.

Originally published in 1520, this work by the Dominican Johannes Romberch describes a number of artificial memory systems.

(OPPOSITE)
Chirologia: Or, The Naturall Language of the Hand… Whereunto Is Added Chironomia: Or, The Art of Manuall Rhetoricke. John Bulwer. 1644.

This table "doth not only serve to expresse the Rhetoricall postures of the *Fingers*; but may be used as Cyphers for private wayes of Discourse or Intelligence."

University of Waterloo Library
Doris Lewis Rare Book Room

Seagram Museum Collection

(ABOVE)
Chromolithographic plate from *Traité général de viticulture: ampélographie.* Pierre Viala and Victor Vermorel. Paris, 1901–10.

(OPPOSITE TOP LEFT)
De secretis remediis. Konrad Gesner. 1554. Title page.

(OPPOSITE BOTTOM RIGHT)
De secretis remediis. Konrad Gesner. 1554. Book cover.

(OPPOSITE BOTTOM LEFT)
De secretis remediis. Konrad Gesner. 1554. Detail.

DISMAY at the news that the internationally-renowned Seagram Museum in Waterloo, Ontario, would be closing in 1997 was tempered with interest by the University of Waterloo Library when it became the beneficiary of two significant portions of the museum's collections.

The "world's finest collection on the beverage alcohol industry"—some 900 volumes dating from 1554 to the 20th century—was donated, accompanied by the only extant archives of the Seagram family and the Seagram plant up to 1929. The book and archival collections complemented the existing research collections in the fields of chemistry, chemical engineering, the history of technology as well as decorative arts, temperance, and the area's urban and local history. Highlighted by traditional as well as electronic exhibits, the collection draws inquiries from around the world ranging from requests for help in identifying "an old bottle of whiskey discovered during house renovations" and clandestine activities during the prohibition era to studies on turn-of-the-century Canadian commercial history.

Earliest of the imprints collected by the former museum, the only one in the world interpreting both wine and spirits, is Konrad Gesner's vellum-bound book on distillation, *De secretis remediis liber* (1554). Among the other often irreplaceable volumes is the first edition of *Livre du vigneron et du fabricant de cidre...et autres vins de fruits*, by Joseph Mauny de Mornay (1838). Superb among the 20th-century imprints is the first edition of the seven volumes of *Traité général de viticulture: ampélographie* by Pierre Viala and Victor Vermorel (1901–1910) illustrated by chromolithographic portraits of grape clusters, all exceptionally beautiful.

In addition, and of importance to social history, the library acquired significant resources on drinking habits and social customs surrounding the beverage industry—thus one finds a 19th-century pamphlet by the "father of the Temperance movement," Dr. Benjamin Rush, next to the rare example of high art deco entitled *The Savoy Cocktail Book* in its 1930 first edition.

Equally noteworthy for researchers in fine and book arts are the decorative features of many books, including the binding of the 1738 edition of Smith's *A Compleat Body of Distilling*, which has wine glasses embossed and stamped in gilt on the spine. Most unique is the treatment of *Instructions for Surveyors of the Distillery and Brandy* (1754) with a companion set of instructions for distillery officers which were bound in a brilliant red leather *dos-a-dos* binding.

The archival collections that were donated by the museum document one of Canada's most prominent, successful, and oldest business families, the Seagrams. Their company's business records, while incomplete in some areas, nevertheless provide information on the liquor industry and include product labels and printed ephemera as well as exceptional photographs. In addition, certain series, such as the 1788–1846 letters of Canadian wine merchants, provide unique insights into the drinking habits of the time and problems with supply and demand of liquor. A significant donation of family material came from the home of Joseph Edward Frowde Seagram, grandson of the company's founder, Joseph Emm Seagram.

DE SECRETIS
REMEDIIS
LIBER AVT PO
TIVS THESAVRVS, EVO
NYMO GESNERO PHI
NYMO Siatro authore.

HIC LIBER NON SOLVM ME
...cis & pharmacopœis, apprime necessarius:
...d omnibus rerū naturalium, alchemiæ atq;
...economiæ studiosis, in varijs tum stillatirijs
...liqueribus, tum vinis medicatis apparandis,
ac singuloru cognoscendis viribus, vti
lis atque iucundus fuerit.

ACCEDIT IAM RECENS
IACOBI BESSONI GALLI
de absoluta ratione olea & aquas è medica-
mentis simplicibus extrahendi.Liber do
ctissimus, nunquam ante hac
in lucem æditus.

In utroque icones ad rerum declarationem paf-
sim adijciuntur.

---

simus per singulas hebdomades semel
ut minimū renouandus est. Idem hoc
fieri potest in uinaceis recens expressis
per uindemiā: Vel in diebus caniculari
bus ad Solem. Potest etiā extrahi quin
ta essentia ex uino turbido immundo
& putrido, modò non sit acetosum. nā
etiam ex corrupto uino, quod in bono
loco natū sit, quanq̃ turbato & mali sa
poris, optimā aquā uitę destillari uide-
mus. ¶ Est & alter modus sine igne &
labore extrahēdi, hu-
iusmodi. Aquam uitę
quam inueneris nobi
lissimā, pone in uitrū
cum collo longo, ha-
bēte in summitate fo-
ramen, quod debet
claudi & lutari cera
rite præparata, ut inferius docet Vlsta-
dius cap.decimo.)Deinde uertatur ui-
trum & cū collo imponatur in simū. sic
crassior materia residebit in fundo de-
stillatorij: quod cum longo tempore
K

Digital Dress: 200 Years of Urban Style

DIGITAL Dress: 200 Years of Urban Style is the result of collaboration among the Wayne State University Library System, the Detroit Historical Museum, the Henry Ford, and Meadow Brook Hall, funded with an Institute of Museum and Library Services grant in 2003. Each of the member partners contributed collections to the initiative to create a study and research collection of urban dress resources now numbering in excess of 5,000 images. This collection includes examples of men's, women's, and children's clothing used for work, play, and formal occasions. The pieces chosen for the digital collection originated in America and Europe with bulk manufacturers, couture designers, and home-based clothing makers.

The catalyst for this particular digital collection came from the Wayne State University College of Liberal Arts and Sciences, the Department of Art and Art History, and its Fashion Design and Merchandising Area, home to the Dorothea June Grossbart Historic Costume Collection. This collection, which emphasizes women's garments and accessories, is used for study and teaching, although access is limited given the fragility of the clothes and the manner in which they are stored for preservation. The capturing of these items with digital images allowed many more students to study the pieces in detail or examine them generally without putting the clothes in further jeopardy.

The Henry Ford's contributions to Digital Dress come from a collection of over 10,000 resources that has received the recognition of the National Endowment for the Humanities. The Henry Ford contributed images to the special collection in the areas it considers its strengths including men's clothing from the 1770s to 1860, undergarments, shoes, couture from the 1940s and 1950s, and children's wear from the 1770s to 1880s.

Meadow Brook Hall was the creation of Matilda Dodge Wilson, a woman who both enjoyed wearing couture clothing and could afford to purchase it. Owing to Mrs. Dodge's interest in particular kinds of clothes, Meadow Brook Hall was able to contribute resources in three important areas for the digital collection: couture from the 1920s and 1930s, Peggy Hoyt-designed clothes, and photographs of the Dodge family in their personal garments.

The Detroit Historical Museum and its clothing collections, in excess of 30,000 items, is particularly representative of Detroit. The selections from this institution reflect five collecting areas: Detroit-made garments, accessories, 20th-century items with an emphasis on the 1940s and 1950s, men's clothing and accessories, and wedding gowns. These are among the special items included: a wedding gown worn in 1821 at a church now located on the Wayne State University campus, the suit worn by G. Mennen "Soapy" Williams for his inauguration as Michigan Governor, and a child's satin flag costume from 1904. The distinct character of this part of the digital collection is found in the mundane rather than the expensive or unique—with such items as pajamas, hats, shoes, and bathing suits—and as a reflection of Detroit as a center of fur processing in the 19th and early 20th centuries.

http://www.lib.wayne.edu/geninfo/units/lcms/dls/grants/ddgrant.php

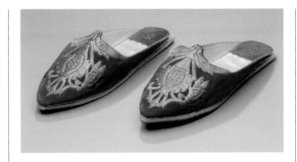

(ABOVE)
Red velvet slippers embroidered in gold thread. Unknown designer. 1935.

(OPPOSITE TOP LEFT)
Woman's light-blue denim coveralls with button drop seat. [1943.]
> These coveralls were worn by Katherine Bogush's mother at McCord Radiator from 1943 to 1945.

(OPPOSITE TOP CENTER)
Black-and-white floral-print satin clocque coat and dress. Designed by Ruth Joyce. [1964–66.]
> This evening ensemble was owned by Mrs. Irving Rose.

(OPPOSITE TOP RIGHT)
Gold tissue evening gown with hand-embroidered lavender flowers and metallic fringe. Unknown designer. 1924.

(OPPOSITE BOTTOM LEFT)
Ice-blue satin wedding gown. Designed by Peggy Hoyt for Frances Dodge. New York, 1938.
> This gown was worn by Frances Dodge on the occasion of her marriage to James Johnson on July 1, 1938. The wedding took place at Meadow Brook Hall, the home of Dodge's mother, Matilda Rausch Dodge Wilson, located in Rochester, Michigan.

(OPPOSITE BOTTOM CENTER)
Off-white satin ballgown with rhinestones and silver beads at neckline and cuffs. Designed by Sarmi for Bonwit Teller. New York, [1970].
> This gown was worn by Helen Milliken at 1970 and 1974 inaugural balls. Her husband William Milliken was Governor of Michigan from 1969 to 1983.

(OPPOSITE BOTTOM RIGHT)
Pale-blue satin-silk gown with embroidered floral patterns of 1/8"-standing silver braid, silver beads, white and gray pearls, blue and silver thread, and cummerbund sash of fuschia faille. Designed by Cristobal Balenciaga. Paris, 1950.
> Worn in 1950 by Elizabeth Parke Firestone, wife of Harvey S. Firestone Jr., son of Firestone Tire and Rubber Company founder Harvey S. Firestone.

The Gustav Mahler-Alfred Rosé Collection

"Gustav Mahler." Gold-toned photographic print in *carte de visite* format from Victor Angerer studio. Vienna, circa 1903.

Symphony no. 1. Gustav Mahler. Detail.
Earliest surviving version of copyist's score in black ink with additions and corrections by Mahler in ink and pencil. N.d.

QUOTING Otto Dietz, visiting Austrian ambassador to the University of Western Ontario in 2004, "Who would have thought to find a piece of Vienna in London, Ontario?" Indeed, visitors to the Gustav Mahler-Alfred Rosé Room are astonished by the richness and variety of the treasures contained therein. From photographs to letters, etchings to sculpture, music manuscripts to published musical scores, the Gustav Mahler-Alfred Rosé Collection (GM-AR Collection) is indisputably one of the largest surviving bodies of primary source material relating to the life and times of Gustav Mahler and his brother-in-law, Arnold Rosé.

A bequest of Mahler's nephew, Alfred E. Rosé, and given to the Music Library by Alfred's widow Maria C. Rosé, the GM-AR Collection was largely assembled by Mahler's sister Justine (Alfred's mother). During the years following their parents' deaths, Justine functioned as her brother's housekeeper, saving some 700 letters, family photographs, and programs of performances conducted by Gustav; she also collected celebrity autographs. Justine married the violinist Arnold Rosé, founder and leader of the Rosé String Quartet; Rosé was also Mahler's concertmaster of both the Vienna Philharmonic and Opera orchestras. The Rosé children, Alfred and Alma, were musically gifted, Alfi studying piano, violin, and clarinet; Alma, the violin. Alfred became a conductor and *repetiteur*; Alma had a career as a violinist, founding a touring women's orchestra, the *Wiener Walzermädeln*.

The GM-AR Collection survived the Nazi *Anschluss*, packed in steamer trunks and accompanying Arnold and daughter Alma on their flight to England in 1938. Alma realized that her father's finances would not sustain him. Leaving the safety of England, she resumed her solo career in Holland, playing house concerts and sending funds to Arnold. While attempting to flee to Switzerland, Alma was captured by the Nazis and sent to Auschwitz, where she was recognized and conscripted to lead the *Mädchenorchester*. Following Arnold's death and the end of the war, the collection was shipped to Cincinnati, eventually accompanying Alfred and Maria Rosé to London, Ontario. Invitations of employment at the Western Ontario Conservatory of Music brought them to their adopted home.

Scholar Henry-Louis de la Grange described the GM-AR Collection as "the finest surviving collection of information about Mahler's early career." Dr. Stephen McClatchie's recent editions of *The Mahler Family Letters* (2005) and *Liebste Justi!: Briefe an die Familie* (2006) make much of this material newly available to scholars. Additional highlights of the collection include manuscript copies of Mahler's songs, a Rodin bust of Mahler, several large etchings by Ferdinand Schmutzer, Maria Rosé's father, and a professional copyist's manuscript of the earliest-surviving version of Mahler's First Symphony, with annotations and amendments in Mahler's hand, which offers insights into Mahler's compositional process. Richard Newman's meticulously researched *Alma Rosé: Vienna to Auschwitz* (2000) represents a major contribution to Holocaust history, and prompted a collaboration with the Jüdisches Museum's *Alma Rosé* exhibit in Vienna (2004), on the occasion of the 60th anniversary of Alma's death at Auschwitz.

http://www.lib.uwo.ca/music/gmar.html

University of Wisconsin–Madison Libraries

Department of Special Collections, Memorial Library

Fry Collection of Italian History and Culture

WILLIAM F. "Jack" Fry, professor emeritus of physics at the University of Wisconsin–Madison, is intrigued by micro history— "common life captured in letters" and the traces of "small town government, the bread baker and shoemaker." He has built the Fry Collection of Italian History and Culture in this spirit. Fry, a specialist in high-energy physics, has long collaborated with Italian physicists and continues to make regular collecting trips to Italy. The Fry Collection—large and still growing—is the product of "endless hours rummaging through piles of discarded papers and dusty old books," as he explains. His finds have included manuscripts dating from the Renaissance to rare pamphlets circulating in Italy following World War II.

In particular, in order to explore Italian life under fascism, Fry has collected a wide variety of books, newspapers, printed ephemera, photographs, and manuscript materials from the period 1920 to 1946. They range from a brochure describing Italian train excursions and programs for the Italian kennel club to certificates of military service and schoolboy accomplishments under Mussolini and books expounding Italian racial policies. The Fry Collection, filled with materials on Italian fascism rarely found in American libraries, complements the UW–Madison Libraries' other strong holdings in modern European history.

The Fry Collection also concerns the history of northern and northeastern Italy from the 15th century through the 19th, with particular attention to the Austrian and French occupation of the Veneto. For example, a recent addition of hundreds of letters from Padua and environs (circa 1810 to 1860) speaks to sanitation, wills and bequests, education, and murder. Genealogical compilations reveal family histories, both grand and modest; ledgers track the fortunes of estates over decades and longer; forms hint at the sad story of foundling wheels, where babies were left to the care of the Church; and broadsides announce governmental decrees and policies as they were posted on Italian walls. Such broadsides might prescribe official rates for gondolas or publicize bread prices.

Other materials offer insights into the rise of Italian nationalist sentiment, the Church and Italian culture, developments in Istria and Latina, partisan movements in Italy during World War II, 20th-century Italian communism, and political culture in postwar Italy.

Fry, who began making gifts to the Department of Special Collections in the early 1990s, supplies extensive collector's descriptions, explaining the appeal of particular items and guiding researchers to related materials in the collection's riches.

An online exhibit filled with strong graphics from the fascist era has generated worldwide attention. The collection provides a wealth of primary sources for history, art history, cultural studies, and history of science and technology, and draws scholars from Italy and elsewhere to Madison to use the collection.

http://www.library.wisc.edu/libraries/dpf/Fascism/Home.html

(ABOVE)
Lo stornellatore della Radio Sociale. C. M. Garatti.
Foligno: Giuseppe Campi, 1940.
    This periodical contains popular verses on a variety of topics.

(OPPOSITE TOP LEFT)
Report card. 1942.

(OPPOSITE TOP RIGHT)
School reader. 1940.

(OPPOSITE BOTTOM LEFT)
"Mussolini Presenting Award to a Boy."
Photograph by unknown artist. N.d

(OPPOSITE BOTTOM RIGHT)
Class photograph by unknown artist. N.d.

Yale University Library
Sterling Memorial Library

Map Collection

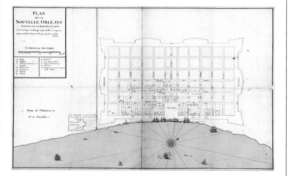

THE Yale Map Collection has the largest collection of print maps in Connecticut and one of the largest university collections in the United States. Its collections are geographically comprehensive and consist of over 200,000 map sheets, 3,000 atlases, and 900 reference books. The Map Collection holds approximately 11,000 rare map prints and manuscripts. These are generally identified as pre-1850 maps and can manifest themselves as large and small flat sheet maps, covers, globes, globe gores, and wall maps, as well as copper- and woodblock-engraved plates. These rare maps cover the world in scope. The majority of the rare collection focuses on North America and includes many maps associated with American history.

Visitors can view maps owned by prominent American figures such as George Washington, early world maps showing geographic perceptions of the period such as Johann Ruyches's 1507 map of the world (*Universalior cogniti orbis tabula ex recentibus confecta observationibus*), claimed possessions of North America such as John Mitchell's *Map of the British and French dominions in North America*, significant historical boundaries such as Charles Mason's *Map of the Mason-Dixon line between Maryland and Pennsylvania* (1768), and the beginnings of American cities such as the 1721 French manuscript map of New Orleans (*Plan de la Nouvelle Orleans*). In addition to the main Yale Map Collection, the Beinecke Rare Book and Manuscript Library contains important collections of rare early mapping, in both atlases and separate sheets. These include such treasures as drawings and charts from the Lewis and Clark expeditions.

The Yale Map Collection is also the central support facility for the use of modern mapping technology at Yale University. At the Map Collection, researchers find state-of-the-art hardware and software resources for the capture, management, and analysis of spatial data, as well as support specialists who provide expert advice and consulting services. The Map Collection staff is well qualified to provide the type of interdisciplinary support required by Yale University's research community. The Map Collection provides instruction in the use of geographic information systems (GIS) for cutting-edge analysis of spatial relationships, as well as the use of mobile mapping technologies such as the Global Positioning System (GPS) to capture the geographic data necessary for the examination of those spatial relationships. The Map Collection is also active in providing services on projects requiring a high level of technical expertise and ranging in focus from the digital mapping of archaeological excavations to the use of 18th-century German postal route maps and modern GIS data to trace James Boswell's route in his travels through Europe.

The Yale Map Collection is a focal point for the collection and availability of cartographic information, regardless of format, at Yale University. The Map Collection augments the collection and use of print maps and atlases with the application of geospatial information systems and imaging software towards a goal of building an internationally renowned collection of cartographic resources in both print and digital forms.

http://www.library.yale.edu/MapColl/

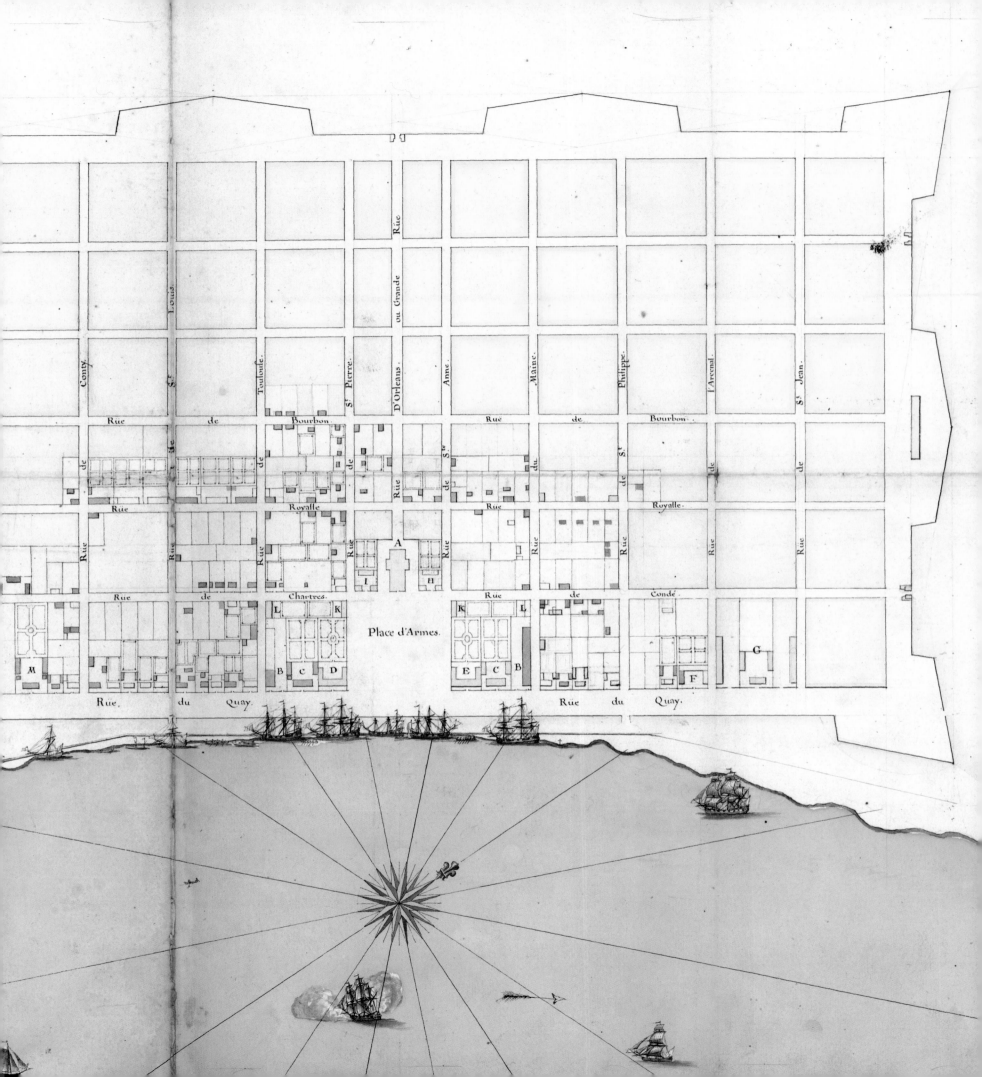

Collection Overviews

Introduction

EACH of the preceding profiles represents only one of many rare and special collections held by the contributing library. The following section provides brief descriptions of these additional collections.

Also presented in each library overview is contact information, credit lines for the collection profiles and illustrations, and a Web address to lead to additional information.

Readers seeking to identify a specific type of collection may search the overviews on the companion Web site to this volume. See http://www.celebratingresearch.org/.

University of Alabama Libraries

From a cabinet in the reference room to a separate named library, Special Collections has grown over the last six decades to become a destination both for students and faculty on campus and for scholars from around the world. Developed by gifts and purchases, the collection includes the world's largest collection of published materials by Alabama authors, works in whole or in part about Alabama, or works published in the state. Additionally, there are works on Southern history and literature, sheet music, sound recordings, maps, and other materials that reflect the culture and history of the South. Within the collections are Confederate Imprints, the works of literary figures such as Lafcadio Hearn, Sir Walter Scott, Mark Twain, Ralph Waldo Emerson, Henry James, and Paul Laurence Dunbar. There are books from the world's leading fine presses and printers as well as contemporary book bindings and unique artists' books by student and leading professional book workers. The University Archives and a historical and literary manuscript collection are housed here. The manuscript collection reflects the history and culture of Alabama from the colonial period to the present, and includes the papers of former congressmen and senators, records of businesses ranging from general stores to iron and coal companies, records of churches and social and professional organizations, and personal papers of individuals and families. A photographic collection includes pictures of individuals, structures, and scenes from the university, around Alabama, and around the nation and world; it contains examples of almost every type of popular 19th- and 20th-century photographic process.

Collection Profile and Overview: Clark E. Center Jr.
Illustrations: Marina Klarić

University of Alabama Libraries
W.S. Hoole Special Collections Library
Box 870266
500 Hackberry Lane
University of Alabama
Tuscaloosa, Alabama 35487-0266
http://www.lib.ua.edu/libraries/hoole/
http://www.lib.ua.edu/libraries/hoole/happenings/events.htm
(205) 348-0500 (t)
(205) 348-1699 (f)

University at Albany, State University of New York, Libraries

The M. E. Grenander Department of Special Collections and Archives includes approximately 600 manuscript collections, 40,000 volumes, and more than 30,000 photographs. Its strengths include the Archive of Public Affairs and Policy, a collection of over 5,000 cubic feet of manuscript collections from individuals and private interest groups concerned with 20th-century New York State political issues, and the German and Jewish Intellectual Émigré Collection documenting the intellectual exodus of the 1930s and 1940s. A recent addition to Special Collections, the National Death Penalty Archive, contains records that document the history of capital punishment in the United States. The University Archives holds the official records and publications of the University at Albany and its predecessor institutions from its origins in 1844 to the present, student publications and memorabilia, and the papers of distinguished faculty and alumni, including those of Pulitzer Prize-winning author William Kennedy, biographer Joseph Persico, and children's book author and illustrator Marcia J. Brown. The department also houses three important book collections. The Miriam Snow Mathes Historical Children's Literature Collection includes over 12,000 children's books and periodicals published between 1800 and 1960. The Elzevier Collection consists of 700 volumes from the printing offices of the Elzevier family, which flourished in the Dutch Republic between 1583 and 1702, and the Mordecai Kosover Collection of Judaica includes materials published between 1584 and 1850.

Collection Profile and Overview: Brian Keough
Illustrations: Larry Gordon

University at Albany, State University of New York
M. E. Grenander Department of Special Collections & Archives
Science Library 350
1400 Washington Avenue
Albany, New York 12222
http://library.albany.edu/speccoll/
http://library.albany.edu/speccoll/collections.htm
(518) 437-3935 (t)
(518) 437-3930 (f)

University of Alberta Libraries

Bruce Braden Peel was Chief Librarian of the University of Alberta from 1955 to 1982. The eponymous Bruce Peel Special Collections Library is located in handsome quarters in the Rutherford South Library. Among its 180,000 volumes are many treasures, including beautiful, rare, and unusual books. Some collections in the Peel Library are tightly focused upon a single author (e.g., D. H. Lawrence) or a printing firm and its output (e.g., Hogarth, Curwen, Grabhorn). Others are more wide-ranging, giving shape to abstract ideas, such as the collection of artists' books and bookworks, which is now the preeminent collection in Canada. Major strengths include the Victorian novel, particularly the first editions of Charles Dickens, but also strong collections in Victorian book art and Victorian and Edwardian children's fiction. Other notable collections include the history of science, featuring many color-plate books, the Alberta Folklore and Local History Collection, the Dime Novel holdings, books focused on the art of William Blake, and the Salzburg Collection, which is one of the most important collections in Canada for historical Central European legal studies. Furthermore, special materials are regularly added to complement the library's collections of fine bindings, modern private press books, and the history and literature of the Prairie Provinces. In the mid-1960s, the library acquired a significant private collection of the works of John Bunyan. On this continent Alberta's Bunyan collection is second only to that of the Huntington Library. To strengthen the overall collection, the Senate of the University of Alberta established a library endowment fund in 1987, which makes possible the purchase of rare materials in a wide variety of disciplines.

Collection Profile and Overview: Robert Desmarais
Illustrations: Karin Fodor

University of Alberta
Bruce Peel Special Collections Library
B7 Rutherford South
Edmonton, Alberta
T6G 2J4
Canada
http://www.library.ualberta.ca/specialcollections/
(780) 492-5998 (t)
(780) 492-5083 (f)

University of Arizona Library

Special Collections is home to one of the nation's finest collections of printed texts on the borderlands of the Southwest and Arizona. These collections document the region's culture and history, including accounts of Native Americans and their ancestors, the impact of Spanish and Mexican settlement, and the influx of Anglo-Americans and others into the region during the 19th century. These vast collections contain volumes in the arts, humanities, social sciences, and sciences, including fiction by Anglo-Americans, Mexican-Americans, and Native Americans; extensive materials on Sonora and Chihuahua, Mexico; state and local documents covering southern Arizona; Western pulp fiction; juvenile fiction; and cookbooks; as well as a large pamphlet and ephemera collection documenting the region.

Established in 1958, Special Collections houses a large number of books, pamphlets, ephemera, broadsides, photographs and significant primary resources in the manuscript and archival collections. Holdings include rare books dating to the 15th century and fine facsimile editions, the history of science, Southwestern Americana and borderlands history, fine and theater arts, British and American literature, and the art of the book.

The manuscript collections also emphasize the history and literature of Arizona and the borderlands of the Southwest. Within these collections, one finds journals of explorers, diaries of settlers, papers of prominent Arizonans, and records of small businesses. It also houses the papers of Arizona politicians, including Morris K. Udall, Stewart Udall, Dennis DeConcini, and Jim Kolbe.

The photograph and graphic collections encompass a variety of research materials such as photographs, postcards, historical maps, and ephemera, most of which are related to various aspects of the history, geography, arts, and industries of Arizona and the Southwest.

Collection Profile: Bonnie Travers
Overview: Patricia Promís
Illustrations: Bonnie Travers

University of Arizona Library
Special Collections
1510 E. University Blvd.
PO Box 210055
Tucson, Arizona 85721-0055
http://www.library.arizona.edu/speccoll/
(520) 621-6423 (t)
(520) 621-2709 (f)

Arizona State University Libraries

The Department of Archives and Special Collections at the Arizona State University (ASU) Libraries hosts seven archival repositories and special collections primarily documenting the diverse history, arts, and cultures of Arizona and the Southwest. These repositories are the Arizona Collection, Chicano Research Collection, Benedict Visual Literacy Collection, Child Drama Collection, Labriola National American Indian Data Center, Special Collections, and University Archives.

Each of the repositories collects current and historical information in a variety of formats including books, periodicals, microforms, photographs, institutional records, personal papers, videotapes, and digital information. The department currently preserves and makes accessible over 20,000 linear feet of archival materials, more than 1 million photographs, and ca. 50,000 monographic titles including rare books. These materials are made available in two reading rooms at Hayden Library, and they are stored at a state-of-the-art remote storage facility at the ASU Polytechnic campus.

Collection Profile and Overview: Robert P. Spindler
Illustrations: Brian Davis, Chris Thompson

Arizona State University Libraries
Department of Archives and Special Collections
Box 871006
Tempe, Arizona 85287-1006
http://www.asu.edu/lib/archives/
archives@asu.edu
(480) 965-4932 (t)
(480) 965-0776 (f)

Auburn University Libraries

The Special Collections & Archives Department of the Auburn University Libraries houses printed materials, manuscripts, still pictures, motion pictures, sound recordings, and maps that merit an extra level of security because of their rare or unique nature. The department collects, preserves, and makes available these materials to support Auburn's instructional and research missions and to further scholarship. Its holdings document such topics as the rough-and-tumble politics of higher education in Alabama; the role of agriculture and agribusiness in the South; the Civil War and its impact upon individuals, families, and communities; the history of flight; and the activities of illustrators and naturalists who studied flora and fauna prior to the development of today's specialized disciplines. Undergraduates, graduate students, and faculty members at Auburn University and other institutions of higher learning use the department's resources to prepare senior theses, master's theses, doctoral dissertations, scholarly articles, and books issued by the academic press. Recent examples of note include Pete Daniel, *Lost Revolutions: The South in the 1950s* (2000); Joshua Buhs, *The Fire Ant Wars: Nature, Science, and Public Policy in Twentieth-Century America* (2004); and W. David Lewis, *Eddie Rickenbacker: An American Hero in the Twentieth Century* (2005). Special Collections & Archives and the Auburn University Libraries' Systems Department have cooperated to produce a growing Digital Library which makes an increasing number of Auburn's rare and unique materials available online.

Collection Profile: Dwayne Cox
Illustrations: Joyce Hicks

Auburn University Libraries
Special Collections & Archives
Ralph Brown Draughon Library
Auburn University, Alabama 36849
http://www.lib.auburn.edu/sca/
http://diglib.auburn.edu/
archive@auburn.edu
(334) 844-1732 (t)
(334) 844-4424 (f)

Boston College Libraries

The Honorable John J. Burns Library of Rare Books and Special Collections houses Boston College's rare books, special collections and archives. It is located in the magnificently appointed English collegiate-style Bapst Library Building, winner of *Interiors* magazine's Annual Award for Restoration (1988). The Burns Library is home to more than 200,000 volumes, some 15,000,000 manuscripts, and important collections of architectural records, maps, art works, newspapers, photographs, films, prints, artifacts, and ephemera. These materials are housed in the climate-controlled, secure environment of Burns either because of their rarity or because of their importance as part of a special collection. While treated with special care, these resources are available for use to all qualified students, faculty, and researchers. Visitors are always welcome, and the library features an attractive and ambitious exhibits program.

Though its collections cover virtually the entire spectrum of human knowledge, the Burns Library has achieved international recognition in several specific areas of research, most notably: Irish studies; British Catholic authors; Jesuitana; fine print; Catholic liturgy and life in America, 1925–1975; Boston history; Caribbeana, especially Jamaican studies; Balkan studies; and Congressional archives. It has also won acclaim for its significant holdings in the fields of nursing, American detective fiction, Thomas Merton, Japanese prints, colonial and early republic Protestantism, and banking.

The library is named in memory of the Honorable John J. Burns (1901–1957), one of Boston College's most successful and respected alumni. A 1921 graduate of Boston College, John Burns attended Harvard Law School, where he excelled as a student and as a faculty member, rising to the rank of full professor in five years. In 1931, at the age of 29, he became the youngest person ever appointed to the Superior Court of Massachusetts.

Collection Profile and Overview: Jill G. Thomas and
    Robert K. O'Neill
Illustrations: Stephen Vedder

Boston College Libraries
The John J. Burns Library
Boston College
140 Commonwealth Ave.
Chestnut Hill, Massachusetts 02467
http://www.bc.edu/burns/
(617) 552-3282 (t)
(617) 552-2465 (f)

Boston Public Library

The Research Library at the Boston Public Library holds extensive special collections in a wide variety of subjects. The Rare Books & Manuscripts Department houses more than 600,000 printed items and 1 million manuscripts. Important holdings include large collections on colonial and revolutionary Massachusetts, anti-slavery manuscripts, the Barton Collection of Shakespeareana, and the Galatea Collection on the history of women. In addition there are many important examples of medieval manuscripts, incunabula, and fine printing.

The Norman B. Leventhal Map Center includes 200,000 historic maps and 5,000 atlases documenting the evolution of the printed map from woodcuts, copperplate engravings, and lithographs to the latest computer technologies. The geographical focus of these maps, atlases, and globes is the world, Europe, and America, with a particular attention to New England, Massachusetts, and Boston from the 15th century to the present day.

The Fine Arts Department holds more than 125,000 titles documenting art, architecture, and the decorative arts, with special focus on Boston and New England. The Music Department houses 150,000 volumes concerning every facet of musical study, including biography, history and criticism, ethnomusicology, theory and composition, and music education; the collected editions of all major composers; musical first editions and other rare items; and important music indexes, encyclopedias, and bibliographies.

The Print Department has built collections totaling over 100,000 prints and drawings and 650,000 photographs. Some of the outstanding holdings include works by Rembrandt, Durer, Rowlandson, Goya, Daumier, and Toulouse-Lautrec. It also houses the Boston Pictorial Archive, the largest public collections of photographs of Boston in earlier days; Civil War photographs; and 19th-century photographs of native peoples and local architecture from all over the world.

Collection Profile and Overview: Beth Prindle
Illustrations: Thomas Blake

The Boston Public Library, Copley Square
700 Boylston Street
Boston, Massachusetts 02116
http://www.bpl.org/
Leventhal Map Center Web site: http://www.maps.bpl.org/
info@bpl.org
(617) 536-5400 (t)
(617) 536-7758 (f)

Boston University Libraries

The African Studies Library began in 1953 as a departmental library of the newly founded African Studies Center. The combination of Cold War–era global politics and the onset of independence in former colonial territories gave rise to interdisciplinary, geographically focused studies programs throughout the United States, with Boston University's African Studies Center one of the earliest. The collection of government documents and other publications acquired by faculty during research in Africa soon outgrew the facilities and resources of the center. When Mugar Memorial Library was built in 1967, the African Studies Library came to occupy an entire floor, with a reading room and substantial stack space for books and journals as well as the documents collection. Today the collection includes over 200,000 volumes, maps, pamphlets, electronic resources, and a small but intriguing collection of archival primary sources. The major strengths of this interdisciplinary collection are in the social sciences, with a broad representation of the humanities and sciences. Most of the collection is included in the Boston University Libraries online catalog, but a significant number of older African government documents have not yet been converted from the in-house classification system used when it was a departmental library. The system encourages browsing the shelf, or items can be located through the card catalog or the published *Catalog of African Government Documents* (1976). Researchers can also draw on the collections of the Cooperative Africana Microforms Project at the Center for Research Libraries.

Collection Profile and Overview: Gretchen Walsh
Illustrations: Vernon Doucette

Boston University
African Studies Library
Mugar Memorial Library
771 Commonwealth Avenue
Boston, Massachusetts 02215
http://www.bu.edu/library/asl/
(617) 353-3726 (t)
(617) 358-1729 (f)

Brigham Young University Library

When the Lee Library's Special Collections was founded in 1957, the collection consisted of 1,000 books, 50 manuscript collections, and 1 curator. Today, 50 years later, the collection has grown substantially to 320,000 books, 10,000 manuscript collections, and 1.3 million photographs. In order to support the ever-expanding collection, the library employs 12 full-time curators, 4 adjunct curators, 2 conservators, 4 paraprofessionals, and 60 students.

In 1999, a new addition to the library was constructed that included a state-of-the-art facility built especially for Special Collections. At that time, Special Collections was named after L. Tom Perry, an apostle of the Church of Jesus Christ of Latter-day Saints.

An array of printed books and pamphlets, manuscripts, maps, music, broadsides, fine artistic printing, posters, and photographs are housed in Special Collections. Among the holdings is one of the nation's foremost collections of Mormon materials, including the 19th and 20th Century Western and Mormon Manuscripts Collection. In recent years, the library also acquired the William A. Wilson Folklore Archives, the largest collection of Mormon folklore in the world, as well as the A. Dean and Jean Larsen Yellowstone Collection, making the Lee Library one of the largest repositories of Yellowstone materials in the nation. Other major collections include Renaissance & Reformation, History of Early Printers, History of Science, Motion Picture Archives, and the Film Music Archives. The Lee Library has also built substantial collections in literature, such as the Victorian and Edwardian Collection and the Fine Printing Collection.

Collection Profile and Overview: David J. Whittaker,
    John M. Murphy, and P. Bradford Westwood
Illustrations: Lee Library Conservation Lab

Brigham Young University
L. Tom Perry Special Collections
1130 Harold B. Lee Library
Provo, Utah 84602
http://sc.lib.byu.edu/
russ_taylor@byu.edu (Reference Services)
(801) 422-2933 (t)
(801) 422-0466 (f)

University of British Columbia Library

Rare Books and Special Collections at the University of British Columbia Library houses significant collections of rare books, archival materials, historical maps, photographs, broadsides, and pamphlets. The principal focus of the collections is British Columbia: history, exploration, settlement, business, politics, ethnicity, literature, culture, and labor. These subjects are covered in considerable depth. Other collections cover Canadian history, Canadian literature, English literature, children's books, and the history of cartography.

Rare Books and Special Collections' holdings of cartographic archives and historical maps are especially strong in pre-1800 world/hemispheres, pre-1900 North America and Pacific Rim, fire insurance plans of BC towns and cities, and Edo-period Japan. Also acquired as parts of larger archival collections and fonds are collections of maps (both printed and manuscript), architectural drawings, and plans and blueprints.

Manuscript collections include materials documenting the economic, political, cultural, labor, literary, and artistic history of British Columbia. Prominent among these holdings are the records of the MacMillan Bloedel forestry company, the British Columbia Electric Railway, and the Malcolm Lowry collection.

The Rare Books and Special Collections reading room provides access to: the *Ubyssey* student newspaper, *The Totem* student yearbook, copies of the British Columbia directories dating from 1882 to 1994, a seminar room, and the Chung Collection exhibition space. The Web site lists and holds inventories for personal papers and private records.

The principal location for University of British Columbia Library special collections is in the Irving K. Barber Learning Centre, with important medical and natural history collections in the Woodward Memorial Room of the Woodward Biomedical Library and Asian language collections in the Asian Library.

Collection Profile: Katherine Kalsbeek
Overview: Ralph Stanton
Illustrations: University of British Columbia Archives

University of British Columbia
Irving K. Barber Learning Center
Rare Books and Special Collections
1961 East Mall
Vancouver, British Columbia
V6T 1Z1
Canada
http://www.library.ubc.ca/spcoll/
spcoll@interchange.ubc.ca
(604)822-2521
(604)822-9587

Brown University Library

Since its foundation in 1764, Brown has accumulated, through gift and purchase, one of the larger academically situated special collections in the United States. Holdings currently consist of some 400,000 books in 300 discrete book collections exclusive of the general rare book collection, several thousand manuscript collections, and the University Archives. Major strengths include American literature, particularly a comprehensive collection of American and Canadian poetry and plays, but also numerous strong collections of prose authors, e.g., Thoreau, Poe, Lovecraft, Pound, and Whitman. In recent decades, the American literature collections, complemented by substantial holdings in sheet music and broadsides, have expanded to incorporate literary sub-genres, including comic books, fantasy literature, and pulp fiction. Another extension has been the acquisition of literary publishing archives, notably St. Martin's Press, Feminist Press, *Conjunctions*, and a number of private fine presses. Paralleling American literature are several important collections in British and Continental literature and history, including over 900 incunabula as well as author collections of Horace, Orwell, T. E. Lawrence, Wells, Shaw, Machiavelli, Dante, and Zola. American history is a major strength at Brown with collections ranging from one of the nation's largest Lincoln collections to major holdings in post-1950 radical and dissenting literature, to the archive of the Gorham Silver Company. The history of science and the pseudo-sciences are well-represented at Brown, with holdings in the natural and physical sciences as well as mathematics and medicine and several recent collections relating to temperance and alcohol addiction. The pseudo-sciences include several collections of occult materials as well as a major collection on conjuring and magic that spans spiritualism, witchcraft, and performance magic. The John Hay also houses one of the largest philatelic collections in the country.

Collection Profile: Peter Harrington
Overview: Samuel A. Streit
Illustrations: Benjamin Tyler

Brown University
John Hay Library
20 Prospect St.
Providence, Rhode Island 02912
http://www.brown.edu/Facilities/University_Library/libs/hay/
hay@Brown.edu
(401) 863-3723 (t)
(401) 863-2093 (f)

University at Buffalo, State University of New York, Libraries

Special collections in the University at Buffalo Libraries reach across a broad range of disciplines at this comprehensive, research-intensive public university, offering students and faculty unparalleled opportunities for study and discovery. The rich offerings also draw in and engage regional, national, and international students and scholars. The Robert L. Brown History of Medicine Collection contains the Edgar R. McGuire Historical Medical Instrument Collection and historical materials in all areas of the health sciences, including dentistry, nursing, pharmacy, and public health. Law Library special collections include rare books, archives, and Tibetan legal manuscripts. Lockwood Library's Polish Room serves as a regional research center for Poland's arts and history. The Music Library holds print, visual, and aural documentation of contemporary music creation and performance at the university. These specialized resources supplement the main Special Collections area encompassing the Poetry Collection, Rare Books, and University Archives. Rare Books holds the great works of literature in their most prized editions, including William Shakespeare's first four folios, first editions of Edmund Spenser's *Faerie Queene* (1590), Robert Burton's *Anatomy of Melancholy* (1621), Milton's *Paradise Lost* (1667), and a signed copy of the first edition of Hawthorne's *The Scarlet Letter*. The collection sustains research in literary history and provides exquisite raw materials for investigating the history of printing and the book. Private presses such as Kelmscott Press and Doves Press are well represented. University Archives' manuscript and archival collections support research on campus unrest; race relations; environmental issues including Love Canal; women's history; political and social issues and the alternative press; and regional architecture, including Frank Lloyd Wright's Buffalo creations.

Collection Profile and Overview: Michael Basinski
Illustrations: James Ulrich

University at Buffalo, State University of New York, Libraries
Special Collections
420 Capen Hall
Buffalo, New York 14260-2200
http://ublib.buffalo.edu/libraries/about/specialcollections.html
lib-archives@buffalo.edu
(716) 645-2916 (t)
(716) 645-3714 (f)

University of California, Berkeley Library

The special collections of the Ethnic Studies Library include over 100 Asian-American archives, including the Kem Lee Archive of historical photographs of San Francisco's Chinatown and the archives of Him Mark Lai, the "dean of Chinese-American studies." It includes important historical collections of Native American serials and posters and a complete set of the research literature on northern California tribal peoples gathered by the California Indian Library Collections project. The H. K. Yuen Social Movement Archive consists of sound recordings of virtually all the civil rights speeches and rallies held on the steps of Sproul Plaza from the 1960s to the 1980s. It was named one of the Ten Treasures of the Ten Million when the UC Berkeley Library reached its ten millionth volume. The library staff continues to be inspired by the courage of the students of the 1960s and 1970s to stand up for their educational rights and is proud to contribute special ethnic research materials to the campus library holdings. The Bancroft Library is a partner in the goal to preserve historical documents relating to ethnic minorities. For example, it holds the Social Protest Collection and the Meiklejohn Civil Liberties Institute Records and many collections on the themes of labor and civil rights related to ethnic minorities and immigrants. Earlier collections include source documents from the Spanish and Mexican periods in the American West, including diaries dating from 1725–1821, transcriptions prepared for H. H. Bancroft from the original Spanish and Mexican archives in California (later destroyed in the 1906 San Francisco earthquake), the Bancroft Dictations with the Californios, and the collected private papers of Mexican Californians.

Collection Profile and Overview: Lillian Castillo-Speed
Illustrations: Dan Johnston

University of California, Berkeley Library
Ethnic Studies Library
30 Stephens Hall #2360
University of California
Berkeley, California 94720-2360
http://eslibrary.berkeley.edu/
csl@library.berkeley.edu
(510) 642-3947 (t)
(510) 643-8433 (f)

University of California, Davis Library

The Department of Special Collections was established in 1966 to house the library's rare and unique collections. Holdings consist of over 150,000 rare books and pamphlets, 17,200 linear feet of manuscript collections and University Archives, and 1.75 million historical photographs. The Special Collections Department houses the J. Richard Blanchard Rare Book Collection with strengths in agriculture, American and British literature, apiculture, botany, British history, entomology, religion, viticulture and enology, and zoology. A major focus of the collection is the history and culture of California's Central Valley and surrounding regions, including the Eastman Photograph Collection of over 13,000 images of northern California.

The department holds a major research collection on the history of agricultural technology, the F. Hal Higgins collection. Other important collections in the agricultural and food sciences include the A. W. Noling Hurty-Peck Beverages Library, the Ferry-Morse Seed Company archives, and fruit crate label collections. Viticulture and enology collections support major programs at the University of California, Davis, and include the Maynard A. Amerine papers, the Bureau of Alcohol Tobacco and Firearms archives on California wineries, and wine label collections.

Special Collections houses a number of research-level collections in the humanities, such as the personal papers of Pulitzer Prize–winning poet Gary Snyder and the Kohler British Poetry Collection. There are especially strong holdings in 20th-century experimental theater including the archives of the San Francisco Mime Troupe and the Living Theater.

The department holds significant collections supporting the study of the political and social movements of the 19th and 20th centuries including radical politics, as well as the contributions and history of women, gays, Native Americans, African-Americans, Asian-Americans, and Chicanos.

Collection Profile and Overview: Daryl Morrison
Illustrations: John Skarstad and Hector Villicana

University of California, Davis Library
Department of Special Collections
General Library
100 North West Quad
University of California, Davis
Davis, California 95616-5292
http://www.lib.ucdavis.edu/dept/specol/
(530) 752-2112 (t)
(530) 754-5758 (f)

University of California, Irvine Libraries

The University of California, Irvine (UCI) was founded in 1965, on 1,500 acres of former cattle-grazing land donated to the State of California to establish a new campus of the University of California. UCI is currently a growth campus, now the fifth largest among the university's ten campuses. UCI is on the move.

The same can be said of Special Collections and Archives, where collecting is particularly focused in five areas of strength, one of which is the Southeast Asian Archive. The Regional History Collection documents both contemporary and historic Orange County. Recent acquisitions have focused on hot topics such as environmental activism, women in politics and the public sphere, and the local gay, lesbian, and transgender community. The Critical Theory Archive supports UCI's groundbreaking, nationally renowned academic programs in theory, and includes the papers of some of the world's most significant scholars in this area, many of whom have taught or lectured at UCI: Jacques Derrida, Wolfgang Iser, J. Hillis Miller, Murray Krieger, Paul de Man, Stanley Fish, Richard Rorty, René Wellek, and Ihab Hassan. The University Archives documents UCI's 40 years of history in great depth and played a prominent role in celebrations of the campus's 40th anniversary in 2005. Dance has long been another academic program of distinction, and the Dance and Performing Arts Collections include not only rare books but also the papers of choreographers Donald McKayle, Eugene Loring, and other significant figures.

These specialized research collections are complemented by a general rare book collection, fine press and artists' books, thousands of heavily used political pamphlets, small-press literary pamphlets, an extensive Thomas Mann collection, and rare books on British naval history.

Collection profile and Overview: Jackie Dooley
Illustrations: Laurel Hungerford

University of California, Irvine Libraries
Special Collections and Archives
PO Box 19557
University of California, Irvine
Irvine, California 92623-9557
http://special.lib.uci.edu/
spcoll@lib.uci.edu
(949) 824-7227 (t)
(949) 824-2472 (f)

University of California, Los Angeles Library

Since its founding in 1946, the Department of Special Collections has become one of the country's leading collections of rare books, manuscripts, historic photographs, and other special materials. Among its 333,000 rare books are the Ahmanson-Murphy Aldine Collection, the Michael Sadleir Collection of Nineteenth-Century British Fiction, the Children's Book Collection, the Elmer Belt Library of Vinciana, the Nitka Collection of Fantastic Fiction, plus extensive holdings of historical and contemporary Californiana and of modern fine-press printing, fine bindings, and artists' books. The department possesses the largest collection of archival materials in the state of California. These include the papers of Susan Sontag, Raymond Chandler, Aldous Huxley, and Nobel Peace Prize winner Ralph Bunche, as well as collections related to Southern California architecture; dance and Isadora Duncan; Asian-American history, particularly the relocation of Japanese-Americans during World War II; and the Orsini, an Italian noble family who, from the middle ages to the 20th century, were crucial power-players in Italy. The department's photographic collections are extensive, and include the works of many of the most celebrated practitioners of the art, such as Julia Margaret Cameron, Eadweard Muybridge, William Henry Fox Talbot, Carleton Watkins, Ansel Adams, and Edward Weston. The department also houses the photographic archives of the *Los Angeles Times* (1920–90) and the *Los Angeles Daily News* (1923–54).

The UCLA Library has separate special collections in the performing arts and the history of medicine and biology. In addition, the William Andrews Clark Memorial Library, housed off campus, focuses on British literature, history, and culture from 1641 to 1760.

Collection Profile and Overview: Victoria Steele
Illustrations: Luna Imaging Inc.

University of California, Los Angeles
Charles E. Young Research Library
Department of Special Collections
Los Angeles, California 90095-1575
http://www.library.ucla.edu/libraries/special/scweb/
(310) 825-2422 (t)
(310) 206-1864 (f)

University of California, Riverside Libraries

Special Collections had its origin in 1958 when a small collection of rare books was acquired and stored in a locked cabinet under the circulation desk in the University Library. Established as a separate department in 1968 with 6,000 volumes and fewer than 400 manuscripts, the collection currently houses almost 200,000 volumes, 150,000 manuscripts, 25,000 photographs, including unique photographs from the Mexican Revolution, and varied archival holdings. The collection comprises eight general subject areas: African-American history and culture, including the Western Region Tuskegee Airmen Archive; agricultural, botanical, and natural sciences, including early records from the citrus industry in Southern California and the original Citrus Experiment Station; California history, including the University Archives; history of the arts, including the papers of music theorist Heinrich Schenker, and the archive of playwright, poet, and art critic Sadakichi Hartmann; Latin-American history and culture, including the Chilcote Archives on Brazil, the Panama Collection, Paraguayan political archives, and the archives of author and poet Tomás Rivera; literary and cultural studies, including the B. Traven Collection, boys' series books from the late 19th and early 20th centuries, Victorian and Edwardian novels, and the Eaton Collection; Native American studies, including the Rupert J. Costo Library of the American Indian; and Western European civilization, including medieval and Renaissance manuscripts, early printed books, the Henry Snyder Collection of 18th-century imprints, the Vernon Duke Paris Collection, and an extensive collection on printing, book history and book arts, including the Dr. Edward C. Petko Collection of antique printing presses used by students taking classes in hand printing and bookmaking.

Collection Profile and Overview: Melissa Conway
Illustrations: Vlasta Radan

University of California, Riverside Libraries
Special Collections
PO Box 5900
University of California
Riverside, California 92517-5900
http://library.ucr.edu/?view=collections/spcol/
(951) 827-3233 (t)
(951) 827-4673 (f)

University of California, San Diego Libraries

For an institution established as recently as 1960, University of California, San Diego (UCSD) has developed special collections of remarkable depth and diversity. Currently consisting of more than 250,000 books, over 500 manuscript collections, the UCSD Archives, and a multitude of items in a variety of other formats, Special Collections from its inception has worked cooperatively with UCSD faculty to build collections that support UCSD academic programs. UCSD places great emphasis on all things related to the Pacific, for example, and Mandeville Special Collections Library (MSCL) has developed the most extensive collection on pre-1850 voyages of exploration and discovery to the Pacific, the renowned Hill Collection. Extensive holdings on California history and culture, Baja California history and politics, and the anthropology and ethnography of Melanesia also contribute to the strength of the Pacific collections. Modern Spain has been a traditional focus of UCSD historians, and MSCL holds the largest extant collection on the Spanish Civil War. With contemporary American poetry a longstanding interest of the literature department, MSCL boasts the Archive for New Poetry, with an emphasis on experimental verse. Through its holdings of unique personal and professional papers, MSCL is also exceptionally strong in 20th-century science, a natural field for a university that has built its reputation on excellence in the sciences. Other areas of collecting strength include artists' books; high-altitude medicine and physiology; San Diego and border studies; culinary history of the American Southwest, Latin America, and the Pacific Rim; Western mining; early meteorology; and Chicano activism.

Collection Profile and Overview: Lynda Corey Claassen
Illustrations: Matthew Peters

University of California, San Diego
Mandeville Special Collections Library
UCSD, 0175-S
9500 Gilman Drive
La Jolla, California 92093-0175
http://orpheus.ucsd.edu/speccoll/
spcoll@ucsd.edu
(858) 534-2533 (t)
(858) 534-5950 (f)

University of California, Santa Barbara Libraries

The Department of Special Collections at University of California, Santa Barbara (UCSB) was established in 1959 and during its relatively short history has amassed more than 250,000 printed volumes, 16,000 linear feet of manuscripts, 150,000 photographs, and nearly 200,000 sound recordings. These materials are contained in five major areas: Rare Books, Manuscripts, and Named Collections; the California Ethnic and Multicultural Archive; the Performing Arts Collection; the UCSB Oral History Program; and the UCSB University Archives. Holdings are predominantly 19th and 20th century. Major strengths include the Stuart L. Bernath Collection, focusing on American diplomatic history and international relations; the Humanistic Psychology Archive, with nearly 200 collections relating to leaders such as Rollo May, Carl R. Rogers, and Virginia Satir; the Lawrence B. Romaine Trade Catalog Collection, with more than 50,000 items, primarily 19th- and early 20th-century American trade and advertising literature; and the William Wyles Collection, the first UCSB "special collection" and still one of the largest, with more than 35,000 volumes and several hundred manuscript collections pertaining to Abraham Lincoln, slavery, abolition, the Civil War, American expansion, travel in America, and the American West. Another rapidly emerging area, the California Ethnic and Multicultural Archive documents the experience of African-Americans, Asian-Americans, Chicanos/Latinos, and Native Americans in California, with major holdings of artists, authors, organizations, and groups such as the Asian American Theater Company and El Teatro Campesino collections. The Performing Arts Collection likewise is a major strength, with manuscript collections relating to music, theater, circus and magic, film and television, and one of the largest historical sound recording collections in the country, with more than 170,000 78 rpm records and 8,000 wax cylinders of classical, popular, jazz, and ethnic music from the United States and other parts of the world.

Collection Profile and Overview: David C. Tambo
Illustrations: Tony Lewis and Alex Hauschild

University of California, Santa Barbara Libraries
Department of Special Collections
Davidson Library
University of California
Santa Barbara, California 93106-9010
Web: http://www.library.ucsb.edu/speccoll/
Email: special@library.ucsb.edu
(805) 893-3062 (t)
(805) 893-5749 (f)

Case Western Reserve University Libraries

Case Western Reserve University was established in 1826 as Western Reserve College in Hudson, Ohio. In 1882, the college moved to Cleveland, sharing the new campus with the Case School of Applied Science. In 1967 Western Reserve University merged with the Case Institute of Technology to form the present university. The Department of Special Collections is located in the Kelvin Smith Library and houses rare books, manuscripts, and special collections. Among the department's holdings are more than 60,000 rare books, association copies, and specialized reference tools as well as over 60 manuscript collections. Major collection strengths include American and continental literature and history of the 18th and 19th centuries and American and European journals in the history of science. There are significant collections in art, architecture, domestic science, history, history of the book and book arts, mathematics, music, natural history, philosophy, science and technology, travel, and exploration. These collections have outstanding examples of books and manuscripts from the 15th to the 21st centuries. The Wilhelm Scherer library of German literature includes rare editions of major 19th-century German authors. Autograph collections contain a variety of documents representing American and British personalities. Also present are several unique collections of local interest including the papers of Charles Brush, inventor of the arc lamp; the urban planning library of Ernest J. Bohn known as the "Father of Housing"; the Warner & Swasey Co. papers, maker of telescopes; WPA posters and prints by Cleveland printmakers; works of Cleveland composers Donald Erb and Marcel Dick; and books from the original Western Reserve College Library.

Collection Profile: Mark A. Eddy
Overview: N. Sue Hanson
Illustrations: Sharlane Gubkin and Tom Steman

Case Western Reserve University Libraries
Kelvin Smith Library
11055 Euclid Avenue
Case Western Reserve University
Cleveland, Ohio 44106-7151
http://library.case.edu/ksl/
http://library.case.edu/ksl/speccoll/
http://library.case.edu/ksl/speccoll/brush/
(216) 368-0189 (t)
(216) 368-6950 (f)

Center for Research Libraries

The Center for Research Libraries (CRL), a partnership of over 200 North American university, college, and independent research libraries, manages and develops a shared collection of primary source materials for advanced research and teaching. The collection offers the rich diversity and depth of resources necessary for the creation of new knowledge. Holdings are especially rich in newspapers, archives, journals, and government documents, many of them from non-US sources. While many of the center's collections are not special collections in the traditional sense, most of the more than 4 million items held by the center can be found in few other North American libraries.

CRL has developed the collection over the past half-century through purchases and deposits, with the aim of supplementing on-campus and local holdings of its member research libraries. Notable CRL collections strengths include holdings of newspapers, government documents and archives, and journals of trade and learned societies.

CRL has one of North America's three largest circulating collections of newspapers from all parts of the world, including newspapers published in Sub-Saharan Africa, the Middle East, South and Southeast Asia, and Latin America, as well as those published in the United States by ethnic and diaspora communities. CRL possesses a vast array of published and unpublished government documents and reports from the early 19th century through 1950, including archival collections, legislative journals, and official gazettes issued by governments on five continents. Dating from the 17th to the early 20th century, CRL's trade journals document ideas, trends, and achievements in the arts, sciences, trades, and industries in the United States and Western Europe.

Collection Profile and Overview: Bernard Reilly
Illustrations: Center for Research Libraries

Center for Research Libraries
6050 South Kenwood Ave.
Chicago, Illinois 60637-2804
http://www.crl.edu/
(773) 955-4545 (t)
(773) 955-4339 (f)

University of Chicago Library

The University of Chicago's founding president, William Rainey Harper, set the course for Special Collections as a "working collection" in 1891. The emphases in Special Collections, now numbering approximately 265,000 books, 30,000 linear feet of archival materials, and 6,000 linear feet of manuscripts, closely parallel the disciplinary and research interests of faculty over the past century.

The core collection included manuscripts and books in philology, philosophy, theology, archaeology, and Renaissance and Reformation studies. The Goodspeed Manuscript Collection was joined by an important manuscript of the *Canterbury Tales*, as well as the Bacon Collection of English Court and Manorial Documents. The Stephen A. Douglas Papers and the Durrett Collection on Kentucky and the Ohio River Valley support the study of 19th-century America; while papers of Edith and Grace Abbott, Saul Bellow, Enrico Fermi, Leo Strauss, S. Chandrasekhar, and many others in the University Archives document the contributions of faculty members, trustees, and students.

Acquiring the first 50 years of the archive of *Poetry: A Magazine of Verse* established Chicago as a center for the study of modern poetry; rare books from the John Crerar Library expanded collections in the history of science and medicine. The Ludwig Rosenberger Library of Judaica supports programs in the social and cultural history of the Jewish people. American drama, children's books, and holdings in American and European history and literature are among the resources mined by faculty and students. The Chopin Collection and its online counterpart, Chopin Early Editions, illustrate the complementary nature of print and digital collections.

Instruction and outreach efforts are enhanced by the media-equipped Marie Louise Rosenthal Seminar Room. Class sessions and open houses introduce undergraduates to the discoveries awaiting them in Special Collections.

Collection Profile and Overview: Alice Schreyer
Illustrations: Ted Lacey

University of Chicago Library
Special Collections Research Center
University of Chicago
1100 East 57th Street
Chicago, Illinois 60637
http://www.lib.uchicago.edu/e/spcl/
SpecialCollections@lib.uchicago.edu
(773) 702-8705 (t)
(773) 702-3728 (f)

University of Cincinnati Libraries

Tracing its founding to the establishment of Cincinnati College in 1819, the University of Cincinnati acquires and provides access to special materials for research and instructional use by its faculty and students, as well as the local community and the scholarly world. The holdings in the Archives and Rare Books Library include the University Archives; the German-Americana collection of both published and archival material; and the Urban Studies Archive of 20th- and 21st-century community organizations, politics, and urban culture. In the Rare Books Collection, major strengths include thousands of 18th-century British anonymous poetical pamphlets, drama, and homiletics; first issues and first editions of Dickens; the Charles J. Livingood Petrarch Collection; the Edward S. Curtis portfolios of American Indians; early travel, and exploration; and the Enoch T. Carson Shakespeare Collection. In recent years, an emphasis on the history of the book has seen additions of incunabula, pochoir-illustrated volumes, William Morris and Kelmscott Press titles, and various works by book artist Barry Moser. The Archives and Rare Books Library also houses the rare volumes of the university's John Miller Burnam Classics Library.

Special collections of the University of Cincinnati are also found in the Chemistry-Biology Library where the Ralph E. Oesper Collections in the History of Chemistry contain more than 3,200 journals and monographs dating from 1600 to 1920, supplemented by the Apparatus Museum and the Oesper Collection of Prints and Portraits. In Langsam Library, the George Elliston Poetry Room is an endowed collection of more than 10,000 volumes of modern English-language poetry. The library of the College of Design, Architecture, Art and Planning holds a large collection of artists' books that represent the work of local artists, University of Cincinnati students, and nationally recognized book artists.

Collection Profile and Overview: Kevin Grace
Illustrations: Dottie Stover

University of Cincinnati Libraries
Administration Office
PO Box 210033
University of Cincinnati
Cincinnati, Ohio 45221-0033
http://www.libraries.uc.edu/
(513) 556-1515 (t)
(513) 556-0325 (f)

University of Colorado at Boulder Libraries

Established in 1877, the University of Colorado Library began with a one-room library in Old Main, the first building on campus. By 1902 the first free-standing library was constructed, but it would not be until 1939, with the move into a new building, that the Treasure Room was established as a separate space staffed by volunteer English Department faculty. While the 1950s brought expansion of the space and formal policies and procedures, it was not until 1963 that the library appointed the first associate director for Special Collections. The department is relatively young in the world of special collections and rare books and has grown through acquisitions and gifts from faculty, alumni, and friends of the university.

The department's holdings consist of 90,000 volumes and several hundred linear feet of manuscript materials, with only 30 percent reflected in the online public catalog. It is strong in 19th- and 20th-century British and American literature and works about travel and expeditions. Manuscript collections focus on the literary papers of authors with a connection to the university or state. The foremost special subject collections are the Mountaineering Collection, the Women of the Romantic Period Collection, the Photobook Collection, and a significant teaching collection of 500 artists' books. The Mountaineering Collection is international in scope, numbers roughly 8,000 volumes, and complements the holdings of the American Alpine Club library in Golden, Colorado. Books in the 450-volume collection of British women poets date from 1770 to 1839. The Photobook Collection, established in the 1990s with the purchase of two separate collections, is a visual record of the 20th century and is a growing collection of 15,000 volumes.

Collection Profile and Overview: Deborah Hollis
Illustrations: Larry Harwood

University of Colorado at Boulder Libraries
Special Collections Department
184 UCB
University of Colorado at Boulder
Boulder, Colorado 80309
http://ucblibraries.colorado.edu/specialcollections/
spc@colorado.edu
(303) 492-6144 (t)
(303) 492-1881 (f)

Colorado State University Libraries

The Archives and Special Collections department of Colorado State University Libraries focuses on documenting the university and areas related to its disciplinary strengths, especially its world-renowned fields of water and agriculture research. Holdings related to the University Archive include institutional records, university publications, and over a half-million photographs and glass plate negatives dating from the university's founding in 1870 to the present day that document the academic and social history of Colorado State University and the state's Front Range region. In addition to its University Archive, the department is also home to two major topical collections: the Water Resources Archive and the Colorado Agricultural Archive.

Beyond its three major archival collections, the department houses incunabula and items of antiquity— some of which were acquired in the mid 1960s from the Grand Trianon, a historic house that is now the Colorado Springs School. Additional holdings of note include: the Equine Collection, the Bailey Botany Collection, the Fore-edge Painting Collection, and the Vietnam War Literature Collection. The libraries' ongoing focus on digital initiatives and access has facilitated the creation of popular online collections such as the Warren and Genevieve Garst Photographic Collection of wildlife still images, the Sidney Heitman Germans from Russia Collection, and the International Poster Collection, a unique online database of over 1,600 posters created by artists worldwide, documenting international events of cultural and political significance.

Collection Profile: Patricia J. Rettig
Overview: Janet Bishop
Illustrations: Joe Mendoza

Colorado State University

Morgan Library
Archives and Special Collections
Fort Collins, Colorado 80523-1019
http://lib.colostate.edu/archives/
specialcollections@library.colostate.edu
(970) 491-1844 (t)
(970) 491-1195 (f)

Columbia University Libraries

Established in 1930, the Rare Book and Manuscript Library (RBML) is the largest of Columbia University's special collections, containing more than 500,000 books; 30 million manuscripts in some 4,500 separate collections; 75,000 photographs; and 40,000 prints, drawings, and works of art; as well as other formats such as papyri, playing cards, and scientific instruments. The other libraries with special collections within the Columbia University Libraries and their affiliates are: the Avery Architectural and Fine Arts Library, the C. V. Starr East Asian Library, the Augustus C. Long Health Sciences Library, the Barnard College Library, the Burke Library at Union Theological Seminary, the Gabe M. Wiener Music & Arts Library, and the Arthur W. Diamond Law Library.

RBML's holdings range from 2000 BCE to the present and include material related to most subject areas. Particular strengths are medieval and Renaissance manuscripts, classical authors, Anglo-American literature and history, the archives of literary agents and of major publishers such as Harper & Brothers, education, mathematics, economics, human rights, social work, history of photography, printing and the allied arts, New York City politics, and theater history. RBML also contains the papers of many of Columbia's distinguished alumni/ae and faculty, including John Jay, Joseph Pulitzer, Frances Perkins, Bennett Cerf, Lionel Trilling, Bella Abzug, Thomas Merton, and Edward Said.

Today, RBML comprises not only the general manuscripts and rare book collections but also the Bakhmeteff Archive of Russian and East European Culture, the Carnegie Collections, including the records of four philanthropic organizations founded by Andrew Carnegie, the Center for Human Rights Documentation and Research, the Herbert Lehman Suite and Papers, the Oral History Research Office, and the University Archives.

Collection Profile and Overview: Jennifer B. Lee
Illustrations: Dwight Primiano

Columbia University

Rare Book and Manuscript Library
Butler Library, 6th Floor, East
535 West 114th Street
New York, New York 10027
http://www.columbia.edu/cu/lweb/indiv/rbml/
rbml@libraries.cul.columbia.edu
(212) 854-5590 (t)
(212) 854-1365 (f)

University of Connecticut Libraries

The University of Connecticut's Archives and Special Collections began in 1965. Early efforts focused on transferring rare books from the main library and building literary collections. Significant early collections included the papers of Charles Olson, Robert Creeley, Fielding Dawson, and Joel Oppenheimer, who taught or were students at Black Mountain College.

A children's literature collection began in the 1960s and expanded with the deposit of Billie Levy's children's book collection which formed the nucleus of the Northeast Children's Literature Collection. Major collections include the papers of James Marshall, Tomie dePaola, Jane Dyer, Richard Scarry, and Ed Young.

In 1978, the library established the Historical Manuscripts and Archives Department, which developed the University Archives, currently its largest collection. It also acquired political papers of Senator Thomas Dodd, Senator Prescott Bush, and 11 members of the House of Representatives. Another major focus is Connecticut history, business, and labor. The library developed a comprehensive labor archives during the 1980s and actively collected Connecticut business records with a special focus on manufacturing and railroad industries.

The two special collections programs combined in 1995 with the opening of the Thomas J. Dodd Research Center, a purpose-built facility designed for special collections and supporting an active program of exhibits and public events. Its public programs include the Edwin Way Teale Lecture on Nature and the Environment, the Raymond & Beverly Sackler Distinguished Lecture, the Greenwich Capital Market Lecture, and the Connecticut Children's Book Fair.

The center's most recent collecting focus is on human rights. This collection builds on Senator Thomas Dodd's involvement as a prosecutor at the Nuremberg Trials. Important collections include the library and records of the Human Rights Internet and papers from the African National Congress.

Collection Profile: Valerie Love
Overview: Thomas Wilsted
Illustrations: Alex Bothell

University of Connecticut

Thomas J. Dodd Research Center
405 Babbidge Road Unit 1205
Storrs, Connecticut 06269-1205
http://www.doddcenter.uconn.edu/
(860) 486-2524 (t)
(860) 486-4521 (f)

Cornell University Library

Cornell University's rare book and manuscript collections date from the founding of the university in 1865. Andrew Dickson White, Cornell's first president, was a life-long book collector who believed that deep collections of primary resources are central to scholarship and teaching. Thanks to White and his first University Librarian, Willard Fiske, the collections grew dramatically in Cornell's early years. White's collection of more than 30,000 volumes reflected his interests in architecture, science, religion, and European and American history. Due in large part to White's collecting passions, Cornell University Library features the largest collection on the French Revolution outside of Paris, the largest collection in North America on European witchcraft, the country's founding collection on the abolitionist movement, and a leading history of science collection. White's gift was followed in 1905 by Willard Fiske's collections on Iceland, Dante, and Petrarch. Outside of Iceland and Denmark, Cornell continues to maintain the most comprehensive collection relating to Icelandic history and culture.

Cornell's rare book and manuscript collections expanded in the 20th century to include the world's second largest collection on William Wordsworth, the Burgunder Collection of George Bernard Shaw, the Noyes collection of Americana, including a copy of the Gettysburg Address in Lincoln's own hand, along with the papers of Lafayette, Lavoisier, James Joyce, Ford Madox Ford, Wyndham Lewis, and E. B. White. In 1942, a collection of regional history was created to document everyday life in upstate New York, and the Cornell University Archives was officially established in 1951. Additional areas of strength include agriculture, Asian studies, city and regional planning, ornithology, human sexuality, and Native Americans. Today, Cornell's special collections include 400,000 rare books and more than 80 million manuscripts, photographs, prints, and artifacts.

Collection Profile: Brenda J. Marston
Illustrations: Rhea Garen

Cornell University Library
Division of Rare and Manuscript Collections
2B Carl A. Kroch Library
Cornell University
Ithaca, New York 14853-5302
http://rmc.library.cornell.edu/
rareref@cornell.edu
607-255-3530 (t)
607-255-9524 (f)

Dartmouth College Library

Rauner Special Collections Library is the primary repository for Dartmouth College's rare book, manuscript, and archival holdings. The collections reflect the long and rich history of the college and feature collections related to eminent alumni, faculty, and others associated with the college. Special Collections holds extensive manuscript and published material related to Robert Frost and Daniel Webster, the Stefansson Collection on Polar Exploration, and the recently acquired papers of Budd Schulberg and the Pilobolus Dance Theatre. The papers of Maxfield Parrish and Augustus Saint-Gaudens are part of a series of related collections documenting the history of New Hampshire's Cornish Colony. There are dozens of named book collections including the Allerton Hickmott Shakespeare Collection, an extensive New Hampshire Imprints collection, the Edward P. Sine Collection of British Illustrated Books, and a deep "Presses" collection that chronicles the history of printing from the 15th century to the present. Students make regular use of the pre-1600 manuscripts for course work, a collection that includes a small but very rich trove of books of hours, a 15th-century prose *Brut Chronicle*, and a strong collection of early musical manuscripts.

A hallmark of Special Collections at Dartmouth has been its longstanding commitment to creating an atmosphere conducive to student use of the collections. Welcoming staff, an open reading room, and access tools invite students to explore what makes Special Collections so "special." Rauner Library has recently expanded its role in curricular support and is now a major component of courses taught throughout the college.

Collection Profile and Overview: Jay Satterfield
Illustrations: Lynn Bohannon

Dartmouth College
Dartmouth College Library
Rauner Special Collections Library
6065 Webster Hall
Hanover, New Hampshire 03755
http://www.dartmouth.edu/~speccoll/
Rauner.Special.Collections.Reference@Dartmouth.edu
(603) 646-0538 (t)
(603) 646-0447 (f)

University of Delaware Library

The Special Collections Department of the University of Delaware Library houses over 100,000 books, over 1,000 manuscript collections, and significant collections of maps, prints, photographs, broadsides, periodicals, pamphlets, ephemera, and realia from the 15th century to the present. The collections complement the library's general collections with particular strengths in the subject areas of art and art history; architecture; the history of printing; English, Irish, and American literature; history and Delawareana; horticulture; and the history of science and technology.

The histories of fine, decorative, and applied arts are collection strengths that complement research interests of the university's programs in art history and conservation. The art of the book, the history of printing and the graphic arts, and the history of papermaking and fine printing are subjects represented in both printed and manuscript collections. Holdings in British, American, and Irish literature are concentrated from the 17th century to the present with particular strengths in Romantic poetry and prose, and 19th- and 20th-century British, American, and Irish literature, including literary manuscripts.

All aspects of English and American history are represented from the 16th century onward, as are significant collections on French political theory and statecraft. The areas of travel and exploration are well represented, and the history of Delaware from its settlement by the Swedes in 1638 to the present is the focus of the Delaware Collection.

Collections on the history of science and technology complement university strengths in chemistry and engineering. Of particular note are holdings for alchemy, dyeing and bleaching, natural philosophy, metallurgy, and military fortification. In addition, the history of American horticulture is richly recorded in books, periodicals, seed catalogs, trade catalogs, prints, broadsides, and manuscripts.

Collection Profile and Overview: Timothy Murray
Illustrations: University of Delaware Library, Newark, Delaware

University of Delaware
University of Delaware Library
Newark, Delaware 19717-5267
http://www.lib.udel.edu/ud/spec/
http://www.udel.edu/cgi-bin/askspec.cgi
(302) 831-6952 (t)
(302) 831-1046 (f)

Duke University Libraries

The Sallie Bingham Center for Women's History and Culture forms one of the constituent parts of the Rare Book, Manuscript, and Special Collections Library (RBMSCL) of Duke University. Housed in the university's original 1928 library building, RBMSCL includes, in addition to the Bingham Center, the Duke University Archives; the John Hope Franklin Collection of African and African American Documentation; the John W. Hartman Center for Sales, Advertising & Marketing History; the Duke Documentary Photography Archive; and the Duke Archive for Human Rights.

RBMSCL's holdings cover a broad range of subjects and a variety of formats. The library's print collections contain over 300,000 printed books, pamphlets, broadsides, maps, and newspapers, while the library's manuscript and archival collections contain more than 20 million items, including diaries, letters, account books, photographs, audio and video tapes, films, digital media, and other formats.

Subjects and materials with significant representation include African-American history, advertising history, comic books and popular culture, documentary photography, English and American literature, the history of economic thought, German baroque literature, medieval and renaissance manuscripts, the history of Methodism, popular American music, American newspapers, papyri, Southern United States history and culture, and women's history.

The library hosts a regular series of public programs and exhibits, offers grants and awards for visiting researchers and to foster undergraduate research, and develops ongoing digital projects that highlight the strengths of the collections.

Collection Profile: Laura Micham
Overview: J. Andrew Armacost
Illustrations: Les Todd

Duke University Libraries
Rare Book, Manuscript, and Special Collections Library
103 Perkins Library, Box 90185, Duke University
Durham, North Carolina 27708-0185 USA
http://library.duke.edu/specialcollections/
special-collections@duke.edu
(919) 660-5822 (t)
(919) 660-5934 (f)

Emory University Libraries

Emory University holds deep collections of rare books and manuscripts with particular strength in modern literature, African-American history, Southern history, the Protestant Reformation, the history of Methodism, and hymnody, among other subjects.

Within the field of modern literature, Emory is particularly strong in W. B. Yeats and his circle, and contemporary British, Irish, and American poetry. Literary collections of special note include the archives of the late poet laureate of Britain Ted Hughes, Nobel Laureate Seamus Heaney, as well as important American poets James Dickey, Lucille Clifton, and Anthony Hecht. These rich archival collections are further strengthened by the presence of the Raymond Danowski Poetry Library, a collection of 20th-century poetry numbering nearly 75,000 titles, the personal library of Ted Hughes, and the library of Wallace Stevens's bibliographer, J. M. Edelstein. MARBL also holds important research collections of 20th-century short story writers and novelists, including a significant Flannery O'Connor collection and the archive of novelist Salman Rushdie.

Emory's Manuscript, Archives, and Rare Book Library has deep collections documenting African-American history and culture. A particular focus of these collections has been Black print culture, that is books, periodicals, and pamphlets written, published, and read within the African-American community. Other strengths include African-American journalists, civil rights and post–civil rights movements, and Blacks and the left. Principal holdings include the Camille Billops and James V. Hatch Archives, the papers of Louise Thompson Patterson and Matt and Evelyn Crawford, as well as the papers of writers, composers, artists, and other African-American cultural figures.

The Special Collections Department of Emory's Pitts Theology Library holds one of the strongest research collections in the country for the study of the Protestant Reformation in Germany to 1570. Other strengths include English and American hymody and psalmody, and extensive archival holdings documenting Methodist organizations.

Collection Profile and Overview: Stephen Enniss
    and Randall Burkett
Illustrations: Jon Rou

Emory University
Manuscript, Archives, and Rare Book Library
Robert W. Woodruff Library, 10th floor
Atlanta, Georgia 30322
http://marbl.library.emory.edu/
marbl@emory.edu
(404) 727-6887 (t)
(404) 727-0360 (f)

University of Florida Libraries

The Department of Special and Area Studies Collections at the University of Florida encompasses primary and secondary source materials in a wide variety of subjects.

The four area studies components emphasize research materials of a geographic and ethnic nature. The Latin American Collection and the African Studies Collection are both recognized as top-level repositories in their respective areas. The Price Library of Judaica focuses on literature of Jewish studies published from 1880 to the present, and the Asian Studies Collection supports research in East and South East Asian language, history, and literature.

The Special Collections unit contains material in eight subject areas that provide primary research resources in support of the university's academic programs and scholars worldwide. The P. K. Yonge Library of Florida History is the state's preeminent Floridiana collection and holds the largest North American collection of Spanish colonial documents. The Rare Book Collection features the Parkman Dexter Howe Collection of New England authors dating from the 17th through the 19th centuries. Among the significant material in the manuscripts collection are the literary papers of Marjorie Kinnan Rawlings and John D. MacDonald and 18 groups of manuscripts relating to Haiti and other parts of Latin America. Three other extensive collections, the Baldwin Library of Historical Children's Literature, the Comic Studies Collection, and the Belknap Collection for the Performing Arts focus on popular culture material. The University Archives collects the university's significant public records, and recent acquisitions have established an African-American collection focused on local history.

Collection Profile and Overview: Rita J. Smith
Illustrations: Ray Carson

University of Florida
George A. Smathers Libraries
Department of Special and Area Studies Collections
Room 208
PO Box 117007
Gainesville, Florida 32611
http://www.uflib.ufl.edu/spec/
special@uflib.ufl.edu
(352) 392-0975 (t)
(352) 864-2746 (f)

Florida State University Libraries

Special Collections traces its origin to 1953, when Louise Richardson, long-time Director of the Library, stepped down to take the helm of the new department, creating it from the wealth of materials already in the library. There are six areas of collecting in addition to general rare books: the Florida Collection; the University Archives and Photo Archives; the Scottish Collection; the John Mackay Shaw Childhood in Poetry Collection; manuscripts; and the Napoleon and the French Revolution Collection. With more than 25,000 volumes, the Shaw Collection gives major strength in English and American poetry from the mid-17th century through the mid-20th century. Within the general rare books are several smaller named collections: the Howard Storrs Kelmscott Press Collection; the Nancy Bird Fore-Edge Painting Collection; the Lois Lenski Collection; the Louise Richardson Herbal Collection; the Tracy W. McGregor Fund Books on the Discovery and Exploration of the Americas; the Julia Stover and Milton Washington Carothers Memorial Collection of Bibles and Rare Books; and the Robert M. Ervin, Jr., Collection of science fiction, fantasy, horror, and comics. Examples of notable manuscript collections include the papers of Nobel laureate Paul A. M. Dirac; the papers of Florida Governor Fuller Warren; the records of the Florida Panhandle's German-American Lumber Company; and the Tallahassee Civil Rights Oral History Collection. In addition, small collections of manuscript books, incunabula, cuneiforms, papyri, ostraka, and Coptic textiles are available for study. Collaboration between Special Collections and the university's Museum Studies Program gives undergraduate students an opportunity to curate and install exhibits based on materials held in Special Collections.

Collection Profile and Overview: Lucia Patrick
Illustrations: Michele Edmunds/Giesele Towels

Florida State University Libraries
Special Collections
Florida State University
116 Honors Way
Tallahassee, Florida 32306-2047
http://www.fsu.edu/~speccoll/
(850) 644-3271 (t)
(850) 644-1221 (f)

George Washington University Library

The Special Collections and University Archives was formed in 1969 to protect, preserve, and make available to scholars the library's most valuable materials. The genesis of the collection was in the form of a gift from W. Lloyd Wright in 1950. The gift included numerous rare books, as well as letters from such prominent individuals as John Adams, Jefferson Davis, Robert E. Lee, and Mark Twain. Current holdings of the department include approximately 60,000 books, over 15,000 linear feet of manuscript collections and university records, approximately 50,000 audiovisual recordings, more than 45,000 graphic images, and over 1,000 maps of various kinds.

The department has a strong Washingtoniana collection, which focuses on the history of the city since the founding of the nation to the present day. This includes items such as city directories dating back to the early 1800s, and the journal of the Historical Society of Washington, DC.

In 1996, through the gift of the I. Edward Kiev Judaica Collection by Dr. Ari and Phyllis Kiev, the Special Collections and University Archives embarked on the building of a world-class Judaica and Hebraica collection. To date, the Kiev Collection has grown from an initial 18,000 titles to over 22,000 titles.

The gift of the Westwood One Mutual Broadcasting System collection marked the beginning of a new area of collecting in the history of American journalism and broadcast communications.

Collection Profile and Overview: Steven Mandeville-Gamble
Illustrations: Jessica McConnell/The George Washington
   University Office of University Relations, 2007

George Washington University
Gelman Library System
Special Collections and University Archives
2130 H Street NW, Suite 704
Washington, DC 20052
http://www.gwu.edu/gelman/spec/index.html
speccoll@gwu.edu
(202) 994-7549 (t)
(202) 463-6205 (f)

Georgetown University Library

In 1789, Georgetown College was founded by Archbishop John Carroll and became the nation's first Catholic university. Its third president, Louis Guillaume Valentin DuBourg, a Sulpician priest, is given credit for founding the institution's library, with more than a hundred of his own books. This was the modest beginning of the library, and its rare book collection, but in time it would grow. In 1815, Archbishop Carroll died, leaving money for "the purchase of valuable works of real learning." The library's growth continued through the presidencies of two Jesuits, Giovanni Grassi and Enoch Fenwick, and in 1825, when Anne Royall visited the campus, she noted the library contained about 9,000 volumes. The acquisition of the library of Thomas C. Levins in 1844 added 1,991 volumes, including 11 incunabula, among the first to enter the collection. In 1891 Riggs Library was built in the Healy Building; this would be the main university library until 1970 when Lauinger Library opened with a collection of 450,000 volumes and a large space for special collections.

Today the Special Collections Research Center encompasses the university's rare book collection of nearly 100,000 rare books; the manuscript collection, 750 separate collections consisting of some 7,000 linear feet of material; the University Archives at over 3,000 linear feet; and the university's art collection, consisting of 12,000 fine prints and some 600 paintings and sculptures. The center actively collects material about the Society of Jesus; American diplomacy and intelligence; European and American history; English and American literature; and European and American fine prints and paintings.

Collection Profile and Overview: Nicholas B. Scheetz
Illustrations: David Hagen

Georgetown University
Lauinger Library
Special Collections Research Center
37th and O Streets NW
Washington, DC 20057-1174
http://www.library.georgetown.edu/dept/speccoll/
(202) 687-7444 (t)
(202) 687-7501 (f)

University of Georgia Libraries

The University of Georgia Libraries' special collections comprise three distinct and distinctive libraries. The Hargrett Rare Book and Manuscript Library consists of the Rare Book and Manuscript Library, the Georgiana Collection, and University Archives. Subject interests include Georgia, book arts, theater, music, history, literature, journalism, and genealogy. Special emphasis is placed on rare books, maps, broadsides, and other printed material dealing with Georgia. The manuscripts area is the repository for over 6 million individual items including family papers, diaries, letters, theatrical papers, and corporate and organizational papers.

The Richard B. Russell Library for Political Research and Studies supports scholarly research in modern political history. Holdings, in addition to the collection of the late Senator Russell, include the papers of former Secretary of State Dean Rusk; former Ambassador W. Tapley Bennett, Jr.; and numerous congressional, state, and local legislators; and political columnists and editorial cartoonists. It is also the official repository for the records of the state Democratic and Republican Parties, Leadership Georgia, the Georgia Public Policy Foundation, and the Georgia ACLU.

The Walter J. Brown Media Archive & Peabody Awards Collection holds film, video, audiotape, transcription disks, and other recording formats comprising approximately 100,000 titles. The Peabody Awards Collection is the flagship collection and contains most of the entries for the first major broadcast award given in the United States. Entries begin in 1940 for radio and 1948 for television. This collection provides a cultural cross-section of television programming from its infancy to the present day, featuring news, documentary, entertainment, and children's programming.

Collection Profile: Mary Ellen Brooks
Overview: Jean Cleveland
Illustrations: Nelson Morgan, Ben McCormick

University of Georgia Libraries
UGA Main Library
Athens, Georgia 30602
http://www.libs.uga.edu/
Hargrett Rare Book and Manuscript Library
    http://www.libs.uga.edu/hargrett/speccoll.html
Richard B. Russell Library for Political Research and Studies
    http://www.libs.uga.edu/russell/
Walter J. Brown Media Archive and Peabody Awards Collection
    http://www.libs.uga.edu/mediadept/
(706) 542-0621 (t)
(706) 542-4144 (f)

Georgia Tech Library and Information Center

Founded in 1885, the Georgia Institute of Technology has played an important and vital role in the development of Atlanta and Georgia. Tech's history reflects its strong commitment to the role of technology, industry, and research, and the library and archives play a major role in that endeavor.

The Archives and Records Management Department promotes research and scholarship through collections relating to the academic curriculum by preserving and providing access to the history of Georgia Tech, its faculty, students, and alumni. These include a 4,332-volume rare book collection, a 4,000-volume science fiction collection complemented by 200 artifacts, approximately 1,000 collections of manuscripts, University Archives, photographs, and architectural drawings.

Collection Profile and Overview: Jody Lloyd Thompson
Illustrations: Katie Gentilello

Georgia Tech Library and Information Center
704 Cherry Street
Georgia Institute of Technology
Atlanta, Georgia 30332-0900
http://www.library.gatech.edu/archives/
archives@library.gatech.edu
(404) 894-4586 (t)
(404) 894-9421 (f)

University of Guelph Library

The University of Guelph's Archival and Special Collections house significant primary source materials that support research in its library's major subject collecting areas. Formed as a separate section in the late 1970s to combine existing, older resources from previous campus libraries, it offers materials that are gathered together separately because of value, uniqueness, condition, or format. Although the unit has been in existence for less than 30 years, it has developed a number of collecting areas that have emerged as important local, regional, national, and international resources.

Guelph's present holdings—25,000 rare books and more than 250 special and archival collections—support university research activities in diverse areas such as Scottish history, Canadian agricultural and rural history, landscape architecture, Canadian theater, culinary studies, and campus and regional history. The Scottish holdings are particularly noteworthy, featuring chapbooks; family, clan, and local histories; emigration; Jacobite rebellions; and church and religious history, especially the Disruption period. The oldest document is a Scottish charter dating to 1332. The basis of agricultural and rural history collections dates to the establishment of the Ontario Agricultural College in 1874 and features the history of Massey-Harris-Ferguson and other agricultural producers such as International Harvester and Cockshutt Plow Co.

A few individual holdings are nationally significant, such as the Dan H. Laurence Collection of Shaviana, Shaw Festival Fonds, Foulis Press Collection, and Una Abrahamson Canadian Cookbook Collection. Rare book holdings contain many publications in disciplines such as horticulture, natural history, veterinary medicine, and Canadian history prior to 1900. Catalog access to all resources is provided by an online catalog and most archival items are searchable at the file level.

Collection Profile and Overview: Lorne Bruce
Illustrations: Dean Palmer

University of Guelph Library
Archival and Special Collections
University of Guelph
50 Stone Road E.
Guelph, Ontario
N1G 2W1
Canada
http://www.lib.uoguelph.ca/resources/archives/
libasc@uoguelph.ca
(519) 824-4120-53413 (t)
(519) 824-6931 (f)

Harvard University Library

The Harvard University Library, the oldest and largest university library in the United States, is a system of more than 90 libraries with collections of more than 15.5 million volumes, as well as journals, primary source materials, images, audio and video recordings, and digital resources that span a wide range of subjects, languages, and dates.

Special collections are integral to nearly every Harvard library and reflect their mission to support the research and teaching of Harvard faculty, students, and researchers from around the world. These special collections are accessible in the Harvard University Library online catalogs and many are heavily used.

Most of Harvard's 11 schools or faculties, including Law, Medicine, Business, Design, Education, and Divinity, have special collections. There are numerous other special collections libraries that focus on particular subjects. These include the Archive of World Music at the Loeb Music Library, the Harvard Film Archive, the Bibliotheca Berenson at the Villa I Tatti in Florence, Italy, the Collection of Historical Scientific Instruments, the Schlesinger Library of the History of Women in America, the Library at Dumbarton Oaks in Washington, DC, and the Library of the Gray Herbarium.

Houghton Library is the special collections library of Harvard College. The collections of Houghton Library focus on the study of Western civilization. Materials relating to American, Continental, and English history and literature comprise the bulk of these collections and include special concentrations in printing and graphic art, and the theater. The collections encompass wonderfully diverse holdings such as ostraca, daguerreotypes and the working papers of novelists and poets. In addition to Emily Dickinson, Houghton Library includes collections of Samuel Johnson, Goethe, Edward Lear, Dante, Lewis Carroll, John Keats, Tennessee Williams, Gore Vidal, and Cervantes.

Collection Profile: Leslie A. Morris
Overview: William P. Stoneman
Illustrations: Imaging Services, Harvard College Library

Harvard University
Harvard University Library
Wadsworth House
Cambridge, Massachusetts 02138
http://hul.harvard.edu/
http://library.harvard.edu/archives/
administration@hulmail.harvard.edu
(617) 495-3650 (t)
(617) 495-0370 (f)

Houghton Library
Harvard Yard
Cambridge, Massachusetts 02138
http://hcl.harvard.edu/houghton/
(617) 495-2441 (t)

University of Hawaii at Manoa Library

Special Collections at the University of Hawaii (UH) includes the Hawaiian, Pacific, and general rare collections. Since the founding of the university in 1907, emphasis has been on research relating to Hawaii and the Pacific Islands. An international reputation for excellence brings visitors from around the world. In recent years Special Collections has been active in digitization projects, including anti-annexation documents of Hawaii and photographs of Micronesia. UH Library also contains the University Archives and Manuscripts Department housing the Hawaii War Records, University Archives, and Hawaii Congressional Papers. The library is the repository for the papers and prints of artist Jean Charlot.

The Hawaiian Collection is a comprehensive array of retrospective and current materials with nearly 150,000 volumes relating to Hawaiian history, culture, art, and science. Recognized as the premier collection of materials on Hawaii, strengths include European voyage accounts, Hawaiian language imprints, travel literature, government documents from the monarchy, republic, territory, and state, and numerous unpublished and unique reports, papers, and manuscript and archival collections. Extensive audiovisual holdings complement the print materials, among them rare recordings of early Hawaiian music.

The Pacific Collection covers the cultural regions of Melanesia, Micronesia, and Polynesia. Over 100,000 volumes contain nearly every published work on the Pacific, including newspapers and periodicals, colonial-era government documents and those of post-WWII independent nations, texts in Pacific languages, and indigenous literature. The Pacific Collection has assembled extensive audiovisual materials representing all the Pacific Islands, and it has obtained numerous archival and manuscript collections, among them anthropological field notes and historical photo albums.

Collection Profile and Overview: Karen Peacock and Joan Hori
Illustrations: University of Hawaii

University of Hawaii at Manoa
University of Hawaii at Manoa Library
2550 McCarthy Mall
Honolulu, Hawaii 96822
http://www2.hawaii.edu/~speccoll/
speccoll@hawaii.edu
(808) 956-8264 (t)
(808) 956-5968 (f)

University of Houston Libraries

The University of Houston (UH) Libraries' Special Collections is a relatively young department that came into being in 1968. Holdings, exclusive of books, across its four units currently number 233 collections.

Major strengths in the Special Collections unit's manuscript holdings include Texas and Houston-area history and politics, American literature, performing arts, and World War II-related collections. Houston-area architecture, the American Revolution, the American Civil War, and the history of quantum theory also are represented.

Book collections focus on Texas and Houston history, US history, English and American literature, the history of the book and of writing, gay and lesbian studies, historic dictionaries, children's literature, history of science and quantum theory, science fiction and fantasy, the occult sciences, and fine-press printing. Faculty and other patrons are pleasantly surprised to find incunabula, as well as the medieval and Renaissance manuscript books highlighted here.

The Women's Archives' original focus was the papers of Houston-area women's organizations across a wide range of subject areas. This collecting focus has expanded to include individual politicians, civic leaders, social workers, and women's movement activists in and around Houston. The Houston History Archives contain the papers of political and civic leaders in the early 20th century, as well as area environmental, commercial, and civil rights collections dating from the latter half of the 20th century.

The University Archives collects selectively, two of its largest collections being its historical photographs and the papers and selected films of KUHT-Channel 8, the first educational television station in the United States. Other collections include UH presidential records, distinguished faculty papers, campus organizations and events, and architectural and construction records.

Collection Profile and Overview: Julie E. Grob
Illustrations: Thomas DuBrock

University of Houston Libraries
Special Collections
114 University Libraries
Houston, Texas 77204-2000
http://info.lib.uh.edu/sca/
speccol@lib.uh.edu
(713) 743-9750 (t)
(713) 743-9893 (f)

Howard University Libraries

Howard University Libraries contain two special collections, the Moorland-Spingarn Research Center and the Channing Pollock Theatre Collection. The Moorland-Spingarn Research Center is recognized as one of the world's largest and most comprehensive repositories for the documentation of the history and culture of people of African descent in Africa, the Americas, and other parts of the world. The center includes more than 175,000 bound volumes and tens of thousands of journals, periodicals, and newspapers; more than 17,000 feet of manuscript and archival collections; nearly 1,000 audio tapes; hundreds of artifacts; and 100,000 prints, photographs, maps, and other graphic items.

The Channing Pollock Theatre Collection contains rare books on the theater, including books by and about Shakespeare and selected first editions by Eugene O'Neill and other American playwrights. There are souvenir programs dating back to 1865 as well as Pollock's manuscripts, published works, and personal correspondence. Extensive material collected by many of his associates in the theater business is also included. The core Pollock Collection is augmented by clippings and photographs of the Howard Players and a host of Black performing artists.

Collection Profile and Overview: Thomas C. Battle, PhD
Illustrations: Donna M. Wells

Howard University Libraries
mmekkawi@howard.edu

The Founders Library
500 Howard Place NW
Washington, DC 20059
http://www.howard.edu/library/
(202) 806-7234 (t)

Moorland-Spingarn Collection
tbattle@howard.edu
(202) 806-7239 (t)

Channing Pollock Theatre Collection
syoon@howard.edu
(202) 806-7252 (t)

University of Illinois at Chicago Library

The Special Collections Department in the University Library at the University of Illinois at Chicago (UIC) contains rich collections of rare books, manuscripts, and photographs. The strengths of the rare books collection include the political, social, architectural, and literary history of Chicago, and the history of medicine, particularly neurology, urology, dermatology, anatomies, herbals, and pharmacopoeias.

The more than 500 manuscript collections contain archival records of individuals and organizations that document the political, social, and cultural history of Chicago, with a focus on the 20th and 21st centuries. The strengths of the manuscript collection include the history of the Hull House settlement, A Century of Progress World's Fair, Chicago politics and government, Chicago design history, Midwest women's history, and the history of African-Americans in Chicago. Access to most of the manuscript collections is through online finding aids.

The photographic collections document a variety of activities of people and organizations. Among those that contain a substantial number of photographs are the Jane Addams Memorial Collection and the Italian-American Collection. Collections that are primarily photographic in content include the Bowen Country Club Collection, the James S. Parker Collection, and the Comer Archive of Chicago in the Year 2000.

The University Archives is the official depository for records with permanent historical value from the University of Illinois at Chicago and includes material from the establishment of the Chicago College of Pharmacy in 1859 to the present day. In addition to the records of the colleges, departments, and campus units at UIC, the University Archives also includes selected professional and personal manuscripts of faculty, staff, students, and alumni that may be given to the university for preservation and use.

Collection Profile and Overview: Ann C. Weller
Illustrations: Roberta K. Dupuis-Devlin

University of Illinois at Chicago
University Library
Special Collections Department
801 S. Morgan (m/c234)
Chicago, Illinois 60607
http://www.uic.edu/depts/lib/specialcoll/
http://www.uic.edu/depts/lib/specialcoll/manuscripts.shtml
(312) 996-2742 (t)
(312) 413-0424 (f)

University of Illinois at Urbana-Champaign Library

The Rare Book & Manuscript Library of the University of Illinois at Urbana-Champaign is one of the largest repositories for rare books and manuscripts in the United States. The collections, which total more than 350,000 volumes and 7,200 linear feet of manuscripts, are strong in the broad areas of literature, history, art, philosophy, and theology, technology, and the natural sciences. Particular strengths lie in early printing (more than 1,100 incunabula) and imprints from the 16th and 17th centuries, with English literature, important editions of the Bible, and Renaissance schoolbooks standing out as distinctive and deep collections. Also noteworthy are collections in the history of science, technology, and economics. The library is renowned for its collection of emblem books and for its extensive holdings of works by and about John Milton. A special emphasis of the library's literature collections is drama, with holdings that encompass neo-Latin plays, Italian baroque drama, Shakespeare, Elizabethan and Jacobean playbooks, 19th-century acting editions, and 20th-century set and costume design. The Cavagna Collection is a significant resource for northern Italian history, and includes material from the 12th to the 20th century. The Spanish Golden Age collection includes more than 1,200 volumes dating from 1472 to 1700, and represents not only Spanish literature, but also religion, law, politics, medicine, and astronomy. The Meine Collection of American wit and humor and the Baskette Collection on freedom of expression are rich resources. Modern literary archival material housed in the Rare Book & Manuscript Library includes the papers of H. G. Wells, Carl Sandburg, and W. S. Merwin, letters of Marcel Proust, and various archival collections associated with numerous 19th-century British authors.

Collection Profile and Overview: Valerie Hotchkiss, Alvan Bregman, Christopher D. Cook
Illustrations: Jason Lindsey, Noah Pollaczek

University of Illinois at Urbana-Champaign
The Rare Book & Manuscript Library
346 Library
1408 West Gregory Drive
Urbana, Illinois 61801
http://www.library.uiuc.edu/rbx/
rbmlref@library.uiuc.edu
(217) 333-3777 (t)
(217) 333-2214 (f)

Indiana University Libraries Bloomington

Holdings of the Lilly Library vary from a Babylonian cuneiform tablet to the New Testament of the Gutenberg Bible; from Shakespeare's First Folio to richly illuminated medieval manuscripts; and from an extensive Abraham Lincoln collection to the personal papers of Upton Sinclair, Ezra Pound, and Sylvia Plath. The library's special collections also include substantial holdings in American and British history and literature, children's books, Latin Americana, history of science, voyages of discovery and exploration, early printing and book arts, and film, radio, and television history. Free public tours and changing exhibitions, printed catalogs, and guides to the collections, public lectures and readings, and an attractive and informative Web site are all part of the library's ongoing effort to make its holdings as widely known and used as possible.

Collection Profile and Overview: Breon Mitchell
Illustrations: Michael Taylor

Indiana University
Lilly Library
1200 E. Seventh Street
Bloomington, Indiana 47405
http://www.indiana.edu/~liblilly/
liblilly@indiana.edu
(812) 855-2452 (t)
(812) 855-3143 (f)

University of Iowa Libraries

In 1847, 59 days after Iowa became a state, the General Assembly established the University of Iowa. Its first academic year was 1855, however, and that year a newly appointed president shipped two boxes containing 50 books purchased for $106 which became the basis of the libraries. Labeled "[Amos] Dean Library," they were stored unopened in a four-foot square room. The library grew steadily over the next 90 years, moving from building to building as space was needed; in the absence of a dedicated building, departmental libraries proliferated, at one time totaling 21 separate collections. Main Library opened in 1951, with space set aside for rare book and manuscript collections. These included the portion of the Daniel Talbot Collection of natural history that escaped a devastating fire in 1897; the Ranney Memorial Library of literature; University Archives, founded in 1931; the Luther Brewer–Leigh Hunt Collection; an embryo Iowa Authors Collection; and a then recently founded Tensions File, now called the Social Documents Collection. Three large inaugural gifts were the James Wills Bollinger Lincolniana Collection, the editorial cartoons of Jay N. "Ding" Darling, and the files of the Redpath Lyceum Bureau. The collections expanded rapidly in the 1960s and 1970s, with continued strong growth over the last 25 years. Existing collections were enlarged, and new initiatives developed significant strengths in railroad history; radio, film, and television, particularly screenwriting and direction; Iowa business and politics; hydrology; the Chef Louis Szathmáry II Collection of Culinary Arts; writers and writing; the John Martin Collection on medicine; the Charlotte Smith Collection of miniature books; Dada and Fluxus; fine printing and artists' books; the Iowa Women's Archive; and the M. Horvat Collection of Science Fiction Fanzines. Special collections today include over 200,000 print volumes and 15,000 linear feet of manuscript and archival materials.

Collection Profile and Overview: Sidney F. Huttner
Illustrations: University of Iowa Libraries

University of Iowa Libraries
Special Collections & University Archives
100 Main Library
University of Iowa
Iowa City, Iowa 52242-1420
http://www.lib.uiowa.edu/spec-coll/
lib-spec@uiowa.edu
(319) 335-5921 (t)
(319) 335-5900 (f)

Iowa State University Library

The Special Collections Department was founded at Iowa State University (ISU) Library in 1969, and its mission is to identify, select, preserve, create access to, provide reference assistance for, and promote the use of rare and unique research materials that support major research areas of Iowa State University.

The collections include nearly 15,000 linear feet of archival materials documenting agriculture, natural history, statistics, veterinary medicine, and women in science and engineering. Included are manuscript collections donated by individuals and organizations not necessarily connected with ISU, but reflective of the university's mission. The department also includes the University Archives, consisting of official records and faculty papers, over 1 million photographs, and 10,000 motion picture films. Finally, there are 50,000 rare books, with strengths in agriculture and the natural sciences. The department is actively digitizing selected priority collections and making them available through the ISU Library's e-Library and also through the Iowa Heritage Digital Collections, an online repository of Iowa history.

The department maintains an active public service, outreach, and tour program to both on-campus and off-campus groups, including academic classes, the Center for Excellence in Learning and Teaching, the Honors Program, ISU Learning Communities, Extension and 4-H groups, and K–12 student groups such as National History Day. The department also creates virtual exhibits for online visitors to its Web site, as well as exhibits for the Reading Room area and other locations on campus. The Reading Room, located on the fourth floor of Parks Library, oversees the central campus, and researchers and visitors are always welcome.

Collection Profile: Tanya Zanish-Belcher
Illustrations: Michele Christian

Iowa State University Library
Special Collections Department
403 Parks Library
Iowa State University
Ames, Iowa 50011-2140
http://www.lib.iastate.edu/spcl/
(515) 294-6672 (t)
(515) 294-5525 (f)

Johns Hopkins University Libraries

The Johns Hopkins University Libraries comprise numerous libraries and resource centers. Special Collections is an integral part of the Sheridan Libraries, the main research library of the Johns Hopkins University. Composed of three separate libraries, the Eisenhower Collection, the George Peabody Library, and the John Work Garrett Library, Special Collections is home to the rare book collection, historical manuscripts and sheet music, and the University Archives. Building on the foundation of early faculty interests, the Eisenhower Collection is strong in economic history and thought, German and French drama, English literature, especially Tudor and Stuart and the romantic poets, and abolitionist literature. The Peabody Library mirrors the interests and scholarship of the late 19th century with strengths in archaeology, British art and architecture, British and American history, biography, English and American literature, Romance languages and literature, history of science, geography, and exploration and travel, including a large map collection. The John Work Garrett Library collection reflects the tastes of several generations of the Garrett family. The collection was started by T. Harrison Garrett, a great collector of prints, engravings, and books, as well as *objets d'art*, and by his son, John Work Garrett. This library has strong collections in natural history including many of the most important and beautiful ornithological works ever produced, illustrated books, Americana, early printed books, and the Fowler Collection of Architectural History. The historical manuscript collections and the University Archives document the history of higher education in America especially as it pertains to the development of graduate education at Hopkins. Supporting the Lester S. Levy Collection of Sheet Music are 37 additional collections of ballads, waltzes, polkas, grand marches, hymns, operettas, and show tunes that have been part of America's musical heritage for two centuries.

Collection Profile and Overview: Cynthia Requardt
Illustrations: Kelly Betts

Johns Hopkins University
Sheridan Libraries
Special Collections
3400 North Charles Street
Baltimore, Maryland 21218
http://www.library.jhu.edu/collections/specialcollections/
(410) 516-8348 (t)
(410) 516-7202 (f)

University of Kansas Libraries

The Kenneth Spencer Research Library was built in the late 1960s, the gift of the late Helen Foresman Spencer in memory of her husband, specifically to meet the needs of users of rare books, manuscripts, regional history sources, and the university's own archives. Holdings include some 350,000 printed books, approximately 500,000 manuscripts, and more than 2 million photographs.

Special collections are particularly strong in medieval and Renaissance studies, economic and legal history, 18th-century France and England, Anglo-Irish culture, natural history, exploration and travel, and various minor literary genres. Major collections focus on the 16th through 17th centuries in Europe, particularly Spanish, French and Italian imprints; 16th- through 19th-century natural history, with notable strength in ornithology, botany and taxonomy, and Linnaeana; 18th-century British studies, particularly Edmund Curll, the Bond Collection of newspapers and periodicals, political and economic history, and various literary figures; the Pre-Raphaelite Brotherhood; and Tennyson and W. B. Yeats.

The Kansas Collection is the regional history division of University of Kansas Libraries, with extensive holdings of primary source materials that document the history of Kansas and the region. Its holdings of African-American materials are nationally recognized. There is a wealth of diaries, letters, scrapbooks, business records, church and club records, maps, architectural drawings and blueprints, books, and more than 1 million photographs. The Joseph J. Pennell Collection consists of some 30,000 glass plate negatives made by this noted Junction City photographer between 1891 and 1923. His often-published images portray many dimensions of life in a special small town at the turn of the last century.

Collection Profile and Overview: Sheryl K. Williams
Illustrations: Robert L. Hickerson (glass plate)/University of
    Kansas Libraries

University of Kansas
Kenneth Spencer Research Library
1450 Poplar Lane
Lawrence, Kansas 66045
http://spencer.lib.ku.edu/
wcrowe@ku.edu
(785) 864-4334 (t)
(785) 864-5803 (f)

Kent State University Libraries and Media Services

The Department of Special Collections and Archives provides access to primary sources and rare materials that support the teaching and research programs of Kent State University. Since its founding in 1967, the department has acquired over 100,000 volumes of books and periodicals and 10,000 cubic feet of manuscript and archival collections in a number of subject areas. Holdings in printing, publishing, and the book arts are punctuated by 12 incunabula specimens, a number of books produced by William Morris's Kelmscott Press, and a nearly complete collection of the hand-press publications of papermaking expert Dard Hunter. The department houses significant collections of 19th- and 20th-century British and American literature with holdings from the personal libraries of noted collectors Paul Louis Feiss, B. George Ulizio, C. E. Frazer Clark Jr., and Matthew J. Bruccoli. A fine collection of 20th-century and contemporary poetry includes books and manuscripts of Hart Crane, Robert Duncan, Cid Corman, James Broughton, Gary Snyder, d. a. levy, and many other noted poets. The true crime and history of crime collection of Albert and Helen Borowitz contains over 12,000 books supplemented by artifacts, manuscripts, and ephemera. During the 1970s and 1980s, the department built impressive collections in theater, film, and the performing arts, most notably including the papers of the avant-garde Open Theater, actor/director Robert Lewis, and film star Lois Wilson. Publications of the Saalfield Publishing Company and a vast collection of Babar the Elephant books and merchandise are high spots of the children's literature collection. University Archives include the historical institutional records of Kent State University as well as the May 4 Collection, which documents the 1970 Kent State shootings and their aftermath. Additionally, the department houses extensive collections regarding Americana and Ohioana, detective fiction, science fiction and fantasy, labor history, and Queen Marie of Romania.

Collection Profile and Overview: Cara Gilgenbach
Illustrations: Hilary Kennedy

Kent State University Libraries and Media Services
Department of Special Collections and Archives
Box 5190
1 Eastway Drive
Kent, Ohio 44242-0001
http://www.library.kent.edu/specialcollections/
(330) 672-2270 (t)
(330) 672-9318 (f)

University of Kentucky Libraries

The University of Kentucky Libraries' Special Collections and Digital Programs (SCDP) is the commonwealth's largest repository of privately generated primary resource material and rare printed resources.

The extensive manuscripts, rare books, and serials holdings in SCDP are particularly noted for the Kentuckiana and W. Hugh Peal collections. The former, documenting the commonwealth's history and culture, contains rare Kentucky imprints and unique primary sources, while the latter is a rich collection of early editions and manuscripts of 19th-century British and American authors. Other notable holdings include the Bert T. Combs Appalachian Collection, which features an array of primary and secondary source holdings supporting Appalachian studies, and the Public Policy Archives, which comprises the collections of many prominent Kentuckians and organizations involved in public policy. In addition, the Louie B. Nunn Center for Oral History contains more than 6,500 interviews representing more than 100 national or Kentucky-related projects. The University Archives and Records Program, also included in SCDP, preserves the institution's historical record and coordinates the management of the university's academic and administrative records. Moreover, SCDP's Audio-Visual Archives houses millions of sound recordings, moving images, and still photographs, including those of the Lexington *Herald-Leader* from the years 1938 to 1990.

The King Library Press, a hand-press publisher, actively perpetuates the book arts as it serves as a centerpiece in the hands-on teaching of printing history. Its electronic counterpart is Preservation and Digital Programs, whose projects include providing material to the statewide Kentuckiana Digital Library, contributing to the National Digital Newspaper Program, extensively reformatting the *Daily Racing Form*, and preserving Kentucky newspapers from across the commonwealth.

Collection Profile and Overview: William J. Marshall
Illustrations: Deirdre A. Scaggs

University of Kentucky Libraries
Special Collections and Digital Programs
M.I. King Building
University of Kentucky
Lexington, Kentucky 40506-0039
http://www.uky.edu/Libraries/lib.php?lib_id=13
sclibraryrefdesk@lsv.uky.edu
(859) 257-8611 (t)
(859) 257-6311 (f)

Bibliothèque de l'Université Laval

The origins of Université Laval can be traced back as far as 1663, with the foundation of the Séminaire de Québec, an institution devoted to the teaching of theology. Parts of the library's collections had their beginning at that time and were steadily developed since then, giving a strong historical value to the library's holdings. Major strengths include philosophy and theology with very strong and/or comprehensive collections. For instance, the rare book section holds many unique documents and, notably, a collection of ancient Coptic liturgical manuscripts, the Alphonse Dain collection, believed to be lost for years by the international community. The same applies to the Aristotle collection, known among the scholarly community for its exhaustiveness, which encompasses dozens of rare documents. As part of the first French university established in America, the library has a special interest in the many aspects and manifestations of North American French heritage, and many collections present substantial holdings that give a unique perspective on it. The law section, for instance, encompasses an all-inclusive collection of all the law texts relevant to both French tradition and common law, from the very beginning of New France to the present. The library also holds extensive visual documentation focusing on French-American architecture, arts, and crafts. Its collection dedicated to school manuals is the second largest in Quebec, after the National Library, and includes thousands of books published between 1765 and the present. Other strengths of Université Laval Library's Special Collections can be found in various disciplines such as music, French-Canadian literature, and Spanish literature. Université Laval Library also has the responsibility of a huge collection of over 800,000 objects and specimens gathered through decades by professors and university staff. This collection includes a wide variety of items, from archaeological artifacts to art pieces, scientific apparatus, and biological specimens, including many extinct species.

Collection Profile and Overview: Jacinthe Guay, James Lambert, Rémi Larochelle, Louise Ranger, Gisèle Wagner
Illustrations: Guy Couture and Arthur Lamothe for "Touladi"

Université Laval Library
Collections Spéciales
Bibliothèque de l'Université Laval
Pavillon Jean-Charles Bonenfant
Local 4484
Québec, Québec
G1K 7P4
Canada
http://www.bibl.ulaval.ca/mieux/decouvrir/
isabelle.archambault@bibl.ulaval.ca
(418) 656-2131 x3227 (t)
(418) 656-7793 (f)

Library and Archives Canada

In 2004, Library and Archives Canada, a new knowledge institution dedicated to collecting, preserving, and making accessible Canada's documentary heritage, was created from the merger of the former National Archives of Canada, founded in 1872, and the former National Library of Canada, founded in 1953. The Canadian Archives and Special Collections Branch at Library and Archives Canada was given the mandate to develop national collections representative of Canada's social, political, economic, and cultural evolution. The branch is responsible for some 13,000 individual collections, dating from the 16th century to the present. The holdings include documents in a wide range of formats, such as textual and digital records, moving images, music and sound recordings, maps, architectural drawings, photographs, documentary art, philatelic records, and rare books. The collections document the lives and activities of prominent Canadian individuals and associations from a variety of fields, many of international standing. Among the many notable collections are those of explorers Samuel de Champlain and Roald Amundsen; authors Lucy Maud Montgomery, Robertson Davies, and Michael Ondaatje; medical scientist and Nobel laureate Sir Frederick Banting; inventor Alexander Graham Bell; photographer Yousuf Karsh; media theorist Marshall McLuhan; pianists Oscar Peterson and Glenn Gould; conservationists Grey Owl and Ernest Thompson Seton; Métis leader Louis Riel; hockey player Maurice "The Rocket" Richard; artists Emily Carr and Frances Anne Hopkins; the records of the National Film Board of Canada; and the Molson business and family records.

Collection Profile and Overview: John Bell, Maureen Hoogenraad, and Marcel Barriault
Illustrations: Library and Archives Canada

Library and Archives Canada
Canadian Archives and Special Collections Branch
550, boul. de la Cité
Gatineau, Québec
K1A 0N4
Canada
http://www.collectionscanada.ca/
robert.mcintosh@lac-bac.gc.ca
(819) 934-7252 (t)
(819) 934-6830 (f)

Library of Congress

Special collections play a critical role in the library's mission to make its resources available and useful to the US Congress and the American people and to sustain and preserve a universal collection of knowledge. Since its founding in 1800, the library has assembled more than 134 million items. In addition to electronic resources and 32 million books and other print materials, the library offers information in such special formats as 2.8 million recordings, 5.3 million maps, 12.5 million photographs, and 59.5 million manuscripts. The purchase of Thomas Jefferson's library in 1815 became a special collections cornerstone that generous benefactors continue to build on. Recent acquisition highlights include the Waldseemüller world map on which the name America first appeared in 1507, the Alvin Ailey American Dance Theater Archive, the Coca-Cola Company television broadcast advertising materials, and Veterans History Project submissions.

The Historic American Buildings Survey, the Comic Book Collection, and the Technical Reports Collection are among the many resources consulted frequently by both the general public and scholarly experts. The special international resources that span many centuries include cuneiform tablets as well as the Archive of Hispanic Literature on Tape. Among the top treasures are presidential papers from George Washington through Calvin Coolidge, a perfect copy on vellum of the Gutenberg Bible, and "Migrant Mother"—Dorothea Lange's iconic photograph of the Great Depression.

Through more than 20 research centers, library specialists help people worldwide connect effectively to the library's collections with onsite services and Web-based resources. Many divisions publish illustrated guides, available online or as printed booklets. The library also hosts such programs as the Kluge Fellowships and the Junior Fellows summer internships to encourage both advanced research for senior scholars and hands-on experience with original historical resources for students.

Collection Profile and Overview: Helena Zinkham
Illustrations: Courtesy of the Library of Congress

Library of Congress
101 Independence Avenue SE
Washington, DC 20540
E-mail, telephone, and fax numbers available at:
http://www.loc.gov/rr/research-centers.html

Louisiana State University Libraries

In 1985, the Louisiana State University (LSU) Libraries organized the Special Collections division to administer its rare books, manuscripts, and other special research collections. The collections, previously dispersed in the libraries' main building, were moved to Hill Memorial Library, which had been renovated for that purpose. Originally constructed in 1925 as the university's main library, Hill stands on the historic quadrangle at the heart of the LSU campus.

Today, Special Collections comprises more than 200,000 published volumes, 10 million manuscript items, 200,000 photographs, 24,000 reels of microfilm, hundreds of oral histories, and other diverse materials for research. Voluminous manuscript holdings document life in Louisiana from the 18th through the 20th centuries. Political papers record the careers of senators Russell Long, J. Bennett Johnston, and John Breaux, among others. University Archives documents the development of a once-small military school into a large research institution. Special Collections is a comprehensive state document depository, houses the Louisiana Newspaper Project, and is the repository for the T. Harry Williams Center for Oral History. It holds treasures of ornithological and botanical illustration, including the elephant folio of Audubon's *Birds of America* (1827–38), Edward Lear's *Illustrations of the Family of Psittacidae, or Parrots* (1830), the Alecto edition of Sir Joseph Banks's *Florilegium* (1990), and watercolor drawings of Louisiana flora by Margaret Stones. Antiquarian holdings are strongest in 18th-century British history and literature, but include high points related to travel and voyages, such as the *Description de l'Égypte* and Kircher's *China Monumentis*. Strong collections of science fiction and comics provide materials for the study of popular culture. Modern book arts flourish, with comprehensive collections of the Janus Press, Circle Press, and books printed by Harry Duncan, as well as works from presses ranging from Arion to Wayzgoose.

Collection Profile and Overview: Elaine B. Smyth
Illustrations: Gina Costello, Adam Hess

Louisiana State University Libraries
Special Collections
Hill Memorial Library
Louisiana State University
Baton Rouge, Louisiana 70803-3300
http://www.lib.lsu.edu/special/
(225) 578-6551(t)
(225) 578-9425 (f)

University of Louisville Libraries

The University of Louisville Libraries offer over 1,000 special collections. The Department of Special Collections within Ekstrom Library includes an internationally known Photographic Archives, with almost 2 million images. In addition to significant collections of regional and historic photographs, the Photographic Archives preserves the papers of Roy Stryker, the archive of the landmark Standard Oil of New Jersey Photography Project, and photographic fine prints. Also within Special Collections, Rare Books collects literature, book history, and popular culture, and boasts the world's most extensive public collections of Edgar Rice Burroughs, creator of Tarzan. Rare Books holds choice collections of rare mathematics books, vintage war posters, and Louisville ephemera.

The University Archives and Records Center serves as the memory of the institution with documents dating back to the 1798 charter of Jefferson Seminary, predecessor of the University of Louisville. University Archives collects records documenting regional history, businesses, ethnic communities, and social action groups. University Archives preserves local political records and is the repository for a number of United States representatives and senators, as well as local officials. The Oral History Center holds nearly 2,000 interviews of regional leaders and activists.

University Libraries' Bridwell Art, Anderson Music, and Kornhauser Health Sciences Libraries each maintain special collections: papers of regional artists and architects, rare art books, 19th-century Louisville music imprints, original scores submitted for the Grawemeyer Award for Music Composition, and documents and artifacts tracing the history of medicine and the university's School of Medicine back to its founding in 1837.

Collection Profile and Overview: Delinda Stephens Buie and
   Thomas L. Owen
Illustrations: Tom Fougerousse, Rachel I. Howard, and
   Amy Hanaford Purcell

University of Louisville
Ekstrom Library
University Archives and Records Center
Photographic Archives
Louisville, Kentucky 40292
http://library.louisville.edu/
Special.Collections@louisville.edu
(502) 852-6745 (t)
(502) 852-7394 (f)

McGill University Library

Beginning in 1859 with the gift of the manuscript Ottawa-French dictionary (ca. 1740) of Pierre Luc Du Jannay and in 1861 with the gift of the extra-large folio of J. J. Audubon's *Birds of America* (1827–38), the McGill University Library has built rich and varied special collections covering many subjects in the humanities and sciences. In some cases these collections were formed by discriminating collectors as with Sir William Osler in medicine and Lawrence Lande in Canadiana. In other cases collections were developed in cooperation with benefactors such as Casey A. Wood and the ornithology collection or have been acquired for the library as in the case of the Redpath Tracts on British history given by Peter and Grace Redpath. In still other cases, collections have reflected academic programs and faculty interest— among these are the holdings of Islamic manuscripts and lithographed books and the David Hume Collection. Finally, some collections are the result of the special interests of librarians to name only the Colgate History of Printing Collection and the Napoleon Collection. Today, among the varied special collections, four general themes standout. The Western philosophical tradition from antiquity to the modern era unites not only the David Hume and Soren Kierkegaard collections but also includes the library of Raymond Klibansky and parts of the Osler History of Medicine Collection as well as materials in the general rare book collection. Canadiana includes not only the Lande Collection but extensive book, manuscript, map, and graphic holdings. The history of the book brings together not only the Colgate Collection on printing but collections documenting the work of book illustrators and the history of bibliography. Finally, the history of science brings together the Osler Collection and collections on geology, ornithology, entomology, and holdings in the general rare book collection. Working together during a century and a half, collectors, benefactors, faculty, and librarians have brought together a body of special collection materials for students and researchers that reflects the diverse interests of a multidisciplinary university and makes evident the university's distinctive collection history.

Collection Profile and Overview: Richard Virr
Illustrations: Eli Brown

McGill University
Rare Books and Special Collections Division
3459 McTavish Street
Montreal, Quebec
H3A 1Y1
Canada
http://www.mcgill.ca/rarebooks/
(514) 398-4711 (t)
(514) 398-2139 (f)

McMaster University Libraries

Although McMaster University Libraries had a small treasure room of rare books in the 1930s and acquired its first archives (the papers of W. J. Bengough, the 19th-century cartoonist) in 1939, the acquisition of rare and unique material for research purposes began in earnest in the 1960s under William Ready's visionary stewardship. The collections include an excellent 18th-century gathering of books and periodicals (Pope, Dryden, Swift, Johnson, and others). McMaster University Libraries is one of the select institutions that offers an annual fellowship sponsored by the American Society for Eighteenth Century Studies. In the category of post-1800 books, there are major collections of Anglo-Irish authors, Canadian poetry, imprints of the Hogarth Press and Canadian publishers, and subject collections pertaining to peace and war, Quakers, temperance, opera, and labor history. The archives are both national and international. There are 90 archives related to peace and war, including Vera Brittain, C. K. Ogden, and the World War II Air Raid Precautionary Committee for Westminster. Other areas of archival collecting include music, represented by Franz Liszt, Hans von Bülow, and Sir Robert Mayer; Canadian literature including Pierre Berton, Austin Clarke, and Leslie McFarlane; Canadian publishers McClelland & Stewart, Macmillan Canada, and Clarke Irwin; the radical left with Canadian Liberation Movement, League for Socialist Action, and the Revolutionary Marxist Group; and student organizations such as the Canadian Union of Students and Ontario Union of Students. The Web site for Archives and Research Collections provides fonds/collection descriptions and finding aids to archives, virtual exhibitions, and blogs about new acquisitions and activities. William Ready, the bibliophilic patron saint of McMaster's research collections, would be proud to know that his dream of establishing a library of rare books and archives has been realized and continues to flourish.

Collection Profile and Overview: Carl Spadoni
Illustrations: McMaster University Libraries

McMaster University Libraries
William Ready Division of Archives and Research Collections
1280 Main Street West
Hamilton, Ontario
L8S 4L6
Canada
http://library.mcmaster.ca/archives/readyweb.htm
(905) 525-9140 x22079 (t)
(905) 546-0625 (f)

University of Manitoba Libraries

Since 1963, Archives & Special Collections has been the fortunate recipient of unique materials from hundreds of donors. Literary papers from such Canadian poets as Dorothy Livesay and Margaret Avison, the mysterious German writer F. P. Grove/F. P. Greve, and journalists including John W. Dafoe and E. Cora Hind provide a glimpse into the writer's mind. Presses—e.g., Thistledown Press, Turnstone Press, NeWest Press—and literary journals—e.g., Prairie Fire, Mosaic—provide the publishers' view.

Records of pioneer farm families, cooperatives such as Keystone Agricultural Producers, commercial organizations such as the United Grain Growers and Ogilvie Flour Mills, commercial publications such as the *United Grain Grower* and *Nor'West Farmer*, and government publications compose the Archives of the Agricultural Experience.

The archives began its collection of materials relating to polar exploration and the search for the Northwest Passage with books from the library of explorer Dr. Vilhjalmur Stefansson. Contemporary accounts of the ill-fated Franklin Expedition as well as Dr. Andrew Taylor's more modern records complement first editions of John Palliser, Alexander Mackenzie, Henry Youle Hind, James Cook, George Heriot, and scores of other explorers, pioneers, and settlers. Other major holdings of rare books pertain to Canadian Prairie literature, early native language syllabics, church history and philosophy, Bibles, English literature (including extensive Rudyard Kipling and Ernest Hemingway collections), children's literature of the early 20th century, and Western Canadian agriculture. The Dysart Memorial Collection on printing and publishing includes late medieval manuscripts, incunabula and early printed books from such well known printers as Aldus Manutius, Johannes Bämler, and Anton Koberger.

The files of the *Winnipeg Tribune*, Archives of the Ukrainian Canadian Experience, University Archives, papers relating to animators and filmmakers Richard Condie, Charlie Thorsen, and Guy Maddin and the architectural photographs of Henry Kalen are a few of the many interesting collections located at the archives.

Collection Profile and Overview: Shelley Sweeney
Illustrations: Bob Talbot

University of Manitoba
Archives & Special Collections
330 Elizabeth Dafoe Library
Winnipeg, Manitoba
R3T 2N2
Canada
http://www.umanitoba.ca/libraries/archives/
(204) 474-6350 (t)
(204) 474-7913 (f)

University of Maryland Libraries

The Special Collections of the University of Maryland Libraries encompass richly diverse formats and subjects, including printed and rare books, manuscripts, still photographs (more than 2.4 million images), audio/visual recordings, and antique maps. Strengths are focused predominantly in the humanities and include major holdings in the areas of Maryland, literature, culture, the book arts, historic preservation, broadcasting, Japan, labor, women, and music. The Marylandia Collection includes more than 65,000 books, newspapers, and periodicals about Maryland, current and historical. Collection highlights are Maryland authors and literary figures, including H. L. Mencken, and more than 3,000 historic maps of Maryland and the Chesapeake region, dating as far back as the 16th century. The vast photo archive of 1.5 million images of the *Baltimore News American* documents the rich diversity of Maryland life and culture.

Among the archival and manuscript holdings are the significant literary archives of the 20th-century writers Katherine Anne Porter and Djuna Barnes. The National Trust for Historic Preservation Library is a national resource center for the study of historic preservation. The voluminous print, manuscript, and photo holdings constitute the most significant collection documenting the theory and practice of historic preservation in the United States.

The Library of American Broadcasting and the National Public Broadcasting Archives represent wide-ranging and unique collections of audio and video recordings, printed publications, manuscripts, and other materials devoted exclusively to the history of radio and television broadcasting in the United States, both commercial and non-commercial. Materials also chronicle the careers of well-known individuals and organizations in the broadcasting industry, including Arthur Godfrey.

The International Piano Archives at Maryland contains one of the world's most extensive concentrations of piano recordings, including vintage piano rolls, books, scores, programs, and artist's archival papers related to classical piano performance. Among the featured archival collections of individual pianists and scholars are Nadia Reisenberg, Leopold Godowsky, William Kappell, and Gary Graffman.

Collection Profile and Overview: Amy Wasserstrom
Illustrations: Nichimy Corp., Thai Nguyen

University of Maryland
Collection Management & Special Collections Division
McKeldin Library, Rm. 4119
College Park, Maryland 20742-7011
http://www.lib.umd.edu/special/
(301) 405-9112 (t)
(301) 405-9191 (f)

University of Massachusetts Amherst Libraries

The Department of Special Collections and University Archives (SCUA) is a center for research in the history and impact of social change in America and the history of western New England. With substantial holdings in African-American history and culture, social and racial justice, organic and sustainable agriculture, the environment, the peace movement, communal and alternative living, and the labor movement and labor radicalism, the department houses approximately 30,000 volumes, 550 manuscript collections, and several hundred historic maps, as well as the official records of UMass Amherst. SCUA has also developed depth in areas as diverse as Revolutionary-era France and Belgium (1789–1848), Scottish literature, the Anglo-American stage (1750–1915), American relations with Meiji-era Japan and the post-war study of Japan, eastern European ethnography, and the literature of American socialism.

Serving a wide range of researchers, from undergraduates to academics and journalists to family historians, SCUA houses a growing collection used by an international audience of students, scholars, and members of the general public.

Collection Profile and Overview: Robert S. Cox
Illustrations: Josh Silver/University of Massachusetts Amherst Libraries

University of Massachusetts Amherst
W.E.B. Du Bois Library
Special Collections and University Archives
154 Hicks Way
Amherst, Massachusetts 01003
http://www.library.umass.edu/
http://www.library.umass.edu/spcoll/
(413) 545-2780 (t)
(413) 577-1399 (f)

Massachusetts Institute of Technology Libraries

The Massachusetts Institute of Technology (MIT) Libraries include five major subject libraries: architecture and planning; engineering; humanities; management and social sciences; and science; as well as several more specialized branch libraries. The libraries maintain and support numerous special collections.

The Institute Archives and Special Collections documents the history of MIT, from its founding in 1861 to the present day. In addition to the administrative records of MIT, the archives maintains the theses collection consisting of over 100,000 theses; MIT publications related to MIT research, teaching, and community activity; and a variety of oral history collections. The archives is one of the primary resources for the study of the development of 20th-century science and engineering, and has been entrusted with the personal papers of some of the most brilliant minds in the world, past and present.

In addition to its vast collection of archives, the MIT Libraries steward rare book collections, including an impressive array in areas of 16th- through early 20th-century science and technology. These include the Vail Collection, an outstanding assemblage of thousands of books and pamphlets in the area of electricity, and the Gaffield Collection, comprised of works relating to glassmaking. Other collections document the development of a broad range of science and technology, such as aeronautics, ballooning, and civil engineering.

The Rotch Library for Architecture and Planning contains a variety of European publications dating from the 16th to the 19th centuries and the professional library of Charles Bulfinch. The Rotch Library also administers the Aga Khan Visual Archive of Islamic Architecture and the Rotch Visual Collection. The Lewis Music Library includes material related to MIT music faculty and recordings of musical activity at MIT, as well as a growing oral history collection.

Less traditional special collections include DSpace@MIT, an institutional repository capturing and preserving the research output of MIT, in digital form, and DOME, the MIT Libraries' digital library.

Collection Profile and Overview: Marilyn G. McSweeney and Thomas J. Rosko
Illustrations: Sean Thomas

Massachusetts Institute of Technology Libraries
Institute Archives and Special Collections
MIT Libraries, Bldg. 14N-118
Massachusetts Institute of Technology
77 Massachusetts Avenue
Cambridge, Massachusetts 02139-4307
http://libraries.mit.edu/archives/
mithistory@mit.edu
(617) 253-5136 (t)
(617) 258-7305 (f)

University of Miami Libraries

Although the Special Collections at the University of Miami Libraries were established in 1978, the libraries have collected rare and manuscript materials since the inception of the University of Miami in 1926. Today, the Special Collections are recognized for extensive holdings relating to the history of Florida and the Caribbean Basin, including the West Indies; the northern coastal regions of South and Central America; and the Gulf Coast states of the United States. The Rare Books Section includes examples of early printing, private press publications, art books, collectible books, fine-press printings, and fine bindings. The Special Collections are also home to the University Archives.

Notably, the Manuscript Collections focus on South Florida and consist of important collections of the papers of Florida pioneers, political figures, authors, businesses, and organizations, social and cultural activists, civic leaders, and alumni and faculty of the University of Miami. Examples include the papers of noted author and environmentalist Marjory Stoneman Douglas and prominent botanist Walter Swingle; the records of the Model Land Company and the Woman's Club of Coconut Grove; the collections of Mark F. Boyd and Charles Deering; and the papers of university faculty such as art historian Virgil Barker and writer Clark Emery.

While Florida materials are the strength of the Manuscript Collections, the Special Collections also hold collections of Latin American materials, such as the collections of Phanor James Eder and Puerto Rican writer José Balseiro, and Americana such as the Historical Manuscripts Collection that includes Thomas Jefferson letters.

One of the most widely used collections in the Special Collections is the Pan American World Airways Inc. Records, and the Special Collections houses several other collections related to Pan Am and Florida's aviation history such as the records of World Wings International and Clipper Pioneers.

Collection Profile and Overview: Maria R. Estorino
Illustrations: University of Miami Libraries Special Collections

University of Miami
University of Miami Libraries
Special Collections
PO Box 248214
Coral Gables, Florida 33124-0320
http://www.library.miami.edu/archives/
asc.library@miami.edu
(305)284-3247 (t)
(305) 284-4027 (f)

University of Michigan Library

Besides the Papyrus Collection highlighted in this volume, the Special Collections Library at the University of Michigan contains rare books in a wide variety of subjects, as well as early books and manuscripts, deep subject collections in various formats, and personal, organizational, and literary archives. The Labadie Collection is one of the world's strongest collections focusing on anarchism and other radical social movements; it covers the period from 1848 to the present day through books, serials, pamphlets, manuscripts, and ephemera, including such diverse topics as free thought, socialism, pre-1930 labor unions, civil rights, campus unrest, peace movements, and transgender issues. The Hubbard Collection of some 3,000 volumes is one of the world's largest gatherings of editions, adaptations, and spin-offs of *Robinson Crusoe* and *Gulliver's Travels*. Other notable literary collections include Shakespeare (ca. 9,000 pre-1900 volumes), Swinburne (books and manuscripts), Dickens and Trollope (published in parts), Faulkner, Frost, archives of post-beat poets (Anne Waldman, Marge Piercy), Hopwood Award materials, and archives of Detroit small presses focusing on African-American literature. Of great rarity is a collection of 1,200 pre-20th-century Islamic manuscripts featuring outstanding specimens of calligraphy and important legal and scientific texts. The Transportation History Collection includes some 70,000 items on canals, bridges, roads, bicycles, carriages, automobiles, and railroads, with special strengths in pictorial material. Several archival and photograph collections relate to the history of American governance of the Philippines in the period 1890 to 1930 and are complemented by additional materials in the Michigan Historical Collections at the Bentley Library. The William L. Clements Library holds manuscript and print collections of great importance for the study of the Northwest Territory and the American Revolution. There are also rich materials in the Music Library with one of the largest collections of 19th-century American sheet music in the United States and the Taubman Medical Library.

Collection Profile: Traianos Gagos
Overview: Peggy Daub
Illustrations: Randal Stegmeyer

University of Michigan Library
Special Collections Library
7th Floor, Hatcher Graduate Library
University of Michigan
Ann Arbor, Michigan 48109-1205
http://www.lib.umich.edu/spec-coll/
special.collections@umich.edu
(734) 764-9377 (t)
(734) 764-9368 (f)

Michigan State University Libraries

The Special Collections Division of the Michigan State University Libraries was established in 1962, and by 1970 had become the university's depository not only for rare books, but also for "sensitive" radical materials, and "ephemeral" popular materials. Given the school's agricultural foundation, it is not surprising that the library's first rare books were primarily in the fields of agriculture, botany, and zoology. Over the years the number of rare book holdings has increased with the addition of outstanding collections in apiculture, cookery, fencing, and veterinary medicine. Rare collections on the French monarchy, the Italian Risorgimento, and German criminology are also held. The Michigan Writers Collection includes publications and papers of authors primarily related to Michigan State University, including Tom McGuane and Richard Ford. The Russel B. Nye Popular Culture Collection is among the best general collections of its kind, holding popular fiction in appropriately great quantities, notably westerns, science fiction, mysteries, and romances, Sunday school books, textbooks, and the Comic Art Collection. The Radicalism Collection includes books, pamphlets, and runs of periodicals from dozens of organizations of the radical left and right, plus files of press clippings and miscellanea on hundreds of causes and movements. Radicalism also includes feminism, lesbian, gay, and transgender materials and a men's movement collection. Archives of materials on the Students for a Democratic Society, the draft resistance movement, the peace movement, and an African Activist Archive are also maintained. The Vincent Voice Library of sound recordings and the Turfgrass Information Center are also nationally important collections in the library, though they are administratively outside of the Special Collections Division.

Collection Profile and Overview: Randall W. Scott
Illustrations: Louis Villafranca

Michigan State University
Special Collections Division
100 Library
Michigan State University Libraries
East Lansing, Michigan 48824-1048
http://specialcollections.lib.msu.edu/
comics@msu.edu
(517) 432-6123 x100 (t)

University of Minnesota Libraries

The completion of the Elmer L. Andersen Library in 2000 brought together 11 distinct collecting entities as the Department of Archives and Special Collections. Underground caverns tunneled into the bluffs above the Mississippi River house nearly 93,000 cubic feet of materials in state-of-the-art environmental conditions. In addition to the James Ford Bell Library featured in this volume, the collections encompass an extensive array of subject areas. The Charles Babbage Institute Archives documents the history of information technology with an extensive collection of oral histories available online. The Children's Literature Research Collections include the Kerlan Collection of manuscripts and original illustrations and the Hess Collection of dime novels. The Immigration History Research Center documents migration, with rich materials from ethnic groups originating in eastern, central, and southern Europe and the Near East. Records of the Kautz Family YMCA Archives encompass national and international Y materials. Records of voluntary-sector social service and social reform organizations and leaders in the field can be found in the Social Welfare History Archives. The Manuscripts Division houses the Northwest Architectural Archives, inlcuding the records of Prairie School architects Purcell and Elmslie; the Performing Arts Archives, which holds the records of the Minnesota Orchestra and Guthrie Theater; the Upper Midwest Literary Collections, including the papers of Robert Bly, Frederick Manfred, and John Berryman; as well as a large collection of World War posters that are available online. Special Collections and Rare Books includes one of the world's largest collections of Sherlock Holmes, as well as political papers and small and fine-press books, and includes the Givens Collection of African American Literature and the Tretter Collection in Gay, Lesbian, Bisexual, and Transgender Studies. University Archives round out the collections. Special collections in other locations include the Andersen Horticultural Library at the University's Landscape Arboretum and the Wangensteen Historical Library of Biology and Medicine, as well as significant holdings in agricultural and life sciences libraries.

Collection Profile: Marguerite Ragnow
Overview: Kris Kiesling
Illustrations: Ahn Na Brodie

University of Minnesota
Elmer L. Andersen Library
222 21st Avenue S.
Minneapolis, Minnesota 55455
http://special.lib.umn.edu/
(612) 626-5776 (t)
(612) 625-5525 (f)

University of Missouri–Columbia Libraries

The genesis of the University of Missouri–Columbia's Special Collections, Archives, and Rare Books Division began with a humble collection of rare books housed in the office of the University Librarian. Since then, the Rare Book collection in Ellis Library has grown both by design and through donations, boasting over 35,000 volumes. The Rare Book collection is particularly strong in the history of printing and the book arts, English political and religious history, *emblemata*, Ovid's *Metamorphoses*, and private press editions. There are an additional 55,000+ volumes in our diverse and rich collections; collections of philosophy, short stories, early American best sellers, and early common school textbooks have enriched the holdings of the division. The Comic Art Collection also contains numerous important gifts, such as the Mort Walker *Beetle Bailey* collection and the V. T. Hamlin *Alley Oop* series. The Comic Art Collection is also strong in graphic novels and underground comic books. The University Archives maintains the official records and publications of the university. More recent collection acquisitions include the Mary Lago collection, which is strong in E. M. Forster and Rabindranath Tagore materials; the Weinberg Journalists in Fiction collection containing over 3,000 novels about journalists; and the Donald Sanders collection from the Senate Watergate Committee.

In addition to the wide variety of print collections, University of Missouri also holds one of the largest microform collections in North America, between 7 and 8 million items. The collection includes materials such as FBI files, women's diaries, historic newspapers, early English books, and American periodicals.

Collection Profile and Overview: Alla Barabtarlo,
    Michael Holland, Karen Witt
Illustrations: Kurt Kopp

University of Missouri–Columbia
Special Collections, Archives, and Rare Books
401 Ellis Library
Columbia, Missouri 65201
http://mulibraries.missouri.edu/specialcollections/
SpecialCollections@missouri.edu
(573) 882-0076 (t)
(573) 884-0027 (f)

National Agricultural Library

Special Collections of the National Agricultural Library (NAL) encompasses a wealth of materials relating to all aspects of agricultural history, discovery, and advancement. It covers a broad range of scientific subjects and was developed to document the history of agricultural research and its worldwide applications and impact. The collection of more than 15,000 rare books; 330 manuscript collections; and original works of art, artifacts, posters, and photographs is particularly strong in botany, horticulture, natural history, zoology, poultry science, and entomology. One of the showcase collections is the US Department of Agriculture Pomological Watercolor Collection. The paintings are beautiful, yet scientifically precise illustrations of new fruit and nut varieties featured in early USDA publications. NAL's rare book collection includes many unique volumes from the world over; the earliest date back to the 16th century. Other unique items include important travel accounts, diaries, field notes, and correspondence by early naturalists such as Mark Catesby, and by USDA plant explorers who identified and collected new and improved plant varieties for introduction into American agriculture. Artifacts such as the electronic egg, Charles Valentine Riley's desk, wool-grading standards, and Smokey Bear memorabilia have been collected to supplement the print collection and provide a complete picture of agricultural research over the centuries. Taken as a whole, NAL's Special Collections forms a premier center for agricultural research in all its aspects including historic, commercial, aesthetic, socio-logical, practical, and organizational. NAL continues to promote and expand Special Collections through collaborative exhibitions, publications, presentations, Web enhancements, and product development.

Collection Profile and Overview: Susan H. Fugate
Illustrations: Bob Nichols

National Agricultural Library
Special Collections
10301 Baltimore Avenue
Beltsville, Maryland 20705
http://www.nal.usda.gov/speccoll/
speccoll@nal.usda.gov
(301) 504-6503 (t)
(301) 504-7593 (f)

National Library of Medicine

The History of Medicine Division holds the special collections of the National Library of Medicine. Formed in 1945 to curate the library's rare books, the division has grown dramatically in its collections and programs. The division has one of the most complete collections of medical works in the country. These include extensive runs of medical textbooks and journals; anatomical books such as those by Andreas Vesalius, Bernhard Albinus, and William Hunter; East Asian language texts; and works on pharmacy, nursing, dentistry, diet, alternative therapies, and public health. The library's collection of medical incunabula is unparalleled.

The division has important collections of medieval Western, Arabic, and Persian manuscripts, and more recent manuscripts in Japanese, Chinese, and Korean. With older collections in military medicine, modern manuscripts collecting now focuses on contemporary biomedicine, public health and health policy, mental health, medical informatics and librarianship, and alternative medicine. The prints and photographs collections comprise over 75,000 items, with digital copies found in an online database, "Images from the History of Medicine." Strong on medical portraiture, the collection now focuses on contemporary medicine and public health, with a large AIDS poster collection. The division's collection of medical films and videos includes some 14,000 titles, with over 500 titles produced prior to 1950. In addition to public health, the collection highlights instructional films, public service announcements, and documentaries.

The History of Medicine Division is digitizing its collections—notably in Profiles in Science (manuscripts in biomedicine and public health); Historical Anatomies on the Web; and Medicine in the Americas (early American medical imprints). The division regularly mounts exhibitions—both physical and online. Recent efforts include "Visible Proofs: Forensic Views of the Body," "Changing the Face of Medicine: Celebrating America's Women Physicians," and "Dream Anatomy." To help reach a broad public, the division also has a full schedule of tours, seminars, film series, and symposia.

Collection Profile and Overview: Paul Theerman
Illustrations: Video Transfer Incorporated

National Library of Medicine
History of Medicine Division
Building 38/Room 1 E-21
8600 Rockville Pike
Bethesda, Maryland 20894
http://www.nlm.nih.gov/hmd/
hmdref@nlm.nih.gov
(301) 496-5405 (t)
(301) 402-0872 (f)

University of Nebraska–Lincoln Libraries

The collections in the University of Nebraska–Lincoln Libraries' Archives and Special Collections are focused on the major teaching, research, and academic programs of the university. The collections are composed of rare and unique documentary materials created by university administration, faculty, and students, with additional collections from individuals and organizations external to the university. Collection strengths are reflected in manuscripts, rare books, ephemeral print materials, photographic collections, and digital texts. Areas of strength include the following: agriculture, ethnic American collections, folklore and folk arts, French Revolutionary War materials, Great Plains history and literature, United States military history, natural history and the sciences, US railroads, Russian history, and social sciences.

Among these focus areas are significant primary resources, such as 14 distinct collections with materials created by and about Willa Cather, the Mari Sandoz Collection relating to Great Plains and American Indian history, and the Benjamin A. Botkin Collection of Applied American Folklore. Numerous collections support quilt-related research and scholarship. Among these collection are the American Quilt Study Group (AQSG) Research Library and Records, and papers from Sally Garoutte, Jonathan Holstein, Michael James, and Penny McMorris. A broad array of collections document military history with a concentration in World War I and World War II materials.

Collection Profile and Overview: Andrew Jewell
Illustrations: University of Nebraska–Lincoln Libraries, Archives and Special Collections

University of Nebraska–Lincoln Libraries
Archives and Special Collections
PO Box 884100
Lincoln, Nebraska 68588-4100
http://www.unl.edu/libr/libs/spec/
(402) 472-2531 (t)
(402) 472-5131 (f)

University of New Mexico Libraries

The Center for Southwest Research (CSWR) is the University of New Mexico (UNM) Libraries' special collections department and UNM's resource center for the comparative and interdisciplinary study of New Mexico and the Southwest. The CSWR includes archival materials, rare books, music, architecture, and photographs; the University Archives manuscript collections document the political, economic, and social history of New Mexico, the Southwest, and Mexico. Most of the collections date from the 19th and 20th centuries and include the papers and records of politicians, historic and literary figures, architects, activists, attorneys, local families, organizations, and businesses. There are more than 90,000 books and periodicals in the Center for Southwest Research rare book collection. Strengths of the collection include New Mexicana and the Southwest, Mexican colonial history, codices, archaeology, Chicano studies, and Native American studies.

The John Donald Robb Archive of Southwestern Music is dedicated to preserving the musical heritage of New Mexico and the Southwest. The John Gaw Meem Archives document the built environment of New Mexico and the Southwest. Materials in the collection also record the works of art historians, architectural firms, and other related organizations. The Pictorial Collection contains over 80,000 images dating from the mid-1850s to the recent past. The collection is subject-oriented with a focus on the histories of New Mexico, the Southwest, and Latin America and Mexico. Also included are important collections of Mexican popular prints by José Guadalupe Posada and a collection of publications from the Taller de Gráfica Popular. The University Archives serves as an information resource for the history and development of the University of New Mexico.

Collection Profile and Overview: Kathlene Ferris and Michael Kelly
Illustrations: Teresa Eckmann

University of New Mexico
University Libraries
Center for Southwest Research/Special Collections
MSC05 3020
Albuquerque, New Mexico 87131-0001
http://elibrary.unm.edu/cswr/contact.php
cswrref@unm.edu
(505) 277-6451 (t)
(505) 277-0397 (f)

The New York Public Library, Astor, Lenox, and Tilden Foundations

The rarity and quality of the special collections in the Research Libraries of the New York Public Library set them apart from other historical archives, and their diversity distinguishes them from the majority of museum collections. The New York Public Library for the Performing Arts contains some of the largest archives in the world for dance, theater, recorded sound, and music; the Schomburg Center for Research in Black Culture is one of the largest repositories in the world documenting the experience of peoples of African origin and descent, with more than 5 million items. They function in turn as museums, documentation centers, cultural centers, and as libraries for the communities they serve. The eight special collection units in the Humanities and Social Sciences Library include the Manuscripts and Archives Division, which alone contains over 3,500 collections. The Print Collection's 18,000 original 19th-century American prints are of special note, as are the Japanese prints from the 10th century to the present. The Henry W. and Albert A. Berg Collection of English and American Literature is world renowned for its manuscript holdings of American and British authors and literary movements; the Pforzheimer Collection of Shelley and His Circle documents Shelley, his contemporaries, and their social, political, and cultural age. The rare book collections are rich in Americana, particularly books printed in the Americas before 1801. The Photography Collection, youngest of the special collections, documents the medium from its earliest years to contemporary works intended for exhibition and the art market. All collections are open to scholars and the public, contribute to a full exhibitions program, and to digitization projects, and provide the basis for public programming, lectures, and classes.

Collection Profile and Overview: Heike Kordish
Illustrations: Various

The New York Public Library
Research Libraries
Fifth Avenue & 42nd Street
New York, New York 10018
http://www.nypl.org/
(212) 930-0711 (t)
(212) 865-3567 (f)

New York State Library

The Manuscripts and Special Collections unit was established within the New York State Library in 1881. Its responsibilities include the acquisition, access and preservation of the library's collections of archives and manuscripts, rare books, maps and atlases, prints and photographs, broadsides and posters, musical scores, and ephemera. Materials are acquired through donation and purchase with the primary focus being on items that document the people, organizations, and history of the state of New York from the 17th century to the present.

The library's collection includes a wide variety of materials ranging from 17th-century works like Adriean van der Donck's *Beschryvinge van Nieuvv Nederlant, (Gelijck het tegenwoordigh)* (1655) and Nicolaes Visscher's *Novi Belgii* (1685) map to a recently created ephemera collection of 21st-century catalogs. Large manuscript collections like the papers of Gouverneur Kemble Warren (1830–1882) and the Van Rensselaer Manor Papers along with diaries and letters written by regular New Yorkers provide information on a variety of subjects. The Factsheet Five Collection includes thousands of zines produced in the 1980s and 1990s, the Players of a Century Collection documents 19th-century theater in Albany, and the records of the Adirondack Forty-sixers give insight about a special group of climbers. Other collection strengths include early American imprints and items illustrative of the history of topics related to American history, literature, science, and the arts particularly the history of agriculture, transportation, New York folklore, and social reform.

Collection Profile and Overview: Janny Venema
Illustrations: Thomas Rocco

New York State Library
Manuscripts and Special Collections
Cultural Education Center
Albany, New York 12230
http://www.nysl.nysed.gov/mssdesc.htm
MSCOLLS@mail.nysed.gov
(518) 474-6282 (t)

New York University Libraries

The Fales Library and Special Collections is the primary repository for special collections materials at New York University (NYU). Its holdings include the Fales Collection of English and American Literature, which documents developments in prose fiction from 1740 to the present; the Downtown Collection, which documents the New York City Downtown art scene from the early 1970s through the 1990s; and the Food and Cookery Collection, which documents American food history with a focus on New York City. The Fales Collection began in 1908 as the private library of DeCoursey Fales, a banker and lawyer. In 1957, Fales donated nearly 50,000 volumes to NYU. The other special collections at the university were brought together in the Fales Library, and the collection now houses more than 200,000 printed volumes, 10,000 linear feet of archival materials, and extensive holdings of media. Other important collections include the Alfred C. Berol Collection of Lewis Carroll, the Richard Maass Collection of Westchester County and New York State, and the personal papers of E. L. Doctorow, Betty Fussell, Pete Hamill, Marion Nestle, Erich Maria Remarque, and Elizabeth Robins.

Collection Profile and Overview: Marvin J. Taylor
Illustrations: Nick Johnson

New York University
Fales Library and Special Collections
70 Washington Square South, Third Floor
New York, New York 10012
http://www.nyu.edu/library/bobst/research/fales/
(212) 998-2596 (t)
(212) 995-3835 (f)

University of North Carolina at Chapel Hill Libraries

Special collections at the University of North Carolina at Chapel Hill (UNC) are the product of more than 160 years of dedicated collection and preservation by scores of UNC scholars, officers, alumni, and library staff. They have served as a resource for generations of researchers and as the basis for both scholarly and popular papers and publications. The Louis Round Wilson Library, which was the main campus library from its opening in 1929 until 1985, is now the home for UNC's special collections. Special collections at Carolina comprise four major areas of focus and a strong conservation program. Digital publications drawing on these collections are supported through Documenting the American South.

The North Carolina Collection, organized in 1844, contains more than 120,000 books and 78,000 pamphlets, as well as newspapers, journals, maps, broadsides, photographs, audiovisuals, microforms, and other materials that document the history, literature, and culture of the state.

The Rare Book Collection, begun in 1929, comprises 150,000 printed volumes, 18,000 broadsides and prints, and 1,200 manuscripts, with strengths in English literature, incunabula, 16th-century imprints, French history, Anglo-Irish literature, and 20th-century American avant-garde collections.

The Southern Historical Collection, built on the manuscript holdings of the library and a strong acquisitions program beginning in the 1920s, was established in 1930 and contains over 15 million items. The Southern Folklife Collection, opened in 1989, contains over 200,000 sound recordings relating to traditional Southern music and its many derivatives, including unique field recordings and very rare commercial recordings. Together these collections provide extraordinary resources for studying and appreciating the history of the American South.

The special collections also feature strong archival and published holdings documenting the history of the university, providing alumni, students, and researchers with primary sources for the study of the nation's oldest state university.

Collection Profile: Natasha Smith
Overview: Richard Szary
Illustrations: North Carolina Collection, Louis Round Wilson Library, University of North Carolina at Chapel Hill

University of North Carolina at Chapel Hill
Louis Round Wilson Library
Campus Box 3908
Chapel Hill, North Carolina 27514-8890
http://www.lib.unc.edu/wilson/
(919) 962-8125 (t)
(919) 843-3480 (f)

North Carolina State University Libraries

Established in 1993, the Special Collections Research Center (SCRC) was formed by combining the newly-created manuscripts and rare books units with the long-standing University Archives. The SCRC contains over 15,000 linear feet of original materials with broad strengths in the history of science, engineering and technology, natural resources, agriculture, the biological sciences, North Carolina State University (NCSU), textiles, veterinary medicine, design and architecture.

Of particular interest for NCSU's Special Collections are disciplines that have emerged and come to maturity in the last half of the 20th century and continue to develop into the 21st—with an emphasis on established and emerging areas of excellence at the university and corresponding strengths within the libraries' overall collection. The collections are managed comprehensively to create strategically aligned special, general, and digital collections with complementary strengths. Signature special collections include plant and forestry genetics and genomics, architecture, entomology, animal welfare, and the history of computing and simulation—with the featured Entomological Archive, the NCSU Plant Sciences Collection, and the Modernist Architecture Collection counted among its most distinguished.

The Plant Sciences Collection includes the papers of groundbreaking researchers in the interdisciplinary spectrum of the plant sciences—from ecology to biology to genetics and genomics. The foundations of the Modernist Architecture Collection consist of the papers of a number of faculty who founded the School of Architecture in 1948 and quickly developed an international reputation for innovation, experimentation, and modernist design. Collectively these holdings contain thousands of drawings and photographs and are rich resources for the study of 20th-century architecture, particularly the development of modernism.

The center also includes a robust digital collections program, a museum-quality exhibition gallery and program, and a new, well-appointed reading room for public service.

Collection Profile and Overview: Greg Raschke and Monica McCormick
Illustrations: Lynn Ruck Photography, Raleigh, NC

North Carolina State University
Special Collections Research Center
2205 Hillsborough Street
Box 7111
Raleigh, North Carolina 27695-7111
http://www.lib.ncsu.edu/specialcollections/
http://www.lib.ncsu.edu/specialcollections/digital/
    index.html#featured/
http://www.lib.ncsu.edu/specialcollections/exhibits/
(919) 515-2273 (t)
(919) 513-1787 (f)

Northwestern University Library

The Charles Deering McCormick Library of Special Collections is home to 80 large and small book collections, numerous archival and manuscript collections, poster collections, periodicals, photographs, and vellum documents. Digital collections of note include the Siege and Commune of Paris (1870–1871), with 1,200 contemporary photographs, and Edward S. Curtis's *North American Indian* (1907–1930), with the complete text and original photographs

The personal library of Johannes Schulze (1786–1869), acquired in 1870, is rich in 15th-century books, Aldines, Elzevirs, and classical authors in first and subsequent editions. There are comprehensive collections of Samuel Johnson, Walt Whitman, Mark Twain, and Frank Lloyd Wright as well as strong author collections of Joyce, Yeats, Eliot, Virginia Woolf, Hemingway, Pound, Maria Edgeworth, Thomas Taylor the Platonist, and Soren Kierkegaard. Archival collections include the entire archive of the Gate Theatre of Dublin from 1928 to 1971. The department is notable for its collections in Dada, Surrealism, Expressionism, Futurism, and Art Nouveau. Recent acquisitions relate to members of the Fluxus movement, such as Jan Herman, Dick Higgins, and Charlotte Moorman, all of whose papers are now at Northwestern.

The department has wide-ranging collections documenting 20th-century alternative movements. The women's movement is extensively documented from 1965 on. A growing collection of gay materials includes underground newspapers and other early serial publications.

Outside the McCormick Library and the Melville J. Herskovits Library of African Studies, prominent special collections at Northwestern include the Music Library, which owns nearly every musical score published from 1945 to the present; the Transportation Library, the world's largest, with annual reports from airlines and railroad companies dating back to the 19th century; the Art Library, especially strong in fin-de-siècle and avant-garde art and architecture journals; and finally University Archives, one of the most extensive university archival collections in the United States.

Collection Profile: David Easterbrook
Overview: Russell Maylone and Jeffrey Garrett
Illustrations: Northwestern University Library

Northwestern University Library
1970 Campus Drive
Evanston, Illinois 60208
http://www.library.northwestern.edu/
(847) 467-5675 (t)
(847) 467-7899 (f)

University Libraries of Notre Dame

The Department of Rare Books and Special Collections holds approximately 150,000 printed volumes with strengths in Roman Catholic studies, medieval studies, Italian and Irish literature, botany and sports, as well as a rapidly growing Latin American collection. Author-based holdings include over 3,000 editions of Dante along with significant collections on René Descartes, Edmund Burke, Eric Gill, G. K. Chesterton, and Jorge Luis Borges, among others. Among the pamphlet collections are about 5,000 American Catholic pamphlets from the 1940s and 1950s and a significant collection of pamphlets from the Irish Rebellion of 1798. Manuscript holdings span the Middle Ages to the present with an emphasis on the 18th through the 20th centuries in the Americas. The department also holds a collection of approximately 1,500 working papers and documents from Vatican II. Further, it owns an extensive numismatic collection, focusing primarily on the colonial period of American history, and also has significant philatelic holdings from around the world. There are major collections of maps of Ireland printed between the 16th and the 18th centuries and maps of the American Midwest Great Lakes region printed up to the mid-19th century. The department also holds an extensive collection of 18th- and 19th-century British and American newspapers and a collection of American Catholic diocesan newspapers. Additionally, the department contains a significant number of posters, broadsides and printed ephemera, primarily related to sports, Irish studies, or Catholicism.

Collection Profile and Overview: George Rugg
Illustrations: Sara Weber

University of Notre Dame
Department of Rare Books and Special Collections
102 Hesburgh Library
Notre Dame, Indiana 46556
http://www.library.nd.edu/rarebooks/
http://www.library.nd.edu/rarebooks/collections/
http://www.library.nd.edu/rarebooks/exhibits/
(574) 631-0290 (t)
(574) 631-6308 (f)

Ohio State University Libraries

Within the Ohio State University (OSU) Libraries, special collections are both numerous and diverse: the Byrd Polar Archives, the Cartoon Research Library, the John Glenn Archives, the Hilandar Research Library, the Historic Costume and Textiles Collection, the OSU Archives, Rare Books and Manuscripts/Charvat Collection of American Fiction, and the Jerome Lawrence and Robert E. Lee Theatre Research Institute. The Medical Heritage Center, which is part of Ohio State University's Prior Health Sciences Library, is a partner with the Ohio State University Libraries. All of the curators of these special collections, the Head of Special Collections Cataloging, and the Collections Conservator meet regularly as the Special Collections Roundtable, chaired by the Assistant Director for Special Collections, to coordinate policies, programs, and services.

For the special collections of the Ohio State University, collecting strengths include literature, visual and performing arts, history of science, popular culture, religion, Ohio, education, public policy, apparel and textile material culture, history of the health sciences, and voyages and polar exploration. Some of the special collections began from a particular significant donation, and several have close ties to other Ohio State University departments, schools, or colleges. All the Ohio State University Libraries special collections have active exhibit programs (locally and on the Web), support classroom teaching, and encourage research by Ohio State faculty and students as well as visiting scholars and the general public.

Collection Profile and Overview: Nena Couch
Illustrations: David R. Barker

Ohio State University
Ohio State University Libraries
1858 Neil Avenue
Columbus, Ohio 43210
http://library.osu.edu/
(614) 688-8447 (t)
(614) 688-4150 (f)

Ohio University Libraries

Established as a separate unit during the 1960s, Ohio University Libraries' special collections department became the Robert E. and Jean R. Mahn Center for Archives & Special Collections in 2002. University Archives, Manuscript Collections, and Rare Book Collections constitute the bulk of the holdings in the Mahn Center.

Collections within University Archives document the corporate memory of Ohio University since its founding in 1804. Minutes of the university's Board of Trustees, administrator and faculty papers, university catalogs, and student life materials ranging from student handbooks, athletic programs, and yearbooks to photographs, scrapbooks, posters, and other memorabilia are well represented. A sampling of images, gleaned from the University Archives buildings files, is available online.

The Mahn Center's nearly 300 manuscripts are gathered from sources far and near. The E. W. Scripps Papers, the Cornelius Ryan WWII Collection, the papers and music of bandleader Sammy Kaye, and the Alwin Nikolais/Murray Louis Dance Collection attract researchers from all over the world. Regional interests are also well served by the United Mine Workers of America District 6 Collection, the papers of Ohio Governor George V. Voinovich, and the papers of Congressmen Wayne L. Hays and Clarence E. Miller.

Broad in scope and age, and strong in uniqueness and aesthetic, the 59 rare book collections are heavily used as both research and instructional tools. Thirty-six author collections include the works of Alfred Tennyson, Dard Hunter, and Charles Bukowski. Although a 13th-century illuminated Bible is the collection's oldest book, 17th- and 18th-century British literature of the handpress period are also represented. Books from the Doves Press and Kelmscott Press, limited editions such as Edward Curtis's *North American Indian* (1907–1930), Victorian trade bindings, artist books, and signed first editions are just a few more of the treasures found in Rare Books.

Collection Profile and Overview: Judith Connick
Illustrations: Rick Fatica

Ohio University
Mahn Center for Archives and Special Collections
Alden Library Room 504
University Libraries
Athens, Ohio 45701
http://www.library.ohiou.edu/archives/
http://media.library.ohiou.edu/cdm4/browse.php
(740) 593-2710 (t)
(740) 593-2708 (f)

University of Oklahoma Libraries

The University of Oklahoma Libraries actively gather and preserve rare research materials and unique primary sources in their special collections. The Western History Collections was begun in 1927 by University of Oklahoma history professor Edward Everett Dale. The collections acquire and preserve scholarly research materials in anthropology, Native American studies, Oklahoma history, and the history of the American West. The collections contain more than 1.5 million photographs including images of Oklahoma and University of Oklahoma history, which are available to individuals seeking a connection with earlier times. The History of Science Collections was begun in 1949 with the loan of 129 books by University of Oklahoma geologist and alumnus Everette Lee DeGolyer. The collections contain over 91,000 volumes, including 55 books published during the first 50 years of printing. The Harry W. Bass Business History Collections were begun in 1955 with funding from Harry W. Bass, a former student at the University of Oklahoma and a leader in the petroleum industry. The collections contain books, journals, microforms, and videos on a number of topics including the histories of business leaders and firms, and the economic, social, and political forces that influence the role of business and industry in society. The John and Mary Nichols Rare Books and Special Collections are comprised of rare books and special research materials in British, European, and American literature dating from the 15th century to the present. The collections feature a number of first edition works by Charles Dickens, Jane Austen, and Sir Arthur Conan Doyle.

Collection Profile and Overview: Marilyn Ogilvie
    and Debra Engel
Illustrations: Sanford Mauldin

University of Oklahoma Libraries
401 West Brooks
Norman, Oklahoma 73019
http://libraries.ou.edu/
(405) 325-2611 (t)
(405) 325-7550 (f)

Oklahoma State University Library

Founded in 1890 as the Oklahoma Agricultural and Mechanical College, the institution acquired its first library volume in 1893. Modest purchases in support of the curriculum and faculty research, primarily in the area of agriculture, continued into the late 1920s. Between 1928 and 1933, the College Library acquired its first rare volumes through the Grolier Society. Much controversy at the then-small land grant college surrounded these purchases, which included *Holinshed's Chronicles* and Audubon's *Quadrupeds*, and no additional items were added until Otto M. Forkert's collection of materials on typography and printing were acquired through a gift/purchase arrangement in 1951. Among the 103 volumes in that collection was a replica two-volume Gutenberg Bible issued as number 43 of a run of 300 sets in Leipzig in 1914. In 1966, the gift of former Oklahoma governor Henry S. Johnston's papers, personal library, and law office was received by the Oklahoma State University Library. This became the first of a number of political collections given to the library that include the papers of former Oklahoma governor and United States Senator Henry Bellmon, United States Senator Don Nickles, and former state representative Hannah D. Atkins, the first African-American woman elected to statewide office in Oklahoma in 1968. In addition to collections documenting Oklahoma history and politics, collecting efforts have focused on Oklahoma natural resources; Oklahoma women; the portrayal of the American West in film, theater, and circuses; and folk music of the southern plains. Shortly after the formal establishment of a Department of Special Collections and University Archives in the library in 1988, the library received the papers of historian and social activist Dr. Angie Debo, a preeminent scholar of American Indian history. Other significant collections include the personal and professional papers of Gannett CEO and AP President Paul Miller and (in process) noted businessman and philanthropist T. Boone Pickens.

Collection Profile and Overview: Jennifer Paustenbaugh
Illustrations: Phil Shocley

Oklahoma State University Library
Department of Special Collections & University Archives
Edmon Low Library
Oklahoma State University
Stillwater, Oklahoma 74078-1071
http://www.library.okstate.edu/scua/
libscua@okstate.edu
(405) 744-6311 (t)
(405) 744-7579 (f)

University of Oregon Libraries

Special Collections and University Archives in the University of Oregon Libraries contains more than 1 million items. Holdings range from medieval codices and rare books to literary and historical manuscripts, university archives, original art, photographs, architectural drawings, and ephemera. These holdings include over 3,000 individual manuscript collections (18,000 linear feet), more than 100,000 monographs, 19,000 linear feet of University Archives, 500,000 photographs, 5,000 architectural drawings, 5,000 original drawings and illustrations, and over 20,000 broadsides and pieces of ephemera.

Collection strengths are Oregon history, politics, and culture; authors and illustrators of children's books; popular literature, with an emphasis on Western fiction; speculative fiction and science fiction; missionaries to foreign countries, especially in East Asia; women's history and studies; photographs, especially pertaining to the Northwest; labor and environmental history; Northwest literature; New Spiritualism (Rajneeshism); and the conservative movement in the mid- to late 20th century.

Among the most notable holdings are the Ursula Le Guin Papers, Damon Knight Papers, Abigail Scott Duniway Papers, Senator Wayne Morse Papers, Paul Wiener Papers, James Ivory Papers, Doris Ulmann Photograph Collection of Appalachia, Lucille Ogle Papers (Little Golden Books), Virginia Lee Burton Papers, Tee A. Corinne Papers and the records of the Oregon women's land movement, Gertrude Bass Warner Collection of Asian art books and photographs, Bill Bowerman Papers (track and field), Major Lee Moorhouse Photograph Collection of Native Americans, and collections of medieval and Renaissance illuminated manuscripts and incunabula.

These collections provide the materials for original scholarship and the resources through which the present generation of scholars can train the next in research methodologies and critical thinking. The collections are at the very heart of the university's research and teaching mission.

Collection Profile and Overview: Linda Long and Marilyn Reaves
Illustrations: Lesli Larson and Rick Gersbach

University of Oregon
Special Collections and University Archives
Knight Library
1299 University of Oregon
Eugene, Oregon 97403-1299
http://libweb.uoregon.edu/speccoll/
spcarref@uoregon.edu
(541) 346-3068 (t)
(541) 346-1882 (f)

University of Pennsylvania Library

Penn, a mid-18th-century foundation, began with what Benjamin Franklin called an "English" (or a secular) curriculum. From the start it aimed to educate people who might, like Franklin, minister to society's non-spiritual needs. Quickly adding faculties, notably medicine, Penn was effectively a university by the time of the Revolution.

Its library grew slowly, like those of other American educational institutions. Early gifts from Franklin, geographer Lewis Evans, and the as yet un-shortened French King Louis XVI, anxious to cock a snook at George III, remain in Penn's collections to this day. They are not numerous.

Real growth awaited the later 19th century. World War II had ended before Penn established a rare book and manuscript department. By then, notable collections already formed its core. Alongside the Furness Memorial were Edgar Fahs Smith's collection of chemistry, alchemy, and history of science, and Henry Charles Lea's library of late medieval and early modern Church history, governance, and the Inquisition. Incunables, Bibles, manuscript and printed Aristoteliana, Elzevier imprints, Leibniz, Meso-American linguistic studies, Americana, Franklin, Jonathan Swift, English fiction through 1830, Italian Renaissance poetry, Spanish Golden Age literature, the French Revolution, 19th-century French drama, cryptology, cookery—these too became strengths.

Archival collections include Theodore Dreiser, Lewis Mumford, Alma Mahler and Franz Werfel, Marian Anderson, Eugene Ormandy, Harry Mathews, and Philadelphia's cultural, artistic, and musical institutions. A large group of manuscripts documents Medici finances, another South Asian religion and philosophy. Individual manuscripts include a 14th-century Wyclif New Testament in English, a 15th-century Apicius, holograph plays by Lope de Vega, Mathew Carey's diary, and a Bartók string quartet.

These collections support Penn's research and teaching mission. The library also reaches out to broader communities through lectures and exhibitions of materials historically important, intrinsically interesting, and also—and frequently!—of simply jaw-dropping physical beauty.

Collection Profile and Overview: Daniel H. Traister
Illustrations: Schoenberg Center for Electronic Text and Image

University of Pennsylvania
Rare Book and Manuscript Library, Van Pelt-Dietrich Library
3420 Walnut Street
Philadelphia, Pennsylvania 19104-6206
http://www.library.upenn.edu/rbm/
rbml@pobox.upenn.edu
(215) 898-7088 (t)
(215) 573-9079 (f)

Pennsylvania State University Libraries

The Special Collections Library of the Pennsylvania State University Libraries contains a large quantity of primary source material in many formats. Reflecting its geographical location in the center of Pennsylvania, there is a strong concentration of Pennsylvania German printing, extensive Amish and Mennonite materials, and German literature in translation (the Allison-Shelley Collection); Pennsylvania Railroad materials and historical records of other lines in Pennsylvania; documents and periodicals of labor unions, including those of the United Mineworkers, the Pennsylvania AFL-CIO, photoengravers, and full-fashion hosiery workers, among others, as well as the comprehensive international archives of the United Steelworkers of America. There are also Pennsylvania county histories, atlases, and regimental histories.

In addition, there is a large collection of emblem books, English literature, and a very strong collection of utopian literature in a variety of languages. There are also important collections of the personal papers of the writer John O'Hara, an extensive collection of the literary critic and philosopher of language, Kenneth Burke, a cache of family correspondence of Ernest Hemingway, and the papers of Conrad Richter.

There has also been an ongoing effort to re-form the 18th-century Williamscote Library, originally gathered by several members of the Loveday family and their descendants in Caversham near Banbury. There are now nearly 3,000 volumes, hundreds of pamphlets, and about 30 manuscript volumes.

The extensive holdings of the University Archives include papers of Fred Waring, a grandson of a founder of Penn State, containing correspondence, recordings of radio and television programs, as well as music by the Pennsylvanians, scrapbooks, and 20,000 photographs. The University Archives also has strong holdings on nuclear engineering, art education, athletics, and campus publications.

For the numerically minded, there are some 130, 000 volumes, 26,500 cubic feet of manuscript and archival material, 23,000 films and videos, several thousand maps, including Sanborn maps of Pennsylvania communities, and hundreds of thousands of photographs.

Collection Profile and Overview: James P. Quigel Jr.
Illustrations: Hughes Photographics

Pennsylvania State University
Special Collections Library
Room 104
Paterno Library
University Park, Pennsylvania
http://www.libraries.psu.edu/speccolls/
(814) 865-1793 (t)
(814) 863-5318 (f)

University of Pittsburgh Libraries

Special Collections at the University of Pittsburgh are housed in four different facilities and focus, primarily, on different themes. They include the Darlington Memorial Library, the Center for American Music, the Archives of Industrial Society, and the Special Collections Department.

The Darlington Memorial Library includes what at one time was said to be the largest private library west of the Alleghenies. The collection, which contains about 11,000 books, is particularly rich in material pertaining to the French and Indian War, and to the history of western Pennsylvania and the Ohio Valley. Letters written by George Washington when he was a young officer are found in the collection. Literature, including many first editions of Charles Dickens, are part of the book collection. A complete set of John James Audubon's *Birds of America* is included, and the University Library System has established a rotating exhibit of the prints from this extraordinary publication.

The Center for American Music includes a broad cross-section of books, manuscripts, sheet music, and sound recordings that document American popular culture, primarily from the 1840s to the 1930s. Much sought-after materials pertaining to the life and music of Stephen C. Foster, the Pittsburgh native who was America's first professional songwriter, are located at the center.

The Archives of Industrial Society include over 650 separate manuscript or archival collections that document the growth and development of Pittsburgh as an urban, industrial society. The materials include union archives, environmental records, ethnic collections, organizational records, and personal papers, primarily from the late 1800s through the 20th century. Together these collections amount to over 25,000 linear feet of materials.

The Special Collections Department was established in 1966. It houses rare books, literary papers, feminist literature, theater collections, and the Archives of Scientific Philosophy.

Collection Profile and Overview: Michael J. Dabrishus
Illustrations: James Burke

University of Pittsburgh
271 Hillman Library
Pittsburgh, Pennsylvania 15260
http://www.library.pitt.edu/
(412) 244-7065 (t)
(412) 244-7077 (f)

Princeton University Library

Princeton University Library's Department of Rare Books and Special Collections supports scholarly research and instruction through extensive holdings that span five millennia of recorded history. Located in Firestone Library are seven curatorial units: Cotsen Children's Library, Graphic Arts, Historic Maps, Manuscripts, Numismatics, Rare Books, and the privately owned Scheide Library. At the Seeley G. Mudd Manuscript Library are units for Public Policy Papers and University Archives. Princeton has been actively collecting these materials since the late 19th century, and collections continue to grow by gift and purchase. Departmental holdings now stand at approximately 35,000 linear feet of materials in Manuscripts, Public Policy Papers, and University Archives; 375,000 printed volumes in Rare Books, Cotsen, Graphic Arts, and Scheide; and substantial holdings of photographs, historic maps, coins and medals, prints and drawings, paintings, objects, and other materials spread among curatorial units.

Notable subject strengths include ancient, medieval, and Renaissance studies, European and American history and literature since the 17th century, including Victorian novelists and poets, travel and exploration, the American West and North American Indians, American foreign policy, civil liberties, and international development; 20th-century American, British, Latin American, Modern Greek, and other authors; modern publishing archives, especially Charles Scribner's Sons; non-Western manuscripts, including Arabic, Persian, Ottoman Turkish, Indic languages, Ethiopic; illustrated children's books in all languages; history of the book, with substantial holdings of medieval manuscripts, incunabula (especially early editions in Scheide), and early printed editions; 18th-century English and American books, illustrated books, and fine-press editions; Greek, Roman, and Chinese coinage; prints; early photography on the Hellenic world, American West, and other subjects; maps and atlases printed prior to 1920; and Princeton University history.

The department annually attracts thousands of researchers worldwide and offers a wide range of services, including reference, digital collections, photoduplication, outreach activities, instruction, publications, public programs, exhibitions, and research grants.

Collection Profile and Overview: Don C. Skemer
Illustrations: John Blazejewski

Princeton University Library
Department of Rare Books and Special Collections
One Washington Road
Princeton, New Jersey 08544
http://www.princeton.edu/rbsc/
rbsc@princeton.edu
(609) 258-3184 (t)
(609) 258-2324 (f)

Purdue University Libraries

The diverse Special Collections of Purdue University Libraries offer a treasure trove of primary source materials for faculty, students, and researchers. Holdings include rare books, manuscript collections, and University Archives. Major subject strengths include the history of science, engineering, and technology; the history of economic thought; the birth of aeronautics and astronautics; time and motion studies; typography and book design. Particular highlights of the manuscript collections include the George Palmer Putnam Collection of Amelia Earhart Papers, the world's largest collection of Earhart papers and memorabilia; the papers of Nobel Prize–winning chemist Herbert C. Brown; the papers of Frank B. and Lillian M. Gilbreth, inventors of motion study whose lives were chronicled in *Cheaper by the Dozen* (1948); over 1,000 original cartoon drawings by "Dean of American Cartoonists" John T. McCutcheon; and the papers of playwright and humorist George Ade and author Charles Major.

Significant rare book collections include the Goss Library of the History of Engineering; the Krannert Special Collection, pertaining to business, economics, and politics; the M.G. Mellon Library on the history of chemistry; the Bruce Rogers Collection; the Bitting Collections on glass and world fairs and expositions; the Indiana Collection, including early and rare works printed in Indiana or written by Indiana authors; and a large collection of finely bound books published by the Limited Editions Club of New York.

Collection Profile and Overview: Sammie L. Morris
Illustrations: Richard Myers-Walls

Purdue University Libraries-SPEC
Archives & Special Collections
504 W. State Street
West Lafayette, Indiana 47907-2058
http://www.lib.purdue.edu/spcol/
(765) 494-2905 (t)
(765) 494-0156 (f)

Queen's University Library and University Archives

Special Collections at Queen's University is a rich and diverse research resource containing a wide range of materials acquired either through purchase or donation. Today, the collection numbers more than 125,000 volumes. Rare materials, early imprints, deluxe editions, fragile and ephemeral items, local history, and items and subject collections with special provenance are located here. Canadiana beyond literature includes works of early exploration, travel and missionary accounts, native studies, early settlement, United Empire Loyalists, the War of 1812, the opening of the West and the North, local histories and Canadian pamphlets—providing a rich resource for the study of Canadian society from the 18th century to the present. Non-Canadiana of significance includes an outstanding 18th-century British Pamphlet Collection; early editions of Dickens, Galsworthy, Masefield, Dante, Hugo, and Disraeli; Anglo-Irish literature including Cuala Press imprints, the works of George Russell and Monk Gibbon; the private library of John Buchan, Lord Tweedsmuir; and three important science collections relating to the history of telegraphy, radioastronomy, and natural history. Maps, plans, broadsides, posters, sheet music, programs, and ephemeral materials are found here as well.

A long archival tradition exists at Queen's University. The first archival document was presented to the university in 1869. The archives preserves records and manuscripts in two general areas—University Records and Private Manuscripts and consists of about 9,000 meters of holdings. The Private Manuscripts program encompasses a number of thematic areas—literary papers, public affairs, business papers, regional collections, genealogy, photographs, architectural drawings, fine arts, and sound and moving images. While most of the literary collections relate to Canadian writers, the archives also have the John Buchan and Monk Gibbon fonds.

Collection Profile and Overview: Barbara Teatero and Heather Home
Illustrations: Derek Cooper

Queen's University
W.D. Jordan Special Collections and Music Library
Douglas Library
Kingston, Ontario
K7L 5C4
Canada
http://library.queensu.ca/webmus/sc/menu.htm
(613) 533-2528 (t)

Queen's University Archives
Kathleen Ryan Hall
Queen's University
Kingston, Ontario
K7L 3N6
Canada
http://archives.queensu.ca/
(613) 533-2378 (t)
(613) 533-6403 (f)

University of Rochester Libraries

The Department of Rare Books, Special Collections and Preservation houses unique, rare, and specialized research materials in all formats. The Rare Book collection numbers approximately 100,000 volumes ranging from incunabula to modern first editions. Four hundred manuscript collections form the basis of the Special Collections; as the repository of the University of Rochester's archives, the department preserves the university's history since its founding in 1850. In addition to book and paper materials, the collections also contain 16mm film, VHS tapes, audio recordings, and more than 100,000 photographic prints, negatives, maps, and other illustrative materials.

The book collection contains first and important editions of books regarded as landmarks in the history of science, religion, medicine, and social and political history; there are over 80 incunabula. There is a broad, representative collection of British and American authors, early American children's books, Tauchnitz editions, and the Roycroft Press. Other book collections with significant holdings include the local history collection, history of law and political theory, Victorian edition bindings, and books illustrated with original photographs.

Although there are excellent examples of medieval, Renaissance, and other early manuscripts, the strength of the manuscript collections lies in 19th- and 20th-century material. The literary manuscript collections include the complete archives of American writers including John Gardner, Frederick Exley, John A. Williams, and Charles S. Wright. The historical manuscript collections hold the personal and public papers of Susan B. Anthony, Frederick Douglass, William Henry Seward, Thomas E. Dewey, and Lewis Henry Morgan.

Collection Profile and Overview: Richard Peek
Illustrations: Christine Elfman

University of Rochester
Department of Rare Books, Special Collections & Preservation
Rush Rhees Library
Rochester, New York 14627-0055
http://www.library.rochester.edu/index.cfm?page=169
(585) 275-4477 (t)
(585) 273-1032 (f)

Rutgers University Libraries

Organized in 1946 but containing materials collected by Rutgers University since shortly after its founding in 1766, Special Collections and University Archives holds the largest, most comprehensive, and most researched collection devoted to the history and culture of New Jersey. Included are over 2,200 manuscript collections and 120,000 volumes which encompass personal and organizational papers, diaries, documents, maps, broadsides, and pictorial materials in fields such as business, labor, politics, religion, medicine, technology, women's history, social welfare and policy, genealogy, utopian communities, and urban planning. The University Archives contains the official records and memorabilia of Rutgers. Other collecting strengths include American women artists, history of the consumer movement, 20th-century Latin American politics and society, 20th-century labor history, and Japanese-American relations during the Meiji period.

The Institute of Jazz Studies (IJS) is a special collection of the John Cotton Dana Library on the Rutgers Newark Campus. It is the most comprehensive archive of jazz and jazz-related materials in the world. IJS was founded in 1952 in New York City by pioneering jazz scholar Marshall Stearns, who selected Rutgers as its permanent home in 1966. Holdings include over 100,000 sound recordings in all formats, more than 30,000 photographs, a comprehensive book and periodical collection, as well as memorabilia and rare musical instruments. Among its extensive archival holdings are the collections of two of jazz's most significant creators: Mary Lou Williams and James P. Johnson. IJS produces two major publications: the *Annual Review of Jazz Studies*, since 1973, and *Studies in Jazz*, a monograph series now numbering over 50 titles. The award-winning "Digital Greats" Web site exhibit is one of several digital projects.

Collection profile: Edward Berger
Overview: Ronald L. Becker
Illustrations: Tad Hershorn/Institute of Jazz Studies

Rutgers, the State University of New Jersey
Special Collections and University Archives
Rutgers University Libraries
169 College Avenue
New Brunswick, New Jersey 08901
http://www.libraries.rutgers.edu/rul/libs/scua/scua.shtml
(732) 932-7006 (t)
(732) 932-7012 (f)

Institute of Jazz Studies
John Cotton Dana Library
185 University Avenue
Newark, New Jersey 07102
http://newarkwww.rutgers.edu/IJS/
(973) 353-5595 (t)
(973) 353-5944 (f)

University of Saskatchewan Library

Special Collections at the University of Saskatchewan Library began with the purchase of the Adam Shortt collection of Canadiana in 1921. Dr. Shortt, a professor and University Librarian at Queen's University was an inveterate collector. Indeed, the collection at the University of Saskatchewan was one of his two personal collections. This collection has been augmented over time and now concentrates on western Canadian history. While it includes old and rare materials, such as 18th- and 19th-century editions of explorers' and missionaries' accounts, it also emphasizes the history of First Nations and Metis people. The library is particularly proud to own an original letter/poem written by resistance leader Louis Riel to his jailer just two weeks before he was hanged for treason.

The work of the English Department has been supported over the years with the purchase of the Conrad Aiken collection in 1972. It contains his novels, poetry, commentaries, and manuscripts. Prior to this, the library purchased collected works by Canadian poets Irving Layton and Al Purdy. These too include published and unpublished materials.

Another important collection consists of the manuscripts, notebooks, and clippings from the private library of Dr. Pitirim A. Sorokin, one of the major social theorists of our era. It includes copious and handwritten annotations in many books, articles by and about Sorokin, lecture notebooks, and research data.

Other collections include the 1,800-plus-volume University Authors Collection; over 10,000 Canadiana pamphlets; and the Arthur S. Morton manuscript collection, which also emphasizes the history of western Canada. The library is also home to the Saskatchewan Music collection and the Rosen Collection of Veterinary Medicine History.

Collection Profile and Overview: Linda Fritz
and Jill Crawley-Low
Illustrations: David Bindle and Luke Sather

University of Saskatchewan
Special Collections Department
Murray Library
3 Campus Drive
Saskatoon, Saskatchewan
S7N 5A4
Canada
https://library.usask.ca/spcoll#1
(306) 966-6029 (t)
(306) 966-6040 (f)

Smithsonian Institution Libraries

Composed of 20 distinct libraries, the Smithsonian Institution Libraries holds over 1.5 million volumes, including 40,000 rare books and manuscripts. These collections support the daily work of the Smithsonian's nearly 6,000 staff, another 6,000 volunteers, and thousands of interns, fellows, and independent researchers. Many of the libraries hold distinctive, specialized collections, but the most valuable are housed in dedicated rare book facilities. The Dibner Library of the History of Science and Technology, established in 1976 at the National Museum of American History, Kenneth E. Behring Center, with a gift from the Burndy Library (created by Bern Dibner), holds major works dating from the 15th to the early 19th centuries in the history of science and technology including engineering, transportation, chemistry, mathematics, physics, electricity, and astronomy. Among them are the 200 "Heralds of Science," the most distinctive works in the history of science selected by Bern Dibner and ranging from Aristotle, Galileo, and Copernicus to Marie Curie and James Watson. The Joseph F. Cullman 3rd Library of Natural History opened in 2002 in the National Museum of Natural History and houses 10,000 volumes on the fields of physical and cultural anthropology; Native American linguistics; ethnology; botany; zoology; paleontology; and geology and mineralogy. Special strengths are 17th- through 19th-century voyages of exploration and the history of museums and scientific collecting. Outside of Washington, the Bradley Room at the Cooper-Hewitt National Design Museum Library contains rare books on the decorative arts and architecture, sample books, pop-up books, and World's Fair material. William Burden's collection of early ballooning works and the Bella Landauer collection of aeronautical sheet music are two special collections in the Admiral DeWitt Clinton Ramsey Room, National Air and Space Museum Library. The libraries of the Hirshhorn Museum and Sculpture Garden and the Freer and Sackler Galleries of Art house precious and rare works in contemporary art and Japanese and Chinese art respectively.

Collection Profile and Overview: Mary Augusta Thomas
Illustrations: Smithsonian Institution Libraries

Smithsonian Institution Libraries
PO Box 37012 MRC 154
Washington, DC 20013-7012
http://www.sil.si.edu/
(202) 633-2240 (t)
(202) 786-2866 (f)

University of South Carolina Libraries

The University of South Carolina, then South Carolina College, started building its library collections in 1803. In 1840, it opened the first purpose-built freestanding college library building in the nation, and by 1850, with 25,000 volumes, it had the largest library collection south of Washington, DC. Many of the books acquired then survive, either in Thomas Cooper Library's Special Collections or in the South Caroliniana Library: incunbula, Theodor de Bry's *Greater Voyages*, Stuart's *Antiquities,* the complete Piranesi, the *Description de l'Égypte*, Kingsborough's *Mexican Antiquities,* Karl Bodmer's *Travels in North America*, and even South Carolina College Book 1.

The focus for acquisition in the earlier 20th century was on South Carolina, on earlier British fiction, and on such high points as the *Nuremberg Chronicle* (1493), the King James Bible, and the Blaeu *Atlas*. Over the past 25 years, Thomas Cooper's Special Collections have grown six-fold, to over 120,000 volumes and several modern literary archives. Areas of significant growth include: philosophy (Hume, Russell); history (Garibaldi); exploration (Renaissance city maps), military history (Civil War, World War I), and military aviation (World War II); natural history (garden books, 18th-century watercolors, Abbot) and the history of science (Darwin, Babbage); English literature (Milton), Scottish literature (Burns, Carlyle, Stevenson), and American literature (Emerson, Fuller, Whitman, Johnson, Fitzgerald, Hemingway, Rawlings, Heller, Dickey, Jakes, Ellroy, Higgins); children's literature (particularly African-American); and the history of the book.

Over the same period, the department has added new initiatives in the areas of teaching, exhibits, digitization, and scholarly and public programs. An extensive series of Web exhibits and Web projects based on the collections has been attracting over 25 million hits a year.

Collection Profile and Overview: Patrick Scott
Illustrations: Keith McGraw and Jeffrey Makala

University of South Carolina
Rare Books & Special Collections
Thomas Cooper Library
Columbia, South Carolina 29208
http://www.sc.edu/library/spcoll/rarebook.html
tclrarebooks@gwm.sc.edu
(803) 777-8154 (t)
(803) 777-4661 (f)

University of Southern California Libraries

The University of Southern California (USC) Libraries' Special Collections form the principal repository of the university's rare books, manuscripts, and archives. The collections hold more than 130,000 volumes of valuable books and serials, over 300 archival collections, and millions of manuscripts, photographs, films, sound recordings, and other primary research materials. Particular strengths include southern California regional history, American literature, Holocaust history, Lion Feuchtwanger and the German émigré experience, and natural history.

The first gift of rare books to the USC Libraries dates to 1911, making the University of Southern California the earliest institutional collector of rare books in Los Angeles. A Department of Special Collections was first organized in 1963 in the Edward L. Doheny Jr. Memorial Library, gathering the rare book and manuscript collections that had previously resided throughout the library. These collections included the American literature collection, a television and cinema collection—including screenplays—maps, wartime posters, and an oral history collection.

Among the rarest, oldest, and most valuable holdings are a 1306 bound-manuscript *Breviarum*, a chapter from an 11th-century Northern Song edition of *Shi Ji*, a fossilized mastodon bone at least 10,000 years old, and a set of plates of John James Audubon's double elephant folio *Birds of America.*

Significant rare items are held in the Hoose Philosophy Collection, the Hancock Natural History Collection, and the Boeckmann Latin American and Iberian Collection. The regional history collections document the history of Los Angeles through more than 2 million photographs from the California Historical Society, *Los Angeles Examiner,* and Dick Whittington photographic collections. The Visual History Archive of the USC Shoah Foundation Institute for Visual History and Education complements these resources by preserving and providing access to unpublished personal histories that otherwise would be lost. Many of these and other collections are accessible online through the USC Libraries Digital Archive at http://digarc.usc.edu/.

Collection Profile and Overview: Crispin Brooks
Illustrations: USC Shoah Foundation Institute for Visual History and Education, University of Southern California

University of Southern California
Special Collections
Doheny Memorial Library Room 206
University Park Campus
Los Angeles, California 90089-0189
http://www.usc.edu/libraries/centers/specialized_libraries/
slac@usc.edu
(213) 740-4035 (t)
(213) 740-2343 (f)

Southern Illinois University Carbondale Library

In 1956, the first official acquisition for the Special Collections Research Center of Morris Library was a small collection of Walt Whitman first editions. Over the past 50 years, Special Collections Research Center has expanded to include manuscript collections, political papers, university archives, and rare books.

Morris Library has a sustained commitment to its manuscript collections, as demonstrated by its extensive collections documenting: American philosophy; First Amendment freedom issues; the Irish Literary Renaissance; American, British, and Irish theater; American and British expatriate authors (especially for the period between World War I and World War II); and southern Illinois history and culture.

The focus on southern Illinois history has resulted in the acquisition of political papers, notably the collections of United States Senator Paul Simon, United States Representative Ken Gray, and Mayor of St. Louis, Missouri, Clarence Harmon. Grass roots politics is also documented.

Southern Illinois University (SIU) Carbondale Archives traces the history of the university, which was one of the first educational institutions in the state to address issues of physical and financial accessibility. It contains a wealth of administrative information including the records of past presidents, as well as campus publications.

The rare books parallel all the other collections. They relate to First Amendment freedoms, as well as to expatriate and modernist literature, the Irish Literary Renaissance, American philosophy, American and British expatriate authors, James Joyce, John Dewey, fine printing, SIU faculty and southern Illinois history and culture. Building on the strengths of all these collections is one of the library's primary strategic directions.

Collection Profile and Overview: Pam Hackbart-Dean
Illustrations: Greg Wendt

Southern Illinois University Carbondale Library
Special Collections Research Center
Morris Library (MC 6632)
Southern Illinois University Carbondale
Carbondale, Illinois 62901
http://www.lib.siu.edu/departments/speccoll/
speccoll@lib.siu.edu
(618) 453-2516 (t)
(618) 453-3451 (f)

Stony Brook University, State University of New York, Libraries

Special Collections at Stony Brook University has been an invaluable resource for the university community, visiting scholars, and the general public for more than 35 years. The depth and uniqueness of the collections offer numerous opportunities for scholarship. Significant archives relating to the arts, literature, and the history of technology have recently been acquired by the department. Highlights include: a letter from General George Washington to his chief spymaster written in 1779 that details spying techniques; the archives of Senator Jacob K. Javits; the papers of the national organization Environmental Defense; the manuscripts of Italian-American author Pietro di Donato; and the largest English-language Chinese cookbook collection in the world, with over 2,600 titles. The Rare Book and Map Collections at Stony Brook University include over 20,000 fine and scarce volumes dating from 1493 to the present. The department is particularly recognized for its extensive Long Island Collection, which documents the history of one of the first planned suburban communities in the United States. Special Collections also serves as a regional resource for maps, atlases, and aerial photography, as it maintains over 2,000 individual items dating back to the 17th century.

The department actively contributes to national efforts to establish digital libraries. In 2003, in collaboration with the Long Island Library Resources Council (LILRC), a digitization lab was established at Stony Brook University Libraries. The materials preserved by the Special Collections at Stony Brook University are unmatched in scope and depth by any other archive on Long Island. The manuscript and monograph holdings have grown significantly in the past five years due to an active outreach campaign and the generosity of donors. There is a new Web site available that contains in-depth information about Special Collections at Stony Brook University.

Collection Profile and Overview: Kristen J. Nyitray
Illustrations: Keith Krejci

Stony Brook University
Special Collections and University Archives
Frank Melville, Jr. Memorial Library, Room E-2320
Stony Brook, New York 11794-3323
http://www.stonybrook.edu/libspecial/
(631) 632-7119 (t)
(631) 632-1829 (f)

Syracuse University Library

Home to more than 100,000 printed works and 2,000 manuscript and archival collections, the Special Collections Research Center (SCRC) holds some of Syracuse University's most precious treasures, including early printed editions of Gutenberg, Galileo, and Sir Isaac Newton as well as the library of 19th-century German historian Leopold Von Ranke (1795–1886). Holdings are particularly strong in the 20th century; they include the personal papers and manuscripts of such luminaries as artist Grace Hartigan (1922–), inspirational preacher Norman Vincent Peale (1898–1993), author Joyce Carol Oates (1938–), photojournalist Margaret Bourke White (1904–1971), and movie score composer Franz Waxman (1906–1967). The center describes itself as a "research center" and, indeed, the repository strives to be much more than a static repository of cultural wonders. The SCRC is more a "humanities laboratory" where librarians and scholars collaborate with the artifacts of history in an ongoing and vital learning process. In this vein, SCRC regularly hosts exhibitions, lectures, and classes focusing on its collections.

Collection Profile and Overview: Sean Quimby
Illustrations: David Broda

Syracuse University
Special Collections Research Center
E.S. Bird Library, Room 600
Syracuse, New York 13244-2010
http://scrc.syr.edu/
(315) 443-2697 (t)
(315) 443-2671 (f)

Temple University Libraries

The Special Collections of the Temple University Libraries encompass several significant collections. The Urban Archives study center was established in 1967 to document the social, economic, and physical development of the Philadelphia metropolitan area from the mid-19th century to the present. It is the home of the *Philadelphia Evening Bulletin* Collection. It also serves as a repository for the organizational records and materials of more than 250 community and political organizations, including the Housing Association of the Delaware Valley, an organization founded in 1909 to address the deteriorating housing conditions in Philadelphia, and the Gray Panthers, an advocacy group that was formed to bring about positive attitudes towards aging. Another collection documenting Temple's rich local heritage is the Philadelphia Dance Collection, which documents the diverse dance legacy of the region.

The Contemporary Culture Collection, primarily documenting the protest era of the 1960s and 1970s, contains 4,000 journal, newsletter, and newspaper titles and 5,000 books and pamphlets. It was established in 1969 and has grown to include microfilm collections, audio-tapes, posters and broadsides, ephemera holdings, and manuscript collections, such as the records of the Liberation News Service, the Committee of Small Press Editors and Publishers, Youth Liberation, Seven Days, and the personal papers of poet Lyn Lifshin.

The Rare Books and Manuscripts Collection includes early, rare, scarce, and valuable books, as well as the Prints, Drawings, Photographs, and Artifacts Collections. The Conwellana-Templana Collection consists of the published books and sermons, manuscripts, correspondence, and memorabilia of Temple University founder Dr. Russell Conwell.

The Blockson Afro-American Collection is one of the nation's leading research facilities for the study of the history and culture of people of African descent. It contains over 500,000 items on the global Black experience in all formats, including books, manuscripts, pamphlets, journals, broadsides, posters, photographs, and rare ephemera.

Collection Profile and Overview: Steven J. Bell, Carol Lang, and Margaret Jerrido
Illustrations: *Philadelphia Evening Bulletin* Collection

Temple University Libraries
Rare Books and Manuscripts
Paley Library
1210 West Berks Street
Philadelphia, Pennsylvania 19122-6088
http://library.temple.edu/collections/special_collections/
(215) 204-4371 (t)
(215) 204-5201 (f)

University of Tennessee Libraries

The University of Tennessee Special Collections Library builds collections of manuscripts, books, and other unique primary research materials in support of the scholarly pursuits of the university community and the residents of Tennessee. With nearly 50,000 rare book titles and 7,000 linear feet of manuscript materials related primarily to Tennessee and the Southeast, the library's collections provide colorful and vivid accounts of the development of the United States from the perspective of the region. Significant holdings include materials from or related to the Civil War and Reconstruction in Tennessee; the Great Smoky Mountains; Native Americans, particularly the Cherokee and Creek tribes; and Tennessee authors, including Alex Haley and James Agee.

The library also contains a strong collection of books and manuscripts related to Tennessee politicians. In 2004, Special Collections, the Department of History, the Papers of Andrew Jackson, and the Correspondence of James K. Polk collaborated to create the Center for Jacksonian America, which specializes in collecting and promoting access to materials related to American history from the beginning of the War of 1812 until the conclusion of the Mexican War in 1848. Additionally, since 2005, the library worked with the Howard H. Baker, Jr., Center for Public Policy to create the Modern Political Archives, a research center focused on documenting the work of Tennessee politicians on the local, state, and national level in the modern era. Among the collections in the Modern Political Archives are the papers of Senators Howard H. Baker Jr., Bill Brock, Estes Kefauver, and Fred Thompson.

Collection Profile and Overview: Erin Lawrimore
Illustrations: William Britten

University of Tennessee Special Collections Library
James D. Hoskins Library
1401 Cumberland Avenue
Knoxville, Tennessee 37996-4000
http://www.lib.utk.edu/spcoll/
special@utk.edu
(865) 974-4480 (t)
(865) 974-0560 (f)

University of Texas Libraries

Special collections are a defining characteristic of the University of Texas, with world renowned collections at the Harry Ransom Humanities Research Center, the Center for American History, and the Nettie Lee Benson Latin American Collection. The Ransom Center has as its major emphasis the study of the literature and culture of the United States, Great Britain, and France. Its collections contain some 30 million leaves of manuscripts, over 1 million rare books, 5 million photographs, 3,000 pieces of historical photographic equipment, and 100,000 works of art, in addition to major holdings in theater arts and film. The Ransom Center offers scholars opportunities for such diverse study as 13th-century Italian verse, early map renderings of the moon, European broadsides, 17th-century English dramatic poetry, early developments in micro-photography, avant-garde theater design, modern French musical composition, literary portraiture, the art of caricature, censorship in Hollywood, and the work of contemporary African novelists. The Center for American History sponsors and supports teaching, research, and public education in United States history. It acquires, preserves, and makes available for research archival, artifact, and rare book collections and sponsors exhibitions, conferences, video documentaries, oral history projects, grant-funded research, and publications. The center's research collections strengths are the history of Texas, the South, the Southwest, and the Rocky Mountain West, the history of the University of Texas, congressional history, and specific national-in-scope topics, including media history and the history of the professional touring entertainment industry.

Collection Profile and Overview: Adán Benavides
Illustrations: Uri Kolodney

University of Texas at Austin
University of Texas Libraries
Post Office Box P
Austin, Texas 78713-8916
http://www.lib.utexas.edu/
(512) 495-4350 (t)
(512) 495-4347 (f)

Texas A&M University Libraries

The collections of the Cushing Memorial Library and Archives reflect the comprehensive nature of the educational and research enterprise at Texas A&M University as well as the wide diversity of interests found among current and former students, faculty, staff, and friends. By preserving and making these collections accessible, the Cushing Library, like the university, seeks to promote intellectual inquiry, cultural enrichment, and the creation and dissemination of research and new knowledge. The library serves the students and faculty of Texas A&M as well as the community of scholarship, learning, and culture beyond the physical boundaries of the campus.

The collections span the breadth of recorded history, from Sumerian clay tablets dating from 2400 BCE to contemporary science fiction paperbacks. These collections comprise over 22,000 linear feet of manuscript and archival material, approximately 200,000 printed volumes, over 300,000 photographs, hundreds of original works of art ranging from oil paintings to pastels to sculpture, and many individual artifacts. The collections include works on paper, film, tape, CD, and other media. Collection strengths and interests of the Cushing Library include military history, science fiction, western Americana, 19th-century American prints and illustrators, modern politics, Texana, natural history, Africana, Hispanic studies, ornithology, nautical archaeology, 18th-century French history and culture, Mexican colonial history, the history of books and printing, the history of Texas A&M, and selected literary collections (including Miguel de Cervantes, John Donne, Rudyard Kipling, Somerset Maugham, the Powys family, Christina Rossetti, and Walt Whitman) in addition to many other subjects.

Collection Profile and Overview: Miguel Juarez,
    Eduardo Urbina, and Steven Smith
Illustrations: Jim Lyle

Cushing Memorial Library and Archives
5000 TAMU Libraries
College Station, Texas 77843-5000
http://cushing.tamu.edu/
(979) 845-1951 (t)
(979) 845-1441 (f)

University of Toronto Libraries

The University of Toronto Libraries comprise over 40 libraries and resource centers ranging from the Architecture Landscape & Design Library to the Zoology Library. The Thomas Fisher Rare Book Library is highlighted in this volume. The Fisher Library collections are many and varied, reflecting the wide diversity of research conducted at the University of Toronto by its own faculty and students, visiting scholars, and the general public. Acquired by both purchase and gift, the holdings currently consist of some 650,000 books and 2,600 linear meters of manuscript material. Chronologically, the range is from a 1789 BCE Babylonian cuneiform tablet from Ur to original drafts and printed works of contemporary Canadian writers such as Margaret Atwood. The general rare book collections include such items as the *Concilium zu Constencz*, printed in Augsburg in 1483 with hand-colored woodcuts, but in addition to these general collections there are over 100 special author or subject collections, focusing on fields as diverse as AIDS, Aristotle, Birdsall Bindings, Lewis Carroll, Darwin, Galileo, Aldous Huxley, incunabula, libretti, Thoreau Macdonald, Shakespeare, Voltaire, and yellowbacks. As a complement to the printed works, the library houses individual manuscripts as well as over 400 manuscript collections covering a wide range of subject areas. Chief among the individual works is the *Codex Torontonensis*, a copy of the four gospels penned in Byzantium around the year 1050 and still in its original boards. Other manuscript holdings range from examples of 13th-century tally sticks to papers of the co-discoverers of insulin, and drafts, research notes, and correspondence of Canadian authors from Mazo de la Roche to Leonard Cohen, Josef Škvorecký, Joy Fielding, Alberto Manguel, and Camilla Gibb. The majority of the manuscript collections date from the 19th century to the present day and pertain to Canadian historical, literary, artistic, or scientific fields. Overall, the great strengths of the library lie in the fields of British, European, and Canadian literature, philosophy, theology, the history of science and medicine, Canadiana, and the history and art of the book.

Collection Profile and Overview: Richard Landon
Illustrations: Jim Ingram

University of Toronto
Thomas Fisher Rare Book Library
120 St. George Street
Toronto, Ontario
M5S 1A5
Canada
http://www.library.utoronto.ca/fisher/
fisher.library@utoronto.ca
(416) 978-5332 (t)
(416) 978-1667 (f)

Tulane University Library

Established in 1889, Tulane University's Special Collections, including Manuscripts, University Archives, Rare Books, Louisiana Collection, Southeastern Architectural Archives, and the Hogan Jazz Archive, is one of Louisiana's older and more heavily used research facilities.

The manuscript holdings comprise more than 4,000 collections covering three linear miles. Among the various strengths of the holdings are 250 collections on the US Civil War from Jefferson Davis to the lowest private; inland waterways, Mardi Gras, medical pioneers, New Orleans authors, New Orleans businesses, social agencies, and Southern Judaica; and the political papers of three Louisiana governors, nine congresspersons, and two New Orleans mayors.

The University Archives preserves the records of Tulane University with 3,600 linear feet of documents, 11,000 slides, and 55,000 photographic negatives.

Rare Books holds 50,000 titles dating from a leaf of the Gutenberg Bible to modern first editions. Special areas of interest are natural history, the American Revolution, American travel accounts, British shire histories, 19th- and 20th-century English language fiction, Russian history and travel, and science fiction and fantasy, with substantial representation of William Faulkner, Lafcadio Hearn, Stendhal, and Robert Southey.

Founded in 1980, the Southeastern Architectural Archives is one of the largest collections of architectural records in the South, including works by antebellum masters, later 19th-century architects, and modernist works and current practicing architects.

The Louisiana Collection holds nearly 25,000 volumes of printed material concerning Louisiana from 1701 onward, plus extensive image, map, and vertical files.

Collection Profile: Bruce Boyd Raeburn
Overview: Wilbur E. Meneray
Illustrations: Harriet Blum

Tulane University
Howard-Tilton Memorial Library Special Collections
6801 Freret Street Room 202
New Orleans, Louisiana 70118-5682
http://specialcollections.tulane.edu/
(504) 865-5685 (t)
(504) 865-5761 (f)

University of Utah Library

The Special Collections Department at the J. Willard Marriott Library consists of six divisions: Manuscripts, Multimedia Archives, Western Americana, University Archives and Records Management, Library Gifts, and the Rare Books and Book Arts Program.

The primary focus for Special Collections is Utah, the American West, and Mormonia.

The Rare Books Division expands this focus to a broad range of topics supporting the teaching and research mission of the University of Utah.

Special Collections collects current, unique, and rare materials including books, pamphlets, broadsides, maps, newspapers, posters, prints, manuscripts, print ephemera, photographs, and other multimedia. Unpublished historical collections include diaries, correspondence, business and personal records, and oral histories. Areas of interest include the Middle East, fine press and book arts, politics, journalism, architecture, science, engineering, medicine, religion, mining, arts, women's organizations, ranching, western travel and exploration, and outdoor recreation. The department's Ski Archives is one of the largest of its kind, providing information on the history of skiing, particularly in Utah and the Intermountain West.

The department provides access to its materials through on-site and online resources. The department staff produces indexes, collection guides, and other finding aids. The staff also provides a strong outreach component, offering classes, lectures, workshops, exhibitions, seminars, and collaborations with campus departments and diverse off-campus organizations. The collections are available to everyone.

The Special Collections Department is one of Utah's most important and valuable assets. Through public and private funding, Special Collections creates, maintains, and makes available important and exceptional collections that have a national and international reputation for depth, breadth, and excellence.

Collection Profile and Overview: Luise Poulton
Illustrations: Borge Anderson & Associates

University of Utah
J. Willard Marriott Library
295 South 1500 East
Salt Lake City, Utah 84112-0860
http://www.lib.utah.edu/
(801) 581-8863 (t)
(801) 585-3976 (f)

Vanderbilt University Library

When the General Library Building was built in 1941, space was allocated in the building for storage of the rare books and manuscripts that had been acquired by the Vanderbilt libraries. A Treasure Room was established on the fourth floor to provide access to these materials and was later moved to more spacious quarters on the eighth floor. Funding for this room was provided by Colonel Granville Sevier as a memorial to John Sevier, the first governor of Tennessee. This space is now occupied by the W. T. Bandy Center for Baudelaire and Modern French Studies.

Special Collections was formally organized in 1965 and focused on collecting materials on the history of the university, manuscripts, and rare books in order to provide primary source material for graduate research. In 1969, the department moved to the new H. Fort Flowers wing and featured the Jesse E. Wills Fugitive/Agrarian Collection, a collection of books by and about the Fugitive and Agrarian literary movements that started at Vanderbilt University in the 1920s. Jesse Wills, a member of the Fugitive literary group and Chairman of the Board of Trust from 1967 to 1976, was the primary founder of this addition to the department and actively sponsored the acquisition of materials to support it.

Today, Special Collections houses one of the finest 20th-century Southern literature collections and is the center for the study of the Fugitive and Agrarian groups. Other subjects collected include Southern history and culture, the Civil War, women's issues, civil rights, religion, journalism, and the performing arts. The collection has more than 50,000 rare books, 300,000 photographs, and over 650 manuscript collections. It also serves as the primary access point for the University Archives. Open to the general public, the department serves patrons worldwide.

Collection Profile: Yvonne Boyer
Overview: Juanita G. Murray
Illustrations: Henry Shipman

Vanderbilt University
Special Collections and University Archives
The Jean and Alexander Heard Library
419 21st Avenue South
Nashville, Tennessee 37240-0007
http://www.library.vanderbilt.edu/speccol/
archives@vanderbilt.edu
(615) 322-2807 (t)

University of Virginia Library

With the opening in 2004 of the Albert and Shirley Small Special Collections Library and the affiliated Mary and David Harrison Institute for American History, Literature, and Culture, which organizes and sponsors exhibitions, programs, and visiting research fellowships, the University of Virginia (UVa) Library has asserted its role as a premier destination for the study and appreciation of the American journey. Known primarily for the Tracy W. McGregor Library of American History, the Clifton Waller Barrett Library of American Literature, and the Albert H. Small Declaration of Independence Collection, the holdings include rare imprints, manuscripts, and maps pertaining to the founding of the American colonies, the early Republic, and the Civil War; papers of UVa founder Thomas Jefferson; records of prominent Virginia families and plantations; early and contemporary African-Americana; as well as primary collections of major American authors, including Walt Whitman, Willa Cather, Robert Frost, and William Faulkner.

Additional literary collections include the Lillian Gary Taylor collection of American bestsellers, the Marvin Tatum collection of contemporary poetry and prose, the Sadleir-Black collection of Gothic fiction, the John Henry Ingram collection on Edgar Allan Poe, the Douglas H. Gordon collection of French books, and the Jorge Luis Borges collection.

Other notable collections represent the wide variety and extent of the holdings, such as the Marion duPont Scott sporting collection, the Paul Victorius evolution collection, the McGehee Lindemann miniature book collection, the Brenda Forman collection of mechanical and pop-up books, and the Edward L. Stone typography collection. American sheet music, shape-note hymnals, WPA folklore, and prominent American composers are also well represented, as are the papers of prominent Virginia politicians and UVa faculty. Including University Archives collections, the present holdings comprise some 311,000 volumes, 15,686,000 manuscripts, 213,000 photographs and prints, 9,000 reels of microfilm, 6,200 audio and video recordings, 3,000 maps, as well as realia and other formats.

Collection Profile and Overview: Christian Dupont
Illustrations: University of Virginia Library staff

University of Virginia
Albert and Shirley Small Special Collections Library
PO Box 400110
Charlottesville, Virginia 22904-4110
http://www.lib.virginia.edu/small/
(434) 243-1776 (t)
(434) 924-4968 (f)

Virginia Tech Libraries

Special Collections at Virginia Tech (VT) welcomes the public in its newly renovated Reading Room in Newman Library, and to a growing number of unique online materials and exhibits. Its wealth of unique resources and rare books largely document 19th- and 20th-century American history and culture. Particularly rich and unique collections include:

The Archives of American Aerospace Exploration document aeronautical and space history through the collections of astronauts (e.g., Michael Collins), artists (e.g., James Dean), NASA administrators (e.g., Christopher C. Kraft), and project managers (e.g., Marjorie Rhodes Townsend), as well as Samuel Herrick, founder of the field of astrodynamics, and John Parsons, the father of numerical control.

Three hundred Appalachian collections include local family papers, oral histories in the Patrick County (Virginia) Project and Blue Ridge Parkway Folklife collections, archives of the Episcopal Diocese of Southwestern Virginia, and more.

The historical records of Virginia Tech, which form the nucleus of the University Archives, extend to statewide activities of the Virginia Agricultural Experiment Station. Scanned yearbooks, historical data, and catalogs are also available online, as are unique digital resources, among them a timeline of Black history, VT in the Spanish-American War, pre-World War II Thanksgiving at VT, 1970 campus unrest, and VT electronic theses and dissertations.

The American Civil War has long been a major collecting focus. Its strength lies in the dual Union and Confederate resources, particularly soldiers' letters and diaries. The backbone of the rare book collection is the Billings donation of 4,500 monographs.

Virginia Tech's rare books are available through Addison, the library catalog, and largely correlate with strengths in the manuscript and archival collections. But also noteworthy are collections such as the Hertzler Children's Cookbook and Nutrition Literature Archive, Peacock-Harper Culinary History, Heron Speculative Fiction, Col. Harry Temple Heraldry, Bailey/Law Ornithology, and John Barnes Victorian Juvenile Literature.

Special Collections welcomes researchers from around the world and encourages undergraduates as well as graduate students, faculty, and others from the university and the wider community to use its resources.

Collection Profile and Overview: Gail McMillan
Illustrations: Digital Imaging, Learning Technologies

Virginia Tech
University Libraries, Special Collections
PO Box 90001
Blacksburg, Virginia 24062-9001
http://spec.lib.vt.edu/
(540) 230-6308 (t)
(540) 231-7808 (f)

University of Washington Libraries

The Special Collections Division at the University of Washington Libraries is the major repository and resource for research in rare and archival materials for the Pacific Northwest region. Special Collections' holdings include rare books, manuscript collections, the University Archives, historic maps, architectural drawings, photographs, broadsides, pamphlets, and other ephemera. The foundations of Special Collections stem from the purchase of volumes for the Pacific Northwest Collection in 1919 and the acquisition in the 1930s of the first manuscript collections. The Special Collections Division was officially formed in 1963, when the Pacific Northwest Collection was combined with the University Libraries' rare book collection, followed in 1967 by the establishment of the Manuscripts and University Archives Division. The two divisions merged into the current Special Collections Division in 1998.

Special Collections serves a worldwide user group comprised of students, faculty, independent scholars, and members of the community. Over 5,000 visitors use the collections annually. Special Collections holdings encompass a broad range of subjects and geographic areas. A major focus is the Pacific Northwest; Special Collections has extensive published materials, manuscripts, and photograph and visual materials collections on this region. These collections contain materials on such diverse topics as politics, pioneer experiences, arts and literature, timber and fishing industries, and environmental and community activism. The University Archives provide historical records of the university and its faculty since its founding in 1861. The nationally known Book Arts Collection includes over 14,000 pieces encompassing all aspects of the physical book. While both historical and modern work is represented, the collection focuses on contemporary artists. Other specialized book collections provide a range of resources for the study of American and English society and culture; these collections include the Hilen Nineteenth-Century Americana Collection of classic American authors and undiscovered women writers and the Historical Children's Literature Collection, which contains over 3,000 17th- to 20th-century children's books.

Collection Profile and Overview: Theresa Mudrock
    and Carla Rickerson
Illustrations: Michael Hilliard

University of Washington
Special Collections Division
Allen Library, Box 352900
Seattle, Washington 98195-2900
http://www.lib.washington.edu/specialcoll/
(206) 543-1929 (t)
(206) 543-1939 (f)

Washington State University Libraries

Manuscripts, Archives, and Special Collections' (MASC) unique holdings consist of manuscripts, historical photographs, rare books, maps, ephemera, University Archives, and other special collections—approximately 17,500 linear feet of primary source material and 40,000 printed items.

Manuscript collections chronicle the exploration, settlement, and development of the Pacific Northwest. Prominent among these are the Pierre Jean De Smet Papers of a 19th-century missionary-priest; the featured McWhorter Collection; the Loran Olsen Papers preserving Nez Perce music; the Frank Chin Oral History Collection documenting Japanese-American resistance to internment during World War II; the Black Oral History Collection; papers of political leaders including Thomas Foley and Catherine May Bedell; archives of Northwest small presses, e.g., Copper Canyon Press; and the Westin Hotels Archives. Also noteworthy are the Regla Papers, spanning over three centuries of Mexican history; the correspondence of such modern British writers as the Sitwells, Roger Fry, and Leonard Woolf; the Moldenhauer Music Archives, papers of 20th-century European and American composers Elizabeth Gyring, Solomon Pimsleur, and Hans Rosbaud; photographs and letters of alumnus Edward R. Murrow; and Frank Matsura Photographs depicting pioneer life in Okanogan County.

Printed materials range from 52 incunabula to modern first editions, small-press books, Washington Territorial Imprints, and early Washington maps. The Walker Library—probably the first private library in the Pacific Northwest—remains intact in MASC.

The core of the Modern Literary Collections is the personal library of Leonard and Virginia Woolf; works by and about "Bloomsbury Group" authors; British and American women authors; 20th-century British authors; and a comprehensive collection of Hogarth Press titles. Historical in scope, the Veterinary History Collection also addresses animal welfare. An extensive collection of angling titles includes first editions of Izaak Walton's *Compleat Angler*. American popular culture is reflected in the counter-culture Comix Collection.

Collection profile: Cheryl Gunselman
Overview: Laila Miletic-Vejzovic
Illustrations: Jeff Kuure

Washington State University
Manuscripts, Archives, and Special Collections
Terrell Library, Suite 12
PO Box 645610
Pullman, Washington 99164-5610
http://www.wsulibs.wsu.edu/holland/masc/masc.htm
mascref@wsu.edu
(509) 335-6691 (t)
(509) 335-1889 (f)

Washington University in St. Louis Libraries

Washington University Libraries' Department of Special Collections encompasses four units: Rare Books, Manuscripts, University Archives, and the Film & Media Archive. Their holdings range from ancient papyri to contemporary documentary film archives. Rare Books has some 50,000 volumes from the 15th century to the present, with particular strengths in graphic design and book arts, 19th-century and modern literature, and semeiology. Another very important collection focuses on British Arts & Crafts fine printing. Manuscripts holds papers of more than 175 contemporary British and American authors—including Samuel Beckett, William Gaddis, and James Merrill—and output from several presses. In addition to these modern literature archives, Manuscripts also holds medieval manuscripts and other historical documents, notable among them a Michelangelo manuscript.

The University Archives document Washington University history and also include other historical archives ranging from modern architectural drawings to St. Louis mayoral papers. The Film & Media Archive is the repository for documentary film archives, including the stellar Henry Hampton Collection and William Miles Collection. The Hampton Collection includes materials from several documentaries, including the landmark *Eyes on the Prize* series; it is a rich resource on African-American life in the 20th century. The Miles Collection features both the history of Harlem and African-Americans in the military. The department's newest effort—the Modern Graphic History Library—encompasses graphic history collections across the department and includes the archives of Al Parker and Robert Weaver, 20th-century illustrators whose work defined the look of many top publications during the heyday of magazine publishing.

Collection Profile: Erin Davis
Overview: Anne Posega
Illustrations: Mary Butkus

Washington University Libraries
Department of Special Collections
Campus Box 1061
One Brookings Drive
St. Louis, Missouri 63130-4899
http://www.library.wustl.edu/units/spec/
spec@wulib.wustl.edu
(314) 935-5495 (t)
(314) 935-4045 (f)

University of Waterloo Library

Opened in 1976 and named in honor of the university's first Chief Librarian, the Doris Lewis Rare Book Room houses the library's special collections comprising some 60,000 books as well as 1,600 linear meters of archival materials. Nationally known for its holdings on the history of Canadian women as well as Canada's only collection of rare books on dance and ballet, the department houses significant treatises in architecture, fine printing, and urban planning as well as aspects of the unique development of the German, Pennsylvania Dutch, and Mennonite heritage of the Waterloo area. Mirroring the university's specialization in developing and making available the most up-to-date innovative technology, special collections maintains collections that document the history of society's developing need and use of mechanical, and finally electronic, devices to aid statistical analysis and calculation.

Developed by purchase and by generous gifts and grants, the Rare Book Room has been able to acquire primary source collections that have been developed systematically around subjects that reflect the goals of the University of Waterloo's major teaching and research programs. Paramount among the research materials used are the family and business papers of prominent local families such as Breithaupt, Dare, Schneider, Motz, and Seagram. Equally as important as their documentary function regarding the Waterloo region, these archives have been viewed as "labs" in which undergraduate and graduate students explore and experience the delights and challenges presented by primary resources.

The University of Waterloo Archives is also part of the special collections and houses the university's official records including correspondence, reports, minutes, publications, architectural and building plans, photographs, and ephemera. These records have been used in a most celebratory manner of recent date as the university observes its 50th anniversary in 2007.

Collection Profile and Overview: Susan Mavor
Illustrations: Chris Hughes

University of Waterloo Library
Porter Library
Doris Lewis Rare Book Room
200 University Avenue
Waterloo, Ontario
N2L 3G1
Canada
http://www.lib.uwaterloo.ca/discipline/SpecColl/Special1.html
LibrarySCRef@library.uwaterloo.ca
(519) 888-4567 x33122 (t)
(519) 888-4322 (f)

Wayne State University Libraries

The special collections at the Wayne State University Library System are best described as newly emerging. Given the leadership of Dean Sandra Yee, the libraries are actively seeking and adding special collections that complement the curriculum and offer members of the university and metropolitan communities access to resources in print or other formats that they might otherwise be denied. Emphasis has been placed on the development of a Detroit-centric African-American Literature Special Collection, which experienced rapid growth with the acquisition of the Dudley Randall Collection, the Ron Milner Collection, and the archives of playwright and poet Bill Harris. Other collections emphasize children's literature, the papers and ephemera of Florence Nightingale, a collection for the study of peace and conflict, and a collection of urban ethnic materials.

Collection Profile and Overview: Barton Lessin
Illustrations: Tim Thayer and Robert Hensleigh for Meadow Brook Hall, Mary Jane Murawka and Rick Bielaczyc for Wayne State University and the Detroit Historical Museum, Alan Harvey for the Henry Ford

Wayne State University Library System
David Adamany Undergraduate Library
Detroit, Michigan 48202
http://www.lib.wayne.edu/
(313) 577-4373 (t)
(313) 577-5525 (f)

The University of Western Ontario Libraries

The first "special collection" at the University of Western Ontario Libraries (Western Libraries) was established in 1934 as the Treasure Room Collection. Thus began the formal development of Western Libraries' antiquarian and rare book holdings that, along with the university archives and local history collection, provide Western with a broad range of primary research resources. In 1999, in recognition of an endowment from the estate of Lillian Benson, a long-service retiree and friend of Western Libraries, it was renamed the James Alexander and Ellen Rea Benson Special Collections in honor of her parents. Currently located in the new Archives and Research Collections Centre, the Benson Special Collections comprises an eclectic mix of major sources, including the G. William Stuart, Jr. Collection of Milton and Miltoniana; H. G. Wells Collection; English Canadian literature to 1939; Canadian Voyages and Travel to 1900; Hannah Collection of the History of Science and Medicine; Beatrice Hitchins Collection of Aviation History; and Richard Maurice Bucke Collection of Medical, Philosophical, and Literary Papers.

Western Libraries' other special collection is located in the Music Library. Its cornerstone is the Gustav Mahler-Alfred Rosé Collection. Received in 1983, it is recognized as one of the largest bodies of Mahler primary source material in North America. Other special holdings at the Music Library include the Opera Collection, a major research resource of over 2,000 volumes of manuscripts and first editions of opera, dating from the 17th to early 20th centuries; the Metastasio Collection of opera scores and libretti based on original libretti by Pietro Metastasio (1698–1782); the Cherubini Collection; and the Delaquerrière Album.

The Benson Special Collections and Music Library holdings are well used by faculty and staff to support teaching and research and are regularly consulted by national and international scholars. Their presence reinforces Western's position as one of Canada's research-intensive universities.

Collection Profile: Lisa Rae Philpott
Overview: Robin Keirstead
Illustrations: Alan Noon

The University of Western Ontario
Western Libraries
London, Ontario
N6A 3K7
Canada
http://www.lib.uwo.ca/

Archives and Research Collections Centre (ARCC)
archives.services@uwo.ca
(519) 661-2111 x81111 (t)
(519) 850-2979 (f)

Music Library
musref@uwo.ca
(519) 661-3913 (t)
(519) 661-3927 (f)

University of Wisconsin–Madison Libraries

Founded in 1946 with the acquisition of the Thordarson Collection of rare science and illustrated natural history books, the Department of Special Collections in Memorial Library, University of Wisconsin–Madison, now features one of the nation's leading collections for the history of science. Holdings in this field include the Duveen and Cole collections of alchemy and chemistry, the Schadewald Collection on Pseudo-Science, the Science and Religion Collection, and the Albert Collection on optics and ophthalmology.

Other strengths include the Little Magazines Collection with runs of more than 7,000 experimental English-language literary magazines (ca. 1900 to the present), the Cairns Collection of American Women Writers before 1920, and numerous author collections. Literary materials also include the Renée Lang Collection on French and German literature, the Ellis Collection of German language textbooks, and an Icelandic literature collection, among others.

Strong collections in European history emphasize 19th- and 20th-century movements on both the left and the right, such as Russian liberal parties, French and German socialists, German workers' theater, cooperatives in Yugoslavia, Cossack émigrés, Nazism, Italian fascism, Vichy propaganda, and French student revolutions. Related collections document the two world wars.

General rare book holdings include decorated publishers' bindings along with many books published up through the early 19th century previously housed in circulating collections.

The university also holds significant special collections in health sciences at Ebling Library; university records as well as personal papers, such as those of Aldo Leopold, in University Archives; a large artists' book collection in Kohler Art Library; rare book collections in the Biology Library and Law Library; and letterpress products and working collections of the Silver Buckle Press. In addition, the Library and Archives of the Wisconsin Historical Society offer extensive research collections in American and regional history.

Collection Profile and Overview: Robin E. Rider
Illustrations: Eric Ferguson

University of Wisconsin–Madison
Department of Special Collections
976 Memorial Library
728 State Street
Madison, Wisconsin 53706
http://www.library.wisc.edu/libraries/SpecialCollections/
askspecial@library.wisc.edu
(608) 262-3243 (t)
(608) 265-2754 (f)

Yale University Library

Yale's special collections offer unparalleled riches. They include written matter of every kind (from books, manuscripts, and ancient clay tablets to unique prints, posters, and even greeting cards), but they also go before and beyond the written word in many ways. Maps, photographs, sound and video recordings, music scores, art works, coins, and other items of great cultural and historical importance await the interested researcher. Set in the context of extraordinary collections of journals, monographs, and reference works, these treasures represent Yale's intense commitment to preserve and know the human past on every continent and in every age of history. The collections continue to grow in size and diversity, supported by the creativity of Yale's people and the generosity of Yale's friends around the world.

The two largest special collections repositories at Yale—Beinecke Rare Book and Manuscript Library (the largest specialized rare book and manuscript library in the world) and Manuscripts and Archives at Sterling Memorial Library—are surrounded and complemented by outstanding special collections in many other libraries and departments:

Beinecke Rare Book and Manuscript Library, Arts of the Book Collection, Drama Library, Faber Birren Collection, Babylonian Collection, Divinity Library, Benjamin Franklin Collection, Lewis Walpole Library, Lillian Goldman Law Library–Rare Book Collection, Manuscripts and Archives General Collection, Fortunoff Video Archive for Holocaust Testimonies, Map Collection, Medical Historical Library, Music Library Special Collections, Historical Sound Recordings, Oral History, American Music , Peabody Museum of Natural History Archives, Visual Resources Collection, Yale Center for British Art, Yale University Art Gallery.

Collection Profile and Overview: Stacy Maples
    and Michael Colavolpe
Illustrations: Courtesy of Map Collection,
    Yale University Library

Yale University
Sterling Memorial Library
PO Box 208240
New Haven, Connecticut 06520-8240
http://www.library.yale.edu/special_collections/
(203) 432-1810 (t)
(203) 432-1294 (f)

Index of Collection Profiles

Page numbers in italics indicate illustrations.